SEEKING
JUSTICE
FOR THE
HOLOCAUST

SEEKING JUSTICE FOR THE HOLOCAUST

Herbert C. Pell, Franklin D. Roosevelt,
and the Limits of International Law

GRAHAM B. COX

UNIVERSITY OF OKLAHOMA PRESS : NORMAN

Publication of this book is made possible through the
generosity of Edith Kinney Gaylord.

Library of Congress Cataloging-in-Publication Data

Names: Cox, Graham B., 1962– author.
Title: Seeking justice for the Holocaust : Herbert C. Pell, Franklin D. Roosevelt, and the limits
  of international law / Graham B. Cox.
Description: Norman : University of Oklahoma Press, [2019] | Includes bibliographical
  references and index.
Identifiers: LCCN 2019004039 | ISBN 978-0-8061-6428-1 (hardcover : alk. paper)
Subjects: LCSH: Holocaust, Jewish (1939–1945)—Germany. | Nuremberg Trial of Major German
  War Criminals, Nuremberg, Germany, 1945–1946. | Prosecution (International law) | World
  War, 1939–1945—Atrocities—Germany. | War crimes. | Pell, Herbert Claiborne, 1884–1961.
  | Roosevelt, Franklin D. (Franklin Delano), 1882–1945.
Classification: LCC KZ1176.5 .C69 2019 | DDC 341.6/90268—dc23
LC record available at https://lccn.loc.gov/2019004039

CONTENTS

PREFACE

This book began as an outgrowth of an examination of the impact of language interpretation on diplomacy. The International Military Tribunal at Nuremberg, 1945–46, an international trial in four languages—French, English, German, and Russian—had offered the perfect case study. There were plenty of instances in which the necessity of interpretation impacted the trial and, more significantly, the negotiations to produce the London Charter used at the trial. Subsequent to my research on the interpretation factor, I had the opportunity to take a graduate seminar on twentieth-century African American history with Professor Gerald Horne. At that time, I knew all too little about the subject, so I wondered if there was a way to connect twentieth-century African American history with something I did know a little about, something I was hoping to research and write on further: Nuremberg.

The connection came easily. I had read it so many times—Section II, Article 6, paragraph (c) of the Charter of the International Military Tribunal:

> (c) CRIMES AGAINST HUMANITY: namely, murder, extermination, enslavement, deportation, and other inhumane acts committed against any civilian population, before or during the war; or persecutions on political, racial or religious grounds in execution of or in connection with any crime within the jurisdiction of the Tribunal, whether or not in violation of the domestic law of the country where perpetrated.[1]

Political, racial, and religious persecution by a government even against its own citizens was apparently an international crime. It was so obvious. As part of the effort to prosecute Nazi war criminals, Allied representatives had pursued and promulgated new international laws declaring, among other things, that racist persecution by a government against its own citizens was an international crime. This simple realization—of course, I was not the first to come to it—began the research and writing that has resulted in this book.

How could it be, I then thought, *that the United States participated in creating a legal code that so obviously pointed out America's own unequal social order?* As I quickly discovered, by connecting "crimes against humanity" to the "conspiracy" and "aggressive war" charges, the charter protected the United States from having this codification boomerang against itself because of its own practice of racist segregation. Although this book shows how and why this connection came about, it is just one aspect of a larger narrative that examines how the Allied powers came to seek justice at Nuremberg for what we now broadly call the Holocaust—hence, the title of this book: *Seeking Justice for the Holocaust.*

What this book reveals, above all, is that the unheralded Herbert C. Pell, as scholar Dan Plesch put it, deserves to be in the pantheon of the creators of modern human rights. But this book also seeks to broaden the discussion of FDR's policies as they relate to Europe's Jews by showing the depth of his commitment to postwar justice in the face of staunch opposition, especially from those in his own administration.

The book builds on the fine work of so many scholars who have previously taken on Nuremberg. Some of the most important to this book must be acknowledged here. First, I am indebted to Dan Plesch and his *America, Hitler, and the UN: How the Allies Won World War II and Forged a Peace* and *Human Rights after Hitler: The Lost History of Prosecuting Axis War Crimes.* Dan has impacted human rights history not only through his scholarship but through his successful effort to get the United Nations War Crimes Commission's archives opened to the public. Thanks to his work, the full significance of the Commission should eventually be recognized. I must also thank Dan for his careful read and insightful suggestions when this book was in manuscript form. Elizabeth Borwardt's *A New Deal for the World: America's Vision for Human Rights* has also assisted immeasurably in helping me understand the meaning of Nuremberg and the role of FDR. Our all-too-brief discussions at conferences over the years on this subject have been invaluable. The staff at the Roosevelt Institute for American Studies, especially Giles Scott-Smith, deserves mention too. Work done in preparation for a 2017 conference on the imagining of a "Rooseveltian Century" contributed significantly in my contextualizing the role of FDR presented in this book.

The list of previous scholarship that has helped make this book possible is too long to list fully here—much of it can be found in the notes and bibliography—but

I must acknowledge these authors directly: Dan Plesch and Elizabeth Borwardt for their works just cited; Leonard Baker, *Brahmin in Revolt: A Biography of Herbert C. Pell*; Michael Steward Blayney, *Democracy's Aristocrat: The Life of Herbert C. Pell*; Arieh J. Kochavi, *Prelude to Nuremberg: Allied War Crimes Policy and the Question of Punishment*; Michael Marrus, *The Nuremberg War Crimes Trial, 1945–46: A Documentary History*; William Schabas, *Genocide in International Law: The Crime of Crimes*, and *Unimaginable Atrocities: Justice, Politics, and Rights at the War Crimes Tribunals*; Christopher Simpson, *The Splendid Blond Beast: Money, Law, and Genocide in the Twentieth Century*; and Bradley F. Smith, *The American Road to Nuremberg: The Documentary Record, 1944–1945*; *Reaching Judgment at Nuremberg: The Untold Story of How the Nazi War Criminals Were Judged*; and *The Road to Nuremberg: The Documentary Record, 1944–1945*. This book could not have been possible without this previous scholarship. Anyone interested in understanding Nuremberg would be well served to start with this list.

I must also thank the following individuals who have helped me in any number of ways: Don Truesdale, Martin V. Melosi, Gerald Horne, Robert Buzzanco, Nancy Young, Peter Linzer, Lawrence Curry, Tom O'Brien, John Moretta, John Q. Barrett, Bill Walker, J. Simon Rofe, Clayton Lust, Alberto Rodriguez, Juan Coronado, Walter Roberts, Shaffer Bonewell, Maddison Craig, Richard Rooks, and all my colleagues in the Department of History, the Military History Center, and Jewish and Israel Studies at the University of North Texas. Special thanks go out to Randolph "Mike" Campbell who read not one but two versions of this book. This book would simply not have been possible without his friendship, support, and editorial skills. Similarly, I am indebted Don Chipman. I am more than happy to report that he caught every error Mike Campbell missed—a feat in itself. Bob Land did a superb job copyediting the manuscript. Any remaining errors in this book, of course, I own fully.

Lasting appreciation also goes out to Don Chipman for connecting me to the University of Oklahoma Press. An introduction to—and brief conversation with—acquisitions editor Kent Calder eventually led me to editor-in-chief Adam Kane, who skillfully guided this book forward in the early stages; many thanks similarly to managing editor Steven B. Baker, who took it to the finish line. I must also express my appreciation to the anonymous readers whose comments and criticism helped immeasurably.

Heartfelt thanks also go out to all the archivists and their staffs without whose unheralded work this book could not have been possible. Particularly helpful have been the National Archives in College Park, Maryland; the Library of Congress in Washington, D.C.; the Franklin D. Roosevelt Presidential Library in Hyde Park, New York; and Distinctive Collections, University of Rhode Island Library. Special thanks go to University of Rhode Island Library archivist Mark Dionne. His help and patience in allowing me to work through boxes of Pell family papers were instrumental.

To my sister, Gail Cox, who suffered through the earliest writing of what eventually became this book, for teaching me one grammar rule after another, I thank you more than you can know—for that and for so much more. To my parents, very simply, thank you for encouraging—and allowing—me to always ask why. And most of all to my wife, Emily Jackson, who has put up with my absences and distractions with work over so many years now, thank you for your love, your patience, and enduring support.

Finally, as we approach the seventy-fifth anniversary of the Nuremberg War Crimes Trial, this book is dedicated to all of those targeted by the Nazis and to all of those who sought to do something about it.

SEEKING
JUSTICE
FOR THE
HOLOCAUST

INTRODUCTION

"The Worst Crime of All"

I believe that we should strongly and firmly run and control the world after the war, suppressing disorder wherever it may arise and protecting justice all over the surface of the globe. This will be a very big thing. It will require serious thought on subjects to which we have given no consideration. It will mean the acceptance of responsibilities for which we have no desire. It will mean sacrifice of life and wealth. . . . I do not think it is a thing desirable in itself, but it seems to me, as it seemed twenty-two years ago, that the cost of abstention will be greater still.

Herbert C. Pell, September 9, 1942

Although Nazi antisemitism was no secret to anyone from the moment Adolf Hitler took power, much of the world found it difficult to believe stories of mass deportation of Jews within Germany and occupied nations at the start of the Second World War in Europe. By the time most of the continent had fallen to the Nazis near the end of 1942, reports of atrocities had become widespread in official circles. Initial thinking about what to do regarding those who committed crimes during the war varied among the Allied powers. U.S. president Franklin D. Roosevelt believed that the Allies should bring war criminals before some sort of trial following the war. But British officials and prime minister Winston Churchill himself considered a trial of the major Nazi leaders a bad idea, favoring summary execution instead. For a brief time in 1944, FDR, too, acquiesced to the proposal. Soviet head of state Joseph Stalin, however, was adamant that all war criminals, including especially the highest leaders of the Nazi state, be brought before a show tribunal and tried publicly for their offenses.

With Nazi Germany conducting an unprecedented racist war seeking global domination, the Allies realized that they must not fail to fully prosecute war criminals after the war, not wanting to repeat the botched attempt to do so at the end of the First World War. The unrestrained looting of civilian property, forced evacuations, slave labor, and the systematic extermination of millions was too much to ignore. On several occasions, the Allies, and in the United States, the president, proclaimed a determination to prosecute Axis war criminals. As a beginning step, in the fall of 1942, the British and the United States announced the formation of the United Nations War Crimes Commission (UNWCC), the first organization tasked with determining war crimes policy and gathering evidence.

A year later in October 1943 with the UNWCC still not yet operational, the foreign ministers of the Allied powers met and outlined a postwar policy on war criminals. Those determined responsible for atrocities, massacres, and executions would be returned to the scenes of their crimes and prosecuted according to the laws of the "Governments which will be erected therein." Those criminals "whose offenses had no particular geographical localization" were to be punished by "joint decision of the government of the Allies."[1] What that last objective meant at the time, no one said—or knew apparently—but it was understood that this referred to the punishment designed for the highest Nazi leaders. Most important, though, the Allies, this time including the Soviet Union, had announced yet again their determination to bring Axis war criminals to justice.

Throughout 1944, seeking justice for war crimes centered on the finally seated UNWCC in London. But then unknown to the public, a battle raged within the Roosevelt administration over war crimes planning, first between Herbert C. Pell, the president's appointee to the Commission, and the State Department, and later between the War and Treasury Departments over whether justice should be sought for what we now call the Holocaust.[2] In mid-1944 the Roosevelt administration turned its attention to planning for the postwar world. Treasury Secretary Henry Morgenthau delivered to the president his ideas on the matter, which included summary execution of major Nazi leaders. Secretary of War Henry L. Stimson delivered to the president a proposal very different from Morgenthau's that called for a public—and fair—trial of the major criminals. Colonel Murray C. Bernays of the Special Projects Branch, the man most responsible for writing Stimson's proposal, recommended that the Allies prosecute Nazi leaders for participating in a conspiracy to instigate and wage a war of aggression and for the commission of atrocities.

At the Yalta Conference in February 1945, the Allied powers confirmed their intention to prosecute war criminals under some sort of yet-unnamed and undecided judicial process. Following the death of President Roosevelt in April 1945, new president Harry S. Truman on May 2, 1945, appointed Supreme Court Justice Robert H. Jackson chief prosecutor for the United States for a still-undetermined postwar war crimes trial, which was to be based on the War Department's original ideas.

Beginning on June 26, 1945, representatives of the United States, Great Britain, France, and the Soviet Union met in London to forge the international law and procedures for a trial. After weeks of negotiations to resolve difficulties in merging two differing legal systems into a single judicial procedure, on August 8 the Allies signed what is commonly referred to today as the London Agreement and Charter—officially, the London Agreement of August 8, 1945, and the Charter of the International Military Tribunal—which became the basis for the trial before the International Military Tribunal at Nuremberg.[3]

The tribunal convened on November 20, 1945, in Nuremberg, Germany, where twenty-two Nazi defendants were prosecuted on four counts: conspiracy, crimes against peace, war crimes, and crimes against humanity. Nearly a year later, on September 30, 1946, the tribunal rendered its judgment. The following day twelve defendants were sentenced to death, three to life terms, four were sentenced to prison terms ranging from ten to twenty years' imprisonment, and three were acquitted.[4]

In the final analysis, the promise of justice brought to fulfillment at the trial has not materially changed the course of history, in the very same way that the threat of capital punishment has not stopped capital crimes from being committed in the United States. Moreover, prosecuting crimes against humanity at Nuremberg—seeking justice for the Holocaust—did not bring about an end to genocide. As the London Agreement and Charter was written, it could not have. There are, of course, several obvious explanations historians have offered regarding the shortcomings of Nuremberg, ranging from the Cold War imperative to the inherent capacity of humankind for evil—something that cannot simply be legislated away. But a part of the reason, as will be suggested here, is that the nation most responsible for authoring the new international laws used at Nuremberg was not completely committed to them.

Most participants in the trial and historians have judged the Allied effort that fashioned international legal precedent for the prosecution of war crimes as a great achievement, despite the unfulfilled promise of a lasting international tribunal.[5] In the largest sense, the trial will forever stand as a testament to the crimes of Adolf Hitler and his Nazi regime. Participants of the trial never forgot the images of unimaginable Nazi excesses. Sarah Klebnikov, widow of Nuremberg interpreter George Klebnikov, who went on to a long career at the United Nations, reflected many years later, "My husband and I, we loved to travel, and of course we got to do so often, but we never—*he never*—returned to Germany. After hearing—and seeing—what he saw—lampshades made of human skin—it is just not a place that he ever wished to return."[6] The charming smile that graced her patrician face as she reminisced about her husband vanished as her voice trailed away, her own personal grief becoming quite conspicuous. Even today for the rest of us, despite the proliferation of violence available in so many mediums, the images both in print and in film of the Nazi death camps have not lost their power to overwhelm.

The world was visually introduced to what happened at the camps during the afternoon of the eighth day of the trial, November 29, 1945. U.S. assistant prosecutor Sidney Alderman interrupted his presentation of evidence on the Nazi campaign of aggressive war and announced, "At this point it is planned by our staff to show a motion picture." Alderman would have to continue his recounting of Hitler's stampede through Europe the following Monday, resuming with "the story of Czechoslovakia." Tribunal president, Lord Justice Colonel Sir Geoffrey Lawrence, then called for a brief recess to prepare the courtroom. When everyone had been reseated, another member of the American prosecutorial staff, Thomas J. Dodd, took over and explained that the documentary film they were about to show was not the "entire proof" of what happened in Nazi concentration camps. It was, he said, "in a brief and unforgettable form an explanation of what the words 'concentration camp'" implied.[7]

According to Dodd, it was appropriate to interrupt Alderman's presentation of events leading up to the launch of Germany's aggressive war because the concentration camps were a fundamental ingredient of the larger Nazi conspiracy that had begun long before the invasion of Poland.[8] Robert H. Jackson had already made that same point in his opening address back on day two when he noted, "This war did not just happen—it was planned and prepared over a long period of time and with no small skill and cunning."[9]

Jackson had hoped the trial would focus the international community on what he considered the greater crime, aggressive warfare.[10] Crimes against humanity, in his (and many of his colleagues') view of what was permissible within the law, was both a fundamental ingredient and consequent symptom of a larger conspiracy to commit an illegal war seeking global domination.

In the weeks leading up to the trial, Jackson tried to explain his position this way: the world wars of the twentieth century, he noted, had demonstrated that limited wars were no longer possible. In any future war, no nation could, therefore, contemplate defeat, negotiated or otherwise, so the only alternative was to win "by being better killers, by killing more and killing more quickly than the enemy, [and] by killing with less risk" to one's own nation. Consequently, any international law governing the conduct of war was unlikely to mitigate the horror of it all. With the abandonment of "honorable and legal" methods to conduct war, Jackson had concluded that the only alternative remaining was to prevent war by declaring aggressive warfare an international crime and promising punishment. Jackson thought that this step was the only rational beginning to eventually outlawing all war. "If we can root out of men's thinking the idea that all wars are legal, and if we can substitute the conviction that aggressive war is criminal," he said, "at last we will have mobilized the forces of law on the side of peace."[11]

Although this American view for the trial had been about prosecuting foremost what they considered the larger crime—the Nazi conspiracy to wage aggressive war—crimes against humanity certainly offered the best evidence of the lengths to which the regime had gone to accomplish it. "The most savage and numerous crimes planned and committed by the Nazis," Jackson had noted in his opening address, "were those against the Jews."[12] He later added that "the conspiracy . . . to exterminate the Jew was so methodically and abundantly pursued that despite the German defeat . . . this Nazi aim largely . . . succeeded."[13]

Nonetheless, Jackson wanted these crimes to be understood as an integral part of the "common plan or conspiracy" of Nazi aggressive war. After all, the legal code the Allies had created for the trial had been structured exactly that way. The last thing Jackson wanted was for the Nazi effort to exterminate European Jewry to be seen as an end in itself, an end for which the Allies must seek justice separate and apart from aggressive war. As Dodd put it to the court, "We propose to show that concentration camps were not an end in themselves but rather they were an integral part of the Nazi system of government."[14] Such an interpretation, as this book reveals, was fraught with complications.

On September 9, 1945, in an editorial he wrote for the *New York Times* just prior to the beginning of the trial, Jackson labeled aggressive warfare—not crimes against humanity—as the "worst crime of all." "We must," he wrote, "teach a lesson to those who plan it." In his construction, crimes against humanity served as both the best evidence and the underlying cause of the Nazi conspiracy to commit aggressive war; it was not—conspicuously—its most disastrous result. Still, Jackson noted, "Another significant principle recognized in this agreement [London Agreement and Charter] is that racial or religious persecutions by a Government against its own people, under some circumstances, may rise to the magnitude of crimes against international society."[15] "Under some circumstances"? What were those circumstances? Jackson did not then specify in his editorial, but they were right there for anyone to read in the Charter of the International Military Tribunal. Racial and religious persecutions by a government rose to international crimes only when connected with a conspiracy to commit aggressive war. But why?

Was it really necessary to subsume crimes against humanity within a conspiracy to commit aggressive warfare? Apparently, yes, it was. Wasn't the enormity of the Holocaust enough to merit consideration separate and apart from the crime of aggressive war? Well, yes—maybe (depending on who you ask)—but it can't be done. Couldn't the trial set precedent, making racial, religious, and political persecution of individuals or minorities an international crime whether it was connected to a larger conspiracy to commit aggressive war? No, it could not. One of my purposes in this book, then, is to explain why American policymakers (not just Jackson) believed Nazi crimes against humanity had to be connected to a conspiracy to commit aggressive war.

So important was the connection between the two that when the American prosecutorial team showed the film of what happened at the camps at that moment of the trial, they did so expecting that it would reinforce their argument: visually connecting crimes against humanity with aggressive war. There was also a growing concern that public interest in the trial had waned. Presenting the film, they hoped, might also dramatically change that. On that account, they were not disappointed.

The film certainly reinvigorated interest in the trial, but it failed to subsume Nazi crimes against humanity within the larger crime of aggressive war. It actually had the opposite effect. The accumulation of evidence presented at Nuremberg, and at several later trials, and the considerable scholarship on what is today called the Holocaust has served to deny what Jackson and his team had sought. Hitler's Nazi Germany had existed for just that end, the destruction of European Jewry. Its entire war effort was built around the annihilation of the Jews and a multitude of other supposed *Untermenschen:* those deemed mentally and physically disabled, Gypsies, millions of Slavic people, Communists, homosexuals, Jehovah's Witnesses, and Afro-Germans—virtually any group that stood in the way of an imagined Aryan purity. The film shown that afternoon in the courtroom only marked the beginning of that fuller understanding of the ends of the Nazi state, and it did so in a way that no other evidence could have.

Following Dodd's explanation, a series of photographs was then projected showing the affidavits of those who had taken or directed the images that were about to be viewed. As each affidavit was shown, the anticipation grew in every section of the courtroom, especially in the defendants' dock, because several of them knew what was coming next.

The previous evening, prosecutors had shown the film to eight of the Nazi defendants and their counsel. Assistant Prosecutor Robert G. Storey later wrote of the prescreening "that the defendants and their counsel were, to say the least, shocked and some even surprised at the horrors, cruelty, and inhumane treatment inflicted upon thousands of unfortunate people by virtue of the directions of some of the defendants in the dock . . . [treatment] which included gas chambers, mass murders, and other unbelievable punishment and torture of defenseless people, especially the millions of Jewish people who were killed or died as a consequence of the ruthless administration of the concentration camps." One of the defendants' counsels later told Storey, "It will be unnecessary for you to show any further captured German films to the defendants and their counsel prior to the introduction of them in evidence."[16]

At Dodd's direction, the final affidavits were presented and then the film, Exhibit USA-79:

> I have carefully examined the motion picture film . . . and I certify that the images of these excerpts from the original negative have not been retouched, distorted or otherwise altered in any respect and are true copies of the originals. . . .
>   (Signed) E. R. Kellogg, Lieutenant, United States Navy
>   Sworn to before me this 27 day of August 1945
>   (Signed) John Ford, Captain, United States Navy.[17]

Although some in the courtroom that day had already been witness to many of the crimes—either at the liberation of the death camps themselves or in preparation of the evidence—the images projected that day were still overwhelming. For the defendants, who certainly knew of the crimes, if not in such a visceral way, the film was a devastating reminder of the malevolent end for which their Nazi regime had existed. *New York Times* reporter Raymond Daniell labeled the presentation "a one-hour nightmare in motion pictures depicting the nameless horror of the concentration camps." Reporting the scene back to American readers, he wrote, "The showing of the film taken at twelve such camps, with horror piled on horror and mounting in dreadfulness as it went along, was almost more than anyone could bear."[18]

No one among those who saw the film that day would ever forget the sight of bulldozers crudely burying thousands of emaciated, wasted bodies that were once human beings. There were mutters of "Oh God—oh God!" and "Why can't we shoot the swine?" reverberating in the courtroom. Daniell observed that those in attendance "greeted the end of probably the most horrible hour that they had ever spent . . . with a gasp of relief."[19] When it was all over, Colonel Storey uttered delicately, "That concludes the presentation."[20] Unwilling—or simply unable—to speak, tribunal president Lord Justice Geoffrey Lawrence failed to announce the adjournment of the court for the day, as had been his practice every preceding day of the trial. He rose, along with the other justices and their alternates, and walked silently out of the courtroom.[21] The silence somehow seemed fitting. Later that night, in tears, defendant Hans Fritzsche told prison psychologist G. M. Gilbert, "No power in heaven or earth will erase this shame from my country—not in generations—not in centuries!"[22]

Because of what happened that day in the courtroom, Nuremberg in public memory has remained associated foremost with seeking justice for the Holocaust, prosecuting Nazi crimes against humanity, and crimes based on political, religious, and most of all racial persecution. Nazi atrocities—literally, the extermination of millions of innocent human beings in Nazi death camps and elsewhere throughout Europe—were so unprecedented, so abhorrent, that the world remembers little else about the trial. "Nuremberg" has become shorthand for the Nuremberg War Crimes Trial, which is itself shorthand for the *Trial of the Major War Criminals before the International Military Tribunal.*

Before the Second World War and the rise of Nazism, Nuremberg was but an ancient medieval city in Bavaria about one hundred miles north of Munich, more famous for the *Nuremberg Chronicle* (*Liber Chronicarum*), a thirteenth-century account of all preceding human history. That Nuremberg, however, is mostly gone, physically destroyed by British Lancaster bombers on the night of January 2, 1945, and psychologically transformed because of what took place at the Palace of Justice that November day in 1945 when the prosecutors presented the footage of what had transpired in the camps. Nuremberg, which had for a time served as Nazi Germany's ideological home, fittingly became a symbol of justice because of the trial that took place there, a trial at which the so-called civilized world stood up for Europe's Jews, and by extension all minorities, and said, "Never again." The disconnect, however, was that the world, represented at the time by the victorious Allied powers—the United States, the United Kingdom, France, and the Soviet Union—almost didn't stand up despite the scale of the horror that took place in Europe.

Seeking justice for the Holocaust, it turned out, had not been an automatic—or an obvious—task for the Allies to pursue, notwithstanding the increasing pace of Allied pronouncements that there would be an accounting at the end of the conflict. Taking on the effort of gathering evidence of so many crimes, creating some sort of legal protocol under which the criminals might be prosecuted, and then carrying out an international trial was burdened with difficulties.

President Franklin D. Roosevelt, as aware of the challenges as anyone, none-theless, remained resilient in his insistence that the Allies seek justice. His public statements on war crimes and atrocities were never contradictory in announcing America's resolve that the Allies would seek justice after the war. Within the administration and among the Allies, he remained unwavering in his determina-tion to seek justice for all Nazi crimes, including those against the Jews. FDR was quite uncertain, however, as to methodology, leaving that to subalterns until the end of 1944. Historian Warren Kimball observed over a quarter-century ago that FDR was remarkable in his consistency, "shrouded as it was . . . in rhetoric and tactical maneuverings."[23] Although Kimball's observation was not directed toward FDR's views on the Holocaust, it certainly could have been. FDR was remarkably consistent in his determination to seek justice for the Holocaust, wrapped as it was "in rhetoric and tactical maneuverings."[24]

FDR's constancy about the certainty of justice came with a belief in the progress of international law and human rights, at least insofar as it served his political agenda, and as such functioned as a forerunner to broader efforts that materialized in the postwar period. A fuller appreciation of FDR's efforts as they relate to war crimes prosecution broadens our understanding of just how important a figure FDR was during the twentieth century and contributes to the debate over whether his administration did all it could to save Jews during the war.[25] His public rhetorical promise of justice never faltered despite behind-the-scenes and often-contentious battles within his own administration and among the Allies generally over the efficacy of attempting to create new international law to bring that promise to fruition. Throughout this struggle, FDR did not waver in his determination, to such an extent that—within limitations noted herein—the Allies delivered on the promise. For his constancy, he needs to be recognized as having a greater impact on postwar human rights advances than previously acknowledged.

During the war years, the rhetoric of justice, once stated by the president, only increased in its intensity—so much so that, by early 1945 a public furor erupted when it seemed as if the United States, and by extension, the Allies, might not live up to presidential pronouncements. That January, the U.S. State Department had forced out Herbert Pell, FDR's appointee on the UNWCC, generating an intense public outcry. Pell had operated as FDR's background bureaucratic voice on war crimes and had become the central character in the struggle to develop Allied war crimes policy during the war, but up to that moment, no one knew it. Thanks in large measure to the ill-advised manner with which the State Department removed him, Pell played a key role in arousing the press and public to what was taking place in Europe. But Pell did much more than ignite public opinion.

Believing he was acting in the name of—and with the support of—his friend the president, Pell had taken up the cause on the UNWCC of seeking justice for European Jews. On the face of it, no one would have expected a man of Pell's class and background to do so—except perhaps the man who appointed him to carry out the effort: FDR. More than anything, this book recounts Pell's effort, against all obstructions, to make sure the Allies lived up to the promise of justice. But it also reveals the importance of the president, not just for his unexpected and what turned out to be inspired appointment of Pell but also for his unwavering determination to seek justice for the Holocaust. Without that determination, of course, Pell—and those who followed him—could have accomplished nothing.

Detractors may point out that FDR had been merely reactive rather than proactive when it came to seeking justice, that he had only ramped up his rhetoric to placate Jewish leaders at home and to quell discontent over increasing revelations in the press about the mounting calamity taking place in Europe. The extent to which these factors influenced FDR is hard to pin down. Even so, he did make multiple announcements when he might otherwise have remained silent. Other than the pressure he received from Jewish leaders, no obvious immediate domestic political reason existed for him to push forward an agenda for postwar justice, especially in the period before victory in Europe was assured.

In fact, an important domestic reason did exist that could have caused him to avoid pursuing justice for the Holocaust altogether: Jim Crow segregation.

Evidence indicates that he did not consider until late summer and early fall 1944 the potential blowback on America's unequal social order should the Allies create international law prohibiting racial, religious, and political persecutions. Surely, he must have anticipated such an issue might arise, but there simply is no evidence to support that he thought about it, much less directed anyone to take it into account before that time. Even after Secretary of War Henry Stimson forced him to acknowledge that seeking justice for the Holocaust might challenge American sovereignty to treat its own minorities as it wished, FDR's constancy about the pursuit of justice remained.

Stimson's revelation came as part of his determination to quash what became known as the Morgenthau Plan, which promised the summary execution of Holocaust perpetrators and the reduction of Germany to an agricultural state. He agreed with Morgenthau that Nazism must be destroyed, but by the legitimate trial and punishment of war criminals, which would expose the underlying depravity of Hitler's vile Nazi regime. Stimson was convinced that the United States must seek justice rather than vengeance. Here, too, Pell played an important and previously unknown role. Unable to convince State Department officials of his plan to seek justice for the Holocaust, Pell turned to the secretary of the treasury, Henry Morgenthau, for assistance in August 1944.

The timing of Pell's approach proved critical. Morgenthau had just become interested in the challenges of postwar planning for a defeated Germany. Morgenthau, if he could have any say in it (and he believed that he could, given his intimacy with FDR), intended to press for the most punitive measures possible against the defeated Nazi state and its leaders, whom he deemed as craven criminals. Consequently, summary punishment for war criminals became an integral facet of the Morgenthau Plan. Summary punishment, however, was unacceptable to a War Department determined to take control of all aspects of postwar planning, including the problem of what to do about the perpetrators of the Holocaust.

FDR briefly acquiesced to the Morgenthau Plan, including its call for lining up the perpetrators and shooting them—hardly a step forward for human rights had it proceeded. His acquiescence does, however, indicate even more just how determined the president was that justice be meted out. Given the many statements promising postwar justice—his own and especially one contemporaneous and prominent statement from Secretary of State Cordell Hull about Hungarian Jews—FDR could hardly have reversed course, even if he wanted to, if for no other reason than concern over the coming presidential election. He came to agree with Stimson that the Allies had to afford the Nazis a fair trial, which had been the plan up to that point, although not approved at any level. Going forward, FDR's determination only increased as he became more personally involved in discovering solutions to the many problems of an unprecedented international trial for unprecedented crimes and for which no international law yet existed—not the least of which was the problem of creating legal precedents that might boomerang on the United States itself because of its own praxis of racial segregation.

FDR's public insistence on postwar justice, beginning with an announcement in the summer of 1942 all the way through to his address before Congress on March 1, 1945, denotes a determination to pursue a human rights agenda and should have created, if at least in public memory, an appreciation of FDR as a forward thinker (in the context of the times) on these issues. For a variety of reasons, however, it has not. Foremost, his untimely death obscured this legacy, coming as it did before the end of the war and especially before Nuremberg. Had he lived through the trial, it certainly would have become a major aspect of his record. The efforts of his wife, Eleanor, before, during, and especially after the war on civil and human rights and justice have also tended to lessen the attention FDR deserves for his own contribution. Where she was outspoken—on racism and lynching, for example—he was not; and he could not be (in a sympathetic assessment) if he wanted to remain politically acceptable to the South. The president's breaking of constitutional guarantees—Japanese internment, most notably, but also other wartime home-front actions—complicates matters. For some, this might forestall any consideration of FDR as a promoter of human rights; many tend to judge the past through the lens of the present, particularly when it comes to issues of morality. The larger the personality—and there were none larger—the more this seems to be the case. Above all, perhaps implicit in calling Roosevelt's reputation as a forward thinker into question is the more obvious failure of the United States, and particularly the president himself, to act more positively on refugee issues before it was too late.

Of course, the problem of rescuing the Jews was a different—though undeniably related—issue than was the problem of seeking justice for the Holocaust. It was certainly more time-sensitive and politically challenging. FDR could and did promise postwar justice while continuing to prosecute the war unfettered. Delivering on that promise could be dealt with later, toward the end of the war or even after, although the longer the Allies waited, the more difficult it would be to capitalize on any outrage for the horror at the crimes' vast scale. Worse still,

Allied leaders might decide that the former Nazis were needed as confederates in the coming Cold War, terminating prosecutions altogether. To a certain degree, the latter happened, but it was not that straightforward, as other considerations also played a role.

While one could wait until the end of the war to prosecute crimes, waiting to rescue the Jews, even in limited numbers, could not. Having chosen to risk little to address refugee issues before the war, FDR could have done something during the fighting, but it would have affected the war effort, at least as he saw it—something he was not willing to allow. After the war, obviously, it would be and was too late. FDR chose expediency or military and political pragmatism over taking any principled stand. Whatever our judgment may be, Roosevelt's choice does not necessarily preclude consideration of his role in promoting the growth of postwar international justice and human rights through his determination to seek justice for the Holocaust. Neither expediency nor pragmatism drove FDR's consistency in this effort. The evidence indicates that, in this case, he was taking a principled stand in accordance with his vision of a postwar new world order.

In the bureaucratic realm, both within the Roosevelt administration and among the Allies, the problem of seeking justice for the Holocaust operated as an ever-growing dilemma. As the war moved inexorably toward its end, pressure mounted to come up with a plan, and little consensus existed, though many came to work on it. There were some, like the U.S. State Department's legal adviser, Green Hackworth, who were convinced it simply should not be done, and he was steering Secretary of State Hull's views. There were those in the British Foreign Office who were similarly inclined, focused more on what seeking justice might mean to maintenance of the empire. Hackworth was part of a cadre of bureaucrats at State who opposed seeking justice for the Holocaust for a mixture of reasons: careerism, antisemitism, a preference for legal positivism, and a general repugnance over FDR's predilection to conduct foreign relations outside of the department. Once Hackworth understood FDR's determination, however, he belatedly altered his position; careerism for him won the day. Hull, for his part, never did grasp the president's resolve and ultimately became only a bit player once Morgenthau and Stimson became involved in 1944.

Setting aside the methodology, the decision to seek justice for the Holocaust itself carried with it significant consequences related to FDR's larger vision for a liberal postwar world order, which included spreading American values and power, dismantling colonialism, and creating what amounted to an executive consortium—headed by the United States—to manage this new postwar world.

The president seemed to understand that should the Allies fail to seek justice, the hopes he articulated in the Four Freedoms, the principles he enunciated with Churchill in the Atlantic Charter, and the determination stated by the Allies in the "Declaration by United Nations" might come into question. Of course, it may have been just as simple as that he believed seeking justice for the Holocaust was the right thing to do.

Obviously, FDR was not solely responsible for seeking justice for the Holocaust any more than he should be held solely accountable for a failure to rescue the Jews. Similarly, the United States was not the only nation facing the problems of rescue and justice. But where FDR failed to take the lead on refugee issues—or attempting to save Jewish lives during the war—he did take the lead on seeking justice. It did not hurt either that his successor, President Truman, made FDR's priority of seeking justice for the Holocaust one of the several aspects of Roosevelt's policy objectives that Truman was determined to see through.

Although this book asserts the importance of FDR's consistency on justice and reveals Pell's remarkable efforts, one person more than any other has remained the face of Nuremberg and seeking justice for the Holocaust: Robert H. Jackson. His brilliant opening statement reverberates still today. "The privilege of opening the first trial in history for crimes against the peace of the world imposes a grave responsibility," he said then. "The wrongs which we seek to condemn and punish have been so calculated, so malignant, and so devastating, that civilization cannot tolerate their being ignored, because it cannot survive their being repeated."[26]

But Jackson inherited Nuremberg and the plan to seek justice for the Holocaust upon Truman's appointment of him in May 1945. He inherited the plan to circumscribe the scope of crimes against humanity to protect American sovereignty, and he carried it out as perhaps no one else could. But before that happened, the central character in the struggle to develop Allied war crimes policy during World War II was Herbert C. Pell, the patrician friend whom Franklin D. Roosevelt appointed to the UNWCC in the summer of 1943. Although this book focuses primarily on one aspect of Pell's work on the UNWCC—seeking justice for the Holocaust—the breadth of his work was far-reaching and contributed greatly to the UNWCC's significance in helping bring about the modern human rights movement.[27] As such, Pell is one of a relatively long line of behind-the-scenes players in U.S. diplomatic history, unknown yet so very crucial to policy making. The early chapters of this book detail Pell's effort to extend—and those of his opponents to limit—a little-understood legal category of "crimes against

humanity" to include atrocities committed against any person based on race or
religion, regardless of the nationality of the victim or perpetrator.

Pell forced the U.S. State Department to take action on war crimes policy.
He brought the Treasury Department into the debate, which, in turn, provoked
Stimson's War Department to intercede and make war crimes an integral part of
the debate over postwar Germany. Pell made Allied war crimes planning part of
a public debate. And it was Pell who—unknowingly—prompted the Roosevelt
administration to consider the need to protect American sovereignty in its
effort to seek justice for the Holocaust. His actions required the administration
to develop a program linking "crimes against humanity" with "aggressive war"
and "conspiracy" to hold Nazis legally accountable for the Holocaust, a program
that simultaneously shielded the United States (and other Allied nations, namely,
the Soviet Union, Britain, and France—who also had internal situations they
wanted to exempt from global evaluation) from being accused of violations
of international law because of lynching and other attacks on blacks, and the
political and social segregation of the races inside the United States.

Pell always believed he had acted in the name of—and with the support of—
FDR. Consequently, he never anticipated or completely understood the persistent
obstructionism he faced in his effort to seek justice for the Holocaust. The U.S.
State Department first fought his appointment and then attempted to trivialize
Pell's position, as well as that of the UNWCC. Finally—and, unbelievably, with
the acquiescence of the president—leaders at State successfully orchestrated
Pell's removal from the UNWCC.

It was a stunning heartbreak for Pell, who had developed a close and trusting
relationship with the president, the man he knew for most of their forty-plus-
year friendship as "Frank." Before that happened, however, Pell had played the
pivotal role in making Nazi crimes against humanity, including and especially
those committed against German nationals, an international offense for which
the Allies would seek punishment. At its most basic level, *Seeking Justice for the
Holocaust* recounts the very human story of Pell's unappreciated effort at the
behest of—and in partnership with—his friend the president to give meaning
to World War II.

CHAPTER 1

FORGING A FRIENDSHIP

"He's Not Such a Bad Fellow"

I can not believe that any one race today is made up entirely of supermen, while none worthy of preservation exist in any other, and I certainly do not believe that it requires a hundred armed Nordic supermen to overcome one unarmed individual belonging to a race destined to succumb.

Herbert C. Pell, August 1924

On the southeastern bank of the Anacostia River near its confluence with the Potomac and within sight of the U.S. Capitol sits Anacostia Flats. Here on the night of July 28, 1932, Herbert Hoover effectively handed Franklin Delano Roosevelt the presidency. The 1932 election was still more than three months away, but a decision taken that day by Hoover was more than enough to convince most Americans, including FDR himself, that he would become the next president of the United States.

Hoping to alleviate some of the pressures of the Great Depression, World War I veterans—the Bonus Expeditionary Forces, as they called themselves—began arriving in the nation's capital in May 1932 to demand of Congress early payment of bonuses that were not due until 1945. Back in May 1920 Herbert Pell was one of a handful of congressmen who had the temerity to vote against future bonus payments. Going so far as to speak out against the bill for veterans, something a politician should never do, he knowingly ruined any possibility of reelection.

Pell during his one term as a U.S. representative from
New York's 17th district (March 4, 1919–March 3, 1921).
*Library of Congress, Prints & Photographs Division, photograph
by Harris & Ewing (LC-H25-62376-BG).*

His last day in Congress was March 3, 1921, whereupon he sent his office equipment back to his home at Tuxedo Park, introducing, he noted in his oral history,
"cockroaches into the house ... which had to be exterminated at some cost."[1]
Pell's actions, though, in no short time politically united him with his old college
friend Frank Roosevelt.

But on that summer day in 1932, Hoover, reacting more out of fear than
compassion and after hearing that shots had been fired that reportedly killed two
Bonus Army veterans, ordered army chief of staff General Douglas MacArthur
to clear out the veterans. This decision, appearing unsupportive of veterans, like
Pell's twelve years before, ultimately ended Hoover's political career.

MacArthur assigned Major Dwight D. Eisenhower as liaison officer to work
with the local police, but it was up to detachments of infantry, several machine-
gun crews, six tanks, and cavalry under the command of Major George S. Patton
to remove forcibly the veterans from the District of Columbia. Around 4:30 P.M.,

Patton's men deployed across Pennsylvania Avenue within sight of the White House and then began moving from Fifteenth Street southeast toward the Capitol. At first, many of the veterans and spectators alike mistakenly assumed the army was merely making a show of force. Some even began to applaud the organizing soldiers. When the army fixed bayonets and donned gas masks, the rest of the veterans were quickly disabused of their instinct to welcome the soldiers. Soon Patton's men were launching tear-gas grenades. Some responded to the assault by throwing bricks and stones; most, unarmed as they were, simply broke and ran, many to the questionable safety of their encampment of crudely assembled temporary dwellings across the river at Anacostia Flats.[2]

Near nightfall, having completed the task of clearing downtown Washington of veterans, MacArthur then exceeded his orders. His army crossed the Eleventh Street Drawbridge, which led into the veterans' encampment. Within hours, the ten-thousand-plus inhabitants of Bonus City at Anacostia Flats—the first of many Hoovervilles to come—had been defeated and dispersed. Only a smoky, smoldering mass of the former makeshift dwellings remained the following morning. Later that day Hoover, completely misunderstanding the mood of the nation, proclaimed victoriously, "A challenge to the authority of the United States Government has been met, swiftly and firmly." Hoover so botched this situation that Roosevelt's victory in the coming fall election was virtually assured.[3]

On Election Day, November 8, 1932, American voters—22,821,277 in all—overwhelmingly selected FDR over the Republican Hoover, Socialist Party candidate Norman Thomas, and the Communist Party's William Foster, thereby making FDR the first popularly elected Democrat to the office of the president in eighty years, since Franklin Pierce in 1852.[4] The 57.4 percent to 39.7 percent popular vote drubbing was ever more sweeping in the Electoral College, where FDR garnered close to 90 percent of the electoral vote, besting Hoover 472-59. Pell tried to reassure his friend, soon to be the president-elect, "Make no mistake, the people are voting for you in hope, far more than they are voting against Hoover in resentment or disappointment."[5]

No one then knew, of course, that FDR would retain the office for slightly over thirteen years, presiding over the breadth of the Great Depression and most of the Second World War. He died just a few months into his unprecedented fourth term on April 12, 1945, just twenty-six days before Nazi Germany's unconditional surrender. Pell sent FDR a letter on November 8, 1932, designed to memorialize election day. He promised to follow it up the next day with a congratulatory telegram. Pell told "Frank"—noting that this was the last time he would ever address him that way—"We all expect from you that justice which can only be the permanent base of prosperity and of peace." Neither knew at that moment that FDR would call upon Pell a decade later to serve in a capacity that had so much to do with the pursuit of justice. In 1932, however, Pell was writing about bringing justice to America's poorest, who were then suffering the most in the Depression, not justice for European Jews.

Pell ended his letter with his "best wishes to a man I have long known on an equal footing."[6] These two men had come from very similar backgrounds and upbringings, and they shared a very similar worldview. Although the footing was forever changed, they remained friends and political allies—at least until 1945. And the expectation of justice that Pell trusted FDR would deliver to Americans in the Great Depression became a very different kind of justice, an expectation of justice for World War II's persecuted millions. This vision for justice was a shared effort, at least for a brief year and a half beginning in the summer of 1943. Before that happened—seeking justice for the Holocaust—FDR needed to revive Pell's political career in the wake of his Bonus Army vote in 1920. It turned out to be a choice that united the two men politically beyond their previous social connection and in a way that neither could have then predicted.

Herbert C. Pell was born on the Upper East Side of New York City on February 16, 1884, his parents having married just one year earlier under mysterious circumstances. A few days after the wedding, the *New York Times* reported, "Society circles" were simply "agog over the unexpected marriage."[7] Rumors abounded, but the likely reason for the secretive nature of the union was that the mother of the bride, Mrs. James P. Kernochan, opposed the marriage. Over the years, she never became comfortable with it—or, to be more precise, with her son-in-law, although she and her grandson Bertie did become quite close. In later years, Pell liked to repeat his much-loved grandmother's advice to the women of the family. "Marry the life you like. The man doesn't matter after a few years. . . . No matter who you marry, you're going to regret it. Better to regret it in a Victoria than in a trolley car."[8]

The Victoria was the most elegant and expensive carriage in the era before the automobile, singularly popular among the wealthiest East Coast families. With a forward-facing seat for two made of the finest leather and a raised driver's seat to display a stylishly clad coachman, New York City's wealthiest families regularly preferred to tour leisurely through Central Park with calash top retracted—all the better to see and, more importantly, be seen. In the latter part of the nineteenth century, it had become the distinguishing symbol of membership in American high society. Pell himself always preferred the ride of a Victoria to that of the trolley—that is, at least until he could replace it with motorized transportation, an all-new symbol of wealth and affluence. To no one's surprise, Pell was an early automobile enthusiast.

In 1905 he had been badly injured when he was thrown out of a moving automobile, but that did not deter his love for this newest symbol of affluence. Beginning the winter of 1908–1909 and lasting until the summer of 1912, Pell traveled by automobile, touring much of Europe. He liked to think of his travels as a solitary journey of a modern-day adventurer. Of course, he was never without a chauffeur, "because cars," he later reminisced, "had those little hard tires that took half an hour to change. . . . You thought you were lucky if you did six hundred miles without breaking a tire."[9] Gentlemen did not change tires, and Herbert Pell, if nothing else, was a gentleman.

Pell learned much about himself and Europe during his travels. It was a satisfying period of wanderlust for a gregarious twenty-something with an endless supply of money and time on his hands; at the same time, his explorations only reinforced his belief in internationalism. To many, he was considered something of a dandy. Pell always preferred the chauffer-driven, peripatetic lifestyle of the gentleman-aristocrat. It had been, he maintained, "a very pleasant way to live."[10] It came as a surprise, then, to the men of his class and upbringing that Pell jumped on the Teddy Roosevelt Progressive bandwagon upon his return to the United States. Pell was a man of his own mind and inclinations, acquiring a serious streak of independence from both his parents, who had regularly encouraged him to above all think for himself.

Pell's earliest memory was of his mother holding him up to gaze out the window of their fashionable Upper East Side home. It was the middle of an impressive New York blizzard, and young Pell spied two immense horses pulling a small sleigh carrying a case of milk to the Pell residence. "Milk," he recalled, "was very important to me at that time." His mother, however—and without comment—pointed through the window toward the figure of William Astor, who was trudging through the snow to his home at the corner of Thirty-Fourth Street and Fifth Avenue, where the Empire State Building stands today, leaving Pell to reach his own conclusions. Many a night William Astor returned home walking, Pell noted, "usually in an advanced state of liquor."[11] Pell was obviously proud of his heritage of intellectual independence. "I've tried to pursue that with my own son [Claiborne Pell]," he later said. "Give a boy anything you can afford to give him, except advice—be awfully stingy with advice. Make him decide everything [on his own] as much as possible."[12]

Throughout his life, Pell remained intellectually self-reliant yet conspicuously well informed. This was especially true during his brief tenure with the United Nations War Crimes Commission (UNWCC) when the layman among lawyers and barristers resolutely sought justice for the Holocaust in the face of sustained opposition. Pell had frequently displayed these traits during his short stints of higher education at Harvard and then informally at Columbia and New York University. At Harvard, Pell judged the studies organized for two types of students. One was arranged "for the drunk who wouldn't study except under compulsion"; the other, for students in attendance only for grades. But Pell saw himself as something altogether different, the student who sought an education for "learning's sake" alone.[13] Consequently, he held little respect for most of his professors. When historian Albert Bushnell Hart suggested Pell drop his course because Pell questioned an interpretation of Hart's, Pell readily did so. Pell's favorite was Columbia historian Charles A. Beard, who later gained celebrity for his *An Economic Interpretation of the Constitution,* as well as for his allegation that FDR goaded the Japanese into attacking Pearl Harbor.[14] Beard appealed to the young but already fiercely independent and progressive-thinking Pell.

It was at Harvard in 1902 that Bertie Pell became friends with Frank Roosevelt, although the families of the two young men had known each other for some time. Of the eight hundred new students entering that year, Pell observed that "there were not forty that had any idea of doing anything with their lives."[15] Presumably, he excluded from that group himself as well as Frank Roosevelt, who was two years his senior and already in his third year at Harvard. At least to Pell, FDR was not one of those attending merely for grades; FDR's grades rarely rose above a C, and his attendance was not regular by any stretch. Like his new friend, Bertie, FDR enjoyed a relatively worry-free childhood full of travel and adventure. With it, nonetheless, came expectations for both men: expectations of their parents and certainly expectations each held for himself.

For most young men of Pell's and FDR's wealth and social standing, college was an opportunity to develop one's sense of self and intellect. Like Pell, FDR gravitated toward economics, government, and history courses. In a spring 1903 English class, already on the editorial board of the *Harvard Crimson,* FDR began honing his public speaking skills. One of the surviving texts of his biweekly efforts was of a speech focusing on the reunification of the nation in the post–Civil War era and the "great problem" of the South: "the Negro." This speech offers a rare insight into FDR's early thinking about African Americans and demonstrates his later 1930s and 1940s distinctive writing and speaking style.

Speaking hypothetically as a Harvard alumnus at some time after the Civil War in rebuttal to a certain former Confederate "Colonel X," FDR considered what divided North from South and the way in which Harvard participated in bridging the divide. It is certainly not true, FDR insisted, that Harvard "represents hostility to the ideals and bringing up" of southerners; Harvard does not represent those Americans "who do not and will not make an attempt to meet the South half-way on their great problem, the Negro." The key for northerners in helping reunite the nation was to "know and sympathize with our brothers of the South more and more." FDR claimed that southerners had suggested education as the solution to the problems created by Congress placing "the ignorant black . . . on the same political footing" with southern whites following the Civil War. That is why Harvard has "done honor to perhaps a half dozen negroes—men all of them who have given their lives for their race," FDR reasoned. "Yes, Harvard has sought to uplift the negro, if you like, has sought to make a man out of a semi-beast."[16]

Had Pell been in the audience for this speech, he would have agreed with FDR on the need for the two sections of the nation to understand each other better, and probably the necessity of uplifting blacks through education as well. But Pell would not have thought Harvard the best institution to accomplish it. Pell, entirely dissatisfied with the school, attended only two years. Initially, he had considered Harvard as preparation for a career in law, just like FDR. The untimely death of Pell's mother's brother, however, significantly changed his fortunes; his mother inherited all his grandmother's considerable wealth. Henceforth, as he later explained to his son, he would never be "obliged to adopt some gainful occupation."[17]

Nonetheless, his time at Harvard, though brief, was exceedingly important, if for no other reason than here he first forged his friendship with FDR. The relationship remained lifelong and consequential for both. Only in the final months of FDR's life did the relationship become strained, when FDR almost inexplicably abandoned his friend to the maneuverings of Pell's enemies in the State Department. At every other step in Pell's political and diplomatic career, FDR sustained his friend. For his part, Pell always and devotedly supported FDR's politics and policies; with rare exception, they were the same as his own. Of course, FDR often made it difficult for those around him to determine just where he stood on an issue.

In June 1921 FDR played a pivotal role in helping revive Pell's then-moribund political career. This was just two months before FDR contracted polio while vacationing at Campobello Island, which threatened not just to derail but also to terminate prematurely the future president's hopes for a long career in government. Pell's political career needed saving because of his own missteps; his heightened sense of duty and honor caused him to do the one thing a politician should never do: he appeared to be unsupportive of American servicemen.

FDR had spent the 1910s as assistant secretary of the navy, appointed by President Woodrow Wilson in 1913, while Pell had become a Democratic member of the Sixty-Sixth Congress at the end of that decade, in March 1919. Just a year later in May, Pell ended any hope of his returning to Congress by voting against—and speaking out in opposition to—making bonus payments to World War I veterans. "I intend to vote against the bonus," he told a small but stunned group of listeners in the House chamber. "I am doing this in the full realization that it means the end of my political career. I can tell you frankly that it is a painful thing to commit suicide, but I do not think that honor will permit me to follow any other course."[18]

Pell believed in giving bonus payments only to those truly needy. He said that he was "perfectly ready—I would have sold the White House and mortgaged the Capitol to get money—to take care of the wounded soldiers, the men who have been injured." But from Pell's perspective, to give money to perfectly healthy men, men more than capable of earning their way in the world, was simply wrongheaded. "I thought it was iniquitous then. I think it's iniquitous now," he remarked later in his life.[19]

Nonetheless, Pell ran for reelection in 1920, certain of defeat, but he felt it his duty to the Democratic Party to run. Pell lost the election to Ogden Mills, as he knew he would, effectively ending his political career for the foreseeable future. Leaving Congress on March 4, 1921, Pell returned that summer to the family residence in Tuxedo Park after a brief stay at his home in New York City. The quiescent gentleman of Tuxedo Park, dressed appropriately in summer whites, found his opportunity to return to politics almost immediately, much sooner than he or anyone had expected. Naturally, it could not come in the form of an elective office. And, naturally, it was his friend Frank Roosevelt who resuscitated him.

In early June the *New York Times* reported that the state chairman of the Democratic Party, William W. Farley, was willing to resign in favor of George R. Van Namee, Al Smith's former secretary and choice as a replacement.[20] According to the *Times,* Van Namee was the preference of Tammany Hall as well, but Pell knew otherwise. After reading the details in his morning paper, Pell reported, "I promptly went upstairs, took off my white shoes and trousers, put on my brown ones and took the second train down to New York."[21]

Upon his arrival, he presented himself to Jeremiah Mahoney, one of "the proper Democratic authorities," as the most viable candidate to take up the post upon the resignation of Farley. Mahoney and Pell became lifelong friends. Mahoney, who later called for the United States to boycott the 1936 Berlin Olympic Games because of Germany's racist policies against Jews, was one of Pell's most loyal supporters when he was American representative on the UNWCC.[22] In the summer of 1921 Mahoney quickly decided Pell was his selection for new chairman of the New York State Democratic Committee.

On June 29 the committee held a preparatory meeting to try to settle on the choice of a new Chairman. Among the power brokers at this informal gathering were some of the most well-known Tammany Hall men: Charles F. Murphy; John H. McCooey; Charles E. Norris; and William Church Osborn, father of Frederick Osborn, who later became FDR's head of the Morale Branch of the army during the Second World War; and several others. Also attending was the former assistant secretary of the navy, Franklin D. Roosevelt.[23] When Mahoney suggested Pell as the best choice for chairman, almost the entire group broke out in laughter. To these men, Pell was the prototypical patrician, a ne'er-do-well aristocrat-socialite certainly unfit to be the leader of the New York State Democratic Party, and they effectively dismissed him.

FDR did not join in the laughter. First, the description of Pell as a socialite idler complete with a Harvard pedigree could have applied to FDR himself. Both men hailed from America's oldest stock of landed aristocracy, and both men, to a certain extent, felt obligated to recompense those less fortunate.[24] Second, FDR likely thought Pell was a good choice for the position, given his experience and connections in the state. Finally, FDR's own future political aspirations could only be helped by having a close friend operating as chair of the New York branch of the party. Attempting to silence those who were ridiculing his suggestion, Mahoney countered that Pell was genuinely well suited for the job.

The former Progressive and Bull Moose committee member–turned-Democrat and one-term congressmen, Mahoney argued, was unaligned and therefore unbiased to any particular faction in the party. He was nothing less than the perfect compromise candidate. Following this, FDR, then brave enough to speak up, carefully told those at the gathering, "Bertie. Bertie. I remember Bertie. We were at Harvard together. He's not such a bad fellow."[25] According to Pell biographer Leonard Baker, FDR's testimonial of support just may have clinched the appointment for the aristocratic Pell.[26] Whatever the case, FDR's endorsement of Pell, if unenthusiastic, left a lasting impression; from this moment on, far from unaligned, Pell remained a steadfast supporter of FDR to the end. For his part, FDR eventually took full advantage of that loyalty.

Herbert Pell never liked being labeled as an aristocrat, but he well understood that most perceived him that way.[27] With a large mustache and well-coiffed dark, wavy hair, the strikingly handsome Pell certainly fit the part. In addition to his meticulous attention to his attire, his conspicuous physical presence dominated most rooms: he stood six-feet-five-inches tall with a fifty-two-inch chest. In a 1943 cautionary note to his son, Claiborne, Pell claimed his inordinate size for the era was the cause for his own periods of temporary idleness. "My worst quality was, of course, an almost uncontrollable unwillingness to work except sporadically. I was reading the other day the life of Charles Croker one of the Californians who built the transcontinental railroad. He was also a very big man and to my surprise given to periods of complete idleness."[28]

Later in life, Pell maintained that his larger-than-average size was due to drinking copious amounts of milk as a youth. Despite his aversion to the label of an aristocrat, he did believe that the ideal twentieth-century man of his class operated under a certain noblesse oblige, albeit with a certain independence of spirit in his case. The reluctant aristocrat Pell, therefore, surprised many of his contemporaries by taking up his new post as chair energetically and performing admirably at a very difficult time for the Democratic Party.

The 1920s brought so much change to the nation, including transformation and division to the Democratic Party. As the national party split into urban and rural factions; pro- and antitemperance factions; Klan and anti-Klan factions; pro- and anti-immigration factions; and Catholic, Jewish, and Protestant groups, Pell had to hold together a New York party similarly divided. Would he operate as an unaligned chairman of the New York party as expected? Would he welcome all factions to his state for the national convention, or would he make obvious his own opinions about what the Democratic Party should stand for?

Herbert Pell made his opinions obvious and unambiguous, proving Mahoney wrong in his prediction that the new chairman would be unbiased. Pell was against Prohibition and committed New York Democrats into making the question into a states rights issue.[29] While a nominal Protestant himself, he was not anti-Catholic, anti-Jew, or anti-immigration. As New York chairman, Pell represented the urban wing of the party. A decade later in 1935 he wrote to a friend that "no intelligent person born on a farm has reached reproductive age without leaving for the city. The natural result of this inverse selection," he concluded, "is the present farming population of the United States, stupid, suspicious, illiterate, dishonest, and superstitious."[30] Perhaps taken in by the social Darwinist discourse of the period but most probably influenced by his experience as New York Party Chairman, particularly during the divisive 1924 Democratic Convention, Pell had grown tired of the anti-intellectual, bigoted, and isolationist tendencies that he had come to associate with the then Klan-centric rural America.

The 1924 Democratic Convention, the longest in U.S. history, was also possibly the most acrimonious. To Pell, it was simply "that terrible Convention."[31] Not since the election of 1860 when the Democratic Party broke into northern and southern factions, thereby ensuring Lincoln's election, had it been so hopelessly divided. The 1924 convention brought together white conservatives from the more rural South and West—Wilsonian Democrats who defended Prohibition, fundamentalism, and the Ku Klux Klan—with a new breed of Democrat produced in the metropolitan North and Midwest. Mostly Catholic or Jewish, these new Democrats cared little for the beliefs or needs of their bucolic counterparts.

The issue of whether to denounce the Klan in the party platform seemed to dominate the convention, or "Klanbake" as some northern papers were derogatorily calling it. On July 4, after ballot number 61 failed to result in the selection of a presidential candidate, twenty thousand–plus Klansmen held a very public picnic in nearby New Jersey, complete with white robes, hoods, requisite speeches about the "Klanvention" in "Jew York," and of course, the compulsory cross-burning. It ultimately took forty-two more ballots, 103 in all, to select a candidate, and those hoping for a stern condemnation of the Klan were left wanting. The final platform vote on the Klan was 546.15 against condemning the group, 542.85 for condemnation.

The 1920s had been a formative period for Pell in politics as he moved seamlessly into the Democratic Party hierarchy while maintaining his intellectual connection to his old Progressive Era days. But it was also an important time for Pell in developing his thinking about racial, religious, and ethnic issues. As chairman of the New York Democratic Party, Pell had responded to a request for a statement from the *Pittsburgh Courier* regarding the growing strength of the Ku Klux Klan in America and in the Democratic Party. This new version of the Klan did not just hate blacks; it was viciously anti-Catholic, anti-Jew, and anti-immigrant as well. Pell, a man already established as not averse to political suicide, was audaciously forthright in his response: "Any group or organization which is attempting to organize for political action along racial or religious lines is fundamentally opposed to the best principles of Americanism." As if he possessed foreknowledge of what was to come in Europe in the next decade, Pell added, "I do not take much stock in the extreme theories of race . . . [and] I can not believe that any one race today is made up entirely of supermen, while none worthy of preservation exist in any other . . . that it requires a hundred armed Nordic supermen to overcome one unarmed individual belonging to a race destined to succumb."[32]

Pell did not offer these views to the small black readership of the *Pittsburgh Courier* for political gain. He was not just telling a black audience what it wanted to hear. He expressed his thoughts openly not just as an individual but also as the chairman of the Democratic Party in New York State. Moreover, he wanted everyone to hear him, white as well as black Americans.

On August 14, 1924, Pell responded to a Long Island newspaper editor[33] who was inquiring about the state party position on the Klan in the aftermath of the convention. The Klan, Pell knew, had considerable support in various areas of Long Island. "The Ku Klux Klan," Pell wrote the editor, "violates the fundamental principles of the American Government by its fight against tolerance and by its interference with and open contempt of the constitutionally organized courts of law." Pell also stated, "I can tell you that there can be no doubt as to the stand of the Democratic Party in relation to the Ku Klux Klan or any other organization gotten up to promote religious or racial prejudice in this country." Of course, judging by the platform vote on the Klan, considerable doubt did exist about the party. Judging by Pell's stance, however, no doubt remains as to his view. Pell concluded his letter observing that he had "hoped never to see the day when my country would need the protection of men too weak, too low, too mean and too cowardly to dare to show their faces."[34]

Pell went so far as to send copies of the statement to every paper in New York "so there could be no possible doubt," he wrote in his 1953 oral history, "where we stood—where I stood."[35] It was prominently reprinted in the *New York Times*—"Klan Is Denounced by Chairman Pell"—the following day.[36] In a 1935 letter, Pell commented to a friend that his efforts in favor of equality and against the Klan had resulted in a threatened kidnapping of his young son, Claiborne.[37]

Threats notwithstanding, Pell had gone so far as to suggest he give a speech at the 1924 convention in condemnation of the Klan and in support of Al Smith, although Pell was not a fan of Smith himself. Pell supported Smith only insofar as FDR did. FDR, Smith's floor leader at the convention, vetoed Pell's proposed speech. It would not do, he thought, for Pell to speak in favor of Smith, a Catholic, and simultaneously against the Klan.[38] FDR was too much a politician to risk alienating any voters, even if he found their beliefs reprehensible, as his friend Bertie Pell obviously did. FDR's denial, however, apparently had helped to motivate Pell to speak so openly and boldly about race in America—that and the circus that was the 1924 Klanvention.

For FDR the convention marked his return to public politics after a nearly three-year hiatus brought about by his contraction of polio in 1921. He wanted to do so by delivering Al Smith's nominating speech. Initially, there seemed to be some debate over who would nominate him. In late May the *New York Times* reported only that FDR might get the nod since he was chairman of Smith's campaign committee.[39] With the seconding speeches already determined—none of whom was FDR—all bets seemed to be on Smith's chairman. When asked about the possible selection of FDR in late June, Smith wryly replied, "It looks that way, although nothing is settled yet."[40] It was, of course; FDR was the choice. But this was only because Joseph M. Proskauer, an adviser and confidant of Smith, reminded the New York governor that a "Bowery mick" could do no better than the "Protestant patrician" Roosevelt.[41] Given the tenor of the convention, it was a smart choice. It was also a good choice to avoid any mention of the Klan in the speech, which was written, to FDR's complete irritation, by Proskauer.

FDR had fully prepared for his public return. FDR asked his son James to serve as his "prop" throughout, which came to include delivering messages and running errands. FDR attended every day of the convention, which required careful choreographing of each entrance and exit. The process for his father was an "ordeal" even after they had "practiced the awkward business," as James put it, many times.[42] For FDR, polio was a relentless ordeal.

Every day at 8:00 A.M. from June 24 to July 9, convention delegate Frederick Osborn arrived at the Roosevelt home on West Fifty-Fourth Street to brief FDR on the day ahead and accompany him to the convention. Osborn was described as having a "Lincolnian presence"—at six-feet-eight, he towered over everyone, even Herbert Pell.[43] The two men met in FDR's bedroom. FDR showed no concern whatsoever with Osborn witnessing the complicated dance he endured every morning. Osborn marveled at his unwillingness to let his handicap defeat him.

> The butler would pull up the shades, Franklin would give me a cheery greeting and sit me in a chair for our morning chat. . . . His behavior was one of character and courage one would never forget. First, he would sit up, lifting his helpless legs over the edge of the bed with a strong hand.

LEFT TO RIGHT: Al Smith, Pell, and Franklin D. Roosevelt. FDR gave the nominating speech for Smith at the divisive 1924 Democratic National Convention. Pell, who supported Smith only to the extent FDR did, foreshadowed his work on the UNWCC by responding to a newspaper query at the time, "Any group or organization which is attempting to organize for political action along racial or religious lines is fundamentally opposed to the best principles of Americanism." Courtesy of the Franklin D. Roosevelt Presidential Library and Museum, Hyde Park, New York.

Then he would reach up to a pulley at the right height above his head, pull himself upright with one arm (he had powerful muscles from the waist up), give a swing and catch the next ring to the bathroom, where he would drop himself down on a chair in front of the washbasin and mirror. Then he would brush his teeth, shave, and comb his hair, talking all the while with intense interest.[44]

The "cheery" demeanor, which was characteristic of the optimism he delivered like a gift to all those around him, belied the very real suffering that returning to a public life meant for FDR. He was quite familiar with the torment that came with a political life, but the physical toll his return to politics brought did not fully show until the last two years of his presidency.

Over time the public tended to forget—even take for granted—just how ardu-
ous each day was for FDR. The delegates at the convention, however, witnessed
it daily. FDR insisted that James help him walk each day to his seat on the
convention floor, one hand gripping James and the other working a crutch. He
was not about to be seen publicly in a wheelchair. "His legs were locked rigidly
by steel braces," his son described, "and his movement actually was achieved
by pivoting with his powerful arms and torso and propelling his body by brute
strength."[45] Even the process of sitting had required practice.

As tough as his daily convention routine was, getting to the podium to deliver
the nomination speech was burdened with danger. Not yet an FDR insider, New
York delegate Jim Farley recalled that his "greatest thrill" of the convention had
been when FDR rose to nominate Smith, "overcoming pain and discomfort."[46]
Any fall could have been disastrous, not just for the moment but for his future
political hopes. Nonetheless, for this speech, he chose to walk as much as possible on his own. He released his grip on James—"his fingers dug into my arm
like pincers," James had written—took a second crutch, and walked, as it were,
on his own to the podium.[47] As Farley described it, despite the pain, "his face
was that of a jubilant marcher."[48] James was "sweating and shaking" until his
father reached his destination and grabbed the podium. In a brief panic, before
his walk, FDR yelled to Joseph Guffey, a Pennsylvania delegate, to "shake the
podium."[49] It would have to hold his weight for the next thirty minutes. "I was
so damn proud," James later wrote, "that it was with difficulty that I kept myself
from bursting into tears."[50]

FDR's appearance to give Smith's nominating speech that day—as labored
and treacherous as it was for him just to get to the podium—was greeted with
thunderous applause. It was hard to know how much was for Smith or FDR;
the delegates obviously appreciated the effort expended. The *New York Times*
noted, "No one who had attended . . . would dispute that the most popular man
in the Convention was Franklin D. Roosevelt."[51] And that observation was notwithstanding that his candidate—Al Smith—did not win the nomination. For
the remainder of the 1920s, at least until he became governor, FDR operated as
the number-two Democrat in the state, second only to Al Smith. Although he
was state chairman, Pell was somewhere further down the line, and that wasn't
to last too much longer.

Disgusted by the experience of "that terrible Convention," as he put it, and
his inability to work well with Al Smith, Pell resigned as chairman of the New
York Democratic Party in January 1926, leaving politics "completely" and by all

expectations, including his own, forever.[52] For Pell, this was not just an expression of momentary frustration; he meant it. Pell was of a class where he did not need to earn a living, nor did he need to participate in politics.

Based on his experience in Congress, his temperament had already proved to be especially unsuited to that kind of public service. Party politics he liked, but it was real work and often quite time-consuming. As he readily admitted, he was not particularly inclined to work hard. So, when he said he was through with politics, he meant it. He much preferred traveling by automobile about Europe. Pell also had a new focus. His son, Claiborne, born just eleven days after the guns of World War I went silent, had turned eight in 1926. It was time for Pell to begin in earnest the long preparation of his son to carry on the work of managing the Pell family fortune and reputation. Pell took both of those things—fortune and reputation—very seriously.

He maintained, however, his close friendship with FDR. And that continuation, as it turned out, was not without its own significance. Pell's self-imposed retirement from politics was destined to be impermanent.

CHAPTER 2

AMBASSADOR TO PORTUGAL

"The Best Listening Post We Have in Europe"

The time may come when a few men, like myself, will be very useful to you, and at that time, you may call on me.

Herbert C. Pell to "Frank" Roosevelt, November 8, 1932

Pell returned full-time to his preferred lifestyle of the traveler after the death of his father in spring 1926. He joined his mother in Italy, observing firsthand the effects of fascism. Looking back, Pell felt the Italian people had accepted Mussolini out "of a combination of apathy, selfishness, and fear."[1] He left Florence, Italy, for Paris early the next year, where he and his wife surprised many by divorcing. Both remarried within two weeks of each other in June 1927. With his new wife, the former Olive Bigelow, Pell spent the remainder of the summer in Vienna. From there and by virtue of his trips into Germany and France, Pell had a ringside seat to the rise of Hitler. Looking back, he remembered, "The Nazi organization was built as openly as Grand Central Station was, with everything explained, every plan advertised."[2]

Pell spent the remainder of the 1920s and early 1930s focused on his two great loves—traveling, and guiding the character and education of his son, Claiborne, who was born November 22, 1918, just days after Pell's surprise election to

Congress. The time and energy it took were well spent. On the first account, Pell's travels—the connections he made and what he learned while on them—would soon enough serve him well as an ambassador and later during his brief tenure on the United Nations War Crimes Commission (UNWCC). On the second, the effort produced a longer-term result. Claiborne came to view his father as the greatest man he knew and, as Michael Blayney put it in his brief book on Pell as aristocrat, "the most profound influence on his life."[3] This is no small matter when one considers the accomplishments of Claiborne Pell, six-term senator from Rhode Island (1961–97).

Still, Pell kept up his friendship with Frank Roosevelt throughout. Thrilled by the latter's nomination for governor of New York in 1928, Pell enclosed a "small contribution" in one of his letters during the campaign. "My Dear Bertie," FDR responded, "I only wish that you were here to take part in the excitement of this close race."[4] No doubt, Pell did too, but any desire to get back into politics remained subsumed by his focus on the upbringing of his son.

Although his first wife had custody of Claiborne, Pell saw him often, electing to live in an oversized mansion in Newport, Rhode Island, close to his son's school. All the while, Pell kept a close eye on New York politics as well as big business and finance. His close attention to what he considered their failings in the 1920s turned to repugnance by the thirties. As someone who saw it as his primary job to maintain the family fortune—to be a "good steward" during his tenure, as he put it to Claiborne—preserving capitalism meant much. Well before FDR was accused of being a "traitor to his class," Pell's wealthy contemporaries had already placed him in that league, although a considerably less impressive term had been applied; with all his demands for restraint and reform, Pell was simply a "rebel."[5]

A few short days after FDR's inauguration as governor of New York on January 1, 1929, Pell urged him to make no concessions to big business. "Of course," he wrote his friend, "I am more of a radical than you, but . . . the national election of 1924 showed very definitely that the business community was not interested in honest government, and the election of 1928 convinced me that the great finance organizations of the country were ready to strain every nerve and stoop to any depth. . . ." Noting their shared effort to limit the excesses of their class, he added, "Every time we have tried conciliating these people we have failed or been corrupted." Agreeing with his friend, the new governor replied, "When that time comes I want to see the Democratic party sanely radical enough to have most of the disgruntled ones turn to it to put us in power again."[6] Of course, that time did come, and it became FDR's task to lead his party and the country.

Among all of FDR's closest friends and advisers, the upbringing, financial status, and political beliefs he shared with Pell created a unique friendship. Pell perhaps was more radical than his friend. But the distance between the two only existed in that from the sidelines Pell was free to speak and act as he wished while FDR, as he suggested for the Democratic Party, had to operate "sanely radical enough." Judging by his response to the 1929 stock market crash and the Great Depression that followed, FDR surely was that "sanely radical enough" in his effort to save an imploding capitalism. Their distanced alliance in this vision to save capitalism through restraint and reform, in a way, later repeated itself when FDR selected Pell for the UNWCC. The "more radical" Pell worked to carry out FDR's call for justice, while the president had to maintain a more politic approach.

Pell was overjoyed by the outcome of the 1932 presidential election. He saw that it might mean an opportunity for him to return to political life. "If in any way, I can help to break up privilege, I shall gladly do so," Pell told him. "The time may come when a few men, like myself, will be very useful to you, and at that time, you may call on me."[7] Although Pell played no role in the campaign, on behalf of the president, Jim Farley approached Pell with an offer to become minister to Bulgaria. Pell declined with no explanation to anyone.[8] Undoubtedly, this post in far-off Bulgaria was not what Pell had in mind when he offered his usefulness. He wanted to help FDR save capitalism for the country and his family.

So Pell remained on the sidelines, publishing a little and writing many letters, particularly to his son. But he continued to reach out sporadically to the president, sometimes dropping in at the White House or Hyde Park. On April 17, 1934, the president hosted the Haitian president, who was in Washington with other officials doing the work to end nineteen years of U.S. military occupation. Pell was among the invited guests at the evening tea to mark the day. Eighteen-year-old Nan Johnson from Cleveland sang for the two presidents and their guests. The occasion was made even more special than the typical gathering because Nan Johnson was a polio survivor like FDR. She had previously written Eleanor, who arranged for her appearance.[9] The day was also noteworthy because, at the luncheon earlier in the day, the first official toasts were made in the White House since the repeal of Prohibition.[10]

For Pell, the day was marked by an unusual conversation—at least for him. He had been in a private discussion with FDR off to the side by a fireplace when the president of Haiti arrived and was formally announced. As he recounted it in his oral history, "I naturally withdrew as these two chiefs of states were in conversation." FDR, however, had none of that and asked Pell to stay, whereupon the three—two presidents and citizen Pell—had a "three-cornered conversation in French." Avoiding any use of English, Pell appreciated FDR's "elementary good manners" toward the Haitian president.[11]

FDR, who hadn't seen Pell in some time, apparently invited him to drop in the next day. According to White House logs, the two met beginning at 11:45 A.M. for an extended visit. An hourlong meeting with several cabinet members scheduled at the time had been canceled.[12] According to Pell, during their meetings, their discussion usually focused on mutual friends past and present—with FDR doing "most of the talking."[13] If anything substantive was discussed this day given the length of their meeting, it would remain known only to the two of them.

Pell's next visit to the White House wasn't until January 22, 1935, for a fifteen-minute chat in the Oval Office; perhaps Pell dropped by simply to wish his friend early congratulations on his upcoming fifty-third birthday, January 30.[14] One topic of discussion must have been the World Court, both having supported American membership since the 1920s. Just the previous week on January 14, the U.S. Senate had taken up the question.

Given the overwhelming number of Democrats in the Senate, five more than the required sixty-four votes needed for a two-thirds majority, FDR expected easy passage. Adding to his confidence was his belief that everyone understood that although the court was part of the League of Nations, adhering to it was not the same as joining the league. All those who feared league membership and the concept of collective security need not be worried. Moreover, as FDR noted in a January 16 message to the Senate, both Republican and Democratic Party platforms "for years" had supported adherence to the court. Numerous groups in the country also recommended joining, among them the American Bar Association and the American Legion.[15]

FDR viewed the World Court as a "concrete realization" of an "obviously sound and thoroughly American policy." It was, therefore, illogical for the United States not to be a part of it. Of course, there was a logic to it; FDR just didn't like it. Cognizant of the reasons behind the failure of Wilsonian internationalism, he reassured the Senate, "The sovereignty of the United States will be in no way diminished or jeopardized by such action [joining the World Court]."[16] The political importance of protecting sovereignty had been made manifest to FDR at the end of World War I, and at this moment with the Senate debate over the court, it was only reinforced. When protecting American sovereignty later became the controlling factor in fashioning the law to seek justice for the Holocaust in 1944–45, no one needed to explain it to the president.

For FDR, joining the World Court was about preventing war, although he publicly couched it in positive terms. "At this period in international relationships," he told the Senate, "when every act is of moment to the future of world peace, the United States has an opportunity once more to throw its weight into the scale of the favor of peace."[17] A short but eventful year and a half later, he was much less restrained when he said plaintively in a speech, "I hate war."[18]

Radio priest Charles Coughlin led the attack against FDR's effort: "Joining the World Court to maintain peace," he charged, "strongly stinks of diplomatic deceit." He preferred the "logic and principles" of Washington "to Wilson and those who follow him with their crude internationalism and their unsound love of minorities."[19] On January 29, amid wheelbarrows of telegrams and messages opposing the court, the Senate voted against adherence. Father Coughlin proudly announced, "Our thanks are due to Almighty God in that America retains her sovereignty." The nation, he said, shall continue to stay "clear from foreign entanglements and European hatreds."[20] If he was including Hitler's hatred of the Jews among them, he should not have called them European hatreds; Coughlin's own hatred mirrored Hitler's, as did, sadly, that of all too many Americans, especially Coughlin's followers.

Outwardly FDR shrugged off this surprising defeat. Privately he vented his anger with a typical reference to one's judgment day. Opponents of the World Court, he said, "are willing to see a city burn down just so long as their own houses remain standing in the ruins." As for the senators who voted against it, "I am inclined to think that if they ever get to Heaven they will be doing a great deal of apologizing for a very long time—that is if God is against war—and I think He is."[21]

FDR's internationalism was out of step with much of the nation. The growing threat of fascism made him only more determined to pursue increased involvement with Europe. It had the opposite effect on most Americans, however, who were determined that the nation needed to isolate itself from Europe even more. Pell was among the few who didn't see it that way, but that must have been of little consolation to the president, who needed most Americans to see it similarly if he were to accomplish his foreign policy goal of an internationally engaged United States.

The following summer, in June, Pell and his wife spent the day at Hyde Park along with Nelson C. Brown, a forestry professor from the New York State College of Forestry. Brown had created and managed a forestry plan for the Roosevelt estate. The highlight of the day, which included a luncheon, was a drive around the grounds in FDR's specially equipped Ford.[22] This visit, of course, was purely social, although Pell and FDR probably found time to discuss their similar views on economics. Three months later the Pells repeated their visit to Hyde Park, this time with Frederick Osborn and his wife. Afternoon tea was marked on the schedule, but it likely included FDR's infamous martinis.[23]

In early 1936, shortly after the death of King George V, Pell wrote his friend, "Many years ago when I expressed the hope that you would be President of the United States and told you that there was only one place that I wanted . . . that of special envoy to the coronation of the then Prince of Wales, you said I could have it." Well, Pell reminded FDR, he "should still like to have it."[24] Calling himself the "last capitalist who is willing to be saved by you," he brazenly commended the president's "efforts" and added, "I am sorry that you have not wanted any assistance from me."[25] It seems he must have been disappointed that his long friendship with FDR had only netted an offer of minister to Bulgaria back in 1932. In any case, this was probably not the best way to make his request, even if his intimacy allowed him to communicate that way with the president.

The coronation Pell wanted to attend for King Edward VIII, the former Prince of Wales, never happened. He abdicated in December 1936 to marry divorced American socialite Wallis Simpson. He was succeeded by his brother, George VI, whose coronation took place on May 12, 1937. Pell did get his invitation, although not as FDR's special envoy, but as the guest of Pierre Cartier.[26]

With his son set to graduate high school in June 1936 and head to Princeton, Pell was apparently ready to return to politics. Pell drove to FDR's home in Hyde Park to see his friend, something he often did, but this time he was upset that the president had done nothing to fend off the many criticisms being lobbed FDR's way. Gentleman Pell could not stand the personal attacks directed at his friend's family and health, recalling later, "I was shocked at the number of false and filthy stories that were being circulated over the country about President Roosevelt."[27] Enough of the party leadership agreed with Pell, so although he had not directly asked for it, he became vice chairman of the Democratic National Campaign Committee. His job was to root out these attacks and respond as necessary. Pell's feeling for his friend and experiences in many political campaigns made him the logical and, as it turned out, best choice.

The most serious attacks focused on FDR's polio. To counter this and the other attacks, Pell composed a standard reply, which included the statement, "I have never seen him in better health. His arms could do credit to a blacksmith. His digestion is perfect, and he sleeps well." Pell noted he had "known him for over thirty years" and that he has "become stronger since his original attack of infantile paralysis." Taking FDR's condition head-on, Pell wrote, "I remember very well the shock to all his friends when he was originally stricken, and the great admiration we all had for his courage in meeting the situation and not retiring to invalidism, as would have been so easy for a man in his circumstance." Pell's defense included the offer of a bet. As "an old friend of the president who is perfectly ready to stake his money on his opinions," he was ready to put up "any reasonable amount that Franklin Roosevelt would outlive his term by two years, barring assassination."[28] Pell would have lost that bet—technically—but in 1936, few could have predicted that FDR would serve into a fourth term.

FDR's victory over Alf Landon was a landslide. Pell's work on the 1936 campaign was no difference maker, although it probably contributed to the lopsided result. And it certainly further cemented the friendship of FDR and Pell. Pell spent the winter following the election in New York, expecting to head to Europe for the coronation the following spring. His brief foray back into politics was over, however, so he prepared himself for a favorite activity: traveling by car through Europe. He arranged to have a newly purchased Ford shipped overseas and left for him at Cherbourg, France. Pell expected to take his wife on a tour through Germany; afterward, she would then head off to Scotland, and Pell would spend the remainder of the summer with his son touring through France and Germany. All in all, for Pell, he could imagine no better way to spend the summer of 1937, except that the well-planned tour never happened.[29]

In April, longtime friend Jim Farley telephoned one morning as Pell was readying himself for lunch with his mother in New York. In an apparent repeat of his 1932 proposition, FDR wanted to appoint Pell to a diplomatic post.

"Would you like to go to Portugal?" Farley asked.

"What do you want me to do in Portugal?" an incredulous Pell replied.

"Be minister there."

"All right. Yes."

As Pell recounted the conversation in his oral history, he added succinctly, "That was the way I was appointed Minister to Portugal."[30] The informality of a phone call likely bothered Pell, a man who generally preferred circumstance and ceremony. Perhaps that was why he said no in 1932. Nonetheless, this time, Pell was very ready to join the Roosevelt administration.

After a brief visit with the president on the morning of April 21, 1937, in Washington, Pell headed to the State Department where he met with Assistant Secretary of State Sumner Welles for instructions.[31] "There's no need to introduce me to Mr. Welles," Pell announced. "I've known him, not all my life, but all of his."[32] Welles was even closer to the president; as a young boy, he had served as an usher in FDR's wedding to Eleanor.

Pell expected to spend an extended time at the department, but after a brief meeting with Secretary of State Cordell Hull, he was cleared to head to Portugal, pending Senate confirmation, which occurred on May 20, 1937.[33] Breaking his observation in his 1932 congratulatory letter that he would henceforth write him as "Mr. President," Pell wrote, "Dear Frank . . . At my age I begin to think of my descendants and it will be a very happy memory to them and they will be as proud of the fact that you selected me as a representative as Olive is that Lincoln appointed her grandfather."[34] Olive Pell's (née Bigelow) grandfather John Bigelow was first appointed as American consul to Paris in 1861, rising eventually to envoy extraordinary and minister plenipotentiary to the Court of Napoleon III.

Pell didn't need another European tour to ready himself for his new post—officially envoy extraordinary and minister plenipotentiary to Portugal. As biographer Leonard Baker noted, Pell knew 1930s Europe as well as anyone.[35] While the president appointed Pell to the post to thank him for his work on the campaign and his many years of loyal support and friendship, no doubt he believed Pell well suited to serve as a European minister—the likely reason he wanted to appoint him minister to Bulgaria. But Portugal wasn't a particularly critical location in 1937, any more than Bulgaria had been in 1932. Pell did little official work in his first year there beyond sending weekly reports back to the State Department.[36]

In one of his early weekly communications to State, Pell offhandedly noted that he had not commented on events in nearby Spain, thinking that was "another man's pitch." The other man was historian Claude G. Bowers, who had written several books on nineteenth-century American politics. FDR had appointed Bowers ambassador to Spain about the same time he had asked Pell to go to Bulgaria. In response to Pell's remark about Spain, the department informed him they wanted all information, so, as ordered, he passed on what he knew. Five thousand German pilots were being rotated every three months into the country. Pell also reported that Mussolini had sent in roughly seventy thousand troops. Pell later recalled that he had "tamed down" those numbers because he "knew they wouldn't believe it back home." His initial estimates were close to correct, but stunned State Department officials, who believed there were only five thousand Italians and an insignificant number of Germans in Spain, thought Pell's information "nonsense."[37] Of course, Pell's estimation of the U.S. State Department later became clouded by what happened during his time on the UNWCC. He wrote sarcastically in his 1953 oral history that "It mustn't be thought, however, that the State Department is particularly incompetent. Every foreign office is."[38]

Pell continued to pay close attention to activities in Spain throughout his time in Portugal. He sent a later report back to the president on January 8, 1940, designed to correct what he considered false information coming from Bowers's successor, Alexander W. Weddell. Pell considered him to be pro-Franco. Notwithstanding the connections Pell reported between Franco and the Nazis, Pell correctly predicted Spain would not join the war. What, if any, impact that prediction had on the president remains unknown.[39]

This 1940 report was just one of many direct personal messages Pell sent to the president about the situation in Europe, subverting usual channels. Having spent several years touring the continent prior to the First World War and again following his tenure as chairman of the New York Democratic Party, Pell was uniquely qualified to report back in this manner. The president appreciated these candid reports from a trusted friend with whom he shared a similar worldview. But at that moment, Pell, more so than the president, was openly pessimistic about what was likely to come.

By the time of his appointment to Portugal in the spring of 1937, Pell had already concluded Nazi Germany was a malevolent—if not criminal—state, and one that was leading the world inexorably into another world war. Discussing the situation with another diplomat, Pell prefaced his comments with "When war breaks out . . ."

The other diplomat interrupted, "Surely . . . you mean *if* the war breaks out."

"No, I said when."

"Do you think then that war is inevitable?"

"Not at all," Pell answered deliberately, "but I am certain that it will not be avoided."[40]

The first of his letters to the president from his post in Lisbon on September 18 was clear and forthright. "The fascist movement is not simply a party tyranny," he wrote, "but a new religion which has already produced plenty of fanatics, a good many hypocrites, some martyrs, and human sacrifices. It can not be combatted as a theory of government or even by an appeal to self-interest."[41] Pell held out no hope whatsoever that the United States, or any other Western democracy for that matter, could ever negotiate an accord with Hitler's Germany or Mussolini's Italy. Pell could not have then known that a short six years later he would delve so much deeper into that Nazi "new religion."

In addition to his forthrightly pessimistic opinion on the menace of European fascism, Pell's letter is striking in that his observations were in the context of a very conversational letter from one friend to another. Moving seamlessly from world affairs to the affairs of Duchess County, New York, the informal tone of the letter reveals the familiarity between the two men. "I have heard a very just criticism of your administration the other day," Pell teased his friend. "It was said that you had been elected on the promise to help the forgotten man and that so far you had done nothing whatever for either Landon or Knox [FDR's Republican opponents in the 1936 election] and who is more forgotten than they?"[42] Pell was part of that small circle of friends who addressed FDR as "Mr. President" but communicated with him as if he were still the man they knew as "Frank." Within that limited number, Pell was among the few who routinely operated without guile, always maintaining his dogged support of the president.

The two friends viewed the situation in Europe similarly. Perhaps Pell may have reached his conclusions about European fascism a little earlier than FDR, or at the very least he was willing and able to be much more vocal about it, as the president obviously could not have been. Pell's next update for the president was not until March 2, 1938, some six months after his previous letter. Again, he moved effortlessly from the international situation to local politics to mutual friends and acquaintances. But this wasn't just a simple letter commenting on affairs of the day; this was a letter about momentous times in Europe to the president of the United States, a man who was keenly interested in all that Pell had to report. The two men just happened to be longtime friends who had already shared much in their lives.

Ever so nonchalantly, Pell began, "The situation is interesting." The Germans and Italians were doing everything in their power "to lower British prestige." From Pell's perspective, the British themselves were also helping "in a good many ways." As if this was of no more import than a discussion about flowers, Pell next related the difficulties of sending museum objects from the Portuguese State Museum to New York's Metropolitan Museum of Art. Pell understood that FDR would appreciate the levity of it all.

Moving from there to mutual acquaintances, Pell related that several of their friends had already visited him, including Philip Archer-Shee and his wife. They had just recently spent the night at the White House on February 6. Because of their "appearance"—Philip Archer-Shee was about an inch taller than the six-feet-five-inch Pell—he told his friend, "I think the Portuguese consider us a race of giants." This kind of double-entendre writing, however, was commonplace for Pell's correspondence.

After writing on their shared views on big business, Pell returned to the more important message of his report. "Looking at the international situation from here, I can only say that everything looks bad and the most hopeful are those who say it has looked bad for a long time. The Fascist countries seem to believe firmly that the British will never abandon their program of surrender . . . that they have enough to continue to buy peace installments year by year." This was just nine days before the Nazi Anschluss of Austria. According to Pell, the British even considered returning German colonies surrendered at Versailles. The British consul general told Pell that "it will be a long time before Great Britain draws the line," adding that he expected the British to do nothing until after Germany had fully rearmed itself. Pell closed his letter, "Let me know if there is anything I can do for you or for the Party."[43]

Pell received a brief reply dated March 18, 1938: "Dear Bertie, It is good to have your letter and I am greatly interested in all you write of. Since you sent it, much water has gone over the dam in Austria." The president then added rhetorically—and poignantly—"Where will it all end?"[44] Pell thought he knew, and if he was reading Pell's communications carefully, so must have FDR. It could end only in war. What that might mean for the United States, however, was something else altogether.

Pell sent FDR another letter on April 22, reporting little of import on the European situation. He did again offer to help the president in any way: "If you want me I hope that you will not hesitate to send for me or to get me to write in defense of your program."[45] On May 12, having just returned from a week at sea, FDR finally had a moment to respond to Pell's offer. "I am wondering," he wrote, "if you and Olive could run over here about the middle of September, and you could then take the opportunity to write letters to newspapers—perhaps a series of them—which might be extraordinarily effective."[46]

It was not atypical for a member of the administration to campaign. The president's postmaster general, Jim Farley, after all, had continued to serve as chairman of the Democratic Party. It was a little unusual, though, for a minister to leave his post in Europe to participate in a campaign at the direction of the president. That might require some maneuvering. But FDR wanted his friend to help. "With your view of things on the other side, letters by you would be even more effective."[47] Already, FDR was doing all that he could to get Americans to understand its European obligations. Pell wasted no time in replying. He would return in September and do all he could. He told the president he had already written Farley in advance to discuss details.[48]

Already sensitive to machinations at State, Pell asked Farley to assist in having the State Department order him back. "I do not want it to appear in their records as deserting my post or as an amateur playing at diplomacy," he wrote. Before closing his letter to FDR, Pell offered a line of encouragement, noting that he fully supported FDR's increasing the size of the navy in response to Japan's invasion of China and Germany's Anschluss. The Naval Act of 1938 authorized a 20 percent increase in the size of the navy. Pell was certain the American people supported it too, given the situation. They would do so, he wrote, because America "can control power as justly as any people known to history." Offering his own rhetorical question, Pell added, "Are we to dodge the inevitable consequences of six generations of American ideals?" Pell was confident Americans would fall in line behind the president even if war came—or, as Pell saw it, when it came.[49]

While he was in London preparing to return for the 1938 campaign—Pell had received his orders—the situation in Europe quickly deteriorated. With Hitler threatening Czechoslovakia, Pell's suggestion to FDR that Germany believed the British would "never abandon their program of surrender" was about to be put again to the test. Given the circumstances, Pell telephoned Washington, suggesting he head back to Lisbon and skip the campaign.[50] He wrote FDR on September 26 to let him know, and to offer a further assessment of the situation, particularly what he had observed recently during a trip over the summer with Claiborne to Italy.

"The majority of Italians," Pell wrote, "do not like the idea of the Rome-Berlin axis." Not much had changed, he believed, since he had been there as a young man when "one of the most popular phrases . . . was 'Death to Germans.'" Such antipathy, perhaps, helps explain the Italian army's ineptitude and general unwillingness to fight later in the war. Writing his letter just a few days prior to British prime minister Neville Chamberlain's now infamous "peace in our time" declaration, Pell remained suspicious of any outcome of the Munich crisis. "I believe Chamberlain has rather divided his own people than united them, but if the crash comes, they will unite quick enough." Offering his larger assessment, Pell concluded, "The only thing that is obvious is that the British are preparing to throw the blame for any failure they may make on France or on the United States. The general trend of conversation seems to be that they would have done more if the French or Americans had done something else."[51]

FDR replied to Pell on October 17. He agreed fully with Pell's choice of staying in Europe. "I think it is entirely right for you not to come over because even with the present appeasement all kinds of things may break out at any time."[52]

Before receiving this response, Pell wrote on October 21 a fuller assessment—six pages—of the situation in Europe, repeating much of what he had already reported to the secretary of state.

Pell was no fan of appeasement, but it was more than that. "It is political pettifogging," he put it, "to deny the basic contention of the Prime Minister that the peace of Europe is worth any price that is asked." But Pell understood the costs of war; he knew that another war that involved all of Europe meant that the United States had to participate. To do otherwise would deny the trajectory of his nation as he understood it—as he knew the president understood it. "The price paid at Munich is cruelly apparent." That was all he needed to write. War was, indeed, now unavoidable. Pell was certain that FDR knew it too. In that context, Pell continued his report.

Having been in France and England recently, Pell had the opportunity to speak to many people. It was what he had always done during his travels, believing it the only way to get to know a country. It was one of the reasons FDR so appreciated his friend's views. "In both countries I found the people hateful of war but prepared to meet the issue," Pell observed. "From the highest to the lowest in both France and England, the people were ready to march to a task they loathed." Pell made comparisons to 1914, and he gave FDR his assessment of how Munich had changed the military situation.

Under the changed circumstances, Pell asked, "Will Hitler use his increased strength to demand even greater concessions within a year or have they crammed him so full that he will forever hate the sight of food?" Recalling their shared youth, Pell answered his own question; "My observation of small boys at Christmas parties has lead [sic] me to the conclusion that a surfeit seldom kills." For Pell, it was now an either-or question in the wake of Munich. Chamberlain had purchased—at a very high price—a great triumph, or he had negotiated his empire into "an almost fatal loss." "Which you think it will be," he told FDR, "depends on your opinion of Mr. Chamberlain's appraisal of Hitler's appetite."

Again, Pell held no illusions when it came to Hitler. "There can be no doubt that Chamberlain bet the future of the British Empire on Hitler's integrity. . . . I think he will lose."[53] FDR had asked his friend six months ago, "Where will it all end?"[54] He had Pell's answer.

Although Pell did not bring it up, in his reply FDR chose to comment first on the dissatisfactory results of the election. Things had gone well in New York State but not so much elsewhere. "Frankly," FDR wrote, "our officeholders and our candidates had not measured up." As to Pell's summary of Europe, FDR was succinct. "You are right about the European situation. Our British friends must begin to fish or cut bait." Making clear to Pell what he thought all of this meant, he wrote, "The dictator threat from Europe is a good deal closer to the United States and the American Continent than it was before."[55] He repeated this sentiment just two months later in his annual address to Congress.

With the events of Kristallnacht (November 9–10, 1938) on his mind, at his five hundredth press conference, November 15, 1938, FDR released a prepared statement: "The news of the past few days from Germany has deeply shocked public opinion in the United States. . . . I myself could scarcely believe such things could occur in a twentieth century civilization." To no surprise, the president was asked about Jewish refugees, specifically whether there was a place for Jews from Germany: "Have you given any thought to that?"

FDR replied that he had "given a great deal of thought to it."

"Can you tell us any place particularly desirable?"

"No, the time is not ripe for that." FDR was not contemplating any change in immigration policy.[56] For his part, Pell made no comment on Kristallnacht when he next wrote FDR, writing what he labeled a "non-business letter."[57] FDR replied on January 10, 1939. Continuing Pell's discussion of politics contained in his "non-business letter," the president related that Congress and their "antediluvian friends" were in a "jam." FDR had just delivered his annual address on January 4, which he knew that Pell would have read by the time he received the letter.

"Three institutions indispensable to Americans," FDR said in his address, were under assault: religion, democracy, and international good faith. In some ways, it was an early conceptualization of the four freedoms to come two years later. Religion "gives the individual a sense of his own dignity and teaches him to respect himself by respecting his neighbors." Democracy, he said, required "free men to respect the rights and liberties of their fellows." And international good faith demanded respect for "the rights and liberties of other nations of men." Calling on Congress—and Americans—out of its isolationist sentiment, he declared, "There comes a time in the affairs of men when they must prepare to defend, not their homes alone, but the tenets of faith and humanity on which their churches, their governments and their very civilization are founded."[58]

To Pell, he wrote, "I have told them some simple home truths and intimated that they had every legal right to go their own way but that if they did, they would bear the full responsibility!" He intimated that he expected Congress to do its part. "I think the session will settle down and be comparatively quiet"; poking fun at his friend, he interjected, "that is if you can keep peace in Europe."

Demonstrative of their closeness, FDR closed, "Love to Olive. I do hope you will be coming back for a little visit to Dutchess County this Summer."[59]

In his February 11 reply, Pell responded directly, "I would not care to bet very much on the continuance of peace." In as dark a prediction as he yet ventured, Pell wrote that Italy and Germany "honestly believe that they will be able to overwhelm, terrify, and starve England and France in a very short time." A simple "show of force" might even get Britain to abandon the French. This was not just Pell speaking from experience and personal observation, although his experience on the ground in Europe was considerable. Pell actively worked toward getting as much reliable information as possible. Before closing this letter, he did assure his friend that he anticipated visiting him the coming summer in Hyde Park.[60]

Pell sent two more letters from his post in Portugal to FDR before returning to the States. In one he reiterated his belief that war was "inevitable," a conviction he had held since 1933. He had also given some more thought to Nazism, marveling at its success as a "political machine." It "was manned right down to the lowest member of the organization by men who have profited from the system, who believe in its principles and who are accustomed to its methods."[61] Some five years later as a representative on the UNWCC, Pell fully discovered just how right he had been.

Back in the United States in the summer, Pell remained sure as ever that war was on the horizon but unsure as to when Great Britain or France would stand up to Hitler.[62] On August 28, 1939, he met with FDR in the Oval Office. It was a brief visit, but given the growing crisis over Poland, the likelihood of war must have dominated their conversation. Pell returned to New York City, staying at the Knickerbocker Club. When a valet awakened him on September 1, 1939, the war he knew was inevitable had begun. He headed to his home in Hopewell Junction later that day, but not before calling Hyde Park. Finding only FDR's mother at home, he accepted her invitation to tea. Pell enjoyed recounting the visit to the president. "She gave me iced tea, which I hate." Nonetheless, Pell dutifully drank it. "Yes," FDR told Pell, "I was afraid of her, too."[63]

Pell headed back to Lisbon via London and Paris. Portugal almost overnight had transitioned from the "dullest and least important post in Europe," as he put it in his oral history, to a place that "really amounted to something." Refugees from all over Europe headed to Lisbon "in all stages of discomfort and poverty," some walking hundreds of miles and avoiding every road for fear of capture. "I have seen men and women who had suffered danger, torture and pain coming from all parts," Pell later recalled.[64]

It is too easy to dismiss the importance of Pell's letters to FDR—or their friendship, for that matter. Judging by FDR's replies, he was paying close attention to what Pell had to say. And judging by FDR's accelerated pace in preparing America for war, he was taking note. Of course, Pell wasn't the only one sharing apprehensions about events in Europe. After all, the president received many reports, including those from William Dodd in Germany, William C. Bullitt in the Soviet Union and later France, Anthony Joseph Drexel Biddle Jr. in Poland, and Joseph E. Davies in the Soviet Union (succeeding Bullitt) and later Belgium.[65] All these men—including Pell—were part of FDR's fraternity of State Department outsiders on whom he relied to offer forthright assessments in the 1930s. But Pell, as much as anyone in FDR's circle, was a longtime trusted friend who was never afraid to share his opinions, which, as it turned out, were often in line with the president's thinking.

Claiborne Pell told author Michael Blayney that he believed the president valued the letters highly for their forthrightness and conversational style, which was very different from the standard fare provided him in State Department reports.[66] Pell obviously believed these letters written directly to the president, subverting the usual channels, mattered—so much so that, when he served the president in the significantly more important capacity as American representative on the UNWCC, he continued the practice.

If we are to believe FDR, Pell's letters carried significant weight. In late October 1940 FDR acknowledged just how important they had been. "It is really more helpful for me than you probably realized to have you in Lisbon at this moment which in my judgment is the best listening post we have in Europe under the present conditions." Pell's time in Lisbon, however, was coming to an end just as he was getting comfortable there. FDR wanted him closer to the action. Secretary of State Hull telegraphed Pell in Portugal in early January. FDR wanted to appoint Pell U.S. minister to Hungary.[67]

Accepting the president's request, Pell returned to Washington in early 1941, meeting briefly with FDR at the White House on February 13. He told FDR to look for his next post after Hungary. Already in early 1941, many expected America at war very soon; Pell certainly did. And when that happened, the embassy in Hungary would close.[68] In a speech to friends in Newport, Rhode Island, prior to his departure, Pell cautioned, "If we refuse the leadership of the world, we are not going to leave the world unled. We are simply defaulting the leadership to someone else." No matter the danger, as Pell saw it, America must take the lead. "The cost will be great," he said, "but I remember saying in a Congressional speech more than 20 years ago, the cost of abstention will be greater still."[69]

Pell traveled by boat on March 22 to Bermuda and then on to Lisbon, where he gathered his considerable luggage and undertook a two-thousand-mile drive across Europe to Budapest. His caravan included a limousine, a station wagon, and a secondhand truck.[70] They traveled through Spain, Switzerland, and Germany to reach their destination. Before leaving Lisbon, he wrote FDR on April 2. Europe had been at war for more than a year and a half, France had fallen, and things did not look very good for the British. Pell reminded his friend uncompromisingly, "World leadership will involve responsibilities which we have never taken, risks we have never even considered, problems of which we have known nothing, but unfortunately there is no hole to which we can withdraw."[71]

Headed toward his second diplomatic post, Pell must have appreciated FDR's trust, and he let FDR know in his inimitable way that such trust was mutual: "During the next epoch of history, the world will be led either from Berlin or Washington. There is no hope of anything else. It will not be the Archangel Michael, but Adolf Hitler and his successors, who will direct a military autocracy from Berlin, or it will be you and yours—not Gabriel, who will direct things from Washington. I see no other alternative."[72] FDR understood this quite clearly, of course, and was confident in his ability to offer that leadership. Pell formally presented himself on May 19, 1941, to Admiral Miklós Horthy, regent of the Kingdom of Hungary, in Budapest.

By the time of his posting to Hungary, Pell and FDR had known each other nearly four decades. Somehow they had managed to maintain a friendship that was both personal and political, and since his appointment to the administration, it was a relationship that had turned professional, with Pell reporting directly to the president. Pell's observations, as FDR told him had been "more helpful" than his friend knew. And notwithstanding all the many communications FDR received about events in Europe, Pell's reports had amounted to "the best listening post" he had. It was little wonder why FDR sent Pell to Hungary. He valued Pell's unfettered view and his integrity, honesty, and loyalty. It wasn't a loyalty purchased in 1921 when FDR told his fellow New York Democrats that his friend Bertie was "not such a bad fellow." It was a loyalty of mutual respect, and certainly, in Pell's case, it was a loyalty built on admiration. FDR understood the value of that kind of loyalty, and he was keen to use it whenever he needed it. Pell's time in Hungary, however, was not destined to last very long.

CHAPTER 3

REPRESENTATIVE ON THE
UN WAR CRIMES COMMISSION

"For a Thousand Who Can Think
There Is Only One That Can See"

*I am not only anxious to serve and to support you, but in my final
account I know that my descendants will count it a point in my favor
that I have enjoyed your trust.*

Herbert C. Pell to Franklin D. Roosevelt, June 24, 1943

At 10:30 A.M., December 7, 1941, Secretary of State Cordell Hull conferred with
Navy Secretary Frank Knox and Secretary of War Henry L. Stimson in preparation for his meeting with Japanese ambassador Kichisaburo Nomura scheduled
for later that day. Stimson wrote in his diary that Secretary Hull was certain
that the "Japs" were "planning some deviltry," which meant, likely, a military
action.[1] Just where an attack would take place none of them knew. Before Hull
left for the meeting, Stimson asked him to dictate his "broad" views on the
situation to a stenographer. With Japan moving to control one-half of the world
and Hitler the other, "this at once places at stake everything that is precious
and worthwhile," Hull said. He then added, rather ironically, given what was
just about to transpire in the middle of the Pacific, "Self-defense, therefore, is
the key point for the preservation of each and all of our civilized institutions."[2]

Stimson went to lunch; around 2:00 P.M., he received a call from the president.
"Have you heard the news?"

"Well, I have heard the telegrams which have been coming in about the Japanese advances in the Gulf of Siam," Stimson replied.

"Oh, no. I don't mean that." FDR interjected. "They have attacked Hawaii. They are now bombing Hawaii."

The master of understatement, Stimson recorded in his diary, "Well that was an excitement indeed." An externally calm Stimson finished his lunch and then went to his office at the War Department. In reflection, Stimson wrote that he was relieved "that a crisis had come in a way which would unite all our people." As the reports arrived at the War Department detailing the extent of the day's losses, Stimson remained sanguine. "The apathy and divisions stirred up by unpatriotic men" that had for some time now been so "discouraging," he believed, would disappear in the face of this Japanese attack.[3] To conclude that Pearl Harbor would unite Americans, as Stimson was suggesting and historians have ever after repeated, was not entirely wrong. Isolationists were quieted, and political squabbles lessened, certainly in the beginning.

The next day FDR called on Congress to declare war on the Japanese Empire. "Mr. Vice President, Mr. Speaker, Members of the Senate, of the House of Representatives: Yesterday, December 7, 1941—a date which will live in infamy—the United States of America was suddenly and deliberately attacked by naval and air forces of the Empire of Japan." Everyone remembers those words, but FDR had something else to say that day: "No matter how long it may take us to overcome this premeditated invasion, the American people, in their righteous might, will win through to absolute victory."[4] In December 1941, even after having spent months in preparation, the United States was still far from mighty.

On December 9 FDR announced over national radio, "We are all in it—all the way. Every single man, woman and child is a partner in the most tremendous undertaking in American history."[5] Saying it, however, did not necessarily make it so. Unification of the American people behind the war effort—maintaining the morale of all segments of the American people—would itself require a maximum effort, particularly when it came to those Americans who might, for one reason or another, be less than disposed to support the goals of the nation unreservedly.

With the United States at last in the war, British prime minister Winston Churchill wasted little time in coming to Washington. Much to his delight, a beaming FDR warmly greeted him at Washington's National Airport the night of December 22. In a rare display of respect, FDR had taken the trouble of driving out to meet Churchill. The ungainly looking pair posed arm in arm in front of a throng of reporters and photographers on the south portico of the White House before finally walking in together.[6] Four days later, Churchill spoke to Congress and thereby to the American people. Having "drawn the sword for freedom and cast away the scabbard," he said, America was now involved in "the noblest work in the world, defending . . . the cause of freedom in every land."[7]

Building on this idea of fighting for the common cause of all humankind, barely a week and a half into FDR's and Churchill's Arcadia Conference, Great Britain, the United States, the Soviet Union, and twenty-three additional governments,[8] including several governments in exile, promulgated the "Declaration by United Nations" on January 1, 1942. Nineteen other nations would become "adherents" over the next three and a half years.[9] Extending the Atlantic Charter, these "United Nations" (a term FDR had devised the previous month) articulated the stated purpose for which the Allies were waging war to defeat the Axis powers.[10] "Being convinced that complete victory over their enemies is essential to defend life, liberty, independence and religious freedom, and to preserve human rights and justice in their own lands as well as in other lands," the United Nations affirmed themselves "engaged in a common struggle against savage and brutal forces seeking to subjugate the world."[11]

The Allied powers had declared World War II a struggle not just to defend but also to extend Western democratic ideals. These values—life, liberty, and freedom—had been enhanced to include the moral principle of human rights and the legal principle of justice for all peoples. However, those ideals, both old and new, were themselves incompletely realized in Allied nations, including in the United States. But here, in this declaration, the signatories were calling for the application of these principles "in their own lands as well as others." As Churchill later noted, "The Declaration could not by itself win battles, but it set forth who we were and what we were fighting for."[12]

FDR's larger vision was the creation of a liberal postwar world order. This included the spread of American values and power, the dismantling of colonialism, and creation of what amounted to an executive consortium to manage the postwar world, of course, led by an American chief operating officer. It was a vision he shared with his friend Herbert Pell. "World leadership," Pell had written FDR just the previous spring, "will involve responsibilities which we have never taken, risks we have never even considered, problems of which we have known nothing."[13]

In a repeat of the First World War, FDR, like Wilson before him, believed that American entry into the war had been necessary to accomplish this vision of a liberal new world order. FDR assumed that once the war was over, the

United States could dominate—politically, economically, and morally—this new syndicate in whatever form it would ultimately take. His friend Herbert Pell was not so confident as the ever-optimistic FDR seemed to be. The United States, as Pell saw it, had defaulted on this responsibility at the end of the First World War; he was not so sure that it wouldn't repeat that failing at the end of World War II. What gave him hope, however, was the man then in the Oval Office.

For Pell, Pearl Harbor meant another end to his career in public service. His brief time in Hungary, however, had been exhilarating. It included, naturally, a continuation of his correspondence directly with the president. As a minister, Pell had hit his stride, and he hoped the closing of the American Embassy in Hungary would not be his final posting with the Roosevelt administration. The president did find him a position, but it did not happen immediately, and as significant as his ambassadorships had been, his next post was even more so. This time, Pell became a participant in determining what a part of the postwar world would be like.

Upon arriving in Hungary—Pell had presented his credentials on May 20, 1941—he sent his first report back to the State Department without delay. His drive through Germany this time had been sobering. He was thoroughly impressed by the size of the German Army, and the automobile enthusiast Pell was in awe of its mechanization: "Neither the German army nor anything else is unbeatable," he concluded, "but it certainly will take a lot to beat them."[14] The early success of the Nazi thrust into the Soviet Union came as no surprise to Pell. He was initially taken aback, however, when Hitler declared war on the United States. He recalled hearing the speech in his office in Budapest. "There was this screaming in the radio which was in a language and accent and at a speed that was far beyond any German of mine."[15] As he expected, German-satellite Hungary broke relations with the United States, declaring war shortly thereafter. Between those two events, Pell and his staff destroyed papers and codes. A good deal of it, incredibly, was a waste of time. Much of Pell's papers and correspondence was already in the hands of German spies.

During his time in Budapest, Pell stayed at the Ritz Hotel. A chambermaid hired for Mrs. Pell took the opportunity to photograph all of her husband's files, which he had kept in his study at the hotel, including all his correspondence with FDR. The Germans never took advantage of what they had. The officer in charge chose not to send the material up to Joachim von Ribbentrop in the foreign ministry. War had already been declared, he wrote, but more than that, Pell's files, especially his correspondence with the president, contained "little except a categorical refutation and rejection of the National Socialist and Fascist ideologies." Consequently, it was "inadvisable to bring them to the attention of the Foreign Minister." This conclusion came notwithstanding that FDR's letters then in German hands noted how important Pell's reports had been to him. His June 23, 1941, note to Pell, for example, had even congratulated him for "spreading the democratic message so well in so hostile an environment."[16]

On December 13 Pell was summoned to the office of Hungarian prime minister László Bárdossy. Just two days previously Bárdossy met with Pell to sever diplomatic ties. This day, it was Bárdossy's task to inform Pell that Hungary considered itself at war with the United States. As Pell recalled it, "He had tears running down his face and, just as I came in, the German Minister walked out of his office in a state of rage, and Bárdossy declared war on me."[17]

Pell was on friendly terms with the prime minister, although back in the summer Pell had asked Bárdossy in the most diplomatic way possible for an "examination" of the treatment of Jews in the wake of an expulsion decree for Jews near the Galician border in Subcarpathia. Pell had received information from the American Joint Relief Association reporting persecutions. On August 2 Bárdossy offered Pell the results of "the matter urgently examined," as he put it.[18]

The decree had "only applied to Jews of Galician origin." Moreover, "All measures have been taken for supplying them with food during their transport." They were even "entitled" to take some of their personal belongings with them. "Furthermore," Bárdossy said, "all those, whose illness could be certified, as well as those who are over 70 years of age, are excluded from expulsion." To counter Pell's harshest criticisms, Bárdossy disingenuously remarked, "A strict order has been given to all competent authorities to strictly respect the expulsion-decree and to carefully avoid anything that would be in contradiction with its principles."[19]

In his summary on the matter—there was not much else Pell could have done given the circumstances but offer protest and demand explanation—Pell expressed his frustration about the attitudes of Eastern Europeans to the plight of the Jews. "Although the treatment meted out to many of these unfortunates has been unnecessarily severe and in some cases flagrantly unjust," he wrote, "roughness on the part of those in authority, and hardship do not shock the susceptibilities of the people accustomed to the habits and standard of living that prevail in eastern Europe." Americans, Pell was sure, would react as he had: helplessly outraged.[20]

Pell remained fond of Bárdossy but to a certain extent found him a pitiable character. Bárdossy appreciated just how well liked Pell and his wife were by many Hungarians—himself included. Pell's counterpart in Romania, Franklin Mott Gunther, described this admiration in a letter to FDR, after a meeting with Bárdossy: "Last week I visited Budapest. . . . I found the Pells in great form. Bertie is already a popular figure with his leonine head and giant stature, and the Buick station wagon in which he generally drives about unfailingly collects a crowd. They are both much liked and appreciated," he wrote, "and the fact that he is an old friend of yours loses nothing in the telling."[21]

Commenting on Olive's considerable talent as an artist, Gunther took the opportunity to transition into his own assessment of Pell: "As [art critic John] Ruskin once remarked, 'For a hundred people who can talk there is only one man who can think; but for a thousand who can think there is only one that can see.'"[22] There is, perhaps, no better description of Pell than Gunther's. It must have been met with agreement and satisfaction in the White House. It was, after all, why FDR had long supported and relied on his friend Bertie. It validated the appointment of Pell to Portugal and Hungary, and it offers the best explanation as to why FDR selected Pell for the UNWCC in 1943.

Back in December 1941, however, nothing was left for Pell to do but inform FDR that Hungary had declared war. Leaving the tearful Bárdossy, Pell returned to the Ritz. Pell's popularity—to the point of being cheered on the streets—pushed the Germans to demand his removal. Pell and retinue were soon relocated to the island of St. Margaret on the Danube, and he remained under guard throughout his time on the island.

At midnight on January 18, 1942, Pell left Hungary to begin his journey back to the United States. The Germans had taken great care to arrange a special train for Pell, his wife, and other diplomats—from Budapest to Croatia, through northern Italy, southern France, and Spain. Finally arriving in familiar Portugal, Pell was relieved to be housed at the Estoril Hotel, except that he was stuck there "day after day, week after week, [and] month after month."[23]

With the Pells in Lisbon, his brother, Clarence, and his wife spent the day at Hyde Park with FDR in February.[24] Judge Sam Rosenman was also there. In the 1920s Rosenman was active in the New York Democratic Party along with Pell, joining FDR in his 1928 campaign for New York governor. In addition to writing the 1932 speech in which FDR pledged "a New Deal for the American people," Rosenman became indispensable in shepherding war crimes policy after Pell's removal in 1945, continuing in that role for Truman after FDR's death.[25]

Pell did not return to the United States until June 1, 1942. According to Pell's biographer, Leonard Baker, the delay was caused by the unwillingness of the

Hungarian delegation in the United States to immediately return home.[26] Pell wasted no time traveling to Washington to meet with FDR. "I explained the situation as well as I could to the President," he recalled in his oral history, "and suggested that I was available for anything and would be very glad to help."[27] Perhaps "the situation" included Pell's observations of deportations and persecutions of Jews. If they did discuss it, neither ever said so. As much as Pell wanted to return to the administration in another diplomatic post upon his return, it seems FDR wanted it more. In a memo to aide Marvin McIntyre, FDR wrote, "Will you tell Bertie Pell that I hope to be able to see him soon and will you check with Sumner Welles about placing Bertie Pell somewhere—I want it done and done quickly."[28] McIntyre, as instructed, contacted Welles. The response was a categorical no. There was "absolutely no place in the Department of State where Bertie Pell could be used."[29] Notwithstanding Welles's assessment, there was a place, but it did not come quickly and not without considerable effort against it.

On August 21, 1942, FDR announced he had received a communication from the governments in exile of the occupied nations regarding an increase in Nazi atrocities in Europe.[30] On June 30, the *New York Times* and *London Daily Telegraph* reported the scope of the calamity; over one million Jews had already perished at the hands of the Nazis.[31] Two days later, a report from the Polish government in exile calling for swift retribution was quoted in the *Times:* "We believe that Hitler's Germany in time will be punished for all its horrors, crimes and brutality but this is no comfort for the millions menaced with death." Before there could be justice, however, the report called for "Allied governments to apply similar treatment against Germans and fifth columnists living in Allied countries."[32]

In his announcement, FDR warned that the United States was "constantly receiving additional information from dependable sources." The Allied powers were sure to win the war, and there would be consequences. "It is the purpose of the Government of the United States, as I know it is the purpose of each of the United Nations," the president promised, "to make appropriate use of the information and evidence in respect to those barbaric crimes of the invaders, in Europe and in Asia." Leaving nothing to doubt, he made the threat explicit: "It seems only fair that they should have this warning that the time will come when they shall have to stand in courts of law in the very countries which they are now oppressing and answer for their acts."[33] The next day's headline on the front page of the *New York Times* read, "President Warns Atrocities of Axis Will Be Avenged."[34]

Then, on October 7, 1942, FDR extended this generic statement of policy into an announcement of an intended procedure that was to "include a provision for the surrender" of war criminals. "With a view to establishing responsibility of the guilty individuals through the collection and assessment of all available evidence," FDR stated that the U.S. government was "prepared to cooperate with the British and other Governments in establishing a United Nations Commission for the Investigation of War Crimes."[35]

Behind the scenes, at the direction of the president, Harry Hopkins had prepared a memorandum for a proposal for creation of the UNWCC (initially called the United Nations Commission on Atrocities), which FDR gave Prime Minister Churchill during a visit to the United States in June 1942. When Churchill returned to Great Britain, he had the War Cabinet Committee on the Treatment of War Criminals formed. The American ambassador to Great Britain, John Gilbert "Gil" Winant, sat in on the meetings. On July 29 this committee proposed a joint commission including representatives from the Soviet Union, the United Kingdom, the United States, China, and the occupied governments in exile. On October 5 FDR informed the British that the United States would announce its joint support for the program, providing a statement was released indicating that no mass reprisals would be sought. Two days later the program was announced in London and Washington.[36]

The Allies followed up their UNWCC announcement on December 18, 1942, with a joint declaration made simultaneously in London, Moscow, and Washington, reporting on the Nazi extermination of Jews throughout Europe.[37] "Numerous reports from Europe" have been received, the declaration announced, "that the German authorities, not content with denying to persons of Jewish race in all the territories over which their barbarous rule has been extended the most elementary human rights, are now carrying into effect Hitler's oft-repeated intention to exterminate the Jewish people in Europe."[38]

The *Times'* front-page report, "11 Allies Condemn Nazi War on Jews," paraphrased the declaration for Americans, reporting that the United Nations issued a statement "condemning Germany's 'bestial policy of cold-blooded extermination' of Jews." The full text of the declaration was reprinted on page 10.[39] The content of the statement, however, made little impact on Americans, although it was at that time the most-publicized statement in America regarding the Holocaust.[40] It remained now for the UNWCC to organize and for the member states to select their representatives. The British acted quickly. The process in the United States was frustratingly slow, creating the impression that the president was unconcerned about the plight of the Jews in Europe, his public statements notwithstanding.

Meanwhile, on October 29, 1942, the British sent an outline proposal for the UNWCC to the Soviet and Chinese governments. When pressed by the U.S. Justice Department in the spring of 1943, State Department officials claimed that the reason nothing had moved forward was that the Soviets had yet to reply to an outline proposal for the UNWCC. According to the State Department, there had been "no communication" between the British and the government of the United States on the subject because of the British desire "to avoid Soviet suspicion that the United States and Great Britain were formulating a plan without full consultation with the Russians."[41] Given that the Soviets never did become part of the UNWCC, the department's claim is to some extent suspect.

On March 5, 1943, the State Department received a communication from the British Embassy requesting that the United States move forward and settle on its representative to the UNWCC.[42] All "concerned" governments, including the Soviet and Chinese, had agreed to the UNWCC proposal. The British had already made public the appointment of its representative, Sir Cecil Hurst. Hurst, if not an obvious choice for the British, was certainly an excellent one, and his appointment met with no opposition on either side of the Atlantic. He had considerable international legal experience and therefore was eminently qualified to sit on the Commission. From 1918 to 1929, he served as legal adviser to the British Foreign Office. In 1919 he attended the Paris Peace Conference. He not only proposed the Permanent Court of International Justice but was also a judge on it at the time of his appointment to the UNWCC; he had been so from 1929 (he would leave it in 1946). Secretary of State Cordell Hull told the president that he would be hard-pressed to find an American representative for the UNWCC, who needed to be, like Hurst, "a man of high caliber."[43]

Hull recommended that FDR consider appointing the attorney general, Francis Biddle. Unlike Hurst, Biddle did not possess a particularly strong international legal background, but Hull told the president such an appointment would "show the degree of importance we attach to the work [of the UNWCC]."[44] Another reason Hull suggested Biddle, however, was to mollify the attorney general, who had expressed his displeasure over having been largely ignored by the State Department regarding war crimes policy and the establishment of the UNWCC.

A State Department committee headed by Sumner Welles, which included three members from the Justice Department, had been working directly with British representatives to define the scope of the UNWCC. Contradicting the early British vision of the UNWCC as a passive evidence-gathering body only, this committee concluded that the Commission should "aggressively seek evidence on all war crimes." Consequently, the UNWCC would have to "adopt policies in the field of international criminal law rather than make recommendations to national tribunals."[45] The British, apparently, were ready to acquiesce to State's more ambitious program.

This plan, as presented in the Justice Department's summary report of the committee's work, matched what Pell would later try to achieve on the Commission, which is what he thought the president wanted him to accomplish. But after Pell's appointment, the State Department had fully come back around to the initial British view of the UNWCC. Secretary of State Hull told Pell in a December 28, 1943, letter that the UNWCC was just "a fact-finding body . . . engaged in the collection of all available evidence with a view to identifying those responsible."[46] Whether this changed attitude was due in full or in part to Pell's appointment remains hard to quantify. There were numerous other factors—including entrenched antisemitism in the State Department, careerism on the part of some of its staff, and a developing desire to control the pursuit of justice among the major powers only.

In any case, the three Justice Department representatives on the committee had been kept in the dark about negotiations throughout. The legal adviser for the State Department, Green H. Hackworth, even prevented them from making copies of a draft agreement. They had hoped to use it to consult with the attorney general and others in the Justice Department.[47] On March 6 Biddle wrote Hull that he was "deeply concerned" and "disturbed by certain impediments which have precluded the [Justice] Department from participating to the fullest extent in the solution of this vital problem."[48] Hoping to deflect Biddle's complaints about the treatment of his staff, Hull replied on March 31, informing Biddle that he was suggesting the president appoint him on a short-term basis to the UNWCC. Hull added deferentially, "I think that your combined prestige and ability would lend great weight to the inauguration of the committee's work."[49]

Assuming that Biddle would not take the post—and that the president had no one else in mind—on the advice of Hackworth, Hull suggested three other people in addition to Biddle for FDR's consideration: Edwin D. Dickinson, Francis B. Sayre, and Manley O. Hudson. All three men had a background in international law. Dickinson was then serving as a special assistant to the attorney general, and Hudson was on the Permanent Court of International Justice with Hurst.[50]

Hackworth had suggested these individuals along with four others, but Hull chose to whittle the list down to men with whom he was familiar.[51]

Hackworth, who had been legal adviser since July 1931, carried considerable influence within the State Department, particularly regarding war crimes policy. For example, he had written Undersecretary of State Sumner Welles on March 16 that the American representative on the Commission had to be "a man of similar caliber" to Hurst. Hull obviously saw the memorandum and repeated almost verbatim the same phrase in his note to the president. Hackworth also wrote Welles, "The person chosen as our representative should be selected not alone on the basis of his knowledge of criminal law or his experience in prosecuting criminals, but also on the basis of his background in the international field and his ability to weigh political implications involved."[52]

Pell had none of these qualifications, save the ability to understand the political score. At precisely the same time that the State Department was considering possibilities for a U.S. representative on the UNWCC, Pell had contacted Undersecretary Welles asking if there was any position available for him, unaware that Welles had already refused FDR's request. Welles brushed him off, recommending he do something with the Office of War Information.[53]

Without question, Hackworth always considered "political implications." Along with his official memorandum to Welles that Hull used with the president, Hackworth sent a "confidential" note regarding the possible designs of the Justice Department as it related to war crimes policy, reflecting Hackworth's overriding concern with protecting the State Department's jurisdiction—and obviously his own control—in the matter.[54] Hackworth advised Welles that prosecution of Axis war criminals was an international issue, "involving negotiations with foreign governments looking to the establishment of international machinery for the application of international law and the enforcement of the laws of war," and, therefore, under the exclusive province of the State Department.[55] But at that moment, no decision had yet been made as to whether prosecutions of war criminals would be the task of individual nations or some international tribunal. It was entirely possible that individual nation-states would try war criminals; consequently, the attorney general was well within his province to want to participate in the planning.

In his confidential memorandum to Welles, Hackworth made it clear that he believed Biddle did not understand the basic qualifications required for the job. Despite making seven suggestions in his nonconfidential letter to Welles for U.S. representative on the UNWCC, Hackworth implied in this private communication that he alone possessed the requisite qualifications and that the wishes of the State Department—and his own—might be best served if Biddle suggested him as a candidate. Hackworth clearly viewed himself as a "man of similar caliber" to Hurst, both men having served as legal advisers for their respective nations. Hackworth had not served on the Permanent Court of International Justice like Hurst, but apparently that was inconsequential. "By requesting the Attorney General to suggest any names he may have in mind," he wrote Welles, "we may tend to regularize the presentation of suggestions to the President."[56]

Hackworth's maneuverings notwithstanding, Hull sent the president on March 30 his suggestion that the attorney general be appointed to the Commission. FDR, upon receiving Hull's letter, forwarded it to Biddle, adding his own two-sentence memorandum for the attorney general: "Will you do it? It would be much the best choice.—FDR."[57] Placated and flattered, Biddle immediately replied to Hull that he appreciated his kindness very much in proposing to the president that he represent the United States on the UNWCC. Biddle told Hull, however, that he required "further word" from the president before he made a decision.[58] Apparently, Biddle being "much the best choice" in the mind of the president was not adequate backing for him to make a decision. Quite possibly, Biddle needed time to consider just whom he wanted to suggest. It is not inconceivable either that Biddle may have believed that Hull was simply trying to exile him to London if he accepted FDR's offer.

Whatever the case, for weeks, no American representative was appointed. Toward the end of May, Hull decided to press the president again for a decision. By then Biddle had let Hull know that he would not be taking it and that he would acquiesce to two of Hull's three suggestions, Francis B. Sayre or Manley O. Hudson.[59]

A month later, on June 22, the attorney general sent the president his own suggestions for the post, either Professor Sheldon Glueck, "a noted expert in criminal law and criminal research," of Harvard Law School, or Charlton Ogburn, a former counsel for the American Federation of Labor who also had some experience in international law.[60] At just about the same time, FDR received via the State Department a forwarded letter from Homer Cummings also suggesting Glueck for appointment to the UNWCC. Cummings had a long history with FDR; he was FDR's first attorney general and, in that role, a steadfast supporter of his New Deal legislation. Incidentally, Cummings was also the man who formulated the compromise plank on the Ku Klux Klan as chairman of the Committee on Resolutions during the 1924 Democratic Convention.

Cummings's June 17, 1943, letter was not the first time he had proposed Glueck's appointment to the Commission; he had sent the president a personal letter the previous December, which included a copy of Glueck's article on the "Trial and Punishment of the Axis War Criminals."[61] FDR already knew of the professor. He had previously read an advance copy of the article Glueck submitted directly to the president in October 1942.[62]

Based on legal background, Glueck had to have been as obvious a choice for the president as Hurst had been for the British. Moreover, any of the other candidates (those suggested by Hull and Biddle) were on the face of it similarly appropriate choices. By the time Biddle and Cummings (for the second time) made their suggestions for the American representative on the UNWCC, however, FDR had already made up his mind.

On June 10 Secretary Hull telephoned FDR wanting to know if he was, in fact, putting his friend Herbert Pell on the Commission. Unable to speak to the president directly, Hull asked Grace Tully, the president's secretary, who had taken the call, to put the question to him in a memorandum. "Secretary Hull's office called to ask if you are putting Herbert Pell on the War Crimes Commission," she wrote. "The other nations are asking who is going to represent the United States." In pencil, the president scribbled on the brief note, "OK, FDR."[63] And just like that, Herbert C. Pell, the man who had absolutely no international legal experience, was the president's choice for the UNWCC, despite the several other eminently qualified individuals he could have chosen, including even the self-promoting career bureaucrat Green Hackworth.

The very next day, June 11, Hull submitted Pell's appointment letter for the president's consideration; it was drafted by Hackworth, which must have infuriated the legal adviser to no end. Three days later the signed appointment letter went out from the White House to the "Honorable Herbert C. Pell." "My Dear Mr. Pell . . . I should be very glad to have you represent this government on the Commission." Pell was to contact the State Department for further details and "proceed to London as soon as possible."[64] That last suggestion—to get to London "as soon as possible"—would quickly cause considerable friction between Pell and several State Department officials, particularly Green H. Hackworth.

FDR may have already decided he wanted Pell for the job back in the middle of April when he sent Hull a memorandum asking, "Do you think there is some place where we could use Herbert Pell? As you know, he is a very devoted friend of the Administration."[65] Pell had been at the White House for an extended lunch with the president on April 8.[66] But like Welles before him, Hull evidently thought there was no place for him. The president must have already had a "further word" with Biddle by then, realizing it was not a good plan for the attorney general to be away in London representing the United States on the UNWCC, if even only for a brief initial stay. FDR had not responded to Hull's other suggestions, and he had made no attempt to suggest Professor Glueck as a viable candidate. Neither Hull nor Hackworth had recommended him, probably because they believed it might be difficult for anyone to argue against the choice, and thus an administration outsider would be representing the United States—a situation the State Department detested every time it happened.

FDR had read and was much impressed by Glueck's work on war crimes policy. The president made sure back in November 1942 that several administration members had read Glueck's "Trial and Punishment of War Criminals," including Supreme Court Justice Felix Frankfurter.[67] Nonetheless, the president made no effort ever to suggest Glueck for the post, despite his clear understanding that Glueck wanted the job.[68] It seemed FDR wanted someone with whom he was familiar, someone he could trust, for the position. Given the timing, FDR probably hoped Hull would make the suggestion of Pell for the job, so he would not have to, and thereby avoid the perception that the appointment was based purely on patronage for an old friend.

Pell was a suspect choice in the eyes of the State Department. Secretary Hull absolutely did not want him. Hull had befriended Pell when he arrived in Congress twenty-four years earlier in 1919, and the two had worked together when Pell was chairman of the New York Democratic Committee and Hull chairman of the national committee, but in 1943 things were different.[69] Hull considered Pell the wrong man for the job, lacking the requisite legal credentials. But more than that, he possessed the one thing that threatened Hull the most: a close friendship with the president. Hull's legal adviser, Green Hackworth, did not want him either. On top of whatever Pell lacked in legal knowledge and abilities, not to mention the resentment his selection must have engendered in Hackworth, Pell was beyond the control of the State Department, a man who could, whenever he chose, go directly to the top to get things done. Such a structure had become standard operating procedure for the president, who in all instances preferred to conduct his own foreign policy and act as his own secretary of state, to the continuing irritation of State Department officials.[70]

Pell became the choice of the president over every suggestion and objection. As Pell later recalled the intrigues surrounding his appointment, "The only real reason I got it was that the president sent down what one of the State Department officers described as a 'ukase' telling them they must give me something and suggesting this particular place."[71] The State Department officer was probably Green Hackworth, with whom Pell met on June 29, once he found out about his appointment.[72] Hackworth obviously wanted Pell to know up front that he was not his or the department's choice.

There were so many other options for the position; Pell was hardly qualified from the standpoint of his legal background or knowledge of the issues surrounding war crimes policy, and evidently no one in the State or Justice Departments wanted him. Nonetheless, the president went ahead and appointed his friend, expecting no opposition. His edict to the State Department consisted of "OK, FDR," with no explanation given.[73] If any opposition to the appointment were to come—and it did, but State Department officials directed it at Pell, not the president—FDR would not have been concerned. He was used to conflict and competition within his administration; he seemed to thrive on it, preferring to keep his purposes ambiguous whenever possible.[74] FDR famously told Henry Morgenthau, secretary of the treasury, in May 1942, "You know that I am a juggler, and I never let my right hand know what my left hand does. . . . I may be entirely inconsistent, and furthermore I am perfectly willing to mislead and tell untruths if it will help win this war."[75]

It also seems that Thomas J. Watson played a role in the president's selection of Pell. Watson was the president of International Business Machines (IBM) and a close friend and confidant of both Pell and especially FDR. Where other businesses and corporations failed during the Great Depression, the New Deal saved IBM, helping the company more than double in size. IBM equipment was needed by various government agencies to manage FDR's public works programs. When Social Security was enacted in 1935, the U.S. government became IBM's biggest customer.[76]

Although Watson had been an early and large financial supporter of FDR—in part to save his company against an ongoing antitrust investigation—he feared that he had destroyed the trust and access to the president his support had given him following the 1932 election. New York bankers and business leaders sent Watson to see FDR in the summer of 1933 to complain that the president's initial New Deal measures were going to destroy business in America. According to Watson's son, FDR told him, "Look here, Tom. You go back and tell your banker and businessmen friends that I don't have time to worry about their future. I am trying to save this great nation. I think I am going to be successful. If I am successful, I'll save them along with everyone else."[77] Whether FDR really said that or not, in the end, the New Deal did do much to save business in America. It certainly saved IBM, and Watson was grateful. He had become a true believer in the president and supported the New Deal throughout the thirties and beyond, and his company was rewarded significantly.

FDR often used Watson as his unofficial representative in New York City, eventually relying on him for advice. FDR even offered to appoint him secretary of commerce or ambassador to the Court of St. James's, a post subsequently given to Joseph P. Kennedy, but Watson turned both down, preferring to remain in control of his company. In addition to the access he then had to the president, Watson went on to develop a friendship with Cordell Hull and other members of the State Department, which turned out to be very helpful for IBM's international activities, particularly with its subsidiary Dehomag in Nazi Germany.[78]

Watson certainly carried the influence necessary to help his friend Pell, if he so chose—and apparently he did. Shortly after his appointment by the president, Pell wrote to his friend Thomas J. Watson at the Knickerbocker Club: "I have no doubt, that you have heard of my appointment, which is due, to such a great extent, to your influence. I am more than grateful to you for your efforts and the trouble you have taken on my account. Of course, I am delighted that they have borne such magnificent fruit. With renewed gratitude, I am, Herbert Pell."[79] Watson wasted no time in telegraphing Pell on July 2: "Greatly pleased with your appointment. Please let me know when you arrive at [the Knickerbocker] club."[80]

It would be exceptionally ironic if Watson played such an influential role in the appointment, as Pell obviously believed he did. In the 1930s, Watson accepted and admired the Nazis. The admiration was mutual. Watson used his position of access to the president and State Department to protect and expand IBM business ventures around the globe, including its subsidiary in Nazi Germany where IBM technology was used throughout; IBM Hollerith tabulating machines, for example, were used to delineate Jews by name in national censuses. IBM, through Dehomag, also provided the Nazis the necessary equipment to keep trains running on time as they increasingly turned their railroads to the service of transporting Jews to death camps rather than ferrying soldiers to the front during the war years. In a very real sense, IBM technology helped facilitate the perpetrators of the Holocaust by bringing increased efficiency to the Final Solution.[81]

The Allied powers also used IBM equipment but for less sinister purposes. After the United States became involved in the war, the German government nationalized Dehomag, and Watson disassociated himself from Germany, thereafter strongly supporting the American war effort. He also returned the medal the Nazis had given him in 1937.[82] In 1945 IBM equipment facilitated the Nuremberg War Crimes Trial. Without the application of IBM's simultaneous interpretation equipment, which allowed for the nearly instantaneous interpretation of English, French, German, and Russian, the trial could not have taken place. IBM provided its Filene-Finlay simultaneous interpretation equipment for use at the trial at no cost to the Allied powers.[83]

Thomas Watson had played a personal role in providing the equipment that helped facilitate the Holocaust, and at the end of the war, his company provided the equipment to help facilitate bringing Nazi war criminals to justice.[84] And it appears that Watson helped Pell become the American representative on the UNWCC—the very individual who would take on the task of asserting that Nazi crimes against humanity, the Final Solution, was an international offense for which the Allied powers should seek punishment.

To whatever degree Watson did or did not influence the selection of Pell, Hull never said, and FDR, for his part, never made any effort to justify his selection. Eleven years into his presidency—longer than any predecessor (or successor)—FDR surely thought he did not have to defend his choice. Pell's appointment letter, drafted by the State Department and signed by the president, offers only basic details of the appointment. First was the official notification that the Commission was about to be established and that the president wanted Pell to represent the United States. He was to be paid a salary of nine thousand dollars per annum plus transportation and per diem. The letter requested that Pell call on "appropriate officials" in the State Department and then travel to London as soon as possible—if he was willing to serve. Of course, the president knew that he was.[85]

It was not surprising that State did not explain Pell's selection and offered nothing complimentary of the man in its draft of the appointment letter; for whatever reason, the president also made no changes or additions to it before signing. In the coming year, this procedure would become standard for letters to Pell from the president. In any case, FDR had chosen him, and now it was only for Pell to accept formally.

Whether it was the White House or the State Department that sent the letter, the June 14 notification went by regular U.S. mail. Pell, a man of multiple residences who also liked to spend time at some of the finest hotels, was also fond of "gentleman's clubs." Consequently, the appointment letter to him was

sent care of the Knickerbocker Club in New York City. During this era, gentle-
man's clubs were still exclusively the haunts of the rich, well-born, and elite.
The Knickerbocker Club was founded in 1871 when members of Manhattan's
Union Club became perturbed by lax admission policies.[86] Pell and FDR were
Knickerbocker members, along with other well-known Americans such as the
Astors and Rockefellers.[87] It could very well have been, therefore, that the letter
was sent to the club at the suggestion of the president. When it arrived, inexplicably, someone at the club forwarded the letter to an old Pell summer residence
in Maine that he had not used for some time.[88]

Only by accident did Pell find out about his appointment. On June 23, he
ran into Sumner Welles in New York City. Pell expressed surprise about the
appointment and told Welles that he had "practically contracted to go on a
lecture tour." When informed about the confusion, FDR instructed Grace Tully
to phone Pell at his home in Garden City, New York, and read the letter to him.
Pell immediately accepted and told Tully to inform the president he would report
directly to Welles or Secretary Hull for further instructions.[89]

Pell replied officially to the president the next day, having finally received the
official appointment letter of June 14. "I am most delighted with the prospect
you offer me," he wrote his friend. "I am not only anxious to serve and to support you, but in my final account I know that my descendants will count it a
point in my favor that I have enjoyed your trust."[90] Typical of Pell's respect for
the president, he addressed his reply as coming from the Knickerbocker Club,
never mentioning his accidental discovery of his appointment when he ran into
Welles the previous day.[91]

Herbert C. Pell was fifty-nine years old when he received this latest and what
would turn out to be final appointment from his longtime friend. Undoubtedly,
Pell meant what he wrote, that he was proud to have enjoyed the president's trust.
At this time of his life, he genuinely appreciated the personal significance of the
appointment. He wrote a family friend not long after, "I look forward as it was
our ancestors' duty, which was well accomplished, to look out for our interests
when 1900 was much further off than 2000 is today."[92] In addition, Pell seemed
to have had a clear understanding that this was probably his final opportunity to
serve the president, who had aged considerably in office. And Pell was obviously
proud to serve the country, which had been quite good to him and his family
since its arrival in North America centuries before.

The presidency and the war, particularly, had been hard on his friend. In
the summer of 1943, FDR had yet to announce any decision to run for a fourth

term. He did not tell Democratic Party chairman Robert E. Hannegan what his intentions were until July 11, 1944, a full year later: "Reluctantly, but as a good soldier . . . I will accept and serve in this office, if I am ordered to so by the Commander in Chief of us all—the sovereign people of the United States."[93]

Pell also understood that this might be his last opportunity to make his mark for his family name, which mattered so much to him. But he was also keenly aware that the UNWCC could be potentially important to the war effort, and more, that it might have a role to play in helping establish American moral authority after the war. He no doubt agreed with what FDR said during the Tehran Conference at the end of 1943: "The maintenance of the moral prestige of the great powers is an essential element in any successful system of international cooperation."[94] The Tehran Conference was also the earliest signal that FDR thought he might have to run for a fourth term, reflecting his awareness of his own role in creating a new postwar world order.[95] Pell was resolute in his conviction that FDR was the man to direct the United States into a solitary leadership role in the postwar world. "From my observation of the United States, and also from what I have seen abroad," he wrote FDR, "it seems to me that your retention of the office of President is almost vitally necessary for the good of the United States and for the future of the world."[96]

Like the president, Pell was an internationalist.[97] He was a devoted reader of history and wanted to avoid any possibility of a third world war.[98] He wrote a fellow Knickerbocker Club friend in the fall of 1944 recalling that when he was in Congress, he was a younger member of the generation that failed to prevent a second world war. "I do not want to see the present generation of which I am one of the seniors fail again."[99] Writing to his brother, Clarence, Pell asserted matter-of-factly that the United States must take the lead and "set the standards of the world."[100] As far as Pell was concerned, FDR was the right man at the right time to lead the world out of the darkness, and Pell was enthusiastic and humbled about having an opportunity to be part of that effort by representing his nation favorably on the UNWCC.

The meaning of FDR's phrase "the maintenance of moral prestige" has remained a matter of historical debate. What "standards" Pell believed the United States should set for the world have been a matter, conversely, of little historical discussion. Given the order of events, and what had been said and left unsaid by the president, at the very least we can conclude that FDR wanted a man he could trust on the UNWCC. He wanted a friend with whom he could communicate directly whenever it pleased him. He knew that Pell agreed with him regarding the place of the United States in world affairs.

If we are to take FDR at his word—something that must be done with care—the punishment of war criminals mattered. Given the consistency of his pronouncements up to and after Pell's appointment, what FDR had said was not just aimed at placating the governments in exile and special-interest groups at home. Beginning with his first statement on war crimes on October 25, 1941, FDR had been keenly attuned to the importance of justice. Denouncing the murder of fifty French hostages in reprisal for the assassination of a Nazi Army officer in Nantes, France—nearly two months prior to U.S. entry into the war—FDR said, "The Nazis might have learned from the last war the impossibility of breaking men's spirit by terrorism." He concluded his statement, forewarning, "Frightfulness can never bring peace to Europe. It only sows the seeds of hatred which will one day bring fearful retribution."[101]

Little doubt exists that war crimes policy fell within the rubric of FDR's vision of a new postwar world order led by the moral authority of the United States. What was taking place on the European continent, what we now know as the Holocaust, was an unprecedented event for which no one was prepared. It would be difficult to explain away the failure to plan appropriately for the prosecution of war criminals, particularly given the failure of the Allies to do so successfully following the First World War. Whatever they may have been lacking in alacrity, the Allies had, at least, taken the first step of organizing the UNWCC to deal with war crimes policy. The president had chosen, against the advice of others, his friend Bertie Pell to represent the United States on the only organization then intended to deal with the problem of what to do about punishing those who were at that very moment committing unspeakable crimes in Europe.

What did the president expect of his latest appointee? Would he take up the cause of European Jewry? Perhaps FDR recalled the stance Pell took on the Klan and racism during the 1924 Democratic National Convention. Could he have remembered that Pell once wrote that he could not "believe that any one race today is made up entirely of supermen, while none worthy of preservation exist in any other . . . that it requires a hundred armed Nordic supermen to overcome one unarmed individual belonging to a race destined to succumb"?[102] We will never know for certain. But common sense requires an appreciation that FDR selected Pell out of the accumulation of his long personal and professional experience with Pell. Maybe FDR fully agreed with Franklin Mott Gunther's assessment of Pell: "'For a hundred people who can talk there is only one man who can think; but for a thousand who can think there is only one that can see.'"[103]

Regrettably, FDR never explained his decision to appoint Pell. Perhaps it was another ornamental appointment for an old, loyal friend as some have concluded. Or, to the contrary, it was an insightfully inspired selection. Given the length and the breadth of their relationship, the degree to which he trusted Pell and his loyalty over the years, it was probably both. FDR would have not have made this selection frivolously.

Too many historians have cited FDR's appointment of Herbert Pell as the American representative on the UNWCC as further proof that the president was not particularly interested in saving the Jews or in pursuing war crimes prosecutions.[104] This conclusion runs counter to the preponderance of the evidence. Pell's résumé included a lifelong friendship with the president, a short stint as a congressman, chairmanship of the New York Democratic Party, and active participation in FDR's 1936 reelection campaign, for which FDR rewarded him with two political appointments: ambassadorships to Portugal and then Hungary. Moreover, these last two appointments were so much more than ornamentation. Of course, Pell was not a lawyer; he had no legal experience at all. And he knew little about war criminals—save what he may have read—and next to nothing about international law, and yet FDR still appointed him. As such, the appointment itself is the best evidence of the degree to which he trusted Pell. That he wanted a man of Pell's character and experience over a skilled legal mind demonstrates that FDR indeed took the plight of Jews and justice seriously. The last thing he wanted as an American representative was a legalist unwilling to look past the lack of precedents. He wanted someone who shared his larger view of the war and the role that justice could play in the postwar world. It only remained to be seen what, precisely, Pell would do now that the president had called on him again.

Pell had sent his friend FDR a telegram of support in early 1943 instructing him to "Read Job Twenty-three, verses three four five six eleven and twelve":[105]

3. Oh that I knew where I might find him!
   That I might come to his seat!
4. I would order my cause before him
   And fill my mouth with arguments.
5. I would learn the words which he would answer me,
   And understand what he would say unto me.
6. Would he plead against me with his great power?
   No; but he would put strength in me. . . .

11. My foot hath held his steps;
     His way I have kept, and not declined.
12. Neither have I gone back from the commandment of his lips;
     I esteemed the words of his mouth more than my necessary food.

The president replied, thanking him and noting, "It's a comfort to know that things got a little easier for that paragon of patience in the last chapter wherein we are assured that 'The Lord blessed the latter end of Job more than his beginning.'"[106] The patience of Herbert C. Pell soon enough would be sorely tested, even before he arrived in London. For the unsuspecting Pell, the latter end would turn out to be no less demanding and challenging than the beginning. Throughout what would become a very difficult tenure as American representative on the UNWCC, just like Job, Pell remained steadfast in carrying out what he believed to be FDR's policy. He would not turn "back from the commandment of his lips," as stated in Job 5:12.

CHAPTER 4

DEPARTURE DELAYED

"Is There Any Reason for the Continued Delay?"

I told him that I expected to do what I could to see to the punishment
of those who had tortured innocent people in concentration camps
and had massacred citizens in the occupied countries.

Herbert C. Pell, 1953

At the suggestion of the president, Pell traveled to Washington on June 28, 1943, to "discuss the details" of the proposed UNWCC with Undersecretary of State Sumner Welles the following day.[1] He was entirely unprepared for the cool reception he received. At State the next morning, he ended up meeting instead with Green Hackworth, who immediately and unceremoniously notified him that the department had already selected Professor Lawrence Preuss to assist him on the Commission.[2] Preuss had been a professor of political science at the University of Michigan, his alma mater, and was then serving in the State Department.[3] The department wanted one of its own working with—and evidently keeping an eye on—Pell, who wanted Harvard Law School professor Sheldon Glueck as his assistant, likely at the suggestion of the president.[4] As Pell later put it, "They insisted on my taking a man called Lawrence Preuss who was not even a lawyer but had, I believe, given some lectures on international law in one of the middle-western universities."[5] Of course, there is not just a little irony in this, given that

Glueck was no lawyer either. He was, like Preuss, a scholar and academic, but Glueck was a Harvard man, not incidentally, like Pell and the president.

For the record, Hackworth wrote an internal memorandum to G. Howland Shaw and Sumner Welles summarizing his June 29 meeting with Pell, falsely asserting that it was Pell who wanted Preuss. Incredibly, Hackworth wrote that he had informed Pell that the appointment of Preuss was pending the "wishes" of others in the department who might object to releasing Preuss to Pell.[6] Pell did not then know about Hackworth's duplicitous actions, nor did he know yet that part of Preuss's duties once he and Pell arrived in London would be to report privately to Hackworth and others in the State Department without Pell's knowledge.[7]

During their meeting, Pell asked Hackworth when he might depart for London. Parroting the president, Hackworth replied that he understood he was to depart "as soon as possible."[8] This was good news to Pell, who was anxious to get to work, having been on the sidelines since December 1941. From State, Pell headed to the White House, where he and his wife had a brief early afternoon visit with FDR. This meeting was twenty-two years to the day that FDR defended Herbert C. Pell's potential for chairmanship of the New York State Democratic Party by saying, "I know Bertie. . . . He's not such a bad fellow."[9]

He was in line for another chair now, this time of the UNWCC. Back on March 5, three months before the president appointed Pell, the British had suggested that the post be given to the U.S. representative, whoever that might be.[10] At that time, Secretary of State Cordell Hull had no problem with an American heading the UNWCC.

In mid-May, after Attorney General Biddle declined the position, Hull still planned on the U.S. representative becoming chair of the Commission.[11] But after FDR appointed Pell, the State Department reversed itself, rejecting the British proposal, Hull alleged, because it "might give rise to some dissension or misunderstanding on the part of other Governments." Deeming Pell unqualified for the job of chair, to say nothing of what he thought about his serving on the Commission in the first place, Hull suggested in a June 28 telegram that the Commission appoint Sir Cecil Hurst, given his standing on the Permanent Court of International Justice.[12]

When Pell met with State Department officials the next day, no one told him that Hull had now rejected the idea of the Commission having an American chair. Quite possibly the president, when he met with Pell later that same day, may have informed him that the British had proposed it. It is also possible that Green Hackworth told Pell of the British proposal. Knowing that Hull had already nixed the idea, it was an opportunity for Hackworth to embarrass Pell in the eyes of the president. Whatever the case, at the time of his appointment, Pell understood that the British wanted the American representative to chair the Commission. The truth was, of course, that the State Department had come to reject the idea because of Pell's appointment.

More than two weeks later Pell still thought becoming UNWCC chair was a possibility. Having heard nothing more about it—or anything else for that matter—from anyone since his State Department visit and meeting with the president, he wrote FDR on July 15 attempting to advance his appointment as chair. "I think this would be a good thing as it would insure [sic] a good deal of firmness in Europe," wrote Pell. "Naturally, I can express this particular point to no one but you."[13] Pell was resuming his practice of communicating directly with the president, which he had done regularly as ambassador to Portugal and Hungary. He would continue this custom as American representative to the UNWCC, frequently to the irritation of officials in the State Department, especially Green Hackworth. Pell wanted the honor of being chair of the Commission, but he was also convinced that America should take a leadership role on war crimes policy. An American chair would signal the nation's resolute commitment to the prosecution of war criminals.

The deceit surrounding the appointment of the UNWCC chair was just the beginning of what would be a year and a half of contemptible treatment of Pell by State Department officials.[14] During the nearly five months between his appointment and departure to begin his work on the Commission in London, State Department officials forced their own choice of an assistant on Pell, repeatedly failed to provide him information regarding war crimes policy planning despite his frequent requests, and continued to leave him in the dark regarding the possibilities of his becoming chair.

Most of all, the interminable delay in his departure to London was exceedingly frustrating to Pell. He was anxious to get started with the work of the Commission, which he considered of utmost importance to the future of world peace. By the time he finally left, Pell had reached the inevitable conclusion that the State Department was directionless when it came to war crimes policy. By mid-spring 1944, Pell believed the State Department was giving him instructions contradictory to those of the president; at least that was how it appeared to him. It was worse than it appeared.

By the end of his appointment, Pell was convinced that State Department officials wanted to engineer not only his ruin but also the failure of the entire mission of the UNWCC, which meant no prosecution of crimes against humanity. Before that happened, before the UNWCC became a sideshow to the planning of war crimes policy, Pell persisted in his effort to expand war crimes to include crimes against humanity, making an extremely important but underappreciated contribution to the advancement of international law and human rights.

Believing he would depart for London quickly—within ten days to two weeks, according to what Hackworth said at their meeting—Pell returned to his home in New York and began preparations. After hearing nothing from the State Department for two weeks regarding a departure date, he appealed directly to the president in a July 15 message, having made a similar plea to the State Department the day before. "I should be very grateful," he wrote, "if you would get me off as quickly as possible."[15]

A short time later, Pell learned that his departure would have to wait. He had been working with Shaw to appoint a secretary for his work in London. In a July 16 letter Shaw wrote him that the "situation had been suddenly changed" by the British Foreign Office. Pell was not to depart until replies regarding the formation of the UNWCC were received from the Soviet, Chinese, and other Allied governments.[16]

The British Foreign Office had informed the State Department on July 13 that "it would be unwise to assume that the commission will be set up in the immediate future." They emphasized that Pell should not come to London, as they put it, "until the position is clearer."[17] Apparently, the British were in no hurry to see the UNWCC established. It was in this message, incidentally, that the Foreign Office acknowledged Hull's suggestion that Hurst be made chair of the Commission. This was quite satisfactory to the British, but any such appointment, they submitted, must be acceptable to the other governments represented on the Commission. Of course, Shaw did not tell Pell any of this, so he continued to wait, trusting that he was to become chair. Shaw told Pell that "a delay of three or four weeks is clearly foreseeable."[18]

On Saturday, July 31, FDR stopped by the Pell residence in Hopewell Junction on the way to Hyde Park. Pell's wife, Olive, wrote FDR adoringly, thanking him for the courtesy of his having sat for photographs. "I was furious," she wrote, "at being coached by my boss before you came to leave the room as soon as I had given you your tea! But 'orders are orders.' . . . ." Even Olive piled on, "I sincerely hope that we get to London soon!" She may have left the room, but she must not have been out of earshot as she told FDR in her note that the sooner the UNWCC was "set up and ready to function," the better. Once Hitler "realizes the game is up," the Commission will be the only thing to deter him from "slaughter[ing] all his prisoners of war."[19]

With no further word and annoyed that the British seemed to be dictating to the United States, Pell telegraphed Secretary Hull on August 6 regarding the delay. Hull did not reply until the eleventh, informing Pell that it was impossible to predict when the Commission would be set up and, therefore, impractical to set a departure date.[20] Growing more impatient, Pell did not wait for Hull's reply before appealing, yet again, to the president.

Pell sent a telegram on August 9 to FDR and followed it up with a letter the next day, inquiring when he might depart and asking for a meeting.[21] "My original understanding was that I was to get ready and go as soon as possible," he reminded the president. "Since then, for nearly two months, I have been waiting, and have received no orders from Washington." Pell added gently that since FDR had been speaking publicly about war crimes and war criminals, it seemed to him there should be no delay in his getting to London.[22]

The president had issued a warning to the Italian people, in a joint state- ment with the British prime minister on July 16, that there would be "inevitable consequences" for war criminals.[23] During his July 28 Fireside Chat, he told Americans that the people of the "conquered" nations had been "reduced to the status of slaves or chattels." Returning to the ideas of his Four Freedoms speech delivered to the Seventy-Seventh Congress back on January 6, 1941, the president declared it was America's duty to restore "these conquered peoples to the dignity of human beings, masters of their own fate, entitled to freedom of speech, freedom of religion, freedom from want, and freedom from fear." And with an important choice of words—words that Pell would not forget—FDR announced that war criminals would be "punished for their crimes against humanity."[24]

Two days later, the White House released a statement at FDR's 912th press conference: "The President Warns Neutral Nations Against Providing Asylum for War Criminals." Reiterating his announcements of August 21 and October 7, 1942, FDR cautioned that war criminals and those aiding them would be brought to justice.[25] None of these proclamations had escaped the notice of Herbert Pell. He could not understand how the president could allow the British to delay formation of the Commission while proclaiming America's intentions to bring war criminals and those who harbor them to swift justice.

Two and a half more weeks went by without word on a departure date. "Dear Mr. President," Pell wrote in another letter to his friend on August 28, "I am still waiting in Duchess County [New York] for permission to proceed to London."

Pell believed the work of the Commission needed to begin immediately, and he considered it vitally important that he get to know the attitudes of the various representatives personally to determine his course—something he could not do until he arrived in London. "I am sure you understand how interested I am to get started in the job which lies ahead of us," Pell added.

As was usual in his correspondence with FDR, Pell then switched seamlessly from the political to the personal.

> I wish you could come over here now and see my place. Since you were here I have been having more fun than a barrel of monkeys directing a bulldozer and a steam shovel, run by the same contractor who excavated for your library. He told me of the obvious enjoyment you got out of watching the machines at work. It is certainly fun seeing it crash through groves of little locusts like a mowing machine across a lawn.[26]

Returning to the purpose of his letter, Pell told FDR that he recently met with a mutual friend of theirs from London at the Knickerbocker Club. "It will be a great pleasure to be in his neighborhood," he told FDR, "and I hope that you will send me there as soon as you can."[27] Pell wanted to get to work, and he was sure that the president must have wanted that as well. What he did not then know, however, was that no one in the State Department had told the president that the British Foreign Office was holding things up.

Pell's August 28 letter accomplished its goal. On September 2, an angered FDR asked Secretary Hull, "Why can't Herbert Pell get off for London? Is there any reason for the continued delay?"[28] Five days later, September 7, Hull sent a formal and detailed reply to the president, covering precisely what had transpired and in what order. Matters had changed, he told FDR, since the time of Pell's appointment, when everyone expected an immediate departure to London.[29]

FDR's evident exasperation that he had had to mediate between the State Department and his appointee forced Hull into updating the president. Hull finally informed FDR about the Foreign Office's July 13 message. The British Foreign Office was displeased that the United States had made the public announcement of Pell's appointment on June 28 without informing the Foreign Office in advance because it had given the impression that the United States was the standard-bearer on war crimes policy.[30] The State Department should have told the Foreign Office in advance. Hull had not wanted the president to know it had failed to do so. A similar unilateral announcement by the United States regarding an increase in Nazi atrocities in Europe had been made earlier in August 1942, and the State Department had failed again to coordinate the announcement with the British Foreign Office. At the very least, the Foreign Office wanted equal billing with the United States when it came to war crimes policy. FDR, finally aware of what was causing the delay, forwarded Hull's September 7 letter the next day to Pell at the Knickerbocker Club with no comment other than a "for your information."[31] Of course, no commentary had been necessary; both Pell and FDR believed they knew the score by then.

The president wanted Pell to get to London "as soon as possible." He wanted the UNWCC up and running, and he would have been quite pleased for the United States to take a leadership position with Pell heading the Commission. Neither man had any idea, even at that late date, that the State Department had already decided that Pell would not chair the Commission. The department had known that piece of information for two months, and still, neither Hull nor anyone else at State had informed Pell or the president.

In an internal September 14, 1943, State Department memorandum, Green Hackworth wrote that "our representative [Pell] is not to become chairman under any circumstances and that he should be instructed to this effect before he leaves the United States." He should be told, not immediately, just sometime before he leaves, as if the timing did not matter. According to Hackworth, Sumner Welles was to have told Pell about the situation "some time ago, but he may not have done so."[32] He hadn't, of course, and he wouldn't be doing so in the future, as Hackworth certainly knew. Hull had seen to it that Sumner Welles was no longer working in the State Department. It was easy, of course, for Hackworth to blame Welles since he was no longer there to defend himself. At any rate, the status of the chair was one of the few things Hull failed to admit in his September 7 letter to the president.

Notwithstanding the treatment of Pell, in the weeks and then months after Pell's appointment, no one in the State Department made any effort to expedite the formation of the Commission or Pell's departure. To the contrary, State Department officials seemed pleased to leave it up to the British, almost relieved that it was taking so much time. All the while the exterminations in Europe continued unabated, and still no organization existed—well, one did exist but neither the British nor Americans seem interested in getting it operating—to gather evidence and suggest procedure. But two Americans in particular were very interested: Herbert Pell and Franklin Roosevelt.

On September 6 the American Embassy in London informed the State Department that the British Foreign Office had received replies from "all the Governments concerned." It was time to get Pell to London. U.S. ambassador Gil Winant wrote

Hull, "I am impressed by the urgency of setting up the Commission without further delay." Winant suggested that Allied representatives meet in London at the end of September to finalize arrangements.[33] This message was received a day *before* Hull informed the president in his September 7 letter that it would be at least four to six weeks before Pell could depart because the other governments had not yet replied. If there was now an "urgency" on the part of the British to set up the Commission, it seemed to make sense that Pell should get to London as FDR had wanted, "as soon as possible." But no one seemed to recognize that. Inexplicably, this message from Ambassador Winant to Secretary Hull was dated September 1 but for some reason was not received in Washington until September 6.

Under normal circumstances, it would be hard to imagine that Hull knowingly kept this information from the president; he was so specific in his September 7 letter, detailing almost every message sent to and received from the British Foreign Office. Given that messages could apparently go undelivered for days, however, it is entirely possible that Hull knew nothing of the changed circumstances when he wrote FDR on September 7. Even so, Hull made no effort to pass this information on to the president or Pell later once he did receive it. In fact, Hull made no immediate reply whatsoever to anyone, including the Foreign Office.

One explanation for the State Department's obduracy in getting Pell off to London—beyond general dissatisfaction with his appointment in the first place—was Hull's most recent confrontation with FDR over the number-two man at the State Department, Undersecretary Sumner Welles. Quite possibly, it was an important contributing factor in encouraging the State Department's efforts to undermine Pell's position on the UNWCC.

By September 1943 the relationship between Hull and the president had gone from a businesslike cool to irreparably frosty. The two men had never been particularly close. In most cases, the president preferred to conduct his own foreign policy. He had selected Hull as secretary of state primarily for the influence Hull could wield with Congress.[34] Hull had served a dozen terms in the House and was in his second year of his first term in the Senate when FDR appointed him secretary of state in 1933. By 1943 FDR's Democratic majority had grown thin in Congress, and he needed Hull politically more than ever. The growing estrangement between the two men reached its zenith when they met at the White House on August 16. As they talked over the typically bland White House lunch fare, Hull presented FDR his ultimatum: Sumner Welles must resign, or he would.[35]

The animosity between Hull and Welles was well known within the State Department. It only continued to grow the longer the two men worked together out of the same office. FDR's continued reliance on Welles over Hull exacerbated the personal differences and difficulties between the two men. As undersecretary, Welles traditionally was supposed to administer the department, leaving Hull to focus on policy. But it was Welles, not Hull, on whom the president relied for policy advice, often having Welles attend important wartime conferences with him rather than Hull. Welles was a member of the circle of friends whom FDR trusted; Hull was not. Hull's own insecurity and inadequacies lay underneath the difficulties between the two men. Not surprisingly, Hull used what he perceived to be Welles's inadequacies as a man—his bisexuality—to force Welles's resignation on the president. In September 1940 on a trip with FDR to House Speaker William Bankhead's funeral, a drunken Welles made homosexual advances to Pullman porters. The incident became well known among several members of the press and administration insiders, including Hull and the president, who chose to ignore it, but Hull obviously did not.[36]

According to Welles's biographer (and son), Benjamin Welles, Hull forged "an unholy alliance" with William C. Bullitt, a former adviser to FDR, in his effort to oust Welles.[37] None other than Green Hackworth had advised Hull in January 1943 that Virginia authorities could prosecute Welles under existing statutes because the 1940 incident had occurred on the return trip while passing through the state of Virginia. Armed with adequate information and allies, Hull forced the issue in late July. Bullitt, apparently at the direction of Hull, met with the president and insisted he remove Welles. Eleanor Roosevelt, in her 1949 book, *This I Remember,* described seeing her husband later that day "shaken with anger" and "white with wrath." FDR recounted the meeting, and, as Eleanor recorded it—using letters rather than names—her outraged husband had told Bullitt the following:

> X [Bill], if I were St. Peter and you and Y [Sumner] came before me, I would say to Y [Sumner], "No matter what you have done, you have hurt no one but yourself. I recognize human frailties. Come in." But to you I would say, "You have not only hurt another human being, you have deprived your country of the services of a good citizen; and for that you can go straight to Hell."[38]

FDR never forgave Bullitt and, according to Eleanor, never spoke with him again. If FDR did not know Hull was behind it at that July confrontation, he had no doubt about it when Hull demanded Welles's resignation in August.

Benjamin Welles called his father's life a "tragedy." Here was an exceedingly talented man who possessed, according to his friend FDR, one of the "finest minds he had ever known." As FDR saw it, the loss of Welles to the country was, indeed, a tragedy. Benjamin Welles blamed the frailties of his father, a man worn out by public service and "crushing responsibility," an alcoholic who allowed his "bisexual urges latent in his nature" to lead to "tawdry advances." Welles himself had provided the means for his own destruction. Cordell Hull, with the help of others, was all too willing to make use of it.[39]

From a twenty-first-century vantage point, Sumner Welles's removal was not just a tragedy *for* the nation; it was representative of the tragedy *of* the nation, an unenlightened, know-nothing intolerance of the other. In this, the United States was not much different from Nazi Germany. FDR was forced to remove the one man he trusted in the State Department because he understood the political implications if what was viewed then as Welles's perversion were known publicly. The extent of the impact of Hull's forcing out of Welles, while hard to measure precisely, unquestionably was extensive.

For a time, Hull was almost giddy with his successful removal of Welles.[40] He never admitted he played any role in Welles's removal, writing in his memoirs only that FDR "decided on his own that in the light of all existing circumstances the efficiency of the Department would be improved by Welles's retirement."[41] Given the way Hull and the Department acted when it came to Pell, it does seem that Hull believed he was now in a stronger position. No longer threatened by Welles's presence, he now had more confidence to treat Pell as he wished. And given Pell's close relationship with FDR, Hull must have thought that the worse he treated Pell, the better. Reinvigorated, Hull apparently had no qualms about stalling the establishment of the UNWCC.

On September 22 Winant, exasperated by the silence and most likely under pressure from the Foreign Office, cabled Hull again: "Embassy hopes soon to receive Department's comments . . . concerning proposed commission for investigation of war crimes."[42] The most important of the British proposals was its call for a "Technical Committee" of "experts" to consider "the sort of Tribunals to be employed" and "the procedure to be adopted and the rules of evidence to be followed."[43]

Finally, Hull replied on September 25, authorizing Winant to attend a meeting of diplomatic representatives to finalize arrangements for the UNWCC and set a date for it to begin sessions. There could be no more objections now to Pell's departing for London, but still, no one in the State Department was in any hurry. Hull even informed Winant that Pell would bring an assistant and a secretary with him, but he made absolutely no mention of when that future event might take place. As to the British suggestion of a "Technical Committee," the State

Department said that "it may be desirable." Conditionals like this were the hallmark of Green Hackworth, who composed the reply for Hull.[44]

Discussion on just who should chair the commission had also morphed somewhat by this time. The Soviets had informed the British that they felt the chair should be held in rotation between Great Britain, the United States, China, and the Soviet Union. Consequently, the British suggested that the choice of chair be left up to the Commission when it began its work. As Green Hackworth wrote it for Hull's signature, "the Department has no objection to the proposal. . . . The Department would, however, desire to be consulted before conferring the Chairmanship upon the American representative."[45] The U.S. State Department, it seems, was doing everything in its power to undercut Pell even before he arrived in London. Hackworth obviously still held out hope that when "experts" were needed for the "Technical Committee," Hackworth himself would be one of them.

Meanwhile, Pell had gone to the State Department sometime during the week of September 12. The only news he had received up to that point regarding the Commission had come in response to his queries to the State Department, so he hoped a personal visit might garner additional information about what was going on about establishing the Commission. What he discovered only added to his frustration. He wrote a letter to Hull on September 17, complaining about the "very lackadaisical way" things were being handled. Green Hackworth had notified Pell "it was out of his hands" and that he "should see Mr. Shaw and Mr. Dunn." But Dunn told Pell "he had nothing to do with it," and Shaw told him it "was a question of policy for someone else." Tired of being given the runaround, Pell wanted Hull to know about it. Surely, if the secretary knew what was taking place, he would correct it.[46] Every moment of delay, Pell thought, only furthered the tragedy then taking place in Europe.

Pell was also irritated over the lack of any concrete vision for how to deal with war criminals, save his conversations with the president. "I have been unable to find any clear definition of the duties and scope of the commission," he wrote Hull. "Twice, as a result of conversations with the President, I have understood that it will have to set up a court ad hoc for the trial of war guilt and gather evidence."[47]

Despite his being passed from official to official, someone did inform Pell about Winant's September 1 telegram. Pell was led to believe, however, that the British still objected to his being sent over at that time, which obviously was not the case any longer. Moreover, Pell discovered no one had yet replied to the message from the Foreign Office. Pell could not believe it, and he told Hull as much in writing. Hackworth had written the reply, but it had not been sent and sat languishing on someone's desk in the European Division of the State Department. And even at this late date, Pell still thought he might become chair since the British suggested the Commission itself decide. He then knew, at least, that department officials were opposed to the idea, but he continued to hope naively that Hull might intercede on his behalf. He had no idea that it was actually Hull who had already decided Pell would not be chair.[48]

Very shortly thereafter, Hull reassured Pell (either in person or by phone), and Pell wrote him on September 23, thanking him for the "trouble" he took on his account.[49] Still, Pell was to wait for his travel orders. Perhaps now, he hoped, the department would keep him better informed, but that turned out not to be the case. Pell had to request again that the State Department provide him copies of correspondence. He contacted Shaw in mid-October, not knowing exactly to whom he should address his request.[50] No one seemed to be in charge of war crimes policy within the State Department. Adding to the difficulty, Hull and Hackworth, along with other department officials, were both off to the Soviet Union, having left Washington on October 7 for the Moscow Conference.[51]

Finally, on October 20, a meeting was held in London at the British Foreign Office formally establishing the UNWCC. At this gathering, Sir Cecil Hurst suggested that an "unofficial meeting be held of those members of the Commission now in London," to which everyone agreed.[52] Herbert Pell was not among those members. He was still at home in the United States, serving an apparently State Department–imposed exile. Undoubtedly, Pell found out about the official formation of the UNWCC in the *New York Times,* which reported on October 21 that a "secret" gathering of ambassadors had met in London organizing the UNWCC. It was expected, the *Times* reported, that the Commission would begin "in a few weeks."[53] On October 26, the first meeting—informal—of the UNWCC was held in London. Hurst noted they could not meet formally until the U.S. representative had arrived.[54] Everyone wanted to know, where was Herbert Pell?

The *New York Times* front-page announcement of the Statement on Atrocities agreed to at the Moscow Conference appeared on November 2.[55] Pell received his own copy from the State Department sometime after November 6, probably when he went there on November 9, again trying to get information about what was happening. Pell was irritated, angry, and bitter that he was still in the United States and decided to do something about it, whatever the consequences.

"Let those who have hitherto not imbrued their hands with innocent blood beware lest they join the ranks of the guilty," read the Moscow Declaration, "for most assuredly the three Allied Powers will pursue them to the uttermost ends of the earth and will deliver them to their accusors in order that justice may be done." The "major criminals" were to be "punished by joint declaration of the Governments of the Allies," which in some ways threatened to undercut the importance of the UNWCC before it even began deliberating.[56] Nonetheless, justice requires evidence, which the UNWCC was to provide—whatever the rank of the war criminal. Still the question remained: where was Herbert Pell?

The president wanted an update. The new undersecretary, Edward R. Stettinius, serving as acting secretary in Hull's absence, told the president on November 4 that it was Pell's own fault that he had not arrived yet in London. "He would not travel," wrote Stettinius, "without his wife," as if this all along had been causing the delay. The charge was false; Pell did expect that he could take his wife with him, as he had done during his previous governmental appointments, but he was entirely prepared to head to London without her.[57]

When Pell reported to the State Department on November 9, he was shown Winant's October 26 telegram that made clear he was needed in London.[58] That department officials had not informed him immediately, that he had to find out through his own efforts, that his State Department–appointed assistant was already on his way to London while he still was not, piled insult upon injury. Winant later told Pell, after he had finally arrived in London, that the British "had been seriously put out" by his delay in arriving.[59] Worst of all, however, throughout this entire ordeal of waiting to go to London, Pell was given absolutely no direction from the State Department regarding war crimes policy. An utterly frustrated and angry Pell told the State Department official with whom he met on November 9 that he would follow any instructions given him from the department, but in the continued absence of any, he would act on his own initiative. And he would do so, he said, with "a strong hand."[60]

Pell wrote much the same two days later to Hull, hoping to receive explicit instructions, or at the very least support, for such a stance. "I hope that you want the War [Crimes] Commission to go as far as it can and to be as tough as possible. I should be grateful if you would write me yourself, and tell me how far you will let me go—how tough I may be." Appealing to someone whom he still mistakenly considered a supporter and friend, he added, "I have in the past, and you have too, shown no fear of responsibility, and we are neither the worse for it."[61] To the president, Pell wrote that same day in a similar vein, "I wanted . . . to know just how tough you will let me be . . . as my inclination is to be as tough as I can."[62]

At long last, Herbert Pell was to travel to London. Befitting the absurdity of the struggle that had gone on for months between Pell and the State Department, he was sent to New York City to depart for England on the *Queen Mary,* along with thousands of American troops. He had to travel alone, without his wife, which aggravated him enormously. His wife was allowed to go to London, but separately, for reasons never adequately explained. Pell blamed the State Department, of course—never sure, he said later, whether it was due to "red tape, rules or malice."[63]

Utmost secrecy surrounded the *Queen Mary*'s departure for fear of Nazi U-boats. Passengers were not to throw anything overboard, and all lights had to be extinguished at night. But the ship departed on November 15 in broad daylight and in view of thousands. Pell later wrote of the episode, "That was the so-called secrecy of departure."[64] State Department officials had done a much better job in keeping the details of the Commission secret from Pell over the last five months than the War Department had done with the *Queen Mary*'s voyage.

The important question was what Herbert Pell would do once he arrived in London. In addition, to what degree did the State Department's outwardly disrespectful treatment have an impact on him? More than anything, the maneuverings of the previous several months had demonstrated convincingly that the State Department intended Pell to do little or nothing while on the Commission. Given no direction and possessing no experience of his own regarding international law and war crimes, State Department officials evidently expected that Pell could—and would—operate only as a perfunctory, even ceremonial representative. This was not lost on Pell.

Pell had attempted to indicate otherwise in his November 9 meeting at the State Department and in his letter two days later to Hull, that he would be taking an active role on the Commission. But Hackworth had orchestrated the appointment of the department's own Lawrence Preuss to implement State Department policy in London while acting, in theory, as Pell's assistant.[65] Moreover, at the suggestion of the British, a "technical committee" of legal experts then planned to work in parallel with the Commission to advise on the creation of a tribunal or tribunals, what policies and procedures would be followed, and, importantly, just what constituted a war crime.[66] Naturally, State expected that Pell would play no role in such a committee of experts and would deal, therefore, with issues pertaining only to the gathering of evidence. Pell, however, had other ideas.

Since his appointment back in June, Pell had endured a five-month ostracism; at every turn, both purposefully and circumstantially, the State Department excluded him from participation. By the time of his long-awaited departure, Pell knew he would not chair the Commission, and worse, he had discovered that the State Department had quashed that possibility. Pell took that decision personally and feared his position on the Commission had been undermined even before he left for London; his fear was not unfounded.

More important, all the delay had led him to conclude that war crimes policy was not high on the State Department agenda.[67] He had suspected as much from the beginning, writing his mother back on July 3, "The work I am to do appears rather vague and it apparently will be very much left up to me." At that time, however, he thought his appointment was providential. Ever the good son, he told his mother, "All together I think I have been very fortunate in my life, and most fortunate in having you."[68] If nothing else, Pell was always cognizant and appreciative of the advantages of his birth, but he was also sensitive to the responsibilities he believed it carried. Many of his later actions while on the Commission may well be explained by this value, one that he shared with FDR.

Whether any of this made him more determined to pursue his own agenda once in London is not all that clear. With the hindsight of history, Pell obviously did have an agenda to pursue while on the Commission. It was not a personal agenda of self-promotion, although he could not have been blamed for having one, given the treatment he had received thus far from the State Department.[69] Pell's mission on the UNWCC was a component of his—and his friend, the president's—larger vision of a postwar American global hegemony based upon a deep-seated commitment to the nation's historical mission and moral authority. Part of achieving that vision, he believed, required seeking justice for Nazi crimes against humanity. It was what the president wanted him to accomplish on the UNWCC.

In the spring of 1944, when Pell undertook to widen the scope of war crimes policy, he summarized his views this way: "We must recognize that there will be a leading nation in the world. . . . Without going back to the dawn of history, the 19th century was directed from London; the center will shift either to Washington or to Moscow."[70] While Pell had been remarkably sympathetic in the past toward the Russian people, and even the Soviet system, he wanted the United States leading the postwar world.[71] His internationalist roots stretched back to his Bull Moose–Progressive Party days in the early 1900s. Pell's appointment as American representative on the UNWCC offered him a chance to pursue that internationalism in an entirely new realm, and he was determined not to waste the opportunity.

Back on June 29, 1943, when Pell met with FDR following his appointment, Pell assured his friend what he would try to achieve on the Commission. Pell recounted a decade later what he called his "interview" with the president:

> I told him that I expected to do what I could to see to the punishment of those who had tortured innocent people in concentration camps and had massacred citizens in the occupied countries. I realized at the time that there was no such thing as international law to cover these cases. These ideas were quite new. I told the President at the time that many people were going to sacrifice their lives in this war and that I stood ready to sacrifice my reputation.[72]

No other record of the men's brief discussion that day exists. Was Pell repeating or responding to the wishes of the president? Or could Pell have been dictating to FDR his own plans? Outwardly, it might appear that he was setting his own course, but to those who knew Pell, these were the words of a gentleman aristocrat, announcing his own steadfast determination to support the wishes of the president of the United States. Whatever FDR and Pell discussed during this meeting—and during FDR's later visit to Pell's home—the record of Pell's service on the UNWCC demonstrates Pell believed this was precisely what the president expected of him.

Pell considered the UNWCC an organization designed to prevent future injustice and future wars, as much as it was an organization intended to gather evidence and suggest a legal protocol for future war crimes trials.[73] Looking back on it, he said, "we were not there to distribute divine justice. . . . It's perfectly clear that the execution of a thousand people couldn't revive one child, couldn't console one widow, and could not remedy the hardships a single individual was suffering as a result of treatment in the camps. Our business, however, was to see that those things did not occur again." Given the enormity of what was taking place in Europe, Pell always maintained the belief that the entire Gestapo should have been hanged. "I believed, and still believe," he said eight years after the war, "that it would have been the best thing."[74]

CHAPTER 5

SEEKING JUSTICE

"None Who Participate in These Acts of Savagery Shall Go Unpunished"

There can be little reason for disagreement on the general proposition that Germany and her satellites should be required to answer for atrocities against the Jews.

Franklin D. Roosevelt to "Bertie" Pell, May 1, 1944

Herbert Pell's arrival in Great Britain was as inauspicious as his departure had been. Onboard the *Queen Mary,* Pell developed a cold that turned into the flu. He had shipped his heavy coat to London months before, along with other items, when he thought he would be traveling in the summer rather than the late fall. Pell concluded that the daily forty-minute lifeboat drills he endured in only a light coat brought on his illness, and not surprisingly he blamed it all on the State Department. After a half-week stay in a Glasgow hospital, Pell traveled to London by rail, where his assistant, Lawrence Preuss, waited to meet him. Still weak from his illness, missing his wife, unhappy with his accommodations, and irritated generally by the London damp and cold, Pell declared, "I was miserable."[1] Undoubtedly, he was also still trying to recover from the rough treatment he had received from various State Department officials over the past five months. Such treatment, however, was not about to subside.

Despite his general state of melancholy, Pell arrived in London with a plan. In preparation for his work on the Commission, he claimed to have read only one book: a biography of Antoine Fouquier-Tinville.[2] As chief prosecutor for the Committee of Public Safety during the French Revolution, Fouquier-Tinville secured convictions and executions of numerous individuals, including Marie Antoinette. When he was later put on trial for his actions while public prosecutor, Fouquier-Tinville used the defense of superior orders, setting an early precedent, ironically, for several Nazi war criminals: "It is not I who ought to be arraigned here, but the chiefs whose orders I have executed. I had only acted in the spirit of the laws . . . passed by a Convention invested with full power."[3] Fouquier-Tinville repeatedly asked, "What would you have done in my place?"[4] Fouquier-Tinville's defense did not work, nor would it work for the Nazis later at Nuremberg.[5] He was put to death by guillotine on May 7, 1795.

Fouquier-Tinville's defense tactic, however, left no lasting impression on Pell. He was more taken with the work of the French public prosecutor and his effort to ensure that the old leadership could not ever return to power. The example, Pell believed, must be repeated in Germany to prevent them from ever setting off another global catastrophe. He was not so nearly impressed with the Thermidorians who brought Fouquier-Tinville to justice for executing so many with so little evidence.[6]

The book, actually, was not the only text Pell read in preparation for his work on the Commission. On July 22, about a month after his appointment, the president forwarded to Pell Professor Glueck's "Trial and Punishment of Axis War Criminals" and an "Editor's Note" to a forthcoming book on war crimes policy.[7] Although Pell never said so, the article and "Editor's Note" apparently had considerable impact on his thinking about war crimes policy even before he left for London. In his final meeting at the State Department in November, Pell had occasion to discuss war crimes policy with Breckinridge Long. Afterward, Pell wrote Long that he was "most heartened" by and "grateful" for his apparent support; Pell was "counting on" it, in fact. That Long was supportive must have come as a surprise to Pell, who knew about Long's nativist leanings. To get in writing just what Long was supporting, Pell wrote him, explicitly stating his goal: "I believe that we should set up, as soon as possible, an adequate tribunal able to try offences against humanity that have occurred in Germany."[8]

Where did Pell get the idea for such a program? Certainly not from officials in the State Department; up to that moment, Pell had received no explicit instructions regarding policy from anyone at State.[9] By his meeting with Long, however, in addition to what he discussed with the president at their two meetings over the summer, Pell had read and obviously digested much of Glueck's "Trial and Punishment of the Axis War Criminals" and the "Editor's Note." Throughout his entire ordeal as American representative on the UNWCC, Pell relied on Glueck's legal views regarding war crimes policy, as FDR obviously desired.

Glueck's own internationalist sentiments reflected in the article must have appealed to both FDR and Pell. The suggestion of creating a lasting "International Criminal Court," for example, "as a vital symbol of the more civilized and orderly international relations we hope to see enthroned after the present war" fit precisely into Pell's worldview—even more so for the president.[10] That such a court was unprecedented in human history was irrelevant. "*All* courts were at one time unprecedented," Glueck asserted [emphasis in the original]. His conclusion that a "more intimate cooperation among nations and the effective enforcement of international justice" was the only defense "against the suicide of the human race" became a guiding principle for Pell.[11] Pell was determined to do his part to prevent anything like the First and Second World Wars from ever happening again.

Glueck advocated an international tribunal that would be able to deal with atrocities previously outside the jurisdiction of any national civilian or military courts. Existing laws, Glueck asserted, "will leave untouched the numerous crimes committed by Axis nationals on their own territory, such as the torturing and killing of American prisoners by the Japanese in Japan, or the merciless cruelties committed by the Nazis in concentration camps inside Germany." Glueck believed that only an international tribunal could prosecute Nazi crimes against the Jews. As he put it, the Allies must stand up for those who could not do so for themselves, "the wretched, friendless victims of Nazi-Fascist sadism."[12]

Herbert Pell believed that FDR wanted him to make a stance in defense of European Jewry. Why else would the president have asked him to read Glueck's article? Pell saw his mission on the Commission as furthering the progress of humanity. He hoped to accomplish what Glueck penned in his last sentence of "Trial and Punishment of the Axis War Criminals": to give "hope to the oppressed and to those who believe that even the horrors of the present war are not too high a price to pay for the structure of the brighter world of the future."[13] Armed with the backing of the president, once in London, Pell acted on this assignment and in so doing took on the task of calling for the creation of all new, unprecedented, international law.[14]

On December 28 Cordell Hull finally sent Pell a response to his November 11 letter in which Pell intimated he would be very proactive as American representative on the Commission. Hull reminded Pell that the UNWCC was conceived as an evidence-gathering body for the Allied powers and was not contemplated as an organization to try war criminals during or after the war. He formally notified Pell that he was to keep the department "advised" on the activities of the Commission, and more, he was to "ask for instructions respecting any questions on which you may need guidance."[15] No mention was made of the British proposal of a technical committee of experts to consider legal procedures and the creation of tribunals, nor, of course, the State Department's earlier determination that such a committee "may be desirable."[16]

If the objective was to rein in Pell, the letter was not nearly explicit enough. After months of inaction and indirection on the part of the State Department, Pell was in no mood to take orders or ask for permission from anyone in the department. He considered himself at the discretion of the president, as had always been his inclination. Moreover, he had a plan, which as far as he was concerned the president endorsed, at least in its general intention. Hull's letter did not prohibit the UNWCC, and therefore Pell, from expanding the scope of crimes for which the Allied powers might hold war criminals accountable. Hull simply replied, "The Commission will adopt its rules of procedure."[17] The UNWCC minutes record that throughout his tenure Pell remained quite active in developing the "rules of procedure," as Hull put it.[18] For at least these reasons, Pell felt free to pursue his agenda, and he did so tirelessly throughout 1944 and the first few months of 1945, even after he had been removed from the Commission. For someone who often expressed a natural proclivity for idleness, Pell remained singularly focused on accomplishing his goal of broadening the scope of what constitutes a war crime and, thus, seeking justice for the Holocaust.

Within the larger objective of promoting American moral leadership and preventing future wars, Pell held the conviction that the UNWCC's mission must be expanded to include the collection and assessment of evidence of atrocities committed by the Nazis against German nationals, specifically Jews. Moreover, Pell argued that the Commission should examine all such acts against Jews in Germany whenever they occurred. Atrocities committed prior to the beginning of hostilities, Pell argued, were perpetrated for the purpose of eradicating an element of society that had undermined Nazi preparations for war. Therefore, Pell also wanted the reach of the Commission extended to include crimes committed from the moment Hitler became chancellor on January 30, 1933. Consequently, although he had not used the word or even likely conceived of its legal significance, Pell was perhaps the first to conceptualize as a conspiracy the Nazi effort to annihilate European Jewry. Such an interpretation ultimately became singularly important in the creation of a legal protocol to prosecute Nazis for crimes of racial, religious, and political persecution while simultaneously safeguarding American racial segregation.[19]

Pell understood that he lacked the legal background that might be necessary to pursue this goal. At the same time, conversely, he also believed this a strength.[20] Writing his son in early 1944 about his activities on the Commission, he said that lawyers tended "to follow every little point to the end; which, if allowed full freedom, would lead to nothing." "My job," he wrote, "is somewhat that of a huntsman who, although he cannot smell a fox in the grass, can at least prevent the hounds from running off in every direction, pursuing rabbits."[21] Besides, as far as Pell was concerned, at least initially, the State Department had provided him with a capable assistant who was sufficiently familiar with international law to deal with the legal details.

In mid-December 1943 Pell considered himself lucky to have Lawrence Preuss on hand. In writing, he thanked G. Howland Shaw, the department official he assumed had suggested Preuss as his assistant on the Commission. While he may have merely been putting forth an olive branch to officials in the State Department, Pell expressed what appeared to be a real appreciation that Preuss was there to assist him. Pell told Shaw, "You could not have judged better or sent someone who could make me feel happier or safer. . . . He is loyal and most intelligent and co-operative."[22] For his part, Preuss expressed a similar appreciation of Pell: "My relations with Mr. Pell both personal and in connection with our work are of the most cordial nature," he reported to Durward Sandifer in the State Department.[23] Pell's letter to Shaw was written December 16, 1943; Preuss's letter to Sandifer on January 22, 1944.[24]

By February 3—a mere two short weeks after Sandifer's letter—everything had changed. Pell discovered Preuss to be disloyal and decidedly uncooperative, and Preuss found his relations with Pell had become increasingly hostile. At some point in late January, but definitely between January 22 and February 3, Pell revealed his ideas to Preuss about extending the scope of war crimes to include atrocities against German Jews. The announcement by the White House on January 22 of the creation of the War Refugee Board (WRB) quite possibly convinced Pell to do so.[25] The executive order stated that henceforth the policy of the United States was directed "to take all measures within its power to rescue the victims of enemy oppression who are in imminent danger of death and otherwise to afford such victims all possible relief and assistance consistent with the successful prosecution of the war."[26] Under such a policy, Pell could have expected nothing less than full support for his plan of gathering evidence of Nazi atrocities against its own nationals. His expectations, however, were far from met.

Lawrence Preuss objected vehemently to every aspect of Pell's plan. In the first place, Preuss informed Pell that his ideas went well beyond the "context of positive international law." No statutory or codified law existed then, or at any time previous, that would allow for the scope of war crimes to be construed in such a way as to include crimes committed by a government against its own citizens on its own territory. According to Preuss, Pell's response to this first objection was that it was "based solely on legalist grounds." The Commission, Pell informed Preuss, "must create new law." Pell had come to believe that the UNWCC was "free to establish precedent where no precedent exists"; at least this was how Preuss put it in his "confidential" report back to the State Department on February 3.[27] Pell was obviously relying on Glueck's "Trial and Punishment of Axis War Criminals," repeating almost verbatim what Glueck had written. "*All* courts were at one time unprecedented," Glueck had asserted, and Pell obviously concurred.[28]

Beyond his legal objections to Pell's plan, Preuss protested that gathering evidence of such acts would "immeasurably" increase the work that would be required of the Commission. Apparently, Preuss at least had some idea of the vast scale of the atrocities committed by the Nazis, but to assert that a crime so huge obviated any attempt to gather evidence for future prosecution must have left Pell flabbergasted. From Pell's perspective, it was precisely the enormity of the crime that demanded the attention of the Commission; indeed, it demanded the attention of the entire civilized world. Pell's reaction to the Holocaust was, first and foremost, a deep-seated emotional response against the incredible cruelty of the Nazis.[29]

Preuss also reminded Pell that the State Department had given Pell no authority to expand the Commission's reach. Pell asserted, however, that in the absence of precise instructions defining war crimes, he was free to interpret broadly what the term encompassed.[30] In any case, Pell was determined to get his orders from the president, not the State Department. Preuss's defiance served only to further Pell's commitment to act on presidential orders rather than State Department instructions. So, on January 27, Pell wrote the president, updating him on the progress of the Commission and communicating his and the Commission's desire to expand their mandate. "There remains," wrote Pell to FDR, "a very large class of people who have committed crimes against the citizens of more than one country, or who have directed inhuman policies in Germany itself. The consensus is that these will have to be tried by an international tribunal which must be able to act pretty freely on the question of evidence."[31]

Although Pell was determined to work directly with the president, thereby circumventing a State Department that by then he had irrevocably concluded was aligned against him—including most recently his own assistant—Pell did believe he had one ally within the department, perhaps the most unlikely candidate of all: Breckinridge Long. Pell was not averse to asking for Long's help. Relying on the support that Long expressed when the two met back in November, Pell explained his plans in more detail than he had in his letter to the president. Hoping that Long might exert some influence, Pell reminded him, "The last thing you said to me [in our November meeting], in reply to my statement that I wanted to be tough, was to go ahead. I asked you then if I could count on your support. You said that you would back me, and I hope that you will do so now."[32] But Long was not about to become involved, even if he had any inclination to do so, which was hardly likely. He told Pell rather curtly in a February 10 reply that he was not "handling the matter."[33] More than ever, Pell understood he had no friends in the State Department.

Pell had no idea that it was Green Hackworth who had composed Long's reply.[34] When Long forwarded Pell's letter to Hackworth, Long told Hackworth it indicated that "a real lack of purpose existed" on the Commission, and he suggested the department give Pell more direction.[35] Unbeknownst to Pell, all correspondence regarding war crimes policy was being referred to the legal adviser.[36] Someone, it turned out, was nominally in charge of overseeing war crimes policy in the State Department. Of course, that had not ever been made clear to Pell.

Having already read Preuss's confidential letters to Sandifer, detailing, among other things, Pell's ideas regarding crimes committed by Nazis against German citizens before and during the war, and most recently Pell's letter to Long, Hackworth composed a memorandum to Long so that he might better reply to Pell. As the State Department's point man on war crimes policy, Hackworth was concerned that he might come under some criticism or, worse, be blamed in the event the UNWCC mission failed. The memorandum amounted to a point-by-point defense of his role in setting department policy and a scolding castigation of Herbert Pell and even Lawrence Preuss as well.

By the time of Pell's confrontation with Preuss, the Commission had decided to forgo a separately constituted technical committee. The work originally envisioned for the technical committee now fell to the Commission itself. As a result, Pell would have the opportunity to suggest policy.[37] Of this new development, Hackworth noted, "While some, and maybe most, of the other Governments are represented on the Commission by lawyers and jurists, Mr. Pell is not a lawyer, nor is Mr. Preuss, his associate. Whether they would be qualified to pass upon rules of procedure in the handling of war crimes before tribunals," Hackworth asserted modestly, "may be open to question." Of course, he left it unwritten, but Hackworth was pointing out that he was a lawyer, and that he alone was qualified to direct American policy on war crimes, rather than Pell or Preuss. With regard to Nazi atrocities against German nationals, Hackworth wrote, "What Germany does to her own nationals is separate and apart from the purposes of the United Nations, which are to punish Axis nationals who commit offenses against nationals of the United Nations."[38]

Pell had become concerned that the UNWCC lacked the necessary power to carry out its mission, as he saw it, or as he hoped to expand it. Conversely, Hackworth was upset that Pell now possessed too much opportunity to carry out his ideas. From Hackworth's perspective, the State Department never wanted Pell to have any input on policy. Furthermore, Pell's assistant, Preuss, was intended to be the instrument through which the State Department—and Hackworth specifically—directed American policy on war crimes. Hackworth closed his memorandum to Long, noting, "In view of the nature of Mr. Pell's duties, as I understand them, I do not know what he means by the statement regarding his being 'tough' and his request for backing." As far as Hackworth was concerned, Pell was to do nothing, "tough" or otherwise, without specific instructions.[39]

In the end, Hackworth thought better of sending the memorandum; instead, he only passed along a suggested reply for Long to send to Pell, which Long did use. At the same time, the president forwarded to the State Department the January 27 letter he received from Pell for preparation of a reply. Hackworth prepared a draft for the president's signature along with a set of proposed updated instructions for Pell. The draft reply, for obvious reasons, contained none of the contempt Hackworth enunciated in his unsent memorandum to Long. Action on cases concerning "inhuman policies in Germany" was to be "taken as rapidly as possible," but the president (per Hackworth) did not specify how, referring Pell to instructions that would be forthcoming from the State Department.[40] As imprecise as this deceptively personal letter from the president addressed to "My dear Bertie" rather than the more formal "Mr. Pell" was, the State Department instruction was just as vague and included nothing regarding crimes committed against German nationals.[41]

Using the Moscow Declaration as a guide, the State Department instructions to Pell suggested that those accused of committing crimes against United Nations' nationals be tried before the courts of the country in which the crimes were committed. Crimes against nationals of more than one country were to be referred to "mixed military tribunals." Since it was not specifically stated, it was not clear what to do about crimes committed against nationals who were not citizens of the United Nations—that is, Axis nationals and those of satellite nations. Were crimes committed against them considered to fall within the jurisdiction of the UNWCC or perhaps some other future legal entity? Pell could not be sure.[42]

Perplexed and probably angry at these incomplete instructions from State, Pell wrote again to the president, this time as explicitly as he could possibly be. "What are we to do about the Jews in Germany? . . . The offences against them certainly seem to be described in your phrase 'crimes against humanity.'" Pell was referring to and reminding FDR what he said in his July 28, 1943, Fireside Chat: war criminals will be "punished for their crimes against humanity."[43] Without directly informing the president about the difficulties he was having with State Department officials, Pell nonetheless indicated as much in his closing remarks: "I sincerely trust that you will be able to have instructions sent to me, or send them yourself, that will permit me to procure justice for these unfortunate people. I have tried to trouble you as little as possible."[44] Again, the president preferred to have the State Department compose his reply.[45]

"My dear Bertie," began the March 1 letter over the signature of the president, "There can be little reason for disagreement on the general proposition that Germany and her satellites should be required to answer for atrocities against the Jews."[46] Presumably, that meant to include atrocities against all Jews, including German Jews. Receiving the letter around March 10, Herbert Pell certainly took it to mean as much.[47] He made sure that the entire letter was duplicated in the text of his 1953 oral history: "That letter gave the green light to the consideration of the punishment to be meted out to those responsible for the cruelty in the German concentration camps, a subject in which I had been very much interested."[48]

Pell's belief that the president wanted to go ahead was no after-the-fact rationalization for his actions on behalf of European Jewry. In the first week of April 1944 Pell used those very words in trying to get Ambassador Winant's support. "A little while ago," he wrote Winant, "I received a personal letter from the president, which I interpreted to [be] the 'green light' on this question [of the treatment of the Jews]."[49] Pell's actions on the Commission unequivocally demonstrate that he believed that the president wanted him to pursue expansion of the scope of war crimes to include those atrocities committed by Germany against German nationals. He would not have taken action without what he believed to be the president's backing.

On March 16 Herbert Pell stood up before the Legal Committee of the Commission and made the following motion: "It is clearly understood that the words 'crimes against humanity' refer, among others, to crimes committed against stateless persons or against any persons because of their race or religion. Such crimes are judiciable by the United Nations or their agencies as war crimes."[50] According to the State Department's summary, "Mr. Pell argued in support of his motion, that the majority of the people of the world had had their indignation aroused by the atrocities committed in Axis countries against the Jews, and that the whole movement to punish war criminals would fall to the ground if the greatest criminals of all were allowed to escape. It is, he said, essential 'to extirpate the roots of Nazi evil.'"[51] To reinforce his point, Pell read aloud a communication he had just received: "There can be little reason for disagreement on the general proposition that Germany and her satellites should be required to answer for atrocities against the Jews."[52]

In the Commission's general discussion following Pell's proposal, British representative Sir William Malkin objected that such action could not be taken without specific instructions from the respective governments, and several other representatives agreed. Pell could not simply imply that he was acting in accord with the highest authority of the United States, especially when his assistant was publicly indicating otherwise. Lawrence Preuss spoke out in the meeting in support of Malkin and in opposition to Pell's initiative, pointing out that the UNWCC could not create new international law without precedent. Moreover, Preuss asserted such an expansion of the Commission's scope might overwhelm the capacity of the UNWCC. Privately, Preuss had informed British representatives on the Commission—and probably others—that the State Department had instructed him to oppose Pell's proposal.[53]

Pell wasted no time in informing the president of his actions, writing him that same day. Although stymied, Pell was nonetheless confident he could get a majority of the Commission's members to support his effort to acknowledge "crimes against humanity" as war crimes, something he believed the president put him on the UNWCC to accomplish. But he did not know of Preuss's behind-the-scenes activities. In his letter Pell took care to make it unmistakable that he considered himself acting directly on presidential orders, repeating verbatim in his letter what the president had written to him on March 1. He added, "Naturally I did not use your name as my authority. I merely said that I had adequate authority."[54]

In this latest letter to the president Pell suggested that FDR might want to make a public announcement on the matter, or at the very least direct the State Department to do so, although he was beginning to suspect that no department official would want to do such a thing unless forced by the president. "There are numberless people in the world, and millions in the United States, who, if you did this, would find their hope renewed and would rise and bless you," Pell informed the president encouragingly. "To extend the definition of 'war crimes' to protect these helpless unfortunates is not only a humane act but a statesmanlike one. To say we are only interested in our own nationals is mere chaffering. If any one is to be sure of justice, justice can be denied to no one." Pell told FDR "there can be no doubt" of the majority of the Commission's support if the president would just make a statement.[55]

Pell must have been thrilled when he read the president's March 24 statement on atrocities; he may even have listened to it over BBC Radio. Initially, he probably assumed it was done at his behest. Although he had no allies in the State Department, at least Pell was not alone in his belief that the promise of postwar punishment might save lives. Returning to a familiar theme, FDR announced in his statement, "The United Nations are fighting to make a world in which tyranny and aggression can not exist; a world based upon freedom, equality and justice; a world in which all persons regardless of race, color or creed may live in peace, honor and dignity."[56]

Events taking place in Pell's last diplomatic appointment prior to the UNWCC provided the motivation for the president's announcement. Hungary had become the latest battleground of the war. The Nazis invaded on March 19, largely to get at Hungary's seven-hundred-thousand-plus Jews, quite possibly the largest population then left in all of Europe. Suggested by Treasury Secretary Henry Morgenthau and written by WRB officials, the president's statement not only decried what was—and had been—taking place, but it also promised swift retribution for the perpetrators.

In a very public presidential statement, Herbert Pell's efforts on the Commission had just become authorized and endorsed: Pell could have interpreted it no other way. It was the furthest the president had yet ventured in any statement on the Holocaust, and it seemed to be correcting a conspicuous omission in the Moscow Conference's "Declaration on Atrocities" enunciated the previous fall.[57] That declaration made no mention whatsoever of Nazi atrocities against Europe's Jews, but here the president was specific and direct:

> In one of the blackest crimes of all history—begun by the Nazis in the day of peace and multiplied by them a hundred times in time of war—the wholesale systematic murder of the Jews of Europe goes on unabated every hour. As a result of the events of the last few days hundreds of thousands of Jews, who while living under persecution have at least found a haven from death in Hungary and the Balkans, are now threatened with annihilation as Hitler's forces descend more heavily upon these lands. That these innocent people, who have already survived a decade of Hitler's fury, should perish on the very eve of triumph over the barbarism which their persecution symbolized would be a major tragedy.[58]

As far as Pell was concerned, the president had announced unambiguously that the Allies would prosecute those committing such crimes, apparently including crimes committed prior to the outbreak of war. "It is therefore fitting that we should again proclaim our determination that none who participate in these acts of savagery shall go unpunished," the president declared. "All who share the guilt shall share the punishment."[59] Herbert Pell, American representative on the UNWCC, believed he was the man appointed to the task. At that point, at least, Pell knew of no other effort under way to deal with war crimes policy and punishment.[60] Moreover, FDR asked "every German and every man everywhere under Nazi domination" to help Hitler's victims evade such a tragic fate, and, critical to Pell's work on the Commission, "to record the evidence that will one day be used to convict the guilty."[61]

In the State Department, the president's statement was met with considerably less satisfaction. Acknowledging that FDR's announcement that "none who participate in these acts of savagery shall go unpunished" supported Pell's proposal on the UNWCC, State still looked for wiggle room, some way to avoid seeking justice for the Holocaust. A later department committee report explained it this way: "It is at least arguable that [FDR's] statement sets up as a prerequisite to punishment some criminal act which is either initiated or consummated in United Nations territory." Their evidence for this was FDR's statement that "All who knowingly take part in the deportation of Jews to their death in Poland or Norwegians and French to their death in Germany are equally guilty with the executioner."[62] As incredible as it may seem, the State Department was grasping at whatever it could find to subvert the president's promise of justice for the Holocaust.

It must have been a proud moment for Herbert Pell. His friend, the president of the United States, had just acted as he suggested—or at least he appeared to be doing so—making a global announcement on atrocities, the Jews, and the assuredness of punishment. What was more, not only was the president declaring Nazi atrocities against all Jews everywhere punishable—State Department efforts to find a way out notwithstanding—he implied that the prosecutable atrocities were not limited to the war years. These crimes, FDR announced, had "begun . . . in the day of peace." European Jews, he pointed out, had already "survived a decade of Hitler's fury."[63] The president had previously written Pell on March 1 (again, per Hackworth) that Nazi atrocities committed prior to the beginning of hostilities might not fall within the scope of war crimes, but from Pell's perspective, FDR now seemed to be including them.[64]

In his address, the president used again the phrase "crimes against humanity," the very words Pell was pushing on the UNWCC to include atrocities against German Jews as war crimes, whenever they occurred. Concluding his statement, FDR said, "In the name of justice and humanity let all freedom-loving people rally to this righteous undertaking."[65] Unfortunately for the president and Pell, when it came to the subject of Axis war crimes, rhetoric was one thing; getting FDR's own State Department—to say nothing of other Allied nations—to act on this farsighted and impassioned call for justice was something else altogether.

Pell was acting at the behest of the president, and this latest address served to reinforce the importance of what FDR had asked him to accomplish. Perhaps the State Department—as unbelievable as it might have seemed to Pell—did not fully understand the president's desires. Pell wrote Hull on March 24, 1944, explaining his actions. Certainly, Pell hoped, if the secretary of state only knew what the president wanted of him, the department would stop issuing contravening instructions. Pell again quoted the "green light" letter from the president, informing Hull of his actions on March 16. They were, he said, "in accordance" with the instructions of the president. Suspecting an entrenched antisemitism as the source for department opposition, Pell noted that Jews were not the only group persecuted by the Nazis, although they had been "the most serious sufferers." There was no getting around the fact, he wrote, that Nazi atrocities were directed initially against German nationals, arousing "the conscience of mankind." These crimes could not simply be ignored. He reminded Hull that he was not acting on just the desires of the president; "There is a universal demand that crimes against these unfortunates should be punished."[66]

On March 27 Pell again stood up before the Commission and reiterated his belief that the scope of war crimes must be expanded and, further, that no additional instructions from their respective governments were necessary. Although other members spoke in favor of Pell's proposal, the representatives agreed that it was necessary to request further instructions from their respective governments, and Malkin was directed to draft the resolution.[67]

Rebuffed by the Commission, Pell then suffered another blow. On March 28 he received a March 13 letter signed by Hull but undoubtedly authored by Hackworth. The department informed Pell that present international law did not allow for the inclusion of atrocities against German nationals within the scope of the Commission, be they Jews or any other persons. Pell had heard this argument before and had already dismissed it. Again, the department turned to the Moscow Declaration, quoting it directly. Hull reminded Pell that it specifically referred to "atrocities, massacres and cold-blooded mass executions which are being perpetrated by Hitlerite forces in the many countries they have overrun," not those within Nazi Germany itself or its satellites. To Pell's way of thinking, such reasoning was not just irrational, it was immoral. How could the Allied powers hold Nazis accountable for crimes against one set of victims but not another simply because of nationality or locality of the crime? But as Hull's letter had it, any action taken by the Nazis "against their own nationals pursuant to their own laws" was legal behavior, and that is apparently all that mattered.[68] For the moment, Pell chose to ignore this legalistic interpretation and did not immediately reply to Hull, believing he had already stated his case in his March 24 letter to the secretary, which he expected Hull would soon receive. Moreover, this letter was dated prior to FDR's most recent statement.

Pell was still convinced that FDR's March 1 letter was all he needed to dismiss any legalistic objection to considering crimes committed against German nationals to fall within the scope of the UNWCC. But he concluded that he would wait for the Commission to officially request further instructions before writing again to the president. What else was Pell to do? As far as he knew, the president was directing him to do one thing and the State Department another. On top of that, his own assistant had spoken out against him at a Commission meeting. As bad as things appeared to Pell at that moment, the situation was far worse than he could have imagined.

What poor Herbert Pell did not know then—probably ever—was that the State Department had been composing the president's "personal" letters to him.[69] The informal "My dear Bertie" that began each letter was enough to lead Pell to believe that he was communicating directly and confidentially with the president. Worse than that, he was receiving first vague and then later contradictory instructions from the State Department. Pell had no idea of the extent to which he was being undermined; nor, it seems, did the president. The State Department was telling Pell one thing over FDR's signature and something entirely different under its own masthead. Pell could never have anticipated such a situation.

The duplicity had begun in earnest back in January and continued through the end of Pell's appointment. At the behest of the president, the State Department composed the reply to Pell's January 27 letter. At the same time, State had also provided a list of instructions they proposed to send Pell. Both were given to the president to peruse, one for his signature, the other for him to approve. He did both—sign and approve—but whether he read them carefully or at all is unknown. Only the most careful of readings and comparisons would catch the differences. Most likely, FDR only read Hull's cover memorandum that went along with the two documents, explaining their contents.[70]

In the letter that was drafted by State, signed by the president, and then sent to London, Bertie Pell was instructed that the Commission was to take action concerning "inhuman policies in Germany . . . as rapidly as possible." The "president's" letter informed Pell that the State Department would send him further "instructions containing suggestions concerning the work of the Commission."[71] The "instructions" he received the following week, however, contained nothing about crimes against German nationals. Nothing in it explicitly prohibited Pell from suggesting the Commission take up these crimes. Conversely, they did not specifically direct him to do so either. The entire tone of the letter was imprecise, containing mere "suggestions" and "recommendations." In fact, the department directives were as noncommittal as they could be.

Prefacing a three-point list contained in the "instructions" sent to Pell was this statement: "The Department's present tentative view as to the procedure to be considered is as follows. . . ."[72] What was Pell to do? As far as he knew at that moment, the president was telling him to move forward on all crimes of racial persecution, including those against German Jews, and the department was offering him ill-defined, "tentative" views for his consideration that said nothing either way.

Pell then received what he considered the critical instruction from the president on the matter, the "green light" letter of March 1. But here again, Pell did not know that this letter was composed by the State Department, rather than the president. "There can be little reason for disagreement on the general proposition that Germany and her satellites should be required to answer for atrocities against the Jews," stated the letter.[73] Pell, quite obviously, took this to mean atrocities against all Jews, everywhere. How could he not? But did the president take it as such at that moment? That question might be difficult to answer, especially considering that FDR did not compose the letter, nor did he give the State Department any written instructions about what the letter—or any other letter to Pell, for that matter—should contain. But we do have FDR's public statement of March 24 that certainly indicates where he stood.

Given what Pell had communicated previously to the president and the State Department, officials there must have known how Pell would view such an instruction from the president. To send Pell directives to the contrary shortly thereafter is almost incomprehensible; consider the March 13 instruction that read, "The Department is of the opinion that to assume to punish officials of enemy governments for actions taken against their own nationals pursuant to their own laws would constitute an assumption of jurisdiction probably unwarranted under international law."[74] It was not as though the department had just come to that conclusion. They had considered atrocities committed against German nationals beyond the purview of the Allied powers from the beginning. Of course, in earlier correspondence, they did not make that at all clear to Pell, whether by design or circumstantially.

By the end of that March, Herbert Pell believed he was receiving contradictory instructions, one set from the State Department and another from the president. As difficult as that must have been for him, at least he had the support of the president—and presidential desires, as far as Pell was concerned, were far more important than any set of strict legalistic interpretations coming out of the State Department. Interdepartmental squabbles were one thing, but here the State Department was acting intentionally at cross-purposes to the president.

Pell may have concluded that the president was deliberately keeping the State Department in the dark about his plans. The March 1 letter, after all, was marked as for his "confidential guidance" only. At the very least, department officials were determined to embarrass Pell—and apparently the president. More likely, they were hoping to force Pell's removal; it was not as if Hull had no previous experience at doing such a thing. And, obviously, justice for the Holocaust was not on State's agenda.

Was Green Hackworth responsible for the department's tactics? Pell certainly thought so then and continued to believe it in the years following his tenure on the Commission, although he never knew that the president was not composing the "My dear Bertie" letters. Pell had discovered early on that Preuss was working to damage his position on the Commission. In addition to the reports he was sending behind Pell's back to Washington, Preuss had indicated to UNWCC members that it was he, not Pell, who was acting on behalf of the State Department and, therefore, the United States. Preuss even openly disagreed with Pell during Commission discussions, specifically contradicting Pell's ideas about including atrocities committed against German nationals. Pell wrote Hull that Preuss made no secret of the fact he was doing so "on the verbal instructions of some member of the State Department."[75] No doubt Pell was convinced that member was Green Hackworth, although he did not say so specifically to Hull at the time.

According to Pell, Preuss had told him—and many other Commission members and their staffs as well—that the State Department selected him "to remedy the President's error in appointing" Pell. Moreover, it was not just a Hackworth-organized effort to unseat Pell. If Preuss is to be believed, a larger conspiracy was at work. He told Pell a "group" existed within the department that had "intended to sabotage" his work in London from the beginning. That was the reason, he said, for Pell's delayed departure in the first place. Exposing all this to Hull, Pell was able to convince the department to recall Preuss. It did not hurt, of course, that Pell caught Preuss copying secret documents after Pell had expressly forbidden him to do so.[76]

In his oral history, Pell submitted that Preuss's activities were part of a "conspiracy . . . engineered largely by Hackworth, who was anxious to have someone else get my place."[77] Pell did not know then, or apparently ever, that Hackworth was also behind the contradictory instructions he was receiving. Pell always believed the president was directing him to do one thing and the State Department another. It is unclear, however, how many allies Hackworth had in the State Department. Both Hull and Stettinius were involved in the drafts of the Pell letters going from the State Department to the White House and then finally on to Pell in London. At least their signatures are on them. It is difficult to believe that these men, and others in the department as well, did not discuss war crimes policy at some length with Hackworth on numerous occasions. Presumably, at least Secretary Hull must have discussed war crimes policy with the president beyond what correspondence remains for the historian to examine today, but the record is not clear. Based solely on the correspondence between the two, it appears that Hull was not entirely forthright with the president regarding instructions sent to Pell in London. To the extent that was the case, and it is difficult to conclude otherwise, Secretary of State Cordell Hull belonged to the "group" that intended to "sabotage" Pell's effort to seek justice for the Holocaust.

Perhaps Hull was simply operating at a certain level of disengagement regarding war crimes policy, leaving it up to Hackworth. Worse yet, perhaps the president was operating similarly in leaving so much up to the State Department. It must be remembered that American war crimes policy was far from the only item on FDR's agenda, and, further, its place was probably well down the list in 1943 and early 1944. War crimes policy was an item then in the planning stages, not execution—beyond early efforts at evidence gathering—and therefore did not have as high a priority as so many other activities of the administration. Only as the war moved closer to its inexorable end did war crimes policy ascend in priority, particularly after the successful D-Day landings and the establishment of another front in June 1944.

More important, when it came to specific war crimes policy-planning goals, Pell's initial efforts on the UNWCC in the first few months of 1944 coincided with a precipitous decline in the president's health. For Pell, this was the most critical period in terms of getting his plans for the UNWCC accomplished. He believed the sooner the Commission acted in clarifying war crimes policy, the more lives they might be able to save.

FDR's failing health had a detrimental effect on his handling of all affairs of state, and unfortunately for Pell, this included war crimes policy planning. Pell probably did not know just how ill the president had become. If he had, it only would have made him more determined to carry out what he believed FDR had sent him to London to accomplish, and to do so as quickly as possible. As it was, Pell believed he possessed a supportive and vigorous collaborator in the White House.

Throughout the winter of 1943–44, FDR endured a lingering bout of influenza. It was not unusual for the president to get the flu, but this infection seemed the worst ever for him and the longest lasting. Eleanor wrote later, "I think all of us knew that Franklin was far from well, but none of us ever said anything about it—I suppose because we felt that if he believed it was his duty to continue in office, there was nothing for us to do but make it as easy as possible for him."[78] But she had never been particularly concerned with FDR's health, and there were others who saw the president almost daily who did not notice his decline. That list included, almost fatally for the president, his personal physician during his White House years, Vice Admiral Ross T. McIntire. McIntire was not only the president's doctor; he was also surgeon general of the navy and chief of the Bureau of Medicine and Surgery of the navy. A charitable account would note that McIntire was overworked, contributing to his failure to examine properly and diagnose the president. In the twenty-first century, McIntire would be an easy target for a malpractice suit.[79]

In February and March 1944, when Pell most needed the president's support, FDR's failing health began to affect dramatically his ability to work and concentrate. Grace Tully observed, among other signs, the president nodding off while reading correspondence. He even appeared to black out in the middle of dictating documents.[80] Finally, but not before his temperature reached 104 degrees, at the insistence of his daughter and with the acquiescence of McIntire, the president went to Bethesda for a thorough physical with cardiologist Howard G. Bruenn on March 28. It may have been, incredibly, the first full medical examination of his presidency. From this point on and through the last year of the president's life, Bruenn served as FDR's de facto personal physician.

FDR was suffering from heart disease and, according to historian Robert Ferrell, had become as "incapacitated" as President Woodrow Wilson had been following his stroke in 1919.[81] Following his March appointment with Dr. Bruenn, FDR's workday was reduced to less than four hours, and many days he did not work at all. The previous months were really no better, but just about everyone took McIntire's word that FDR was only suffering from a particularly formidable bout of the flu.

Around the same time that the president was finally getting proper care for his condition, Eleanor interrupted FDR and his longtime friend and former law partner Harry Hooker, discussing compulsory military service during peacetime. She noticed a significant change in FDR's management style and his ability to consider matters in depth. FDR "could no longer bear to have a real discussion," she noted. When she offered her own opinion, as he had so often encouraged her to do in the past, FDR became visibly bothered. Eleanor later wrote that she had "forgotten that Franklin was no longer the calm and imperturbable person who . . . had always goaded" her on.[82] Undoubtedly, the weariness his condition produced in him had changed things with all his advisers and appointees, not just Eleanor.

Considering the president's declining health in March 1944, his most recent public announcement on European atrocities and the assurance of punishment could not have been followed up by presidential attentiveness, to whatever degree FDR might have been inclined to do so. It is worth noting, however, that despite his illness, he did take the time to address European atrocities to the exclusion of other duties that his illness was causing him to neglect. And what he said remained consistent: the United States intended to pursue justice for all crimes, including "crimes against humanity."

Although Dr. Bruenn had discovered the reason for the president's declining health, the then-available medical treatments could not cure the condition; only extensive rest could substantially alleviate the problem. The prescribed reduction in schedule and consequent inattentiveness to detail continued until the end. Later, as war crimes policy moved up in importance, the president would have precious little time to give his attention to it. During the important months of the first half of 1944, the president's deteriorating physical condition not only facilitated the effort of State Department officials to obstruct Pell's activities on the UNWCC, but it also set war crimes policy planning adrift at a time when no one was particularly concerned about it in the Roosevelt administration, except, of course, Pell and the president. Meanwhile, "the wholesale systematic murder of the Jews of Europe," as the president put it, the horror then taking place in the death camps, continued "unabated every hour."[83]

Although Pell was unaware of the president's condition, he was becoming much more cognizant of the duplicitous actions of the State Department as the spring of 1944 wore on, saying so very pointedly to Hull that April. Deception, therefore, could not last much longer. If the intention of the State Department was to place Pell in an almost untenable position in London, they were certainly succeeding, whoever was behind it. If the goal was to remove Pell, at least at that point in the late spring of 1944, it had failed. Pell was going nowhere, and he seemed more determined than ever to pursue his plan of extending international law to include crimes against humanity, as he believed the president wanted.

Was antisemitism the explanation for State Department actions? Pell certainly thought so. He blamed the avarice of self-promoting State Department careerists, specifically Green Hackworth (and to a lesser degree G. Howland Shaw), whom he believed shared a generalized antisemitism with the rest of the country.[84] But Pell was always careful to point out that Nazi atrocities were not committed solely against Jews, indicating his belief that Americans might not fully support prosecution of Nazi atrocities against Jews unless other groups were included.[85]

According to David S. Wyman in The Abandonment of the Jews, a generalized antisemitism did exist in the State Department, but he noted that little direct proof existed to support the claim.[86] When it came to dealing with refugee affairs, anti-immigrant and antialien views prevailed within the department and to a degree with the president as well, who always seemed overly concerned with fifth columnists, but the extent to which these nativist views may have affected war crimes policy is difficult to determine. Whatever the reasons or motivations for the

State Department's actions regarding the UNWCC and Pell, one thing was sure; no matter what they tried to do, Herbert Pell was not about to abandon the Jews.

For Pell, there was something larger than his own personal reputation at stake. The reputation of the United States was at risk—everything he believed it should stand for, and everything for which he believed his nation was then fighting was about to be jeopardized by what was taking place, or more correctly, by what the UNWCC was not doing. It seemed so obvious to Pell that the Commission, even the entire philosophy underpinning the effort to defeat the forces of fascism, was at a crossroads.

Pell told Hull as much in his March 24 letter, and he did so pointedly, reiterating what he said during Commission meetings: "It was these offences committed in Germany that first aroused the conscience of mankind against the Nazi regime and which first suggested its horrors to the world. There is universal demand that crimes against these unfortunates should be punished."[87] Pell believed that racial and religious persecution was, in his words, the "essential evil" of the Nazi regime.[88] To say one thing publicly about crimes against humanity, as the president had done, and to take no action on it with the UNWCC or any other organization was pure hypocrisy. American morality was not supposed to be selective, at least as far as Pell was concerned.

Pell stated what by then had become an obvious conclusion for him to make: "It seems to me an unduly narrow point of view to say that we are interested only in our own nationals, and hypocritical if, at the same time, we say we are fighting for humanity and justice."[89] Pell was a man of books, what we would call today an "armchair historian." He had read enough history to know that hypocrisy was no stranger to the United States, and he wanted no part in adding to and extending that sad legacy. What he did not recognize then, or ever, was that if he could succeed in removing this hypocrisy, he was adding to an even larger one. If he could get the Allies to agree that Nazi Germany be brought to justice for the crime of racial persecution against its own citizens, what might that mean with respect to America's own system of racial persecution against her own citizens?

Pell did not yet know it, but the direction of American war crimes policy was about to be moved to other people with different ideas and other departments with different agendas. Still, even after Pell discovered this, he persisted in his belief that Nazi crimes based upon racial and religious persecution, including those against German nationals, were crimes for which the Allied powers must seek punishment. As for his growing exasperation with the State Department, it, too, would not just persist but grow ever stronger.

CHAPTER 6

FURTHER STATE DEPARTMENT OBSTRUCTION

"The War Crimes Commission Might Be Authorized"

We have promised to protect humanity. Do we dare face the Jewish community, or any other people interested in justice and humanity, with the statement that we will do nothing to protect these innocent victims; that all we have said on the subject is mere propaganda? It will be a test of the sincerity of the governments which we represent.

Herbert C. Pell, April 3, 1944

As the spring of 1944 wore on, Herbert Pell began to consider the advantages of viewing American war crimes policy within the context of domestic politics. It was an election year, FDR had not yet announced whether he would run, and Pell did not like the prospect of the United States or the world facing such momentous issues and problems under anyone else's lead. In the midst of all of his problems with the State Department, Pell wrote the president on March 8 expressing this concern and encouraging him to seek an unprecedented fourth term. He told FDR that he was doing so not as the U.S. representative on the UNWCC or as his old friend but as "an American citizen interested in the future." It was, he wrote, "vitally necessary for the good of the United States and for the future of the world" that FDR retain the presidency.[1] Pell meant it sincerely. However, time and events had also convinced him that it was imperative that FDR retain the presidency so that Pell himself could retain his post and succeed with his objectives.

Pell did know something about domestic politics. As New York State chairman of the Democratic Party in the 1920s and later as vice chairman of the national party during FDR's 1936 reelection campaign, Pell had become well acquainted with the requirements of electoral campaigns and the degree to which race and ethnicity could play a role. Although he believed that FDR would win in the coming fall election if he ran, Pell understood that it was bad politics to alienate any constituency, particularly American Jews. He was sure that FDR knew this himself; perhaps no one understood the American political landscape better than the president. Pell was not concerned that any failure on the part of the UNWCC to deal effectively with atrocities against European Jews might detrimentally harm FDR's reelection chances, but he did hope the implication might coax FDR into pushing the State Department to support his cause.

Pell closed his letter by reminding the president that he was in London at *his* request, doing *his* work. "I am pleased and proud, as will be my descendants," Pell noted, "to say that I took a part in your work."[2] Why Pell never exposed the State Department's contravening orders directly to the president is a mystery. Why he resisted explicitly asking FDR to instruct the State Department to support him is equally puzzling. Quite possibly, Pell simply considered it improper behavior for a gentleman-aristocrat to do such a thing. Had he known that FDR may have been too ill to focus on war crimes with clarity, perhaps Pell would have been more straightforward with him, but he did not know of the president's condition. Few did; it would remain a carefully guarded secret.

FDR did not reply to Pell's March 8 letter. He had probably already concluded he needed to continue in office for the very reason Pell presumed, although he had not announced his intentions. The question at that moment was his health. FDR had yet to see Dr. Bruenn, and in the latter part of March he had become too ill to do much of anything.

For Pell, this same period was just as difficult as it was for the president, but for entirely different reasons. He had failed to get the Commission to move on his March 16 proposal; worse, a majority of the representatives had concluded that they could not even consider it without specific instructions from their governments. April arrived, and Pell had heard nothing from the president in reply to his latest letters. The last word he had received from FDR was the "green light" letter of March 1, and he had received contradictory instructions from the State Department since then. Nevertheless, Pell decided to push forward with the Commission again but now under the changed circumstances. On April 4, at

Pell's insistence, the Commission agreed to seek further instructions on crimes against humanity: "The Commission is of the opinion that the question of the punishment of offences committed in enemy territory against enemy nationals or stateless persons on account of their race, religion, or political opinions, requires immediate consideration."[3]

Pell informed Secretary Hull, Ambassador Winant, and the president of this pending action in separate but similar letters on April 3.[4] To Hull, Pell wrote, "I do not believe, however, that it would be a wise policy to allow the Catholic and Jewish communities, and indeed any people interested in human justice, to believe that the United Nations, with our country at the head, were not interested in these outrages and did not intend to extirpate the soul of Nazism. We must either consider this question or allow them to reach the conclusion that everything we have said on the subject is mere propaganda."[5] To Winant, Pell wrote, "We have promised to protect humanity. Do we dare face the Jewish community, or any other people interested in justice and humanity, with the statement that we will do nothing to protect these innocent victims; that all we have said on the subject is mere propaganda? It will be a test of the sincerity of the governments which we represent."[6] And to the president, he wrote in the strongest tone he had yet risked taking: "I would not dare to face the Jewish community, or any other people interested in human justice, if I left a stone unturned in my efforts to punish the crimes committed against them." Pell closed this message writing that he trusted the "necessary instructions" would be forthcoming.[7] As Arieh Kochavi notes in his *Prelude to Nuremberg,* Pell was conspicuously reminding the president that war crimes policy was not just an issue of international law but also one of domestic politics.[8]

Pell had previously demonstrated a willingness to use the domestic political situation to further his goals. Back in January, on Pell's invitation, representatives of the World Jewish Congress (WJC) called to impress on him the necessity of the UNWCC doing something on behalf of Europe's Jews. Pell's then-assistant, Lawrence Preuss, sat in on the meeting and recounted every detail to the State Department in early February in one of his many clandestine reports.[9]

Pell and Preuss had both met with representatives of the WJC in Washington shortly after Pell's appointment the previous summer, but at this meeting in London, Pell was very assertive in encouraging the WJC to publicize its cause. According to Preuss's report, Pell proposed that the WJC "'build a fire' under their respective governments by means of a vigorous press campaign." Preuss objected to this idea immediately, but Pell overruled him. Pell was convinced, Preuss wrote, that mobilization of "Jewish support would alone ensure success of the entire plan of brin[g]ing war criminals to justice."[10] Based on the efforts of WJC representatives, Pell had succeeded in building the fire, but they really needed no encouragement. The president, however, seemed to be another matter. Inexplicably to Pell, FDR's supportive letters and his public rhetoric had not produced comparable instructions from the State Department.

By the time Pell wrote on April 3 to the president outlining his next move, FDR had finally responded to Pell's March 16 note, but FDR did what he had been doing all spring with Pell's letters; he forwarded it to the State Department for preparation of a reply.[11] It is not clear when Pell received the response, although it was probably around the middle of April.

The reply, again addressed personally to "My dear Bertie," seemed to be calculated to mislead and confuse. The letter informed Pell that the president felt he "should not undertake to pass upon the jurisdiction of the Commission or become involved in its work."[12] If the president of the United States should not "undertake to pass upon the jurisdiction of the Commission," who could? Again, unknown to Pell, Green Hackworth composed the reply, repeating, but in a strengthened version, what he had previously inserted into the March 1 "green light" letter: "I [FDR] do not undertake, however, to pass on the extent of the jurisdiction of your Commission in these matters." Of course, in the March 1 letter, that statement followed one that informed Pell, "Germany and her satellites should be required to answer for atrocities against the Jews."[13] The alteration from "I do not undertake . . . to pass on *the extent* [emphasis added] of jurisdiction" to "I do not undertake to pass on the jurisdiction . . . or become involved" was subtle but significant to Pell.[14]

It seemed as if Hackworth was seeing just how far he could push the State Department's position without FDR's notice. In this letter, importantly, there was no broad statement that "Germany and her satellites should be required to answer for atrocities against the Jews."[15] It wasn't as if FDR had changed his views. If anything, he had become more resolute in his view given his March 24 statement, yet this letter went out to Pell signed by the president.

Herbert Pell must have thought this was madness. Adding to all the confusion— as if the duplicity of the State Department was not enough—communications were generally taking place through regular diplomatic air-mail pouches, not via telegram. Days, and in some cases weeks, would pass between letters being sent, received, and replied to. Only time-sensitive messages were sent telegraphically. Perhaps it was intentional on the part of the State Department, but more likely it was just standard procedure for diplomatic communications.

In any case, from Pell's perspective, nothing had materially changed in the conflicting directions he was receiving from the president and the State Department. But things had indeed changed; Pell just did not yet know it. The change was for the better, given how the State Department had been handling things, because the War and Navy Departments were becoming involved in war crimes policy planning, and very soon, so would the Treasury. As American troops continued their drive eastward toward Germany proper, war crimes policy increasingly, and by necessity, fell under occupation planning. It had to; at the very least, American troops and other Allied forces on the ground were needed to gather evidence. Pell would carry on bravely until the end, and he had other moves still to make, but he was on his way to being removed from American war crimes policy planning.

On April 28 the Commission discussed the possibility of the creation of an international court.[16] No one seemed sure just whose responsibility it would ultimately be, but it was obvious to nearly everyone on the Commission that some form of international court or tribunal would be necessary. At that moment, no other organization could take up the task. Shortly thereafter, during the first few days of May, separate committees of the Commission continued to propose and debate the inclusion of atrocities against non–United Nations persons while waiting for their respective governments to offer instructions one way or the other.[17]

Meanwhile, Pell tried to enlist Undersecretary of State Edward Stettinius in helping Pell secure formal instructions from the State Department.[18] Pell asked Hull in a March 24 letter if he could see Stettinius when he was in London so that Pell could press his case personally.[19] Hull acquiesced and told Pell so in a March 31 telegram.[20] Simultaneously Hull sent Stettinius a "strictly confidential" telegram informing him of Pell's desire. He suggested that Stettinius should ask Pell to examine FDR's March 1 letter because Pell "may want to discuss the authority of the War Crimes Commission to deal with atrocities committed prior to the beginning of hostilities." Hull added, "The President, while carefully refraining from passing upon the jurisdiction of the Commission, indicated his views on the subject."[21]

Judging by this telegram, Hull seemed to suggest that the jurisdiction question, as he wanted Stettinius to understand it at least, was only over whether to include pre-1939 atrocities, not over whether war crimes included atrocities against Jews generally. The March 1 letter stated explicitly that "Germany and her satellites should be required to answer for atrocities against the Jews." As to prewar atrocities, the March 1 letter suggested atrocities against the Jews "occurring before the war period . . . may not fall within the category of war crimes [and] will have to be dealt with by the United Nations."[22] Of course, the question on the table at that moment for the Commission was whether atrocities at any time against the Jews were war crimes for which the Allies could seek punishment. After all, Pell's own State Department–appointed assistant, Preuss, was arguing they were not per Department instructions.[23]

Of course, we are left to wonder, given that the telegram was marked "strictly confidential" and "no[t for] distribution," why Hull told Stettinius to get Pell to show him FDR's March 1 letter to Pell, which was, by the way, written by Hull's own legal adviser. Why Hull failed to explicitly state where he stood on the matter—which, not inconsequentially, was different from the Hackworth-defined State Department position—is hard to understand. Hull could have suggested that Stettinius have Pell give him his signed March 13 instruction to Pell, which suggested all atrocities against the Jews were not war crimes, at least not crimes that fell within the jurisdiction of the Allies under international law.[24]

This March 13 communication also offered a similar, yet more byzantine, answer to the question of prewar atrocities: "As to the earliest date on which a war crime could have been committed . . . It is suggested that the determination of the date as of which war crimes shall be made punishable the Commission might desire to consider the possibility of adopting different dates for the European and Far Eastern theaters of war. Perhaps the date . . . might be considered . . . September 1, 1939 . . . for the war in Europe."[25] Of course, this March 13 letter from Hull to Pell was also written by State's legal adviser, Green Hackworth. In any case, nothing in the record indicates when or if Pell and Stettinius met. Assuming they did, nothing of consequence came out of it, as neither reported a meeting.

Whatever happened as it related to Stettinius, Pell took a similar opportunity to enlist the assistant secretary of state for Latin American affairs Adolf Berle, who also made a visit to London. After meeting with Berle, Pell believed he finally had an ally in the State Department, but Berle would turn out to be no more help to him than Breckenridge Long, or, apparently, Stettinius. At their London meeting, Berle suggested he would try to get the department to produce some sort of "brief" on the matter.[26] Pell needed a department instruction that atrocities against Jews, especially German Jews, could be considered war crimes and thus fall within the jurisdiction of the UNWCC. He hoped Berle might be able to speak on his behalf back in Washington and convince State to issue the instruction.

When May arrived and nothing had come of Berle's suggestion, Pell wrote him and inquired about it.[27] When Berle received Pell's latest query, he chose to consult Hackworth. Berle let the legal adviser know that he agreed with Pell, but he was apparently unwilling to go any further and take a stand on Pell's behalf—on behalf of European Jewry—so Berle simply asked Hackworth how he should reply.[28] Hackworth told him that "two officers" of the State Department's legal department were working on it, preparing to bring the problem before a newly created State "Policy Committee" on war crimes. As for a reply to Pell, Hackworth suggested he "tell Mr. Pell that the matter is being studied and that an official communication from the Department will probably be sent without too great [a] delay."[29]

Berle replied to Pell on May 16, "The brief on the subject of Jews in Germany from the Legal Department is duly at hand." Practically repeating verbatim what Hackworth had told him, Berle assured Pell that the legal adviser's office was working on it and would send him instructions "without much delay."[30] This was the last thing Pell would have wanted; the legal adviser had been against him from the beginning. Pell's May 23 reply to this development was immediate and quite abrupt, indicating the anger and frustration he must have felt over Berle's note. Without intervention from Berle, Pell was sure it would turn out badly for him. He was alarmed, and rightly so, that State was about to deliver a fait accompli.[31]

By this time Pell knew full well that Hackworth was against him, and worse, his former assistant, Preuss, was now back in Washington; Pell had him removed just that April. Pell was certain that Preuss was conspiring against him in concert with Hackworth. He reminded Berle that Preuss "was bitterly opposed to doing anything for the German Jews," and now that Preuss was back at the State Department "and apparently in the confidence of the Legal Adviser," Pell expected the worst. Unaware that Berle had simply left things up to Hackworth, he then asked Berle to speak on his behalf in opposition to Hackworth and Preuss's plotting. "Watch the brief through its course and keep an eye on it," adding vainly that he was "hoping we will be successful."[32] But the policy committee had already produced its brief. Berle had been correct; the brief, such as it was, was "duly at hand."[33]

On May 19, the policy committee produced a summary report titled "The Definition of War Crimes in Relation to Crimes against Jews in Axis Countries," which detailed Pell's activities on behalf of European Jews over the previous several months.[34] Lawrence Preuss likely authored this report, which provided background "facts." It supplemented a second report, "The Scope and Definition of War Crimes—Summary," which laid out "The Problem" and the Committee's "Recommendations."[35] Presumably, the information contained in this document would outline U.S. war crimes policy for Pell's use on the UNWCC.

At last, the State Department appeared to be taking some action without conflicting instructions; at least it seemed that way to Pell. "The problem" was stated plainly: determining "the nature and scope of war crimes" as it related to the nationality of offender and victim, and the location and date of the crime. The "recommendations" called for the UNWCC to restrict its definition of war crimes to acts committed in violation of existing laws of war by Axis military forces or civilian leaders against United Nations nationals no earlier than July 7, 1937 (the date Japan attacked China). For each United Nations' state, the actual date of Axis invasion was to delineate the earliest date for which a war crime could have been committed.[36]

The policy committee then stated unequivocally what was to be done—or, rather, not to be done—regarding German Jews. The report stated, "That acts committed by Axis authorities against their own nationals should not be assimilated to war crimes." But did this mean that crimes against Axis nationals would be entirely ignored? The committee suggested that "the problems of punishment of war crimes and of acts of Axis persecutions committed against their own nationals or committed prior to the outbreak of war [should] be considered as separate problems, and that the question of the means by which retribution for the latter category of offenses may be ensured be reserved for further consideration." Lastly, the report recommended that these instructions be delivered to Pell for his use on the Commission. While this final recommendation might seem superfluous, up to that time the State Department had not offered specific instructions to Pell, and the Commission had asked its representative states to provide them.[37]

There was no immediate consequence of these recommendations. International law did not allow for consideration of atrocities against Axis nationals, and, if the policy committee was to have its way, what to do about them was "reserved" for a later decision. When Hull saw the proposals is unknown; he chose not to send anything immediately to the White House for presidential approval.

Unaware of the Committee's recommendations, Pell, still frustrated, wrote again to Berle on June 5: "I am still waiting for the instructions of which you spoke."[38] Apparently, no one in the State Department was in any rush to send anything to Pell.[39] Berle simply forwarded Pell's latest letter to Green Hackworth. This time, Hackworth told Berle that instructions to Pell "regarding atrocities against Jews" awaited consideration of the War and Navy Departments.[40] Pell, of course, did not yet know of this new development.[41]

The same day Pell wrote Berle, he wrote again to the president. Pell had a new piece of ammunition to use with FDR. Sir Cecil Hurst, chairman of the

Commission, had provided Pell a copy of a May 31 letter he had sent to Anthony Eden, Hull's counterpart in Great Britain. Hurst wrote Eden that a legal "distinction" existed between war crimes and atrocities committed by the enemy against United Nations' nationals and those who were not. However, he noted that most Commission members agreed that "the need to exact retribution is as great in the one case as in the other." The public expected that the UNWCC would investigate all these crimes, Hurst noted, particularly "the atrocities which have been committed on racial, political or religious grounds in enemy territory" against the Jews. The UNWCC required support and instructions, Hurst told Eden, "to ensure that the authors of these atrocities are brought to justice."[42]

Using Hurst's note to Eden as his backdrop, Pell reminded FDR of his March 1 letter. Pell wrote, "I have your letter telling me that you believe the powers of the Commission are already broad enough to cover the case of crimes against Jews in Germany which occurred after the declaration of war." Pell had been trying since receiving that letter to convince the rest of the Commission, but as he told FDR, "A good many of them, fearful of responsibility, feel that they should have additional instructions." Therefore, Pell wanted specific instructions, "direct orders to go ahead," which he could use on the Commission.[43] FDR's March 1 "views," which Hackworth wrote for him and were for Pell's "confidential guidance" only, were not sufficient.[44]

Following a procedure that had by then become standard, the president sent Pell's letter to the State Department for preparation of a "My dear Bertie" reply. Hackworth composed not only a reply to Pell for the president's signature but also a memorandum to be signed by Hull explaining the status. The memorandum informed the president that the State Department had begun consultations with the War and Navy Departments on June 1 to finalize instructions for Pell, including those "relating to atrocities against the Jews." Hackworth even wrote that State had asked the War and Navy Departments to "expedite" their replies, notwithstanding that State had done nothing remotely expeditious regarding war crimes policy at any time over the previous year. Hull told FDR that the "contemplated instruction" was of such "broad character" that it required presidential approval. As soon as he could, within the next "two or three days," Hull said, he would submit it.[45] Hull was waiting for Navy and War to approve a memorandum of instruction for Pell.

Pell probably received the latest Hackworth-composed and FDR-signed "My dear Bertie" letter on or shortly before June 20. FDR's June 13 reply succinctly told Pell that both the War and Navy Departments were involved in war crimes policy planning. With their "collaboration," Pell was to receive "adequate instructions" shortly, noted the president's letter.[46] Aware that new players were involved in the game but unsure of what that might mean, Pell sent another letter to Hull pleading the rectitude of his case.

The relentless Pell told Hull that the London papers were preparing to publish a new account of "another wholesale slaughter of the Jews by Germans." Repeating what he had already told Hull numerous times, Pell argued, "It seems to me manifest that something will have to be done to punish such actions, and the clearer we make it that certain punishment will follow, the more effective will be our effort to prevent the repetition of such things."[47] Pell was not about to give up on his effort to move beyond existing international law, even if other men in other departments were involved in the decision-making process. Pell closed this letter with one final appeal to Hull: "I believe that such orders . . . would not only clear our consciences, which is a personal matter, but would settle the whole affair in conformity with the conscience of the United States and the world."[48]

Clearing individual consciences was one thing; unburdening the conscience of the entire world—and the United States specifically—was another altogether. It did not occur to Pell that clearing the national conscience might expose it to a more distinctively American problem, unchecked racial discrimination at home. To be fair, there was probably no reason that it should have occurred to Pell, given the underdeveloped state of American public morality at the time and the social environment from which Pell had emerged. In a few short weeks, however, someone would notice the problem, someone in one of the highest positions of the U.S. government. For that to happen, however, Pell would have to take it upon himself to involve the Treasury Department and the War Refugee Board. In particular, he needed the involvement of the Treasury secretary, Henry Morgenthau, who, like Pell, was a personal friend of the president.

By the third week of June, both the secretary of the navy and the secretary of war had given their approval to the State Department's policy on war crimes and the jurisdiction of the UNWCC.[49] The substance of the suggested policy had not materially changed since the State Department's policy committee produced it in May. Hull sent the "proposed instructions" for Pell along with a summary memorandum on June 28 to the president for his authorization. "OK FDR," was the president's response; he made no comment whatsoever on the contents.[50] He probably did not read it closely, especially since both the Navy and War Departments had signed off on it.[51] Moreover, the president almost certainly felt he had made his position clear, at least from a public perception, in his several announcements on European atrocities, particularly his most recent statement of March 24.

Surely FDR was sincere when he announced his "determination that none who participate in these acts of savagery shall go unpunished," or when he said, "All who share the guilt shall share the punishment."[52] FDR would not have made this statement only for momentary political gain, whether to satisfy the demands of his treasury secretary or as an appeal to the Jewish electorate in an election year—as important as both those things were, particularly the latter. FDR had before acted primarily based on political motivations, but in this case, the gravity of the subject matter merited a serious response. Moreover, demanding justice for atrocities fit within FDR's and the Allies' larger wartime aims as verbalized in the January 1942 "Declaration by United Nations," which stated a "complete victory . . . is essential to defend life, liberty, independence and religious freedom, and to preserve human rights and justice."[53] Finally, given his March address, should the president have expected that War, Navy, and State would present a policy for him that ran so obviously counter to his announced desires? If had he been carefully reading the letters he received from Pell or the Hackworth-composed "My dear Bertie" reply letters composed for him, maybe he should have expected it. To some extent the burden and scope of the job explains much of the inattention, but it was more than that.

FDR cared about the plight of Jews in Europe and American war crimes policy in general. Like Pell, he was a victim of State Department duplicity, but he also suffered from the consequences of his often deliberately enigmatic administrative style and continuing estrangement with the State Department, which had been made worse by FDR's confrontation with Hull over Sumner Welles.[54] At a press conference in late July, FDR told a reporter that questions regarding war crimes policy were "a little premature." Pausing and thinking over the statement he had just made, he said it again, "premature—that is a good word to use," indicating that he thought it was too early for him to be discussing it with the press.[55] The administration was, in fact, working on war crimes policy. The president was not indifferent, but he was not prepared to offer any formal statement of policy on war crimes.[56] The problem was that no one in the Roosevelt administration, except perhaps Pell, was willing to do what was necessary.

More important, this planning period coincided—disastrously—with the onset of FDR's failing health. In any event, with the involvement of the Navy and War Departments, and later the Treasury, more focus would soon be brought to the issue, but not immediately. Yet the president had publicly announced the determination of the Allies to bring war criminals to justice while he simultaneously signed off on a set of instructions for Pell that declared otherwise.

Not until July 15 did the State Department send its latest set of War-, Navy-, and President-approved instructions to Pell. State Department duplicity was not, however, over; the memorandum to the president had listed instructions for Pell in active, declarative pronouncements, but the letter to Pell was written in conditionals. Indefinite to the level of equivocation, the department instruction to Pell began this way: "Having in mind your several communications and discussions in the War Crimes Commission, it is deemed desirable that the position of this Government be stated for your guidance." Pell required instructions, specific orders, not more "guidance" on policy.

This was decidedly not the way to begin a letter to a man of Pell's independent nature. Hull did not tell the president he was sending Pell a guide; he told FDR he was sending a set of "instructions." What Pell ultimately received was a set of "for the present purposes," "it is believed," "are believed to be," and "might be" statements, all approved by the State, War, and Navy Departments, as well as the President.[57] The instructions did provide Pell a list of starting dates for the commission of war crimes in various nations—July 7, 1937, in the Far East, and September 1, 1939, in Europe. At least, Hull wrote him, "For the present purposes . . . it is believed" that those were to be considered the dates. More to the point, yet still conditional, Hull informed Pell, "Punishment for war crimes and atrocities committed against individuals or minority groups prior to the outbreak of war *are believed to be* [emphasis added] separate problems." They were "reprehensible," and everyone wanted "proper retribution," Hull stated, but for the Allies to treat them as war crimes would be "unwise."[58]

Such words must have been difficult for Pell to accept, although it was hardly the first time he had heard them. He had argued previously that persecution against Jews prior to the outbreak of war could be treated as war crimes because they were carried out in preparation for the war that followed.[59] In other words, Pell had concluded well before it became American policy that the Nazis had planned and perpetrated a conspiracy on a vast scale prior to the beginning of actual hostilities.

While Hull presumably offered what came next as a consolation for Pell, Pell probably found no solace in it: "The War Crimes Commission *might be authorized* [emphasis added] by the participating governments to examine the question of punishment of offenses committed in enemy territory against persons on account of their race, religion, or political opinions." If such a case arose, however, the Commission was authorized only to formulate recommendations as to the method of dealing with the subject. Additionally, most of the perpetrators of prewar atrocities also committed crimes during the war and therefore would be dealt with as war criminals. In this way only, Hull suggested, would "the arch offenders" be prosecuted.[60]

One can only imagine Pell reading "might be authorized" and wondering what he was to do with that. Did that mean the possibility existed that the Nazi Final Solution might not be prosecutable? That the "arch offenders" committed crimes later during the war could have been little consolation. What about all those who were something less than arch offenders? Were they simply to be ignored? And what exactly constituted an "arch offender"? In almost every respect, this long-awaited set of instructions presented more questions than answers.

Finally, Hull offered Pell direction regarding German crimes against German nationals: "The Department is of the opinion that to assume to punish officials of enemy governments for action against their own nations pursuant to their own laws would constitute an assumption of jurisdiction probably unwarranted under international law."[61] This was, as Hull conspicuously noted for Pell, precisely the same instruction, word for word, sent to him previously on March 13.[62] Bear in mind, Pell received that instruction from the Department two weeks after the president (via Hackworth) wrote Pell, in essence, that the Nazis would be held accountable for atrocities against the Jews.[63]

Arieh Kochavi in *Prelude to Nuremberg* noted that Hull "illustrated" this last instruction in his July 15 letter with a "relatively trivial example" of internal sabotage.[64] It was Pell, actually, who had first linked saboteurs and German Jews. Pell made the mistake of connecting the two in his February 16 letter to the president, asking then, "What are we to do about the Jews in Germany and the German saboteurs?" Pell went on to discuss the two cases separately. The only thing they had in common was German territory. He argued that German nationals "to a certain extent" had been encouraged by the Allies to commit acts of sabotage, and therefore the United Nations was bound to offer them protection.[65]

Certainly, Pell did not mean to imply that German Jews had committed the "crime" of being Jewish at the instigation of the Allies. While the Nazis may have considered Jews saboteurs (worse actually, they were regarded as a "plague" on the body politic),[66] Pell absolutely would not have made the comparison. Quite obviously, he was not linking the two beyond their territorial connection. Offenses against Jews in Germany, he reminded the president in his letter, seemed to fall within FDR's phrase "crimes against humanity." Consequently, it seemed to Pell—and he said so pointedly to the president—the UNWCC must protect "these unfortunate people [persecuted] on account of their religion and their race."[67]

In FDR's "green-light" reply of March 1 saboteurs and German Jews were addressed separately, just as Pell had done. The March 1 letter began, "I [FDR] am in receipt of your [Pell] February 16 letter regarding the jurisdiction of the War Crimes Commission with respect to German saboteurs and Jews in Germany." As for the case of German Jews, the letter continued, "There can be little disagreement on the general proposition that Germany and her satellites should be required to answer for atrocities against the Jews." As for saboteurs, however, the letter stated, "We [the Allies] would be going rather far to undertake to punish officials of an enemy country for penalizing its own nationals for acts of sabotage against that country."[68] Quite obviously, in March, FDR—and thus the State Department, since they composed the letter (although Pell did not know that)—considered the two separately and, moreover, had come to markedly different conclusions as to what to do about each.

In the State Department's July 15 instruction for Pell's "guidance," Hull used the case of German saboteurs as an example to follow with regard to German Jews.[69] The two cases were no longer "somewhat different" as they had been in March.[70] Hull treated the case of German saboteurs as no different from that of German Jews. Atrocities against either, for whatever reason, were not punishable. But here, too, the State Department made this a conditional declaration: "To assume to punish officials of enemy governments for action taken against their own nationals pursuant to their own laws would constitute an assumption of jurisdiction *probably* [emphasis added] unwarranted under international law."[71]

Arieh Kochavi may be right that when Hull used the "trivial example" of saboteurs, he "blurred the fact" that such an interpretation excluded atrocities against Jews from consideration by the UNWCC, particularly in the case of Hungarian Jews who were then being exterminated.[72] It certainly "blurred" the distinction for the president, who had signed off on the policy, but the War and Navy Departments were not confused when they agreed to it, nor was Pell when he received it. Hull had now made the unconscionable and almost preposterous connection of the two, and moreover, he had done so with the approval of the War Department, the Navy Department, and apparently the president. Perhaps Hull had in mind Japanese Americans held in internment camps on the West Coast when he chose to equate German Jews with saboteurs.

Undeterred, Pell sought to involve another arm of the U.S. government, the War Refugee Board, the most obvious U.S. government agency to which he could turn. Pell and the WRB shared in part the same goal, to save as many victims of the Nazis as possible. Pell hoped further that the WRB might assist him in his larger effort of expanding the scope of the UNWCC.[73] To get to the WRB, Pell took advantage of an opportunity to visit with Treasury Department secretary Henry Morgenthau, who had traveled to London in August 1944.

CHAPTER 7

ENLISTING THE
TREASURY DEPARTMENT

"Pell Called on Me in London and Told Me His Troubles"

*The London papers today print the story of another wholesale slaughter
of the Jews by Germans. It seems to me manifest that something will
have to be done to punish such actions, and the clearer we make it
that certain punishment will follow, the more effective will be our
effort to prevent the repetition of such things.*

Herbert C. Pell, June 20, 1944

On July 6, 1944, Treasury Secretary Henry Morgenthau had asked FDR if he
could make a trip to Europe primarily to check on the currency situation in
France. Precisely one month later, Morgenthau was on his way. Accompanying
the secretary were staff members Josiah DuBois, Fred Smith, and Harry Dexter
White. DuBois had played an active role earlier in the formation of the War Refugee Board (WRB) and was then serving as its general counsel. Smith, described
as a "cheerful (if that is possible) Richard Nixon" by Henry Morgenthau III,
primarily functioned as the public relations adviser to Morgenthau. And White
was Morgenthau's most trusted adviser, principal architect of the World Bank
and International Monetary Fund established at the Bretton Woods Conference
that had just concluded on July 22, and in general the least liked of the bunch.[1]

Given that DuBois and Smith were junior members of Morgenthau's inner
circle, the two sat toward the rear of the plane on the sixteen-hour flight to
Europe. They were apparently not out of earshot, however, from an extended

conversation taking place between White and Morgenthau during the flight. DuBois later recalled White telling Morgenthau, "What we ought to be doing is making Germany basically a deindustrialized nation, not rebuilding them and making them a strong nation."[2] And thus was born the Morgenthau Plan, "conceived in the mind of Harry Dexter White," wrote Henry Morgenthau III.[3] The treasury secretary took this idea, made it his own, and expanded it with the support and assistance of a variety of individuals, among them General Eisenhower, Winston Churchill,[4] and, unexpectedly, Herbert C. Pell.[5]

Following a very positive and supportive meeting with Eisenhower at his headquarters in northern France, Morgenthau and his staff returned to Great Britain. On August 16, Pell took it upon himself to try to involve the Treasury Department in war crimes policy planning, calling on Morgenthau shortly before he departed London.[6] Although Pell did not know it then, his decision to approach Morgenthau was critical for him and a pivotal moment for war crimes policy planning. That policy had languished for months in a bewildering succession of memoranda and letters emanating from an outwardly feckless State Department. From this point forward, Morgenthau and his staff treated war crimes policy planning as an inseparable element of postwar planning, something Morgenthau believed had been given little consideration in the Roosevelt administration up to that time and, therefore, required the vigorous attention of the Treasury Department.

In January 1945, when Sam Rosenman complained about continuing Treasury interest in war crimes policy, Morgenthau reminded his staff at a group meeting what had happened and why they had become involved in war crimes policy planning: "Pell called on me in London and told me his troubles, and I got in good. We stayed on it until it looked as though we had a distinct part in shaping this very important policy." Morgenthau wanted someone in Treasury to write the story, to show what Pell had put in motion by telling him "his troubles."[7] Morgenthau quite obviously wanted no doubt to exist, within or without government, about the role his Treasury Department played in furthering war crimes policy planning.

Although Morgenthau would not have wanted to admit it was so, Treasury Department involvement in war crimes policy did little at first other than motivate Secretary of War Henry L. Stimson and Assistant Secretary of War John J. McCloy to oppose Treasury ideas vigorously. War Department opposition to Treasury views on war crimes was equal to, if not greater than, their opposition to the rest of the Morgenthau Plan once it became fully known to them. A major proposal in the plan called for the summary execution of the highest criminals of the Axis powers. Punishment for war crimes in the view of the War Department required careful attention to relations with the Allies—the Soviets especially—to say nothing of developing a well-defined legal procedure that would bring Axis war criminals to justice for all their crimes.

Stimson's resistance, even outright hostility, to Treasury's war crimes plan, however, forced the secretary to come face-to-face with an intrinsic problem in attempting to extend existing war crimes law to include atrocities committed by a nation against its own nationals, a problem no one had yet dare mention: namely, that such an intrusion on sovereignty might boomerang on the United States. It may have simply been a problem that had not yet occurred to anyone, given the entrenched state of racism in the United States—a nation, likewise, that possessed long-standing presumptions about its own moral superiority.

Of Pell's own doing, war crimes policy planning was finally moving beyond the confines of a do-nothing State Department and consequentially ineffectual War Crimes Commission to an overactive Treasury and ultimately proactive War Department. No one bothered to inform Pell about the significance of this development, and he would toil on for several months more, unaware of what was taking place back in Washington or his role in instigating it. Not until the middle of the summer of 1945, long after the State Department—with the apparent acquiescence of the president—unceremoniously discharged him from his post on the UNWCC, did Pell come to understand just how far removed he had become from war crimes policy planning. But what he had set in motion in August 1944 by speaking with Morgenthau in London finally altered the status quo. The problem he had been working on for months was at last about to be addressed.

Ambassador Winant, who had met with Morgenthau on August 12, 1944, probably informed Pell that Morgenthau was then developing his ideas on postwar planning. Perhaps Pell was hoping that Morgenthau would incorporate his views on war crimes policy within his developing plan. Pell was quite aware that the WRB was chiefly a Treasury Department entity, and he was undoubtedly desirous for its support and help. Whatever the immediate goal of this first meeting with Morgenthau, Pell's ultimate purpose was to convince someone to coax the State Department into supporting his effort to expand the scope of the Commission to include Nazi atrocities committed against their own nationals and those of their satellites.

Reacting positively and instantaneously to what Pell had to say, Morgenthau arranged for Josiah DuBois to meet with Pell the following day, August 17.[8]

Morgenthau, in fact, probably concluded at this very meeting with Pell that his postwar plan required a section on war criminals; it must have been obvious to Morgenthau, who was already utterly determined that Germany must pay harshly following the war, that retribution for war crimes was a prerequisite.

At his meeting with DuBois, Pell was interested in conveying the problems he had thus far faced and proposing how the WRB might help him overcome them. In DuBois, Pell believed he had found himself a fellow traveler, given all he understood about the mission of the WRB up to that time. But Pell thought he had supporters before—Breckenridge Long and Adolf Berle, for example—and neither had provided any assistance. Pell was still convinced, and rightly so, that he had the president in his camp despite FDR's failure to overtly intercede on Pell's behalf. Pell asked DuBois if he had any knowledge of "machinery" having been established "to deal with crimes being perpetrated by the Nazi[s] against minority groups." DuBois told him that he understood that the UNWCC had jurisdiction over such crimes, but beyond that, he was not familiar with the work of the Commission. Morgenthau must not have prepared DuBois very well for what he was hearing, especially given what Pell was about to tell him.[9]

Pell explained to DuBois that his understanding was incorrect. The Commission had jurisdiction only over Nazi crimes committed against enemy citizens and neutrals. Under this view, DuBois reported Pell telling him, "acts against German citizens by Germans, Hungarians citizens by Hungary, etc., or crimes by Germany against Hungarian citizens, Rumanian citizens, etc." were not war crimes. DuBois was staggered at this information, given his intimate knowledge through his work on the WRB of what was taking place in Europe at that very moment. DuBois told Pell that such a view was simply "unacceptable in the face of the facts of the present war." It did not make any sense. "Whatever the definition of 'war crimes' may have been in the past," it must be "re-examined . . . rather than endorsed as binding precedents developed in past wars," DuBois argued. Pell must have thought he was listening to a recording of himself. He obviously agreed wholeheartedly with what DuBois was saying and told him so directly at their meeting.[10]

Pell asked DuBois for whatever help he and the WRB could give; specifically, Pell told DuBois that he needed a definitive directive "from the Government of the United States" regarding the inclusion of all atrocities within the jurisdiction of the Commission, regardless of the nationality of the victim. It appears from the Treasury record of their meeting that Pell neglected to inform DuBois he had already received instructions from the State Department to the contrary, which had been approved by the War and Navy Departments as well as the president, although that probably would not have deterred DuBois or Morgenthau from acting on Pell's behalf.

Pell did not consider Hull's July 15 instruction as the final word on the matter, conditional as it was. According to DuBois, Pell "specifically mentioned" the issue "might be brought to the attention of Secretary Hull" so that Pell could obtain "the proper instructions."[11] Certainly, Pell knew Hull was already aware of the matter. It is not inconceivable, though, that Pell had convinced himself, and rightly so, that Hull was ignorant of the importance of the issue or the legal details, and that Hull had been simply signing off on Hackworth-composed policies. It was, after all, what the president had been doing, although Pell did not know it. Moreover, a recent statement by Hull on atrocities in Hungary gave Pell reason to believe that Hull intended that Axis crimes against Axis nationals be prosecuted, despite department instructions to the contrary.

Pell discussed with DuBois the appropriateness of publicizing the threat of punishment. He told DuBois there were "two schools of thought." On one side were those who believed that public threats of punishment only made things worse because assured punishment would likely expand and accelerate the Nazi killing machine. The other believed that the threat of punishment might save lives. FDR, both men well knew, had already come out publicly threatening punishment, most recently with his forceful March 24 statement. The general attitude within the State Department, however, was that no publicity should be assigned to the UNWCC.[12]

Toward the end of July, Pell had informed the department in two separate communications that a recently created publicity committee of the UNWCC had scheduled a press conference for August 3. At the conference, the Commission planned to issue a "specific statement" announcing, among other matters, that the Allied powers had not yet authorized the Commission to consider crimes committed by Axis authorities against Axis nationals "because of race, creed or politics."[13] It was, in fact, Pell himself who had proposed the formation of the committee for the very purpose of making such an announcement.[14] Pell reminded Hull in his second message that these very crimes included "Jews in Hungary, about whom you made an excellent and clear statement a few days ago."[15]

At the very same time that Hull had acquired approval for instructions to Pell that prohibited the UNWCC from considering crimes committed against German nationals and those of its satellites, he had publicly announced that those guilty of persecuting Hungarian Jews would be prosecuted. "Let them [the Hungarian puppet government] know that they cannot escape the inexorable punishment which will be meted out to them when the power of the evil men now in control of Hungary has been broken," Hull declared.[16] Given Hull's statement, Pell felt confident enough to tell him on July 29, "At the press conference, unless otherwise instructed, I shall express what I believe to be your opinion: that is, that the United States government would be willing to entrust this duty to the Commission, if satisfactory to the other governments."[17] If Hull did not act quickly, UNWCC jurisdiction and the definition of "war crimes" was about to be greatly expanded, something the State Department had opposed from the beginning.

The department's response reached Pell the morning of August 1 in the form of a telegram, which Pell dutifully paraphrased for the Commission members the same afternoon.[18] At least on this occasion, the department was now communicating with Pell via telegram, greatly speeding things up and, theoretically, lessening confusion. Green Hackworth, who composed the response, advised that he had discussed the matter with "people" in the War Department, who were "outspoken in their condemnation of the proposed procedure as outlined by Mr. Pell." A certain "Colonel Bernays who is handling war crimes matters in the War Department," Hackworth added, had officially approved the telegram.[19]

The department did not want the UNWCC to publicize its activities in any way. But it was more than that. Pell wanted his fellow Commission members also to know he had received the following set of instructions: One, the duties of the Commission were mainly advisory to the Allied governments; therefore publicity was unnecessary. Two, no statements were to be issued without prior approval. Three, the Commission should refrain from mentioning persecutions in Germany because "they might inspire future excesses."[20] Pell had just declared that he had been denied any authority whatsoever. Furthermore, he was informing everyone present that the Commission itself had no authority either in the eyes of the U.S. Department of State, other than the limited ambit to gather evidence and carry out policy.

Unwilling to submit to the unilateralism inherent in Pell's announcement, Commission chairman Sir Cecil Hurst offered only that the British censor would examine the Commission's statement prior to its being issued. Hurst was then asked by another representative on the Commission if the proposed statement was for public consumption, "which might start agitation" and controversy, or if it was merely intended as an outline of the Commission's work that the press was to treat as "confidential." "Critical articles about the Commission had been published implying that its work might end in a fiasco," Hurst replied. Therefore, he reiterated that the press conference would take place as scheduled on August 3, totally ignoring Pell's announcement that his government considered "publicity unnecessary."[21]

Hurst announced that the press would be provided a statement outlining "the powers and the work of the Commission" in order to "clarify the situation." It was obvious to everyone present that Hurst had not answered the question about confidentiality. Pell was asked then if the U.S. government really meant that "all statements" must be submitted prior to their release. Pell replied succinctly in a manner befitting this most recent and resounding failure to bring public attention to his and the Commission's troubles: "That was my understanding." Despite the position of the United States, Pell had been unable to persuade Hurst and the other Commission members to cancel the press conference.[22]

The next day, accompanied by his new assistant, Lieutenant Colonel Joseph V. Hodgson[23] from the Judge Advocate General's Office of the War Department, Pell met with Hurst to insist that he "postpone" the scheduled conference that was only a day away and not release the statement.[24] But Pell himself had little influence in changing Hurst's determination to go on with the press conference. The State Department had asked Ambassador Winant to intervene with British foreign secretary Anthony Eden. According to Winant, "notwithstanding the dissent and protest of Mr. Pell," only the intervention of Eden terminated the proceedings.[25]

Pell did not want to see the press conference canceled, despite his orders from the State Department to the contrary, but in this case, he acted as instructed. He could hardly have done otherwise, but he was determined that the work of the Commission be publicized; that was the reason he brought it up with DuBois a little more than two weeks after the row over the proposed press conference. Pell could not understand the absurdity of it all. Who could blame him? If his friend, the president of the United States, could so very publicly demand punishment of Axis war criminals, and on numerous occasions no less, why did the State Department demand the silence of the UNWCC? Moreover, the secretary of state himself had just come out demanding justice for Jews in Hungary. Perhaps someone should have informed both FDR and Hull that the State Department believed that announcements on atrocities in Europe "should not be referred to as they might inspire future excesses."[26]

What exactly was going on? From Pell's perspective, either the State Department was hopelessly fractured, or the government of the United States (and Great

Britain as well) had decided the Commission was at best tangential to war crimes policy, preferring to keep specific policy decisions monopolized among the Big Three—and, if at all possible, between the United States and Great Britain only. The answer, evidently, was yes to both.

Pell chose to carry on with what he believed was the necessary next step, despite orders to the contrary. He was convinced that publicity was necessary and that it could act as a deterrent to further atrocities. Moreover, at least in terms of his immediate goal, Pell believed publicity might produce the pressure necessary to alter State Department intransigence. DuBois assured Pell at their meeting that he personally believed publicity was a "healthy thing." The WRB, DuBois added, had already "adopted the view that publicizing the threat of punishment for crimes against Jews and other persecuted minorities, of whatever nationality, served as a deterrent to further criminal conduct."[27] DuBois was evidently unaware of the State Department's opinion to the contrary, and Pell was not inclined to let him know.

Pell did convey to DuBois his belief that many of the other nations represented on the Commission had concluded that both the United States and Great Britain "would probably be very soft hearted" about punishment.[28] This was the logical conclusion for the other members to make, given what had just transpired over the aborted press conference. However, the commissioners generally assumed, Pell said, that the "arch criminals of the Hitler, Göring, Goebbels, [and] Himmler class" were to be dealt with on a "political level" by the Big Three.[29] Presumably, that meant summary execution. Pell probably knew by then such a plan fell precisely within Morgenthau's desires, having met with the Treasury secretary the previous day.

Throughout their discussion, as DuBois noted in his "Memorandum for the Files," Pell "continually" pointed out that Jews were not the only European group the Nazis were persecuting. With the 1944 fall election drawing ever closer, Pell remained cognizant of the domestic political environment. His understanding that he had just approached the most visible Jewish member of the Roosevelt administration—Morgenthau—made it even more important that Pell include as many groups as possible. It would not do for the public to perceive American war crimes policy solely as a response to the persecution of the Jews. The more policy was focused on the underlying criminality of racial, political, and religious persecution regardless of the minority, the better. DuBois reminded Pell, "However true this might be [that other groups had been persecuted], the Jews of Europe were the only group with respect to which the Nazi[s] had adopted a systematic policy not only of persecution but also of extermination." "This was probably right," Pell replied, but he told DuBois that he nonetheless "hoped that Secretary Morgenthau would actively pursue the matter of expanding the scope of the Commission's jurisdiction over 'war crimes.'"[30]

It did not occur either to Pell or DuBois that focusing on the criminality of racial persecution generally rather than specifically might expose the United States to accusations about its own treatment of minorities at home. It did not occur either to Morgenthau, who, upon his return from England, began immediately to put all his and his staff's energy to work on the Morgenthau Plan, which included a set of draconian proposals for Germany as well as the summary punishment of Axis war criminals.

On August 14, 1944, in the midst of everything going against him on the Commission, Pell wrote a personal letter to FDR's secretary, Grace Tully, describing the benefits of an electrically powered wheelchair. He had noticed a man motoring around in such a device in Hyde Park, a 350-acre historic commons in central London. Pell struck up a conversation with the man. Before long, Pell had the name of the company that made the vehicle and had written away for a catalogue. Finding the "machine" both "simple and practicable," able to "climb high gradients, and travel over rough ground with safety and comfort," Pell told Tully that it struck him, therefore, "as the perfect thing for the President." The one he saw in operation, he added, "was an old one, but still working extremely well." On top of that, it was "still going well after seven years of work, and has actually covered ten thousand miles," Pell's description of the machine accurately summarized the average American's vision of the president, although FDR was considerably less "simple and practicable" than Americans believed him to be; moreover, FDR was no longer "working extremely well," but no one knew that then.[31]

Given the lack of support he had received lately from FDR, perhaps Pell was trying to send his friend another symbolic message. If Pell was to climb his own "high gradient," he desperately needed his sponsor who had championed the cause publicly to become more involved. Pell went so far as to offer to provide one of the machines as a gift to FDR. English landowners, Pell said, used the machine to inspect their estates, so he thought FDR might make use of it on his own grounds at Hyde Park. FDR already owned a modified Ford sedan with special hand controls, which he famously used to drive guests around Hyde Park, including Pell. Perhaps Pell was suggesting that FDR should prepare for retirement.

Whatever the case—sincere offer or subtextual message—FDR did not think much of the idea. He told Tully to notify Pell, "I think I get along all right with my old Ford."[32] Tully wrote Pell back, informing him that the president, while "appreciative" of the offer, declined. Tully added, "The President is most grateful to you for your kind thought of him and asked me to send you his very best wishes."[33] Reminding FDR of his incapacitation was probably not a good idea, although Pell was probably one of the few who could do it.

CHAPTER 8

JUSTICE, NOT VENGEANCE

"A Lawless Conspiracy against the Decencies of Modern Civilization"

I don't see any more reason in law or in justice why we should intervene in the matter to punish the Germans who had been guilty of killing the Jews than Germany would have the right to intervene in our country to punish the people who are lynching the Negroes.

Henry L. Stimson, September 8, 1944

Upon returning to Washington on August 17, 1944, Morgenthau summarized his European trip for several members of his staff at a noon conference at the Treasury Department. General Eisenhower was prepared to treat Germany "rough," Morgenthau told everyone. "He was perfectly willing to let them stew in their own juice." But much to his displeasure, the treasury secretary found that little had been done in preparation for the occupation, little anyway that was to his liking. "It took me days, and days, and days, but I got the story," he announced. "I didn't go over for that, but I made that my business." Part of the "story" that he had made his "business," the punishment of Axis war criminals, he acquired from Herbert Pell. Morgenthau's next step back in Washington was to confront the secretary of state with what he had discovered while in Europe. "I don't know how much Mr. Hull knows," he told his staff, "but he is certainly going to get an ear-full."[1] In the coming days and weeks, Morgenthau made sure that Hull was not the only one.

The next morning Morgenthau recounted for Hull the highlights of his trip; first, that Eisenhower felt the Allies should treat the Germans harshly; and second, that Churchill was similarly inclined. Morgenthau told Hull he "had done a lot of probing" and feared a reconstructed Germany might still be ready to wage another war in as little as ten years' time. Morgenthau was sure, however, that both the president and Churchill did not intend to allow such a thing. Morgenthau also met with Foreign Minister Anthony Eden and learned that the Allies agreed at the Tehran Conference (November 28 to December 1, 1943) to dismember Germany into at least three parts; he had Eden read that point to him directly from the conference minutes. To study the possibility of dismemberment, a European Advisory Commission (EAC), which had been agreed upon at the Moscow Conference (October 18 to November 11, 1943), was confirmed at Tehran. At this, Morgenthau reported, "Mr. Hull literally gasped." Recovering, a deflated Hull admitted to Morgenthau that he had not ever heard this: "I have never been permitted to see the minutes of the Tehran Conference."[2]

Morgenthau wanted Hull on his side, but he did not know the secretary's position on postwar planning. Most members of the Roosevelt administration understood that inconsistency and vacillation were Hull hallmarks.[3] To Morgenthau's questioning, Hull commented first on war criminals. "You know the reason I got along so well with the Russians," Hull said, "was because when I was in Moscow [for the Moscow Conference] I told the Russians that I would hold a secret trial before which I would bring Hitler and his gang and Tojo and his gang and I would shoot them all, and then I would let the world know about it a couple days later."[4]

Morgenthau must have been taken aback by this non sequitur. Herbert Pell certainly would have been. From what Pell had told Morgenthau back in London, Hull had taken an exceedingly legalistic stance on war crimes policy and had given no indication he supported harsh measures. Hull had not been reading those Hackworth-authored letters and instructions very closely after all. By his response, did Hull want Morgenthau to infer that he was for a harsh peace and the partitioning of Germany? It certainly seemed that way, but Morgenthau wanted a straightforward answer. What about Germany? An obviously frustrated and embarrassed Hull simply replied, "I don't have any chance to do anything. I am not told what is going on. That's on a higher level. I am told that that is a military affair. . . . I am not even consulted."[5]

Morgenthau did not press the issue, although he seemed to have reason to believe that Hull would support him, if Hull's apparent zeal for the execution of

Nazi war criminals was any indication. He wanted Hull as an ally, although he did not yet know just how much he would need him, so Morgenthau dropped the matter. But he had already told Hull that he was to broach the subject with the president the next day. Morgenthau confided to Hull, what Pell might have, in part, said himself: "I appreciate the fact that this isn't my responsibility, but I am doing this as an American citizen . . . and I am going to stick my nose into it until I know it is all right. I am more interested in my responsibility as a citizen than I am in holding my job."[6]

On August 19, 1944, Morgenthau met with the president. He told FDR that the State Department was working on a study of what to do about postwar Germany, but that they did not know about what Churchill, Stalin, and the president had agreed to in Tehran. Now it was the president's turn to be embarrassed. Morgenthau even repeated the State Department's ignorance of the Tehran agreements, "so that he would be sure to get it." He then told FDR that no one—not anyone on the EAC, the State Department, or the War Department—"has been studying how to treat Germany roughly along the lines you wanted."[7]

His confidence restored, FDR replied, "Give me thirty minutes with Churchill and I can correct this. . . . We have got to be tough with Germany and I mean the German people not just the Nazis." FDR then added, turning Nazi eugenics back onto the citizens of Germany themselves, "We either have to castrate the German people or you have got to treat them in such a manner so they can't go on reproducing people who want to continue the way they have in the past." Morgenthau left the meeting convinced, he said later, that FDR wanted him "personally . . . to be tough with the Germans." Of course, this was just what Pell believed the president had wanted him to do in London. Back at Treasury, Morgenthau wasted no time in putting Harry Dexter White, John Pehle, and Ansel Luxford to work drafting what became the Morgenthau Plan.[8]

On August 21 presidential assistant Harry Hopkins called Stimson and suggested that the secretary discuss postwar plans for Germany with Morgenthau.[9] Morgenthau's meeting with the president had served its purpose. Not only was FDR moving on postwar planning, but he was also allowing Morgenthau to become intimately involved. More than that, he was instructing Stimson to see Morgenthau, indicating to the secretary of war, therefore, that the Treasury Department was speaking for the president.

Stimson had not yet given nearly enough thought to the problems of the postwar world, including the punishment of war criminals.[10] From the time the War Department had agreed to the last set of State Department instructions to Pell, nothing else of any importance had been discussed on the problem. In addition, Stimson had not considered how war crimes punishment fit into the larger issue of the postwar treatment of Germany, as Morgenthau had already begun to do—thanks to Pell's urging. Stimson then held only the most basic idea that the primary purpose of any postwar plan was to keep Germany from launching another world war.[11] He told Morgenthau as much when the two lunched on August 23. Before he did so, however, Stimson arranged to meet first with the president.

Stimson's discussion with FDR was brief—only twenty minutes—but he thought it was one of the best talks they had had in a long time—commenting in his diary on FDR's improved physical condition. Stimson believed that he had succeeded in conveying to the president the importance of setting postwar policy for Germany as quickly as possible. FDR told Stimson that the upcoming Quebec Conference would settle things with regard to Germany, never clearly indicating his position, however, as was customary for him. Before leaving, Stimson arranged for another, longer meeting with the president two days later on Friday, before the cabinet meeting.[12] This would give him time to consider the problem of postwar planning more carefully, which included meeting and discussing it with Morgenthau.

Both Stimson and Morgenthau seemed pleased with the results of their late afternoon lunch. Stimson called it "a very satisfactory talk."[13] Morgenthau, although he did not come right out and say it, was delighted that Stimson had not done much thinking on postwar planning because this allowed Treasury to take the lead. Assistant Secretary of War John J. McCloy, who also attended, was concerned with the immediate problems generated by American troops heading into Germany proper. Stimson seemed more interested in the long term, in how the immediate postwar period might determine future peace.

Sensing an opportunity, Morgenthau suggested turning Germany into an agricultural state. The present population in Germany, Stimson believed, was too large to be self-sustaining. He told Morgenthau that such a plan might require moving large numbers of Germans out of their country. Morgenthau replied pointedly, "Well, that is not nearly as bad as sending them to the gas chambers." None of this particularly fazed Stimson, whom Morgenthau thought tired easily (not unlike the president), but it did motivate Stimson to put his ideas together more diligently so that he would be ready to present them at the cabinet meeting the following Friday.[14] He did not arrive empty-handed for his meeting with the president. With the help of his staff, Stimson came prepared with a four-page brief.

Of the six "Urgent matters of American policy" on Stimson's agenda, four dealt broadly with the problems of war criminals. One related to zones of occupation, reflecting Stimson's growing concern over the potential for future conflict with the Soviet Union.[15] Another concerned the partitioning itself, whether it was to be "limited" in scope or "radical." In line with what he told Morgenthau at their earlier meeting, Stimson was worried about "creating [a] major humanitarian issue," considering Germany's large population.[16]

Points three through six dealt with war criminals. Should "Hitler and his gang" simply be "liquidated"? Or should there be a judicial procedure? The brief stated that "if shooting [is] required it must be immediate; not postwar," indicating Stimson's early preference for some sort of trial structure, however that might be accomplished. What should the Allies do about the Gestapo?[17] How far down the chain of command should they go? How were the Allies to prevent war criminals from escaping into neutral nations? Lastly, Stimson was worried about thwarting retributive attacks by Allied soldiers against Nazis, both civilian and military. "How far do U.S. officers go," he wrote, "towards preventing lynching in advance of law and order?" Although Stimson had yet to form any specific ideas about war criminals, his preference is obvious; he was sure that some form of legal procedure was needed.[18] That he was worried about American soldiers "lynching" Germans rather than preventing a more generalized retribution is notable. While it may have been just some offhand notation, given what he would soon grapple with, there may have been some deeper significance to that word choice.

Stimson thought his meeting went well, and he believed he had made a major point with the president that not nearly enough had been done thus far in preparing a policy for the postwar period. Stimson took an earlier suggestion of Morgenthau's that a committee be appointed by the president to prepare such a policy, made the idea his own, and recommended the president do so. FDR did just that at the cabinet meeting that followed, appointing Secretaries Hull, Morgenthau, and Stimson. Harry Hopkins, FDR's principal foreign policy adviser, was to sit in on the meetings for the president. Stimson, however, probably should not have told FDR so resolutely that too little had been done up to that point, because Morgenthau also had his own meeting with FDR earlier that same day, which only reinforced his position that the Treasury Department must be involved in postwar planning, since so little had yet been contemplated.[19]

Just two days after Stimson had described FDR as looking better than he had seen him in a long while, Morgenthau was "shocked," finding him "a very sick man, and [one who] seems to have wasted away."[20] Despite his concern over the president's health and ability to deal with a matter as important as postwar policy, Morgenthau provided the president with the War Department's *Handbook of Military Government for Germany,* which he knew Stimson had not yet approved.[21] It did not include anything along the lines of what Morgenthau and the president had already discussed, and Morgenthau hoped it might aggravate the president into taking further action. Although Morgenthau probably did not intend it to work out this way, one result was that Stimson had made his own department look a little careless. When Stimson met with FDR later that day and complained about too little being done on postwar planning, from the perspective of the president, it was wholly the fault of Stimson's own department.

The letter FDR wrote to Stimson the next day, unambiguous and itself harsh, was not unlike the kind of peace Morgenthau wanted imposed on Germany. "This so-called Handbook is pretty bad," wrote the president. Reflecting something similar to Morgenthau's bitter attitude toward Germany, FDR added, "It is of the utmost importance that every person in Germany should realize that this time Germany is a defeated nation. . . . The German people as a whole must have it driven home to them that the whole nation has been engaged in a lawless conspiracy against the decencies of modern civilization."[22] Although Stimson then knew FDR's position on postwar policy, at that moment he was more concerned with Morgenthau. The president, Stimson well knew, was often flexible about things, whereas Morgenthau was generally not, and Morgenthau at this moment and on this topic seemed to hold considerable influence over FDR.[23]

While Stimson busied himself formulating a strategy for defending the War Department's position, Morgenthau put his staff to work drafting a comprehensive plan for the occupation of Germany in the postwar period. At that moment, no one seemed to notice that FDR had hit upon the method that the Allies would ultimately utilize to overcome the legal difficulties surrounding the issue of prosecuting Nazis for crimes against their own citizens both before and during the war—a method that, not incidentally, would simultaneously protect American sovereignty. FDR probably did not notice it himself either. That "the whole [German] nation has been engaged in a lawless conspiracy against the decencies of modern civilization" was, in the end, a very important realization. Of course, Pell, too, had come to that same conclusion without appreciating how important placing Nazi atrocities within a framework of conspiracy might be.

Meanwhile, Josiah DuBois had returned from London and reported his conversation with Pell to the executive staff of the WRB. Based on what Pell told both DuBois and Morgenthau while they were in London, John Pehle, executive director of the WRB, drafted a memorandum to Undersecretary of State Stettinius dated August 28, 1944, a copy of which was sent to the secretary of war.[24] Pell would now be heard, in a stronger and clearer voice than at any time previously, and very importantly not just in the State Department (they had heard it all before) but in the War Department as well.

The WRB, Pehle wrote, was created "to induce and persuade the enemy to cease the persecution of Jews and other minorities." The State Department, the War Department, the Office of War Information, and just about every other agency had been expected—or so Pehle had concluded—to cooperate in the effort to get out the word that "every Axis war criminal" participating "in such persecution" would be punished. Moreover, and even before the WRB had been created, the government of the United States had numerous times made this very threat publicly, he noted, "with increasing tempo." Pehle attached copies of the many declarations. And why? He got right to his point—which had been a premise of Pell's all along—"those declarations . . . specifically set forth the determination of the United States and of other United Nations to punish the perpetrators of atrocities and other crimes against Jews and other minorities even where the victims are or were nationals of Germany or of a satellite power."[25]

Pehle wrote that the WRB had assumed that the UNWCC would see to "the gathering of evidence and the ascertainment, trial and punishment" of those participating in atrocities and war crimes, but they had learned from "Mr. Pell" that the Commission had determined they could not do so under existing international law without instructions from the respective governments. "Needless to say," Pehle concluded, "it would be a fearful miscarriage of justice if such war criminals were permitted to escape punishment for their inhuman crimes."[26]

Pell needed appropriate instructions along with suitable publicity. Therefore, on behalf of the WRB, Pehle suggested that the State Department instruct Pell appropriately. In fact, Pehle attached a suggested memorandum that the State Department should send Pell. It was all very straightforward and simple, from Pehle's perspective anyway. The United States had already announced its determination to punish all war criminals, including those who committed crimes "against Jews and other minorities whether or not they are nationals of enemy countries," he wrote. The State Department simply needed to inform Pell of the decision, so he could act.[27] Of course, it was not, and had not ever been, as easy as that. The State Department replied to Pehle's letter on September 4. The "matter was under consideration."[28] Later inquiries from the WRB returned the same pat response.[29] To the contrary, the War Department—Stimson, in particular—took the memorandum seriously, especially the difficulty of prosecuting Nazis for crimes against its own citizens.

On August 28, the same day Pehle sent his letter to the State Department and a copy to Stimson, Morgenthau spoke with Harry Dexter White on the phone, filling him in on what had happened at the last cabinet meeting. He also told White that Stimson "just hasn't a thought" other than some vague idea that the Allies should take the members of the Schutzstaffel (SS) and "put them in the same concentration camps where the Germans have had these poor Jewish people . . . and make an exhibit of them."[30] Morgenthau quite liked that idea, but Stimson already had an additional thought.

Also speaking by telephone that same day but with McCloy, Stimson added the prerequisite of a swift trial and punishment of all war criminals to the idea he shared earlier with Morgenthau about detaining the SS in concentration camps. "We should always have in mind," he told McCloy, "the necessity of punishing effectively enough to bring home to the German people the wrongdoing done in their name, and thus prevent similar conduct in the future." Prevention, not vengeance was the important thing, Stimson thought.[31] At least outwardly, Morgenthau completely agreed. Both men believed in the priority of preventing Germany from ever initiating another global conflict. But Stimson thought this had to be accomplished in a manner that would not extinguish hope for Germany's future. Morgenthau's ideas, as Stimson then understood them, allowed little hope for the future of Germany. Whether or not Stimson instructed him to do so—it is not clear—McCloy copied the summary of his telephone conversation with Stimson to both Harry Dexter White at the Treasury Department and Freeman Matthews at State, suggesting to the latter that he show it to Hull for future meetings of the Cabinet Committee on Germany.[32]

On September 2 the president and his wife visited Morgenthau at his family home not far from Hyde Park in Fishkill, New York. While his staff continued revising what was to become the Morgenthau Plan, he delivered to the president that day a preliminary copy. The president, Morgenthau noted later in his diary, "was keenly interested in the memorandum and read it very slowly and carefully."[33] (If only he had done so with the "My dear Bertie" letters of the previous spring.) In this version, what to do about war criminals was not yet very well thought out, but the men drafting the document had given considerable attention to the ideology underlying the entire Nazi system.

Under the heading of "Treatment of Special Groups" in the preliminary document titled "Suggested Post-Surrender Program for Germany" appeared this one-sentence instruction: "A particularly intensive effort must be made to apprehend and punish war criminals." Any steps between apprehension and punishment remained unspecified, and the method of punishment was similarly open to interpretation. Members of the SS, the Gestapo, high police officials, the Sturmabteilung (SA, the Brown Shirts), all "high officials" of the government and Nazi Party, and "all leading public figures closely identified with Nazism" were to be "detained," presumably in the former concentration camps, but again the document did not specify. They were then to serve in a "compulsory labor battalion."[34] No one seemed to notice—at least Morgenthau made no mention of it in his diary entry that day—that such a plan was nothing less than a replication of wartime Nazi slave labor. If either FDR or Morgenthau then found the suggested plan for war criminals lacking, neither said anything.

Among the additional proscriptions regarding the "Treatment of Special Groups," appeared the following blanket statement: "There should be abrogated and declared null and void all pre-surrender laws, decrees, regulations or aspects of the same which discriminate on the basis of race, color, creed or political opinions."[35] The men drafting the document evidently deemed this requirement so important that they repeated it again in a slightly expanded form in a later section under the "Political Guide."[36] Despite this proposed interdiction having appeared twice and the president's having read the document "slowly and carefully," this directive made no obvious impression on FDR. Both men certainly knew that these Nazi dictates had to go; they had to be removed from Germany. They were, after all, the very basis through which the Nazis conducted the Final Solution. Any ideas about denazifying Germany, at the very least, needed to begin here. Did FDR or Morgenthau recognize then, or ever, that such a prescription for Germany could be equally applied in the United States? Did they understand that discriminatory laws and regulations were similarly entrenched in America and, moreover, that some might question why it was necessary to remove them in Germany but not at home? Certainly, they had to see that.

Maybe both FDR and Morgenthau had concluded that it was not necessary in America; no Final Solution had been undertaken here. Or perhaps they did believe it was needed, but the nation was not yet ready. Maybe they implicitly understood through the experiences of their own lives as national leaders that the morality of the nation was still so underdeveloped that direct assaults against racism in

America were impossible at that time. The man who had spoken so eloquently about the Four Freedoms back in 1941 must have recognized something in that part of the plan for Germany. Certainly, the man who was forced to send federal troops to Detroit in 1943 to end a race riot—and kept them there six months to ensure that racial violence did not again break out—must have noticed that a similar recipe was needed in America. About this, we can only speculate. Neither FDR nor Morgenthau said anything about it that day.

FDR did have three rather innocuous suggestions for Morgenthau: "Germany should be allowed no aircraft of any kind, not even a glider." No German "should be allowed to wear a uniform." And, finally, "marching" in Germany must be prohibited. "That would do more to teach the Germans than anything else that they had been defeated." Whether FDR was sincere about this or merely deflecting a serious subject with humor is not clear.[37] It would not have been out of character for FDR to do such a thing, of course, but Morgenthau took FDR at his word and incorporated all three of those suggestions into the next version of the Morgenthau Plan.[38] The significance of abrogating all laws "which discriminate on the basis of race, color, creed or political opinions" was apparently not worth mentioning.

Back in Washington on the morning of September 4, Morgenthau met with his staff regarding the updated version of the Morgenthau Plan. During the meeting, Harry Dexter White brought up the punishment of war criminals, suggesting that the plan needed to be "revised." The War Department official overseeing the planning of Allied occupation, Major General John H. Hilldring, had suggested in an earlier meeting with White that a list of about twenty-five hundred criminals could be drawn up. Allied soldiers could then shoot them, White offered, and they could then avoid the problem of "discretion by the military." The exact size of the list and who was to be placed on it, no one was prepared to say. DuBois had informed White earlier that he had learned from Pell in London that the UNWCC had done "next to nothing" about it. Morgenthau already knew that. He was the one who had arranged for DuBois to meet with Pell, and he told White as much.[39]

White then offered that it was his understanding that Harry Hopkins had inquired of both Matthews and McCloy what the UNWCC had accomplished thus far. The answer Hopkins received was that they had no idea, but that summary execution was one of the options the Commission had been considering. Just who and how many were to be shot was not yet clear, White then said, but in any case, "American soldiers wouldn't shoot them." American troops would only identify the criminals; some other entity would have to do the shooting.

Morgenthau interjected that that was not the case. Churchill, when he was last in the United States, had informed him that soldiers were to shoot anyone on such a list "on sight." That, Morgenthau noted, was problematic. It had been attempted in Italy, and soldiers do not like to execute other soldiers for having carried out their orders, criminal or not.[40]

Pehle spoke next. DuBois, he said, had been studying the last war and the Allied failure to deal properly with war criminals. Any list of criminals in this war, therefore, needed to be ironclad—"a list of names about which there would be no question." All others, Pehle said, "would be subject to trial." At that, Morgenthau announced, "Stalin has a list with 50,000." Perplexed and not seeing any humor in Morgenthau's interjection, Pehle responded, "But we wouldn't get that, I don't think." Morgenthau then directed the conversation away from war criminals.[41] Following a second meeting that afternoon to discuss final changes with his staff, White accompanied Morgenthau to his home for a dinner with Stimson and McCloy. The newly updated Morgenthau Plan was ready to be presented and discussed.

"Treatment of Special Groups" had been expanded to "Punishment of Certain War Crimes and Treatment of Special Groups." As for "arch-criminals," a list was to be drawn up of those "whose obvious guilt has been generally recognized by the United Nations." Such criminals were to be apprehended, identified precisely, and "put to death forthwith by firing squads." "Certain Other War Criminals" were to be detained and brought to trial before military commissions for "certain crimes which have been committed against civilization during this war." Among those crimes for which trials would be held included the following conditions:

(i) The death was caused by action in violation of the rules of war.
(ii) The victim was killed as a hostage in reprisal for deeds of other persons.
(iii) The victim met death because of his nationality, race, color, creed or political conviction.[42]

Noticeably absent from this updated and expanded draft was the requirement of the abrogation of all "laws which discriminate on the basis of race, color, creed or political opinions." Who removed it and why are unknown. War criminals, however, were to be brought to justice. Some—although it was still not clear who or how many—were to be summarily shot, while others would get their day in court. Apparently, it was no longer necessary to specify that discriminatory laws be removed, only that those who had carried them out be punished.

During dinner, Morgenthau read aloud portions of his plan. Stimson appeared most interested in war crimes policy, stating his belief that all war criminals should be given an opportunity of a fair but not necessarily public trial. At a cabinet committee meeting held the next morning at Hull's office in the State Department, the discussion was significantly less restrained. Stimson expanded on his ideas from the night before, adding with some emphasis that Germany should be treated with "Christianity" and "kindness." Hopkins, who chaired the committee at the request of the president, confided to Morgenthau after the meeting that Stimson's ideas were both "terrible" and "ridiculous."[43]

At that moment, Stimson alone seemed to be seeking justice rather than vengeance. Not only was Hopkins supporting Morgenthau's plan, but it was now clear to Stimson that Hull, too, supported it. In supporting Morgenthau's ideas about turning Germany into an agricultural country, Hull announced, "This Nazism is down in the German people a thousand miles deep, and you have just got to uproot it, and you can't do it by shooting a few people." Hull then repeated for everyone what he had told Morgenthau back on August 18, that the Soviets were quite pleased with his suggestion that all war criminals be summarily shot. Just a few simply would not do. This sentiment came from the same man who for months had been signing memoranda and instructions putting off Pell on the UNWCC. An increasingly frustrated Stimson set off on what Morgenthau described as "a long legal discussion of how you would have to have [a] legal procedure before you shot the people, and [how you] had to do all this on a legal basis."[44]

Back at the War Department later that day, Stimson composed a memorandum for the president summarizing his opposition to Morgenthau, Hopkins, and Hull. Stimson had this to say about the proposal to turn Germany into an agricultural state: "I cannot conceive of such a proposition being either possible or effective, and I can see enormous general evils coming from an attempt to so treat it." It would, he noted, destroy any "hope that the future peace of the world can be maintained," which they had all agreed was the ultimate aim of any plan for Germany. Then he turned, lastly, to the problem of war criminals, again in direct opposition to Morgenthau's ideas that then seemed to have the full support of Hull and Hopkins. "It is primarily by the thorough apprehension, investigation, and trial of all the Nazi leaders and instruments of the Nazi system of terrorism . . . with punishment delivered as promptly, swiftly and severely as possible," he wrote, "that we can demonstrate the abhorrence which the world has for such a system and bring home to the German people our determination to extirpate it and all its fruits forever."[45]

On the afternoon of September 6, the cabinet committee met again, this time at the White House. Hull presented his views, which were similar to Morgenthau's but considerably less detailed. He had his own memorandum for the president dated September 4. While Hull's memorandum contained nothing about war criminals, it did contain the same clause that appeared in the first version of the Morgenthau Plan: "All laws discriminating against persons on grounds of race, color, creed or political opinion should be annulled."[46] Again, no one cared to discuss the hypocrisy of this suggestion. Stimson spoke next, followed by Morgenthau.

Hull later concluded that the results of the meeting were "inconclusive."[47] Stimson, however, believed that he had made some progress. Hull, he thought, was "easing up" in his attitude, and most important, Stimson thought that the president was moving away from Morgenthau's position, if only just slightly.[48] Morgenthau took the meeting as a considerable setback, requesting a longer "rehearing," which was set for the end of the week, Saturday, September 9.[49] Disappointed but still confident in FDR's support, Morgenthau told his staff that he "had a very unsatisfactory meeting over there with the President."[50] In none of the maneuverings at the brief meeting, however, did these men have any time to discuss punishment for war criminals.[51]

Back at his office at the War Department the next day, Stimson showed U.S. Army chief of staff General George C. Marshall his latest memorandum as well as Morgenthau's. Marshall agreed entirely with Stimson's demand for a more moderate treatment of Germany in the postwar period, but he rejected outright Morgenthau's suggestion that war criminals be summarily shot without a fair trial. Stimson told Marshall that while he was not surprised at Morgenthau's attitude, he was, however, "appalled."[52] It was very important to Stimson to get Marshall's take on things. He believed that Marshall, a man whose opinion the president certainly trusted, could turn out to be an important ally on the issue of what to do about Germany after the war.

After a lunch with McCloy that same day, Stimson began an all-out effort within his department to prepare the counterargument to the Morgenthau Plan, busying himself, he later observed, "in collecting resources for the coming battle." In addition to Marshall, one of those "resources" was Justice Felix Frankfurter. Stimson invited him to a dinner that night to "enlist him in this battle." Frankfurter fully supported Stimson, particularly Stimson's view that war criminals must be given a fair trial. In his diary, Stimson wrote, "We discussed a little the limitations of jurisdiction which are involved in the fact that most of these Nazi crimes have not been directed at the American government or at the American Army but at the people and armies of our Allies."[53]

At that moment, Stimson was thrilled to have Frankfurter's input, particularly on the problem of "jurisdiction." Herbert Pell had been fighting that battle with the State Department for months. Back in July the War Department had either agreed or acquiesced to State's position that Allied jurisdiction did not cover atrocities based on racial, religious, and political persecution committed against German nationals or its satellites. Stimson had just been reminded of the entire problem when he received a copy of Pehle's memorandum to the State Department of August 28, which recommended that Pell be given instructions to consider such crimes within the compass of the UNWCC.[54] In addition, Stimson had just that week finally taken note of the clause in Hull's September 4 memorandum about the necessity of removing all "laws discriminating against persons on grounds of race, color, creed or political opinion."[55] Stimson could hardly have favored a policy directive that called for the abrogation of racial laws in Germany and then at the same time come out against jurisdiction for crimes committed on that same basis. It was nonsensical to do so. Stimson was so moved by that incongruence that he took the time to research the exact origin of the policy.

The policy directive first appeared in April 1944 in a document titled "Directive for Military Government in Germany Prior to Defeat or Surrender" produced by the Combined Civil Affairs Committee for the Combined Chiefs of Staff. Stimson's penciled notation on the document stated it was a "result of low level cooperation of State, Treasury, War (including CCS and JCS) & Navy." Under "Political Guide," it contained the following statement: "You will take steps to prevent the operation of all Nazi laws which discriminate on the basis of race, color, or creed or political opinions. All persons who were detained or placed in custody by the Nazis on such grounds should be released subject to requirements of security and interests of the individual concerned."[56] This statement had found its way into both the initial version of the Morgenthau Plan and Hull's September 4 memorandum, which was discussed at the cabinet committee meeting before the president on September 6.

The problem of what to do about crimes based on "race, color, or creed or political opinions" against German nationals and satellites had just reached critical mass for the secretary of war. The State Department had pushed Pell— and the president—around and aside for months on the issue of jurisdiction, although Stimson did not know any of this. At that moment, Stimson believed that Hull preferred summary execution but that he was not necessarily resolute about it. With summary execution, one did not particularly have to worry about jurisdiction. Of course, that was the plan Morgenthau was pushing—the plan Stimson was determined to "battle" against, and bitterly so.

If Stimson were to succeed in his "battle" against summary execution in favor of fair trials, he had to deal with the problem he termed "jurisdiction." Most legal experts maintained that Nazi crimes against German nationals and satellites were not prosecutable under existing international law. If any trial or trials were to be held—fair or even something less than fair—the Allies would have to prosecute Axis war criminals for *all* their crimes, including crimes of racial, religious, and political persecution against German nationals and nationals of satellite nations; that would require creation of new international law. Moreover, the president of the United States on numerous occasions had announced the Allied determination to bring Nazi war criminals to justice for just such crimes. Prosecuting Nazis or any other Axis nation for crimes of racial, religious, or political persecution presented a seemingly insoluble problem for the United States that no one, up until September 1944, apparently had recognized. Or perhaps it had been recognized, and no one wanted to own up to it. Whatever the case, the secretary of war assumed the task.

Faced with all these issues and considerations, Stimson sat down with Assistant Secretary McCloy on September 8, only one day before the next meeting of the cabinet committee, to attempt to articulate the problem. The purpose of their meeting was to prepare the "skeleton of a statement" for FDR at the committee meeting the next day. McCloy was then to spend the afternoon fleshing it out.[57] The first portion of their discussion covered the proposed destruction of future German industrial capability. Stimson was still "unalterably opposed to that," but he wanted McCloy to point out that his opposition did not mean he wanted Germany to become a world power again. "We are all trying to devise protection against recurrence by Germany of her attempts to dominate the world," he told McCloy.[58]

Stimson then turned to the punishment of war criminals. Between the last cabinet committee meeting and his conversation with McCloy that morning, Stimson finally had an opportunity to read Morgenthau's latest proposal regarding treatment of war criminals in its entirety—because there had not been time for Morgenthau to bring it up during the last meeting. Stimson told McCloy, "It [the plan's treatment of war criminals] seems to me violative of our entire constitutional history," and he suggested McCloy give this a larger hearing in the statement he was to prepare that afternoon. "Give [the] whole story," Stimson said.[59] But what did he mean by that? The "entire constitutional history" of the United States was a rather large topic. Perhaps Stimson wanted McCloy to present a discussion of the enduring belief in justice in America and the right to a fair trial. Most probably, however, Stimson wanted McCloy to "give the whole story" of the War Department's position on punishment, whatever that was at that moment.

What came next was an admission shocking in its straightforwardness. The problem of jurisdiction—what to do about crimes against Axis nationals—had floated around the War Department for some time, since at least June. Pell had fought that battle with the State Department for months. And why had State been so unalterably against it? Outwardly, State held to the position that no international law existed to do such a thing. But why couldn't the United States take the lead and call for the creation of new international law and set precedent? What problem would that cause? Up to that time, no one in the State Department had said, nor had anyone in any other department either. Moreover, the State Department had even suggested that doing such a thing would "immeasurably" increase the work that would be required of the UNWCC, as if that was a proper reason for passing on the problem.[60] Finally, on July 15, Pell was sent an instruction with which the War Department agreed: "As reprehensible as those acts were and as much as we all desire to see proper retribution in those cases, it is the view of this Government that to try to bring such offenses into the category of war crimes and to treat them as such would be unwise."[61] But why really was it "unwise"? Why couldn't the United States put forth a new legal precedent to account for those crimes against humanity?

The secretary of war had an answer, and he was now willing to put it in writing. The United States could not put forth new legal precedent covering the prosecution of Axis war criminals for crimes based upon racial, religious, and political persecution for one simple reason: the United States had its own deeply rooted system of persecution, namely, racial segregation and all its associated evils. Stimson probably had the July 15 memorandum to Herbert Pell in front of him when he voiced the following to McCloy that Friday morning; it certainly seems that way based upon his choice of words. It was the first open acknowledgment that the racial persecution of Jews and "other undesirables" in Europe was connected intrinsically with the United States' own domestic environment of racial persecution:

> While we appreciate the abhorrence of those crimes against civilization,
> I have yet to see any way by which we can treat them as a crime against

ourselves or as a crime in the punishment of which we can participate.
I don't see any more reason in law or in justice why we should intervene
in the matter to punish the Germans who had been guilty of killing the
Jews than Germany would have the right to intervene in our country to
punish the people who are lynching the Negroes.[62]

Of all the members of the Roosevelt administration, the secretary of war was
the first one willing to enunciate the real problem of suggesting that Germany
be held accountable for crimes of persecution against its own nationals. This
statement, which first appears in the notes of the conversation between McCloy
and Stimson, was not meant to languish as an observation between the two,
never to see the light of day. Stimson wanted it put into a memorandum that he
would present to the president at the cabinet committee meeting the next day.[63]

Stimson was pleased with the final document McCloy put together that
afternoon.[64] He was not, however, pleased with the outcome of the committee
meeting the next morning. The planned two-hour meeting turned into a meager
forty-five-minute affair with FDR doing most of the talking, and again, war
crimes policy was not even discussed. At least Stimson was able to provide the
president and the other members of the committee his expanded memorandum.
Of course, Morgenthau provided the same group with another updated version
of his plan.

It was Stimson's turn to be disappointed. "It was a very discouraging meeting
and I came away rather low in mind," he recorded in his diary at the end of the
day, but he was not the only one left dissatisfied. No one was particularly happy
about the futile meeting, except perhaps the president, who, to all those present,
seemed determined to evade discussing anything of importance.[65]

As far as Stimson was concerned, no matter how poorly things went, at least
his memorandum was out and in the president's hands. Stimson only hoped
that FDR would read it. As it applied to war criminals, Stimson reiterated his
opposition to summary execution. "The method of dealing with these [so-called
arch criminals] and other criminals," he noted, "required a careful thought [out]
and well-defined procedure." The accused must be given a fair trial that embodied
"at least the rudimentary aspects of the Bill of Rights." What he wanted was the
"punishment of these men in a dignified manner consistent with the advance
of civilization."[66]

Stimson called for the United States to participate in an "international trial"
of the "chief Nazi officials." In accordance with the Moscow Declaration, lesser

criminals were to be returned to their respective subjugated territories where their crimes took place. But Stimson made a tactical error by admitting that bringing war criminals to justice for all their crimes presented a dilemma for which he had no solution. This was certainly not going to work with FDR. Stimson had to have a workable plan of his own if he was to sway the president. He was, at least, willing to tell FDR what the real problem was, but in so doing, he was reminding the president of the moral and political challenges presented by the pervasiveness of racism in America, a deep national wound that had divided and disgraced the nation since its founding. FDR well knew that no Democratic candidate could speak out—much less act—against racism and segregation, even in a small way, and hope to win the South in an election year.[67]

Despite informing FDR that the "moral position" of the country required the nation "to take our share" in the conviction of all war criminals, Stimson openly confessed that he had "great difficulty in finding any means whereby military commissions may try and convict those responsible for excesses committed within Germany both before and during the war." He was quite prepared to "construe broadly what constituted a violation of the Rules of War," he wrote, "but there is a certain field in which I fear that external courts cannot move." But why? As McCloy had reworded it for him, "Such courts would be without jurisdiction in precisely the same way that any foreign court would be without jurisdiction to try those who were guilty of, or condoned, lynching in our own country."[68]

Protecting the sovereignty of the United States to police its own was a concern, but more than that, American sovereignty had to be protected from international assaults against its own system of racial persecution, a system that had been masquerading under the guise of Jim Crow segregation since the 1890s. If the United States was to participate in an international effort to prosecute Nazi war criminals for racial, religious, and political crimes against its own citizens, that left the United States open to attacks on the very same basis. That simply would not do.

At least the problem was out there, plainly written. As it turned out, it wasn't just antisemitism that had held back Pell from moving forward on the UNWCC; it was a different racism, or rather, the need to create a system to deal with Nazi war crimes that would not expose America's domestic system to external assaults. Certainly, the United States did not have to worry about some foreign power or group of foreign powers meddling in America's homegrown system of persecution. No nation would have the temerity—or capability—to do such a thing. Stimson himself was not worried about that scenario in the short term, but as a lawyer he was troubled by the legal precedent that would be set.

At this point in 1944, America was well on its way to becoming the world's most powerful nation. For Stimson, the most pressing issue was the hypocrisy of it all. While foreign powers could not materially attack the nation's sovereignty, they could criticize in the court of world opinion the moral authority of the United States. This would not bode well for the coming postwar battle with the Soviet Union to win over hearts and minds. But more important, what would Americans say—what would African Americans say—once they found out the United States was participating in the prosecution of Axis war criminals for crimes based on racial, religious, and political persecution when analogous crimes—albeit to a lesser scale—were routinely occurring at home without the same consequences? Wouldn't black Americans and other minority Americans rightfully demand the same justice be meted out at home? If "all pre-surrender laws, decrees, regulations or aspects of the same which discriminate on the basis of race, color, creed or political opinions" were to be "abrogated" in Germany, shouldn't they be abolished in the United States as well?[69] The secretary of war, the head of the world's largest military—more precisely, the head of the world's largest segregated military—had been the first to realize, or at least the first to document, why it was a problem to hold Nazis accountable for all of their crimes.

If Stimson had any hope now of fighting off Morgenthau's demand for summary execution and replacing it with some sort of trial system, he had to find a solution—and quickly. By the fall of 1944, there was no doubt about which side was going to win the war in Europe, and before long, the Allies would have to announce publicly how they would deal with war criminals. Stimson put McCloy to the task of getting the best advice available from within the War Department. In fact, the War Department had begun that process even before Stimson brought the issue to the cabinet committee meeting with the president that Saturday.[70] For whatever reason, however, Stimson wasn't particularly concerned with what the UNWCC had or had not accomplished over the last nine months. And despite what he knew from Pehle's August 28, 1944, memorandum about Herbert Pell's efforts, Stimson seemed singularly focused on a War Department solution to Nazi war crimes.

CHAPTER 9

A CONSPIRACY
AGAINST CIVILIZATION

"How to Make Good This Government's
Frequently Announced Intention"

*To let these brutalities go unpunished will leave millions of persons
frustrated and disillusioned.*

Murray C. Bernays, September 15, 1944

Although Stimson had been disappointed over the nonoutcome of the September 9, 1944, cabinet committee meeting, he seemed more apprehensive about the president's health and appearance. FDR was preparing to travel to Canada for the coming Quebec Conference with the British, beginning September 11. The president's deteriorating physical condition worried Stimson deeply. In addition to his concern for the man, Stimson was concerned for the nation, writing in his diary, "I am particularly troubled . . . that he is going up there without any real preparation for the solution of the underlying and fundamental problem of how to treat Germany." Stimson confided in his diary that he hoped the British were bringing "better trained men" to the conference. His hope that the British might take the lead over his own country demonstrated how much confidence Stimson had lost in the president, whether because of FDR's failing health or Morgenthau's influence—or probably both. In the largest sense, this anxiety masked Stimson's own frustration that he would not be at the conference himself.[1]

Back in his office at the War Department on September 12, Stimson sat down to the task of composing notes for yet another memorandum in response to the latest version of the Morgenthau Plan.[2] Stimson's first difficulty was that he still had no solid counterproposal to offer, so he was merely repeating what he thought was wrong with Morgenthau's approach. When it came to war crimes punishment, jurisdiction was still high on Stimson's list of priorities: "Call attention to the fact that the present Treasury memo contains the same features in respect to the trials of war criminals which we discussed in our first memo," he told McCloy, "perhaps calling attention again more specifically to the analogy of its attempt to punish anti-semitism [sic] with an attempt to punish American lynching." His observation was correct; Morgenthau had not altered his position on war criminals. Why should he? Stimson still had no comprehensive, positive program to offer in its place. Still another difficulty Stimson faced in trying to get his case heard was the president's poor health, which made any extended memorandum superfluous; FDR could not take the time to read it.[3]

Meanwhile, comments and recommendations began to filter in to McCloy from lower War Department officials, many of whom were commenting on earlier drafts of the Morgenthau Plan. Harvey Bundy, special assistant to the secretary of war, wrote McCloy that Stimson should remind FDR about the Four Freedoms.[4] He thought Stimson had "covered adequately" the problem of punishment—both McCloy and Stimson, of course, knew he hadn't—but Bundy thought Stimson could improve his overall argument if he focused on "the basic rights of a man as a human being in a free society."[5] This was all well and good, but it was of no help in solving the problem of jurisdiction. Focusing on the rights of free people in a free society would only make more obvious the underlying problem.

At about the same time, the comments of several officers in the Military Intelligence Division (G-2) of the War Department arrived on McCloy's desk. McCloy had asked for their responses to the Morgenthau Plan back on September 5. One respondent took a larger, more philosophical view of what needed to be done. "The question at the moment," an unspecified (at the time) "Colonel H" wrote, "is not merely what should be done to Germany but what can be done to preserve our Western civilization of which Germany is only a part." This same colonel also made an observation that served only to reinforce what both Stimson and McCloy were already taking into consideration: "The crowning consequence of a dismemberment of the German Reich, and with it German industry, would inevitably be the emergence—without restraint or rival—of the Communist State as the dominant power in Europe and ultimately also in Asia."[6] As significant as that prediction may have been as far as it related to early Cold War planning for the postwar period, it was of no help to the problem of jurisdiction. None of the comments from G-2 (and there were many) offered anything substantive on war crimes planning. A document dated September 15, 1944, from another officer, however, did have something to say about it. This officer, little known at the time, was Lieutenant Colonel Murray C. Bernays, chief legal specialist for the War Department's Personnel (G-1) Special Projects Branch.[7]

In the summer of 1944 Bernays had been spending his days investigating Nazi war crimes against American troops. By the end of July, he was already aware of the jurisdiction problem and of Pell's attempt on the UNWCC to overcome it. Bernays had been the signatory for the War Department on a specific instruction that Pell received on August 1. The UNWCC was planning to acknowledge publicly that they had yet to receive authorization to consider crimes committed against Axis nationals based on race, religion, or political persecution. According to Green Hackworth, several members of the War Department, including Bernays, had been "outspoken in their condemnation" of the plan.[8]

Bernays began to formulate his ideas about the problem of war criminals at this time, from the end of July forward, working throughout August on it at home on Sundays and "the tail end of evenings," the only free time he could find to deal with what he knew was a complicated subject.[9] By early September, after Stimson and Morgenthau had begun their battle over postwar Germany, Bernays was coming closer to a possible solution to the problem of the punishment of war criminals generally and the dilemma jurisdiction presented particularly. By then, he had in his possession Pehle's memorandum to Stettinius outlining what had transpired the previous months between Pell and the State Department. That memorandum, produced as a result of Pell's meeting with DuBois in August back in London, played an important role in Bernays's thinking as he composed the initial draft of what ultimately became the Nuremberg trial plan.[10]

Bernays had discovered a method to accomplish what Herbert Pell had not—to set forth a workable legal approach to hold Nazis accountable for all their crimes, including atrocities against their own nationals. But what that might mean in America, and how African Americans might respond, was not a concern for Bernays.

Murray C. Bernays was born in Russia on November 2, 1894. He came to the United States six years later, becoming a naturalized citizen in 1905. At that time, however, he was known by another name, Murray Cohen, a Russian Jew of Lithuanian descent.[11] In August 1917, just before heading off to Europe to fight in the First World War, Bernays married "Hella"[12] F. Bernays, niece of Sigmund Freud. According to the *New York Times'* report of the wedding, "The change of the name of the bridegroom was made by Mr. Cohen in deference to their mutual desire to keep alive her family name." Hanna Bernays had three sisters, but only one brother, Edward L. Bernays, who had announced his intention never to marry.[13] Edward L. Bernays, "the father of spin,"[14] had convinced the entire family of his determination to remain a single man. Of course, that did not stop him from marrying five years later.[15] Although Murray C. Bernays was just another nameless officer in the War Department during World War II (to a certain degree, he is still largely unknown today), he was not without his own interesting pedigree, at least by marriage.

Like FDR and Herbert Pell, Bernays possessed a Harvard education (BA, 1915). He briefly attended Columbia Law School (1915–17), but World War I interrupted his education. He finished at Fordham Law School (1919–20) upon his return. His then still-unmarried brother-in-law gave him his first job in New York City in 1919. At seventy-five dollars per week, Murray Bernays was the highest-paid employee of Edward L. Bernays.[16] Ten years later, Bernays became a partner in the law firm of Ernst, Gale, Bernays & Falk. By the time he returned to the service in the Second World War, Bernays was earning on average in excess of fifteen thousand dollars per year.[17]

When Bernays began to work on the problem of war criminals, he was not so sure that it fell within the War Department's sphere. Up to that time, Bernays and his colleagues had limited themselves to immediate military matters, issues such as how to avoid enemy retaliation against prisoners of war and instructions to soldiers in the field on how to apprehend and detain enemy combatants. The other possibility was to construe their task as something much larger and important. As Bernays put it the following summer, "We could consider that our responsibility ran to the entire question of how to make good this Government's frequently announced intention, which had become American policy, to see to it that after victory the Axis criminals were punished as they deserved."[18] Ample grounds existed for Bernays not to become involved in the larger issue, not the least of which was that no one had specifically instructed him to do so. Moreover, he had no significant background in international law.

Bernays listed several motivating factors for his involvement. First, by the summer of 1944, he had become one of the few people in government who was aware just how mired in red tape the problem of prosecuting war criminals had become. He knew that the British were against Pell's ideas, and he knew the State Department had no solution for the problem Pell's ideas presented. With the war in Europe progressing favorably, pressure had mounted for the announcement of specific plans both inside and out of government circles, but no one had any answer. So why not, he thought, take a stab at finding the solution?[19]

At the time, the Civil Affairs Division of the War Department had been working on postwar planning, and Bernays knew that they were having difficulty with one aspect of it—war crimes. According to Bernays, it was actually worse than that. As he put it, they had no "answer to what they recognized as a major problem in reaping the fruits of victory; vis., the punishment of 'war criminals,' so called." But Bernays had confidence in those around him, the Special Projects Branch (G-1), and, although he never said so, he certainly had confidence in himself, and not just a little ambition to go with it.[20]

By his own admission, Bernays's initial thinking on the problem was far off the mark. He had accepted the arguments of "traditionalists," that major criminals should receive political justice and that the Allies could not consider Axis crimes committed against enemy nationals. Bernays apparently sent a memorandum along those lines to the Navy Department and one other department, perhaps State. In the end, Bernays believed that what he had written was "hopelessly wrong," and he concluded that it "would have done a great deal of damage had it gone through." He was pleased to write his wife that the report never found the light of day. In the Navy Department it had been "held up," he believed, "by the sickening professorial pettiness" of the officer assigned to work on it. In the other instance, he "surmised" politics had held it up. In any case, Bernays believed he would have lost any opportunity to participate in war crimes planning if this memo had made it to higher levels in the War Department.[21]

While his first, ill-advised attempt was still in low-level consideration, Bernays "began to see some light," he recalled later. His insight occurred during a conversation with Colonel David Daniel "Mickey" Marcus, chief of planning for the Civil Affairs Division. Marcus had asked Bernays to give him some help with a directive he was putting together regarding categorization of Germans for possible future war crimes trials. Bernays recollected these came to a "tidy" number. Their discussion turned to how to deal with them all. This was the first moment Bernays tried out his new, "rough ideas" on anyone regarding the possibility of utilizing "conspiracy" to deal with war criminals. What he "stressed" to Marcus, he later wrote, was that failure "to try these beasts would be to miss the educational and therapeutic opportunity of our generation."

More important, he argued, Nazi war criminals must be brought to justice not so much for their "specific crimes but for the bestiality from which those crimes sprang." The underlying ideology of racial, religious, and political persecution defined for Bernays and many others Nazism itself.[22]

Of all the men Bernays could have chosen to whom to divulge his conspiracy idea, Marcus was perhaps the most fascinating. His story is almost too much to believe. He grew up on the mean streets of the Brownsville section of Brooklyn. He went to West Point and, following his required service, entered law school, later working as a federal lawyer in New York through the 1930s. Expecting the Second World War eventually to involve the United States, Marcus rejoined the army in 1940. From there, he became executive officer to the military governor of Hawaii following Pearl Harbor. In 1942 he took over the post of commander of the army's newly created Ranger school. Not content with deskwork, Marcus parachuted into Normandy on D-Day with the 101st Airborne, having never parachuted before.

With Marcus back in the War Department's Civil Affairs Division by the end of the summer, Bernays revealed his conspiracy ideas to him. Marcus was a man with a weighty résumé. While in the Civil Affairs Division, he attended the conferences at Cairo, Dumbarton Oaks, Tehran, Yalta, and Potsdam. The citation for his Distinguished Service Medal included the following accomplishments: "negotiation and drafting of the Italian Surrender Instrument, the Instrument of Unconditional Surrender of Germany, and the international machinery to be used for the control of Germany after her total defeat." To this should be added that he was an early sounding board and supporter of what ultimately became the London Agreement and Charter.[23]

Back in September 1944 Marcus told Bernays he would take his plan directly to McCloy. Although Bernays heard nothing more about it at that time, he later discovered that Marcus did take the idea to McCloy, but McCloy apparently did not then act on it. Nonetheless, Bernays was encouraged by Marcus's "enthusiastic" support and set out to prepare his thoughts into something more definitive. Bernays outlined his plan to his commander, who also liked it, suggesting that other staff members be recruited to offer comments.[24]

Meanwhile, at about the same time, probably during the first week of September but no later than the fourteenth, Bernays had an opportunity to discuss his latest ideas with the legal adviser in the State Department, Green Hackworth. Based on his history with Pell, Hackworth was a man not likely to give Bernays much of a hearing. Hackworth had acted not just as the voice of moderation in the State Department but, for all appearances, as the voice of know-nothing narrow-mindedness. To Bernays, Hackworth was a "sound, well-trained civil servant." The only criticism Bernays had of Hackworth was that he tended to act too "deliberately." He was, therefore, quite unlike Bernays, who often acted by his own admission with the "ill-considered rashness of inspiration." (At least that was the way he immodestly put it to his wife.) Outwardly, Bernays routinely tended to downplay his own importance.[25]

Hackworth showed Bernays a reply he was composing to a British aide-memoire that, he said, was giving him "a great deal of trouble." "It dealt with," Bernays later recalled, "the question of punishing the Nazis for their atrocities against fellow Germans, notably the German Jews, even before the outbreak of war."[26] Green Hackworth, of all people, told Bernays that day that the United States could not simply "wash our hands of the matter." FDR had already made so many statements promising punishment that the reputation of the United States was at stake. Hackworth's reply proposed that both Great Britain and the United States had a responsibility to seek justice for everyone and that they must find a way to carry it out.[27] But how could they carry it out, and moreover, who was this man? He sounded just like Herbert Pell. If only Pell had heard Hackworth make this statement, he would, at least, have had the consolation that his nemesis had actually been listening to what he had been saying—and what FDR had been saying—over the last several months. That is, of course, if we grant that Hackworth was being truthful with Bernays.[28]

"Common morality and public policy," Hackworth continued, required that the United States do something. Yet Hackworth had no answer. Bernays, of course, completely agreed with Hackworth and told him so. The United States must find a way to be as good as its word. Bernays then "suggested" that "there might be a solution." He believed he had an answer and set about outlining it for Hackworth.[29]

Just like Marcus, as unbelievable as it seems, Hackworth was "enthusiastic" about Bernays's plan, so much so that he wanted to schedule without delay a meeting between Bernays and Sir William Malkin, who was then in Washington attending the Dumbarton Oaks Conference. Just six months previously, in opposition to Pell, Malkin had demanded that UNWCC representatives must have instructions from their respective governments to consider atrocities against German nationals. As to meeting with Malkin, Bernays demurred. He had not submitted his ideas in writing to his own department. He could hardly place something like this before a British representative without first moving it through proper channels. Hackworth agreed. The ideas of Bernays did not yet represent U.S. policy. That was going to take some time. According to Bernays, from this moment forward, Hackworth was "uniformly sympathetic to the plan and helpful in forwarding it against the opposition it ran into."[30] As far as Pell was concerned, however, Hackworth would remain an enemy to the end, personally and politically. Pell never knew that his ideas had had some influence on Hackworth.

Bernays then set out to put his ideas on paper. As he later recounted, he "outlined one Sunday" (probably September 10, 1944) and delivered it to his commanding officer, who "forwarded it the day he got it" to the Civil Affairs Division, which also immediately approved it. Someone in the deputy chief of staff's office criticized the draft for not making clear why the War Department should take the lead in war crimes planning. Bernays recalled that he "answered that question to the satisfaction of the Deputy's office and rewrote the letter as desired." Whatever this change was is unknown, but Bernays's initial plan, "The Trial of European War Criminals," finally arrived in McCloy's office around mid-September with Bernays's recommendation that the secretary of war send a copy of it to the State Department. Given his previous discussion with Hackworth, Bernays was confident his plan would be well received there.[31]

The "Trial of European War Criminals" contained five sections and was written in simple-to-comprehend language even though the topic was legalistic. First came the "General Problem": how to prosecute such a vast number of crimes committed by a vast number of persons and accessories. "Trial on an individual basis, and by old modes and procedures," was at best impractical and probably impossible, Bernays wrote. In addition to that basic obstacle, there was what Bernays titled "The Minorities Problem." This was not a new issue to anyone who had been privy to the Pell communications with the State Department, nor to anyone who had received John Pehle's August 28 memorandum. Bernays's document followed along a simple syllogistic reasoning.[32]

First, numerous atrocities were committed by the Axis powers prior to the beginning of World War II. Under existing law, these could not be considered "war crimes." Second, "Some of the worst outrages were committed by Axis powers against their own nationals on racial, religious, and political grounds," but the accused could claim to have acted in a legal manner under domestic laws. In addition to that difficulty, Bernays also pointed out what Stimson himself had already discovered: "To call these atrocities war crimes would set the precedent of an international right to sit in judgment on the conduct of the several states toward their own nationals." He added, "This would open the door to incalculable consequences and present grave questions of policy." Third—and this was a major part of the problem—Allied leaders had publicly assured such atrocities would be prosecuted. Fourth, even if most of the Axis war criminals could be brought to justice for acts that were already considered war crimes, some war criminals would go untouched. This was not acceptable, and furthermore, "it will not satisfy the insistence of the minority groups," Bernays wrote. "Successor governments" could not be relied upon to undertake the task following the conclusion of the war. Consequently, Bernays cautioned, "To let these brutalities go unpunished will leave millions of persons frustrated and disillusioned."[33]

After briefly dismissing the existing suggestions regarding war criminals, Bernays then set down the three "Basic Objectives" of his plan: establishing that national interest was not an adequate justification for war crimes and atrocities, "bringing home to the world the realities and the menace of racism and totalitarianism," and awakening the German people to their own guilt and responsibility for the crimes of their government. For Bernays—and he was not the only one—if war criminals were not prosecuted for all their crimes, "Germany will simply have lost another war." Although it remained an unwritten understanding, no one from FDR on down wanted to repeat the mistakes of the First World War and allow Germany to rise again to bring about another.[34]

Finally, Bernays offered his solution. Bring the Nazi government, the Nazi Party, and all its agencies—the SS, SA, and Gestapo, in particular, among them—before an international tribunal for participating in a "conspiracy" against civilization. Under this conspiracy/criminal-organization plan, as it has become known, it would then be unnecessary to indict every member of these criminal organizations, but only representative individuals. Once the representative individuals and organizations were tried and convicted, all other individual members could be considered coconspirators and be adjudicated by later summary trials. Whether the conspiracy/criminal-organization plan could protect the United States against accusations about its own racist culture was not yet clear.[35]

Bernays's solution, while novel, was at that moment superfluous, considering what was taking place at the Quebec Conference from September 11 to September 16.[36] Due in large part to the activities of the UNWCC over the previous year, Great Britain had been struggling with many of the same issues regarding war crimes prosecution as had the United States. Invited to Quebec by FDR, Morgenthau had been able to introduce his plan for war criminals—namely, summary execution for Hitler and his top staff. Britain responded by submitting its own memorandum dated September 4 that also called for summary execution. Without any strong cautionary voices present at the conference, FDR and Churchill agreed to send a copy of the British memorandum to Stalin with a suggestion that a list be prepared of those criminals to be shot.

As far as the treatment of postwar Germany, Stimson learned from McCloy over the weekend of the sixteenth that both FDR and Churchill had agreed with Morgenthau's demand for harsh treatment. Stimson confided his reaction in his diary: "It is Semitism gone wild for vengeance and, if it is ultimately carried out (I cannot believe that it will be), it as sure as fate will lay the seeds for another war in the next generation."[37] In light of the major decision on the treatment of postwar Germany, what to do about war criminals merited a distant second best in importance, if that. Only on September 20 did Stimson learn from McCloy that FDR had come out strongly in favor of summarily executing Nazi leaders. Perhaps worst of all, it was British representatives in Washington who had filled in McCloy about this development.[38]

Once back in Washington, Morgenthau delivered the news of his victory at a cabinet committee meeting on September 20.[39] While Stimson recorded in his diary that he was pleased that Morgenthau "did it modestly and without rubbing it in," it was a devastating blow. Felix Frankfurter, who had come to dinner that night, offered needed consolation to Stimson's difficult day. The idea of shooting war criminals without trial "was preposterous," Frankfurter told Stimson. With Frankfurter's encouragement and support, Stimson vowed to fight it with all means available.[40]

Part of the means available arrived on September 27, during a meeting in McCloy's office. Although Stimson himself was not there, Bernays presented his plan for war criminals to McCloy and his assistant executive officer, Colonel Ammi Cutter. Like Marcus and Hackworth before him, McCloy was similarly enthusiastic about Bernays's ideas, even after Cutter submitted his criticisms a few days later on October 1. The plan, while "ingenious," was too "radical," so Cutter advised it not be adopted as policy without further considerations. For the next three weeks, Bernays's plan circulated throughout the War Department.[41]

On the same day that Bernays laid out his plan to McCloy and Cutter, FDR, back from the Quebec Conference, telephoned Stimson at his home on Long Island.[42] The purpose of the call was to prepare the way for the president to dissociate himself from his previous alignment with the Morgenthau Plan. The divergence within FDR's cabinet on the treatment of Germany had leaked to the press.[43] Press reaction strongly favored Stimson's views, and by this point, Hull had switched sides, allying himself marginally with the views of Stimson but definitely against those of Morgenthau. By the time of their conversation, FDR had also taken the time to read Stimson's latest memorandum on the treatment of Germany.[44] While that memorandum was essentially a repetition of arguments Stimson had expressed previously, this September 15 document contained a pointed appeal to the maintenance of the moral authority of the nation. As Stimson and McGeorge Bundy put it best in *On Active Service in Peace and War,* the memorandum "was designed to appeal . . . to Franklin Roosevelt, the farsighted and greatly humanitarian President of the United States" rather than to "FDR, the hasty signer of ill-considered memoranda."[45]

Largely composed by McCloy from Stimson's rough notes, this latest appeal to the president contained numerous rhetorical flourishes not too dissimilar from statements FDR had made previously on a variety of topics, including war crimes. The Morgenthau Plan of "enforced poverty . . . would be just such a crime as the Germans themselves hoped to perpetrate upon their victims—it would be a crime against civilization itself." Reference was made to the Atlantic Charter and the Four Freedoms. The United States "since its very beginning has maintained the fundamental belief that all men, in the long run, have the right to be free human beings and to live in the pursuit of happiness." The degree to which these interpositions affected FDR is difficult to determine. The political fallout of the publicity surrounding the breach in the Cabinet over postwar Germany, barely more than a month before the election of 1944, was likely motivation enough for FDR to distance himself from what Stimson labeled a "Carthaginian" plan.[46]

At a lunch in the White House on October 3, FDR's dissociation with the Morgenthau Plan was completed. Stimson had a long list of things to discuss with the president, but he immediately scaled that back to the essentials. "He was ill again with a cold," Stimson wrote of FDR, "and [he] looked tired and worn." When Stimson confronted the president about what had transpired at Quebec, FDR "grinned and looked naughty and said 'Henry Morgenthau pulled a boner' or an equivalent expression." He told Stimson he had "no intention of turning Germany into an agrarian state." After Stimson abruptly informed FDR that he had agreed to do just that at Quebec, the president responded that he "had no idea how he could have initialed [it]." All he was really after—all the Allies should be after—Stimson told FDR, was "preventive punishment, even educative punishment, but not vengeance."[47] Stimson wanted these principles to form the basis of all postwar policy toward Germany, and, of course, that included the punishment of war criminals. But Stimson still could not discuss war crimes policy with the president in any detail. At this point, Bernays's plan had not yet reached as high as Stimson's office. That changed on October 24, 1944.

At 11:00 A.M., McCloy brought in a small army of ten men who had been considering the problem of war crimes planning and Bernays's proposed solution. Among them was Lieutenant Colonel Joseph V. Hodgson, Pell's deputy on the UNWCC. Hodgson filled in those who did not know what had transpired on the UNWCC, but Bernays was the most important presenter that morning. The "deeply interesting" meeting lasted an hour and a half, Stimson wrote in his diary. By the meeting's end, Stimson was as enthusiastic about Bernays's solution as anyone had been.[48]

Bernays recalled that he "pointed out the difficulties of trying to bring to justice millions of Nazi criminals by the leisurely traditional methods by which we try individual pickpockets" and the "futility of proving all the crimes (even if we could) and never proving the one great crime." He quickly got to the bottom line: "I pointed out that the Nazi plan for total war, going back to 1933 and before, was a conspiracy of gangsters who had taken over a complaisant or conniving or ineffectual Government for their own criminal purposes." The entire Nazi experiment in Germany from the beginning was nothing less than one large criminal conspiracy. It was all so very straightforward to Bernays. Almost instantly, it was just as obvious to Stimson. Having stated his central position, Bernays needed to say little else. "Mr. Stimson immediately saw the point," Bernays later wrote, "and took the matter out of my hands."[49]

Stimson went on to expand on the effectiveness of using the conspiracy/criminal-organization plan to prove the "real crime." As he put it in his diary, the essential crime was a "Nazi scheme of terrorism" based upon racial, religious, and political persecution.[50] But did this solution—the utilization of a criminal conspiracy—completely obviate the problem of jurisdiction for Stimson? Was conspiracy the "reason in law or in justice" for which the Allies could "punish the Germans who had been guilty of killing the Jews in Germany"? It certainly seemed to be. However, what did this mean, as Stimson had put it just the previous month, for the possibility of opening the door to other nations to "intervene in our country to punish the people who are lynching the Negroes"?[51] Couldn't someone claim that a conspiracy existed in the United States to keep minorities, and African Americans in particular, in a perpetual state of secondary citizenship? Was it possible for an argument to be offered that American minorities were not altogether different from Nazi *Untermenschen*?

Based on his enthusiasm for the solution to prosecuting Nazis for all their crimes, the jurisdiction problem was at least halfway solved, as far as Stimson was concerned. His problem now was to bring the president over to his new vision, but he would have little opportunity to accomplish that immediately. One other thing was then obvious. The "jurisdiction" problem had become a Roosevelt administration problem to be solved separate and apart from the authority of the UNWCC. Almost by osmosis, since the Treasury and War Departments became involved with war crimes policy, the focus had shifted to solving the issues rather than how any solution might be carried out on the UNWCC. If Stimson had his way, his department would come up with a plan to seek justice for all Axis crimes, including especially crimes against humanity, in a way that would protect American sovereignty.

Over the next several days, Stimson promoted widely among his associates the moral and legal virtue of the plan. On the very day of the meeting with Bernays, McCloy, and the rest, Stimson confided to Marshall the jurisdiction solution, just in case FDR raised the subject during upcoming talks with the general.[52] He spoke with Hopkins as soon as he could the next day, writing in his diary, "I want[ed] to get across to him the picture I have now in my mind as to the proper way to handle the war criminals so as to make a dramatic record of the whole Nazi system which we have been fighting." Stimson wanted Hopkins to present the solution to the president before he committed to some other course.[53]

On Friday, October 27, Stimson discussed it with Ambassador Winant. Recalling the exchange, again in his diary, Stimson wrote, "I explained at length to Winant the work we were doing . . . in regard to war criminals and . . . my picture of a big trial for conspiracy involving the leaders and actors all the way down who had taken part in the different atrocity camps and mass murder places." One person with whom he did not discuss his enthusiasm for the plan was Herbert Pell, destined to carry out the final month or so of his time on the UNWCC still in the dark about the changing complexion—and direction—of war crimes planning.[54]

Stimson was anxious, as he had been with Marshall and Hopkins earlier in the week, that the president not commit the nation to some other plan before Stimson had a chance to present the War Department's solution to the problem.[55] With FDR in the final days of the 1944 campaign, Stimson knew he would have no opportunity to meet with the president personally until after the election.

Stimson left no record of whether he believed the conspiracy/criminal-organization plan solution solved the jurisdiction problem in its entirety, specifically whether it closed the door to other nations that might wish to demand a similar legal course be taken against the United States and America's system of racial persecution. Throughout the war years, Stimson felt constantly pressured by the dilemma of prosecuting the war with a segregated army. On October 3, for example, the very day he met with FDR to put to rest the Morgenthau Plan, Stimson was greatly troubled about what to do about troops returning from the front. "It is a question which is complicated by the question of segregation of the Negro troops," he wrote.[56] The problem of segregation in the army—the problem of racism at home—while fighting a war against an ideology based on racism posed a continuing challenge for the secretary of war.

In the days and weeks after he became an outspoken proponent of Bernays's conspiracy/criminal-organization solution, surprisingly, Stimson made no reference to what it might mean to those racially persecuted in America. It must have been obvious to Stimson that if the Allies prosecuted Axis war criminals for crimes against humanity, crimes based largely upon racial persecution, American minorities might find this ironic and hypocritical, and demand similar justice at home or, at least, a swift end to segregation.

Stimson had always held that war crimes policy—indeed the complete policy for postwar Germany—must be based upon traditional American values. In an even larger sense, his entire prosecution of the war demanded an approach that was both legal and moral whenever possible. Winning the war always came first for the secretary of war, but like FDR and Pell, he remained ever aware of the necessity of preparing the way for American dominance in the postwar world. Both men understood such leadership required both a legal and moral authority in securing the peace. This fundamental belief explains Stimson's previous attention to what impact proscriptions against racism internationally might have at home. But once he was delivered the solution of conspiracy to the problem of war crimes, he failed to consider again—at least in the remaining record—what this solution might mean to African Americans in the United States, or any other minority, for that matter. A growing, overarching political concern with the United States' future relations with the Soviet Union in part explains this omission.

Just the day before his group meeting on war crimes policy, Stimson met with the ambassador to the Soviet Union (1943–46), Averell Harriman, who had previously served FDR as a special envoy to Europe.[57] Harriman had come to the War Department to report on the recent conference he had attended between Stalin and Churchill in Moscow on October 9. Listening to Harriman and his report on Soviet "domination" of liberated areas by using secret police forces, Stimson discovered that "his mind was cleared up a good deal upon the proper solution of which the success of our relations with Russia will ultimately depend." Stimson already had come to believe that the Soviets were materially no different from the Nazis in their methods.[58]

While contemplating the meaning of all this alone in his office after Harriman left, Stimson began to consider how this realization influenced everything within his department. He thought about a film he had recently seen, which the morale branch of the army had prepared. Stimson did not like the film in the least "because it was an indiscriminate condemnation of Germany and Germans without giving the reasons why or the methods we should use in the future in curing their evil methods." He wrote succinctly in his diary, "Now I begin to see the light." He immediately called in the chief of the morale branch, General Frederick Osborn, to convey his displeasure.

Like Herbert Pell, Osborn was another FDR upper-crust friend moved to serve the country. Back in August 1940 Osborn was vacationing with his wife in Maine when he received a call from his good friend, sociologist Stuart Rice, then working in the office of the director of the budget. He asked if Osborn would be willing to fill one of the "dollar-a-year man" positions just recently allowed by Congress. The very next day an eager Osborn found himself back in Washington for a personal meeting with the director of the budget, Harold Smith. Smith informed Osborn that he wanted to put his name before FDR as a possible member of the committee on Selective Service. War seemed imminent, and like so many patricians of his day, service in Washington, therefore, seemed to offer a "wonderful opportunity." Osborn told Smith, yes, he could place his name before the president.

The next day Smith sent for Osborn. As Osborn recounted the meeting years later—no doubt with a smile—Smith asked him directly, "Is your name Fred?"

"Yes," he replied.

"Well, the President said that Fred was to be chairman of this committee and that must be you."[59]

The chagrinned Smith obviously did not know that the patrician families of both men had been close for several generations, and more, that the two were on a first-name basis with one another. Osborn, of course, was also a friend of Pell's, with whom he shared a similar background. For a brief time, they were childhood neighbors residing on Thirty-Sixth Street in the then elegant Murray Hill Section of New York City.[60] Both had spent much of their formative years growing up north of the city along the Hudson, the most fashionable area of New York State at that time. Osborn spent his summers and most weekends in Garrison with its panoramic view of the valley of West Point and the distant Catskills. His red-roofed estate, identified sardonically by locals as "the castle," was perched on one of the highest hills in Garrison, overlooking the imposing gray walls of West Point Military Academy across the Hudson to the west.[61] Garrison was just twenty short miles to the northeast of Pell's home in Tuxedo Park. Just thirty miles to the north sat FDR's estate at Hyde Park, with its own panoramic view of the Hudson.

While today these distances seem close, at the turn of the century, this area of New York State was still a wilderness, where distance tended to separate each community and delineate one's standing within the social hierarchy. But still, these three men grew up in communities within the same universe, a universe defined by the privileges of economic and social status, where manners always remained formal. The informality of addressing one another with first names was to be used only after long acquaintance, and it said something about the closeness of relationships. As Osborn later wrote, "In those days and even later, much more than today, people of a certain standing knew each other wherever they lived."[62] Osborn, like Pell, on account of that "certain standing"—and the personal relationship forged with his fellow Hudson River Squire, FDR—had landed a post in the government of his friend.[63]

Osborn served as chairman on the Committee for Selective Service for a short but busy five months. He then became the new chair of the Army Committee on Welfare and Recreation, the group responsible for providing education and information services for army personnel. It was in this position that he began working closely with the army brass and got to know General George C. Marshall, who commissioned him as brigadier general and chief of the morale branch of the army in September 1941 at FDR's request. During the war years, Osborn came to know Secretary Stimson and many of his staff quite well; Robert Patterson, John McCloy, Robert Lovett, and Harvey Bundy were "a wonderful group of men," said Osborn.[64]

Osborn would not have wanted to disappoint the secretary, but Stimson's thinking on the postwar world had changed since the morale branch's film had been first put together. The United States should not convict the "German people as a hopelessly evil race," he told Osborn at their meeting. The film needed to be reshot, thought Stimson, to indict Nazi leaders and accessories for the underlying ideology for "which this evil has been accomplished."[65] The nation might need a reconstituted Germany in the postwar world as an ally in the battle against the potential spread of communism.

Stimson called McCloy in on his meeting with Osborn. He wanted McCloy to hear what he had to say next. Stimson reminded both men what his mentor Elihu Root had said in his June 15, 1915, speech on the meaning of the Magna Carta.[66] Root had served President William McKinley and President Theodore Roosevelt as secretary of war (1899–1904) during the Spanish-American War and Philippine Insurrection. Shortly thereafter he served as secretary of state (1905–9). Almost everything Stimson knew about the law he credited to Elihu Root. In many ways, Stimson's entire legal and moral view of society was nothing less than an expression of Root's own beliefs under nominally changed circumstances. Root argued that there were but two theories underlying man's social relation to the state: one in which individual rights derive from the state, and the other in which individuals possess inalienable rights. In the first case, the state is sovereign and "free from those rules of morality by which individual men are bound." In the second, the people are sovereign; consequently, the state itself is bound by the same "rules of morality which the individual recognizes."[67]

To Stimson's way of thinking, this was, in fact, what the Second World War was about, two separate ideologies fighting it out for world supremacy. One operated under the same Christian morality expected of its citizens, and the other operated free from moral requirements. Stimson told Osborn and McCloy that day that "two agencies" were responsible for destroying freedom and liberty in fascist nations, whose citizens had delegated too much unrestrained power to the government: the loss of a "free press" and the loss of "the liberty of the citizens through the secret police." The second was, Stimson added, "the most [sic] abhorrent of the two."[68]

From this point forward, Stimson's thinking on everything relating to the creation of a new postwar world order reflected this basic understanding, and more important, his rising belief that Stalin's Soviet Union was materially no different from Hitler's Nazi Germany. Individual citizens in both of these nations possessed "rights only as a member of the state." Consequently, the Soviet Union was no less an enemy than Nazi Germany. Reinterpreting Root, Stimson was convinced that both states had operated "free from those rules of morality by which individual men are bound." When Bernays presented Stimson with a solution to the jurisdiction problem the following day, it was not just a solution to a vexing legal problem; it was an opportunity to place the United States unambiguously within Root's type of nation, in which morality matters. Of his meeting with Osborn and McCloy, Stimson concluded in his diary, "The result of the talk was that I felt I had had an interesting and stimulating afternoon and I have been thinking of ways of spreading the gospel in the future."[69]

While Bernays's conspiracy/criminal-organization formula certainly provided Stimson a novel way to "spread the gospel," he could only do so by ignoring that the United States incompletely reflected his own worldview, inherited as it was from Elihu Root. Stimson had recognized the problem on September 9. He had been willing to reveal it to the president, but Stimson could hardly attempt to deal with it then, or even rationalize it; to do so would be to undermine everything for which he had lived and worked. Besides, when Stimson did bring up the comparison between Nazi atrocities and American lynching, no one seemed to notice.

Perhaps Stimson was the only one within the Roosevelt administration who understood. Perhaps he was the only one who realized that prosecuting Germans for atrocities committed against its own nationals based upon racial persecution might have an impact at home. Perhaps he was the only one who realized the importance of race and racism in the coming Cold War conflict with the Soviet Union. Time would reveal that another man, Justice Robert H. Jackson, also understood; he would very soon play his own pivotal role in preserving America's social order, but his involvement was still several months away. In any case, the United States had managed quite well ignoring that national actions did not always live up to national rhetoric. Why should anyone expect our international actions to be any different?

The comfort zone provided by the professed belief in the traditional American values of freedom, liberty, and equality had made it possible in the past for American leaders to ignore that those very ideals remained incompletely realized at home. To announce a dedication to these values was all that mattered. In seeking justice for Axis war crimes—for the Holocaust—the security of American idealism offered an opportunity to demand that others outside the United States live up to those same values. For the vast majority of Americans who believed that freedom, liberty, and equality were the guiding principles of the nation, the basis for the nation's founding, and the reason for its continued existence, such dedication perennially obscured the inequitable application of those ideals.

American minorities, African Americans in particular, well understood the incomplete application of national ideals; they had lived it. The demand that Axis war criminals be held accountable for carrying out a system of terror based upon racial, religious, and political persecution would have great implications for those Americans who faced discrimination based on the same ideology at home. At that moment, however, the American public had no idea of the battle that had taken place over war crimes policy within the Roosevelt administration and on the UNWCC. The battle was not yet over, but the ideas of Bernays would be shepherded by McCloy, whom Stimson had assigned to administer the formation of war crimes policy.

One man, who remained purposely excluded from the interdepartmental deliberations over war crimes policy taking place in the fall of 1944, was determined to bring the issue before the American people, despite orders and even threats from his superiors that he not do so. That man was the U.S. representative on the UNWCC, Herbert C. Pell.

CHAPTER 10

THE SACKING OF PELL

"We Had No Reason to Suppose That the President Would Not Have the Matter in Mind"

It was perfectly obvious that all this was designed to get me out because I had so vigorously upheld the cause of the victims in Germany.

Herbert C. Pell, May 5, 1954

On November 9, 1944, Assistant Secretary of War John McCloy brought in representatives from State and Navy, as well as members of his own War Department, to discuss the efficacy of using the conspiracy/criminal-organization plan as the basis for prosecution of war criminals. Judging by the discussion at the meeting, support for the plan appeared universal. Murray Bernays was put to work immediately, drafting an updated memorandum. It took him only two days to produce it. After laying out the difficulties of war crimes prosecution, the heart of Bernays's revised November 11 document summarized how conspiracy was to be utilized to bring war criminals to justice. Finally, the document recommended approval by the secretaries of the three departments and subsequent submission to the president, whose approval was expected to come as a matter of course. Although the proposed memorandum did receive considerable criticism and suggested additions over the next few weeks, it ultimately formed the basis for American policy on war crimes.[1]

Within the War Department, McCloy moved forward with Bernays's plan immediately, inserting it into JSC 1067, the department's political directive for army occupation of Germany.[2] In the State Department, Green Hackworth offered several criticisms. He had asked his assistant, Katherine Fite, to examine the document closely for problems. He also asked her to research whether the conspiracy/criminal-organization plan was "cognizable" under international law.[3]

Basing his remarks almost entirely on the work of his assistant, Hackworth sent a November 16 memorandum to McCloy suggesting that Bernays revise his November 11 draft to remove minor ambiguities. In addition, he thought its proposal calling for a treaty among the Allies to establish the international court was a bad idea. The British were against it, but more important, in the United States, treaties required Senate approval, which took time and came with unwanted publicity. Many in the State Department, especially Hackworth, were concerned that any undo publicity given to war crimes policy might produce repercussions within Germany, specifically reprisals against Allied prisoners of war or those unfortunates held in concentration camps.[4]

Hackworth had one final, minor suggestion, again per Fite: the November 11 draft listed several earlier statements of war crimes punishment—FDR's October 7, 1942, declaration; the United Nations Declaration on Persecution of Jews of December 17, 1942; and the Moscow Declaration on Atrocities of November 1, 1943. Hackworth believed that FDR's March 24, 1944, statement must also be included.[5] FDR's very public pronouncement on what he called "one of the blackest crimes of all history," which declared America's determination "to pursue the guilty and deliver them up in order that justice be done," needed to be included.[6] It was the president's strongest public statement on atrocities and American war crimes policy up to that time—and for all time, as it turned out.

Although he did not reveal it to McCloy at the time, Hackworth was having second thoughts about Bernays's conspiracy/criminal-organization plan. He was troubled by the inclusion of "prewar atrocities." In an unsent draft to McCloy, Hackworth noted that he agreed that some method must be found, as he put it, "to require the Axis to atone for the atrocities committed by them since they launched their campaign of ruthlessness." But he was concerned that the conspiracy/criminal-organization plan exposed the Allies "to attack from the point of law and order."[7] It is difficult to know precisely what Hackworth meant here, but if nothing else, he was very doctrinaire when it came to the law. Consequently, this was surely an expression of his concern over the maintenance of law enforcement, laws themselves, and social conventions. If that is true, then this is the closest Hackworth ever came to an admission that seeking justice for crimes based on racial, religious, and political persecution threatened American sovereignty to treat its own as it wished.

Prosecution for traditional war crimes had never been an issue for Hackworth, nor was prosecution of the Axis for crimes against Allied nationals, and Hackworth said so in this unsent memorandum intended for McCloy. For Hackworth, however, attempting to "exact punishment for the maltreatment by a foreign state within its own territory" of its own nationals prior to the war was, he wrote, particularly problematic. Of course, Pell had pushed for this from the beginning. The United States had, Hackworth wrote, "in times of peace . . . occasionally voiced . . . disapprobation on general principles of humanity, oppressions against minority groups on the basis of religion, race, etc., but [has] not seen fit to go further." To seek punishment for crimes on this basis, he believed, might constitute an "unwarranted interference in the domestic affairs of a foreign nation."[8]

Hackworth just could not let it go, in spite of Bernays's belief that Hackworth was "uniformly sympathetic" to his plan.[9] And it was more than his enmity toward Pell that had driven him. What was it that bothered him so? Was it antisemitism? Perhaps it was, but the evidence does not exist beyond his effort against Pell. (And it is likely never to be found; Hackworth "destroyed" the bulk of his papers before depositing them at the Library of Congress.[10]) Could it have been fear over what such a legal extension might have meant in the United States? Here again, perhaps it was, but he never directly said so, notwithstanding his overriding concern for the protection of sovereignty. Or was it more banal than that? Perhaps to Hackworth the law was the law, and it was not to be confused with morality. Even the Holocaust, as unprecedented as it was, was not enough for Hackworth to move past international law *as it was* to international law *as is it needed to be*. That had never been an issue for Pell. In any case, Hackworth let the matter of jurisdiction, as it had come to be known, drop and did not send this memorandum to McCloy. But he was not yet done with his effort against Pell.

The November 11 Bernays draft had inspired Hackworth. His belief that publicity regarding war crimes policy might bring about retaliation against Allied personnel in Axis custody presented him an opportunity. He might finally have found a basis with which he could bring about Herbert Pell's removal from the UNWCC. Because many seemed to agree that publicity was a bad thing when it came to war crimes planning, why not make known, perhaps even to the president, how Pell had attempted to publicize his activities as U.S. commissioner on the UNWCC?

Coincident with the November 16 memorandum Hackworth sent to McCloy—
and the one he didn't—he also put down on paper the basis for which he hoped
State might accomplish Pell's removal from the UNWCC. This document had
no title other than a typed "SECRET" in the top right corner. At some point, it had
been stamped as "SECRET." Someone—it had to be Hackworth—prefixed the stamp
with a handwritten "TOP," but crossed it out. In blue grease pencil, a handwritten
"Pell" was scribbled above the typewritten "SECRET." Although it contains no date,
the content of the document reveals the timing of its authorship. There is also
no indication that Hackworth ever sent it, but every indication that he shared its
contents with Undersecretary of State Stettinius, who may have even shared its
contents with the president. Innocuously, it was filed under "Pell Correspondence,"
when it clearly was not correspondence. It contains no secretarial initials, like so
many other documents, in Hackworth's files. He typed it by himself to lay out all
his accusations against Pell. The document contained three headings: "PUBLICITY,"
"INSTRUCTIONS," and "Delay in keeping the Department informed of matters on
which action is necessary." They represent Hackworth's reasoning to sack Pell. All
three were designed to paint Pell as a person who refused to carry out or follow
State Department directives, and even subvert them.[11]

As Hackworth saw it, Pell had deliberately ignored State Department instructions not to publicize the work of the Commission. Back in the summer of 1944
Pell had been the driving force behind the creation of a UNWCC Publicity
Committee. At Pell's suggestion, that committee scheduled an August 3 press
conference to publicize the reluctance of the Allied powers to authorize the Commission to consider persecutions and atrocities committed by Axis authorities
against Axis nationals and satellite citizens.[12] When the department ordered Pell
to try to get the press conference called off, Pell acted as ordered, attempting
to get it canceled even though he wanted it to take place as planned. With the
help of Ambassador Winant, it was stopped, but Hackworth had good reason to
believe that Pell did not let the matter drop there. In his "SECRET" document for
his file, Hackworth noted that Pell gave the department "a minimum amount
of time in which to instruct" him to cancel the press conference. Further, the
document stated, "He [Pell] was instructed on July 31 that he was not to associate
himself with any publicity that had not been approved by the highest political
and military authorities."[13]

A little more than six weeks later, United Press reporter Frederick Kuh revealed
the problems of the UNWCC in two separate articles dated September 17 and
September 25 in the leftist New York newspaper *PM*. Datelined London, these

articles praised Pell and his effort to force the Commission to consider crimes against all individuals on the basis of race, religion, or politics regardless of nationality or location of the crime.[14] According to Kuh, Pell had been "fighting a losing battle for speedy justice" against other representatives on the Commission "whose brains are a judicial crazy quilt . . . retarding everything."[15] As a result of these articles, Commission members discussed the "leakage of information" on September 27.[16] As Hackworth quoted Kuh's articles, "One of the articles stated that Mr. Pell was no jurist, that his mind was 'not cluttered with dead clauses of mummified legalistic conventions,' and that 'in the opinion of the State Depart.' this might 'render Pell unworthy of serious attention.'"[17] Kuh actually singled out the "legal division" of the department. Of course, Pell's lack of legal knowledge was one of Hackworth's reasons to oppose Pell's appointment in the summer of 1943. While at first glance an indictment of Pell's legal abilities—which must have pleased Hackworth—the article also seemed to condemn the State Department for having such an inexperienced man represent the United States on the Commission.[18] But the subtext here was significant. Pell had let many officials at State know that he considered his lack of legal knowledge an advantage. Since this issue appeared in the article, the implication was obvious; Pell had spoken to Kuh.

Kuh reported to a Norwegian official in London that he had received his information from two unnamed sources, both members of the UNWCC. Pell was obviously one of them, although Hackworth didn't spell it out in his "SECRET" document.[19] The other may have been Sir Cecil Hurst; if that was true, it might have played a role in his leaving the UNWCC as well. Whether Pell thought it was Hurst is not clear, but Hackworth had more ammunition as it related to Pell's contraventions of orders through publicity efforts.

In addition to Pell's August attempt for a UNWCC press conference, he was already on record promoting publicity for his views. The previous February, Hackworth had learned from one of Lawrence Preuss's secret reports to Durward Sandifer that Pell had then "urged" Jewish leaders in American to "build a fire" back home "by means of a vigorous press campaign."[20] It was a campaign, Hackworth noted, designed to push for "the inclusion of Axis crimes against Axis Jews within the category of war crimes.[21] Although Hackworth did not record it in his "SECRET" document, his colleagues at State and others also knew that in August Pell had encouraged the involvement of the War Refugee Board (WRB) in promoting his cause. Pell had carefully asked permission from State to speak with Stettinius in April 1944 and Berle in May, but he asked for no approval to speak with Morgenthau that August.

On October 5 the counselor of the Norwegian Embassy in Washington went to the State Department to complain about these leaks to the press, specifically one of the articles that appeared in *PM* and was later reproduced in an abridged version in the *Washington Post*. Katherine Fite typed up a "Memorandum of the Conversation" for the record, which Hackworth used for his summary of the conversation in his "SECRET" document. According to Fite's recitation, Hackworth assured the counselor that the government of the United States "was of the opinion that the concept of war crimes did not extend to atrocities by Axis Governments against Axis nationals." Moreover, Hackworth "agreed" that the publication of the story "was embarrassing since it showed that someone had been talking." But Hackworth noted "that it was impossible to determine how the reporters got the information on which they elaborated and that the Department paid no attention to the articles in question." Duplicitous as ever, Hackworth already knew one of the sources—Pell; moreover, he knew that the department undeniably did pay attention. He certainly did.[22]

Hackworth now had irrefutable evidence that Pell was continuing his campaign to have his views aired publicly in America against departmental orders. In his "SECRET" document, Hackworth added that the Norwegian representative, Ambassador Erik Colban, "protested before the Commission against leakage of information." For effect, Hackworth wrote, "All Commission documents are "Secret," adding, "We are told that Mr. Colban was trembling with anger when he spoke before the Commission."[23] It must have pleased Hackworth to no end that he could accuse Pell of revealing secret documents, the very issue Pell had used to have his assistant, Lawrence Preuss, recalled in late April 1944. If Hackworth had his way, he would do the same thing to Pell.

Next in his "SECRET" document, Hackworth offered a blow-by-blow recitation of Pell's subverting of State Department instructions by trying to extend the Commission's jurisdiction to include "atrocities against the Jews." As Hackworth had it, Pell had gone way beyond his orders by stating on the Commission, "It is clearly understood that the words 'crimes against humanity' refer, among others, to crimes committed against stateless persons or any persons because of their race or religion."[24] This, manifestly, had been what Hackworth was against all along, seeking justice for the Holocaust: the very thing FDR had promised when he said that "none who participate in these acts of savagery shall go unpunished," the very thing Pell had tried to bring within the compass of the UNWCC. "The United Nations are fighting," the president had said, "to make a world in which tyranny and aggression can not exist; a world based upon freedom, equality and justice; a world in which all persons regardless of race, color or creed may live in peace, honor and dignity."[25] It was obviously lost on Hackworth that he—not his adversary Pell—was the one who had been subverting instructions all along—the president's instructions.

For good measure, Hackworth recited two further instances of what he considered Pell's dereliction of duty, matters that were outlandishly petty in comparison to the momentous issue of seeking justice for the Holocaust. According to Hackworth, Pell had failed to get Ambassador Winant's signature on a document related to financing the Commission's activities. It is worth noting that financing—this time Pell's salary—would become the modus operandi to remove Pell. It's quite likely Hackworth had already decided upon this methodology at the time he wrote the document. The final instance related to an October 17 Commission vote regarding the question of "whether or not the preparation and launching of the war could be considered a war crime." The Commission tabled discussion of the question for six weeks, after which time the members would take a vote based on instructions from their home governments. According to Hackworth, Pell waited until November 2 to refer the question to State, and the request did not arrive on the legal adviser's desk until November 14, leaving Hackworth "only two weeks in which to consider the question." Hackworth's apparent perturbation over this would be comical were it not for the subject matter, given that he already knew the War Department had been considering this issue for some time, and that the UNWCC was no longer important to war crimes policy beyond evidence-gathering.[26]

Pell seems to have had no idea the work that had been taking place in Washington regarding war crimes. No one had informed him about Bernays's conspiracy/criminal-organization plan or the generalized support for it. No one had told him that the secretary of war was worried about what the prosecution of Axis atrocities against Axis nationals and satellites might mean with respect to racism at home in America. Hackworth never confided to Pell—or anyone, it seems—that he apparently had the same reservations. Pell's assistant, Lieutenant Colonel Hodgson, had returned for a time to Washington and even participated in some of the discussions, but the documentary record is unclear as to what degree—if at all—he conveyed anything to Pell about those deliberations.[27] Pell's later actions and statements, however, indicate that Hodgson told Pell nothing of what he knew. It seems that a homegrown conspiracy—whether intentional or circumstantial—among the War, Navy, and State Departments had been put in place for keeping Pell and other members of the UNWCC in the dark about U.S. war crimes policy deliberations.

Back on October 20 Pell had written to Hull about the latest developments on the Commission. The UNWCC had produced a recommendation to the various governments regarding setting up courts, which Pell forwarded to Hull the previous day.[28] Pell informed Hull that the issue was "rather complex and that it would be a good thing if I were ordered back to the United States for consultation in this and other subjects."[29] What Pell really wanted was to meet with the president. Still, without specific instructions of any kind from the State Department that would allow him to pursue what he understood FDR had sent him to accomplish on the Commission, he believed it was time to report directly to the president.

Pell received no response from Hull to this request. Three weeks earlier, on October 1, 1944, Hull had informed the president of his intention to resign. Hull was a sick man. After spending eighteen days laid up at home, Hull was transferred to Bethesda, where he spent the next seven months for treatment of a throat ailment and exhaustion.[30] Discovering that Hull was ill, Pell wrote to Stettinius, who was serving as acting secretary in place of Hull: "For the moment, I see no very serious work coming up . . . and I believe it would be a very good thing if I were ordered to Washington, as soon as possible, to explain the case [of setting up treaty courts] to the Department viva voce." Always the good son, Pell also wished to visit his eighty-seven-year-old mother, whom he had not seen in a year.[31]

Stettinius cabled Pell on November 9 that he thought it unwise for him to return to the States just then. But Stettinius had been unwilling to make his own decision and answer Pell directly, well aware of the close friendship between Pell and the president. Stettinius understood that the president was keenly interested in the activities of the UNWCC and that of his personal appointee and friend, despite the many demands on his time. He asked the president during a telephone call the previous week how he should respond. FDR told Stettinius to check first with Ambassador Winant, who had told the acting secretary that it was "inadvisable" at that moment for Pell to leave London.[32]

Undeterred by Stettinius's negative response, Pell still expressed his desire to return to the States, adding another reason. His son, Claiborne, by then a lieutenant in the U.S. Coast Guard, was to be married in New York on December 16.[33] On November 24 Stettinius again denied the request. As had been explained to Pell in a previous telegram, Stettinius told him this time that Attorney General Biddle and McCloy might soon travel to London to discuss war criminals with him.[34] This was the first indication that Pell, finally, might be brought into the loop. When those plans failed to materialize, Pell was allowed to return to the States. It is not clear whether Stettinius again sought and received FDR's approval for Pell a second time.

It is entirely likely that by the end of November, Hackworth had discussed Pell's actions with Stettinius, particularly the leaks to the press. It is even conceivable that Stettinius took that information to the president. Given recent leaks about the Morgenthau Plan, such a transgression might disturb him. That was not very likely, however, because disclosing Pell's leak to the press would have to have been handled delicately, as it might reveal the extent to which State had undermined Pell's efforts on the Commission to carry out FDR's wishes. Neither Hackworth nor Stettinius was very good at handling things delicately. Moreover, if one or both had decided it was time to remove Pell ostensibly to stop the leaks, they should have considered the possibility that their plan might backfire. If he was let go, the irrepressible Pell—no longer as an unnamed source—would be free to issue direct, public statements as the former representative, unless, of course, he was ordered otherwise.

On the third anniversary of the attack on Pearl Harbor, December 7, 1944, Herbert Pell called on Green Hackworth at the State Department in Washington. The two spoke for nearly an hour. Pell had returned from London the previous day. Leaving his wife behind, he believed his visit would be for only a few short days. Pell had an all-new angle from which to present his case, a Cold War perspective. Unknown to Pell, the War Department was already considering the implications of that possibility. "[If] the United States did not take the lead promptly in these [war crimes] matters," he told Hackworth, "such countries as Greece, Yugoslavia and Czechoslovakia would gravitate toward the Soviet Union." If Pell had been speaking with Stimson, unquestionably, this statement would have had considerable impact, but Green Hackworth was not Henry Stimson, and the statement made no impression on him at all. Hackworth was focused on something else.[35]

Pell proceeded to work through a long list of issues with Hackworth, who offered nothing specific in reply. As Hackworth recorded it, Pell "discussed" the Gestapo and other German organizations. Hackworth did not note it plainly, but Pell wanted to know if they were to be considered criminal organizations. Pell "also discussed the situation with respect to minority groups." Hackworth recorded it as if it was of no more significance than any other item on Pell's list. British commissioner Lord Wright, Pell told the legal adviser, "was interested in German Jews." And although "there might be some difficulty in dealing with prewar crimes . . . certainly war crimes against minority groups . . . should be dealt with." If Hackworth responded to this assertion of Pell, he didn't record it. Pell also told Hackworth that the Supreme Headquarters Allied Expeditionary Force (SHAEF) should be ordered "without delay" to get courts ready to "get hold of members of the Gestapo." The remaining issues Pell relayed were that State had not yet responded to the Commission's October request regarding the establishment of an international court and military tribunals.[36]

Once Pell finished, Hackworth dismissed all he had said with one sweeping statement. "The whole situation," he said, "was being considered by the [State] Department and the War and Navy Departments. . . . It was somewhat involved and . . . it had to be thought through and worked out carefully in order that we might not be accused of taking illegal and strong-armed methods such as those for which we are now condemning the Axis powers."[37] Why didn't he tell Pell what, precisely, the three departments had been considering? That would have been the easy solution. If Hackworth had informed him about the conspiracy/criminal-organization plan, Pell would have been mollified. Of course, Hackworth was not inclined to divulge secret information to someone he considered an inferior legal mind and, more than that, a security risk. Above all, Hackworth was already working on his plan to have Pell removed from the UNWCC. At that moment, the last thing he would have wanted was a silenced Herbert Pell. An angry and vocal Pell would help Hackworth in his effort to force out his adversary.

Further insulting—and angering—the unsuspecting Pell, Hackworth added that he intended to have additional meetings on the subject within the next few days, hoping Pell would take the bait—and he did. For obvious reasons, Hackworth knew that Pell would want to sit in on the meetings, even participate. At the ready, the self-important Hackworth replied condescendingly, "The discussions would be along technical lines and I doubt whether you would be interested."[38]

Hackworth then took up with Pell what was most pertinent to his primary purpose that day, and he made sure to record it carefully in his "Memorandum of Conversation" for later use in having Pell fired. Assuring Pell that they "were all of one mind as to the desirability of dealing with the different types of atroci-ties," he then reminded him that war crimes planning was a complicated matter that must be addressed cautiously. If the result of their work was "to be above reproach, it was necessary to be sure of our ground before undertaking to reach conclusions," he said. Pell must, therefore, wait patiently for instructions. Then Hackworth came to his main objective, setting the trap and putting it in writing: "I impressed upon him the confidential nature of the whole subject and finally said that if any word were dropped as to any phase of the matter . . . it might give rise to speculation and inquiries of an embarrassing nature which neither he nor I would wish." According to Hackworth, Pell "professed to understand thoroughly" and "was glad to have had this talk." The two agreed to meet again in about two weeks' time.[39]

Underneath his gentleman-aristocrat exterior, Pell must have been seething. He was the president's appointee, doing the president's work. Hackworth was a careerist and commoner, a man of no social standing. Pell later observed venomously of the legal adviser, "Hackworth was well named. He was a little, legal hack of no particular attainments. He was manifestly not a born gentleman and had acquired very few of the ideas of a gentleman on his way up in the world. His manners were bad, his fingers were dirty, he was clearly unused to good society."[40] But what was Pell to do? His only choice was to do what he had always done: communicate directly to the president. This time he would do so by meeting with FDR as soon as he possibly could. He was sure the State Department would not attempt to get him an audience, so he would have to do what he had always preferred to do: go directly to his friend.

On December 11 Pell sent a telegram to FDR. A crisis was developing on the Commission over the issue of atrocities, he wrote, and he needed to bring it directly to the president's attention.[41] That same day—very possibly motivated by Pell's telegram—FDR authorized former ambassador to the Soviet Union Joe Davies to travel to London to undertake a survey of war crimes work.[42] Earlier that December—in typical FDR style of appointing multiple constituencies to work on the same problem—he had asked both Davies and Sam Rosenman to serve as White House go-betweens on war crimes policy.[43] Over time in the spring of 1945, Rosenman came to take precedence over Davies. But FDR wanted to meet with Pell. On December 14 he asked Edwin "Pa" Watson to work Pell in for a half hour the following week. But on December 27 Watson wired Pell that the meeting would have to be postponed. Finally, on December 30, Watson sent Pell a letter informing him that a meeting was scheduled for 12:30 P.M., January 9, 1945.[44]

By this time, however, Hackworth had convinced his new boss, Stettinius, that Pell had to go. FDR had accepted Hull's resignation on December 1, appointing Acting Secretary Stettinius his official replacement. The initial problem for Hackworth—even with the approval of Stettinius—had been how to bring about the sacking of a personal friend of the president. In the end, it turned out to be far easier than he anticipated, at least the firing part. Getting Pell discharged was one thing, but silencing him was another matter entirely.

Before his meeting with the president was set, Pell met again with Hackworth on December 21. This time, Stettinius sat in on the meeting. Pell made the mistake of telling the new secretary what he was going to speak about with the president. At the top of his list of complaints was inadequate support from the State Department, insufficient staff in London, and the department's failure to give him instructions regarding two important issues: whether atrocities against German nationals could be considered war crimes and U.S. policy regarding the establishment of some form of international court to try war criminals. Thanks to Pell's revelations at this meeting, Stettinius was able to defend the department against these charges even before Pell presented them to the president.[45]

On December 27 Stettinius sent to the president a Hackworth-authored summary of his conversation with Pell. He assured FDR that war crimes policy was being discussed within the War, Navy, and Justice Departments as well as with the British. When they reached an agreement, he noted, a report would be forwarded. There was an additional matter, however, that Stettinius wanted to bring to the president's attention.[46]

"A complication has arisen in connection with Mr. Pell's work which I have not mentioned to Mr. Pell," he wrote, "but of which I think you should be informed."[47] Expenses for the American delegation on the UNWCC, which included Pell's salary of slightly less than six thousand dollars,[48] had been originally covered by an allocation of thirty thousand dollars from the president's emergency funds, but new congressional restrictions forbade the use of emergency funds for more than one year. Pell's salary and his delegation's expenses for 1945, consequently, would have to be provided in a regular appropriation.

The department went through all the motions to make it happen. In November, an appropriation bill came before a House committee to cover Pell. It was not approved. The bill moved to the Senate, and the appropriation for Pell was restored at the written request of Stettinius, again authored by Hackworth.[49] When the appropriation bill went before a conference committee of the House and Senate shortly thereafter, the committee members sought advice from the State Department. Did they want this appropriation, minor as it was, to remain in the bill? The answer was no, and the appropriation was eliminated. One of the members of the conference committee later told Pell that inquiries to the State Department, presumably to Hackworth, returned an answer that "any attaché in the Embassy" could handle Pell's work.[50]

Putting all the blame on Congress, the Hackworth-authored Stettinius letter to the president carefully explained everything that had happened and why— except, of course, that State was really to blame. The documentary record indicates that Hackworth never told Stettinius that State was responsible for the failure of Congress to appropriate funds for Pell. Even when Hackworth, Pell, and Stettinius met on December 21, Hackworth said nothing of the appropriation problem. Unless Hackworth told Stettinius privately in some other conversation, Stettinius acted in ignorance of what Hackworth had done. It would not have been out of character for Hackworth to have acted so duplicitously, especially given his vision of the law, his conception of the UNWCC, and his attitude toward Pell. Hackworth met with several of his staff members on December 22 to discuss the appropriation problem. At Hackworth's request, a memorandum of explanation was sent to Stettinius, detailing what had happened—that Congress, not State, had eliminated Pell's position.[51]

The letter to the president recommended that Pell be notified of the situation. In addition, Stettinius's letter, which was a word-for-word copy of Hackworth's draft, suggested that Pell's position on the UNWCC be "carried on" by his assistant, Lieutenant Colonel Hodgson, "or someone else."[52] Of course, Stettinius did not tell the president that Pell could be retained merely by making him an employee of the State or War Department.[53] Certainly, FDR should have known that. As if this appropriation problem was a matter of the highest secrecy, Stettinius then asked a bizarre question: "May I have your approval to discuss this with Secretary Stimson or Mr. McCloy?"[54] Hodgson was part of the War Department. If he were to serve in place of Pell—temporarily or permanently—the State Department would obviously have to discuss the matter with either Stimson or McCloy. Was informing Stimson and McCloy really a decision requiring presidential approval?

Stettinius was a dismal replacement for Cordell Hull. He had little experience in foreign affairs, but more than that, he had little interest in taking any position on any matter before the department. In addition, he was not respected in other departments. Morgenthau, for example, referred to Stettinius as "what's-his-name" in meetings with his staff.[55] To the extent this was true, and all evidence indicates that it was, it might not have been difficult for Hackworth to orchestrate Pell's removal without fully informing Stettinius.

FDR, of course, had never shown any interest in a strong State Department, so in that respect, Stettinius's appointment only furthered the State Department's insignificance. For his part, Stettinius would do nothing to alter the unimportance of himself or his department. Even before his official appointment, when he was still just acting secretary, he had already begun the process of relinquishing State Department oversight of war crimes policy.

When Pell had cabled the department in early November asking for instructions on whether the UNWCC could consider the preparation for or waging of aggressive war as an international crime, Stettinius's initial reaction was to ask the War Department how he should answer. As far as Stettinius was concerned, war crimes policy was no longer solely under State Department control. The answer that the War Department suggested be given to Pell might as well have originated in the State Department; it was no different from what they had been advising Pell all year long: "It is recommended that the United States member on the War Crimes Commission be instructed that this Government is not at present prepared to express an opinion on this matter."[56] By the end of December, as the issue of aggressive warfare was still being discussed among various departments, Stettinius simply took the advice of his legal adviser and, in so doing, handed over all authority on the matter to other departments.

In preparation for an upcoming meeting with Stimson and the secretary of the navy, Hackworth told Stettinius to take no stand of his own—on anything. With regard to the conspiracy/criminal-organization plan, Hackworth informed the secretary that it had "already been discussed and largely agreed upon." He should say, therefore, nothing further about it. On the issue of aggressive war, Hackworth advised Stettinius to take the following position: "I think you could say that the question is one on which there are divergent views among writers and students of the subject; that if the War and Navy Departments feel that such a criminal charge may reasonably be made, and particularly if the Attorney General feels that there would be justification, you would be prepared to go along with them."[57]

Neither Hackworth nor Stettinius was apparently interested in directing war crimes policy. Their new strategy was to leave it to better minds in the War, Navy, and Justice Departments. However, one man nominally in their employ was still determined to have something to say about war crimes policy, and he had to go. In no circumstance, Hackworth held, should Pell and the UNWCC be allowed to direct or even advise on policy. The best way to ensure that was to remove Pell from the Commission and replace him with his assistant, a member of the War Department.

In his December 27 letter to the president, Stettinius had one last question about the appropriation problem: "I would appreciate if you would let me know whether you prefer to tell Mr. Pell of this yourself or would rather have me talk to him."[58] Who was going to tell Pell about the budgetary problem? That was what Stettinius wanted to know. Did it really mean Pell was finished? Surely, somewhere within the budget of the State Department, nine thousand dollars could be found to fund Pell's continued service on the UNWCC. Why not just hire Pell as a regular employee of the department?

Sometime between December 30, 1944, and January 1, 1945, FDR was informed that his meeting with Pell was scheduled for January 9. On the night of the first, FDR directed his son-in-law, Lieutenant Colonel John Boettiger, to compose a memorandum to Stettinius asking for an update on the UNWCC.[59] Whether the president had read Stettinius's December 27 memorandum by that point is not clear. He may have seen it and forgotten its contents. Whatever the case, in a January 3 memorandum, FDR asked Stettinius to send him a "brief report" on Pell's activities on the UNWCC, apparently in preparation for his upcoming meeting with Pell. Specifically, FDR wanted to know what his appointee to the Commission thought. The president requested "the status of the proceedings before the War Crimes Commission, particularly the attitude of the U.S. representative on offenses to be brought against Hitler and the chief Nazi war criminals." In this memorandum, FDR suggested that "the charges should include an indictment for waging aggressive and unprovoked warfare, in violation of the Kellogg[-Briand] Pact.[60] Perhaps these and other charges might be joined in a conspiracy indictment."[61] FDR well knew that many people in several departments—State, War, Justice, and Navy—were working on these very issues, and yet he still wanted to know what his appointee—his friend Pell—thought.

This was not the first time FDR had put in writing his belief that Hitler and his top personnel had participated in a conspiracy. He wrote Stimson exactly that on August 26 when criticizing the War Department's *Handbook of Military Government for Germany*. "The German people as a whole," FDR wrote then, "must have it driven home to them that the whole nation has been engaged in a lawless conspiracy against the decencies of modern civilization."[62] The reference to the Kellogg Pact originated from Colonel William C. Chanler, deputy director of civil affairs under Major General John H. Hilldring, and peacetime law partner with the secretary of war.[63] He first suggested the idea to Stimson in late November, but the secretary had been lukewarm to the idea.[64] But when FDR's son-in-law presented Chanler's aggressive war plan on January 1 to the president, FDR liked it and gave his approval.[65]

In the weeks between Chanler's proposal and FDR's approval, McCloy and Bernays, like Stimson, both expressed doubts about its usefulness. In a memorandum to McCloy on December 1, Chanler expressed his own reservations regarding Bernays's suggestion of using the conspiracy/criminal-organization plan to gain jurisdiction over Nazi crimes against German Jews. He feared it might "establish a precedent that . . . lynching or Jim Crow Laws" would become subjects of "international concern." Adding that such a thing might be good from a moral standpoint, Chanler nonetheless told McCloy that he thought using Bernays's approach "might cause unnecessary opposition to the whole plan."[66] Chanler was repeating the very objection Stimson had put forward to the president back on September 9.[67] It is quite likely that Chanler discussed the problem with Stimson before bringing it up with McCloy, indicating that Stimson himself was still quite troubled about what prosecutions of Nazi crimes against humanity might mean in America. Although no one yet recognized it, Chanler's aggressive warfare idea when paired with Bernays's conspiracy/criminal-organization plan offered a promising solution.

FDR's apparent approval of conspiracy and aggressive warfare in violation of the Kellogg-Briand Pact did not go unnoticed by leaders in the various departments. Presidential support did not end all criticism of Bernays's conspiracy/criminal-organization plan or Chanler's aggressive war idea, but it did make possible the endorsement of these basic ideas by Stettinius, Biddle, and Stimson, which were presented to the president in a January 22 memorandum.[68] Before that happened, however, FDR was to meet with Pell.

On January 6 FDR finally replied to Stettinius's December 27 memorandum. FDR answered each of Stettinius's questions, adding a little something extra. In his own hand, FDR wrote the following in the margin and returned it to Stettinius: "ERS Jr, OK—You do it—at last, FDR."[69] So apparently, it was "OK" for Stettinius to discuss with Stimson and McCloy the budgetary problem and the possibility of Hodgson replacing Pell. As to which one of them—the secretary of state or the president—was to tell Pell he was not to return to London and his place on the UNWCC, FDR wanted Stettinius to do it. But what about those two words: "at last"? Why did FDR write them? What did they mean? Was FDR referring to Stettinius's assurance that war crimes policy was being discussed within the War, Navy, and Justice Departments, as well as with the British and that "a proposal will be laid before" the president shortly? Was FDR simply expressing his satisfaction that he would soon have something in writing to examine? Good reason exists for this interpretation.

Nearly two months had passed since the secretary of war had first informed FDR about the conspiracy/criminal-organization plan on November 21, 1944. Stimson found that FDR was "greatly interested" in what he had to say then, and more than that, the president had given "his very frank approval" to the conspiracy/criminal-organization plan. Stimson had expected some opposition from the president, considering his approval of summary execution at the Quebec Conference the previous September, but in his diary he wrote, "In fact he was very nice about it."[70]

Since there was, as yet, no official document covering war crimes policy for the president to approve, by January he was probably quite anxious to see something in writing. The United States needed to have a reasonably firm grasp on war crimes policy prior to FDR's trip to Yalta. Stettinius's suggestion that one was soon to be in his hands, then, explains those words "at last." Pell and the UNWCC were no longer important or even necessary to war crimes policy. Of course, FDR still wanted to meet with Pell and get his thoughts. The budgetary problem simply gave FDR a convenient way to take Pell off the Commission, which would surely signal to everyone that war crimes policy would be directed from Washington but in consultation with Churchill and Stalin at Yalta.

A more sinister interpretation of the meaning of those two words, "at last," is worth considering. The State Department had never wanted Herbert Pell and had sought his removal from almost the moment of his appointment. In the spring of 1944, the department had delivered to Pell what he interpreted as contradictory instructions—one set from the State Department and another from the president. Believing that the president wanted him to do one thing and the State Department another, Pell understandably chose the higher authority. Faced with continued State Department intransigence, Pell took other measures to promote his (and what he believed to be the president's) cause by attempting to publicize the Commission's problems. He also enlisted the help of Jewish organizations, the Treasury Department, and the War Refugee Board. Finally, in the fall of 1944, Pell leaked his story to the press. Given this final transgression, the State Department was able to force the president to remove his appointee, "at last." Lack of appropriations was simply an efficient reason to fire Pell.

Two documented opportunities existed for Stettinius—and one for Hackworth—to discuss Pell and the appropriations issue in person between the Stettinius letter to the president of December 27, 1944, and FDR's January 6, 1945, response. The first was a fifty-minute meeting, from 2:10 to 3:00 P.M. on December 30, when Stettinius met with FDR at the White House; also present was Charles E. Bohlen.[71] At the time, Bohlen worked on Soviet issues for State. He had also been FDR's interpreter at Tehran in 1943 and would do so again at the upcoming Yalta Conference. The likely and obvious topic of discussion at this meeting was Yalta. Nothing exists in the record to indicate that the issue of war crimes arose.

A meeting on January 2 most likely covered war crimes policy at least in part—again, probably in preparation for Yalta. According to Grace Tully's appointment calendar, the forty-five-minute meeting began at 12:15 P.M. and included eight members of the State Department, among them: Stettinius, Undersecretary of State Joseph Grew, Assistant Secretary of State Dean Acheson, Bohlen, and legal adviser Green H. Hackworth.[72] The extent to which war crimes policy was discussed is unknown, but one thing for certain never came up. No one present at the meeting—not Stettinius, not Hackworth, not FDR—brought up the appropriation problem.

After Pell was removed, Dean Acheson sent Hackworth a memorandum demanding an explanation as to how and why Pell was not returned to London and his position on the UNWCC. Acheson was not a man to be forgetful. If the issue had been brought up at the White House on January 2, there would have been no need for Acheson's inquiry or Hackworth's four-page explanation, which, not incidentally, exaggerated the lengths to which Hackworth and his staff went in trying to keep the funding for Pell.[73]

One final opportunity existed for Stettinius to bring up Pell and the appropriations issue. Again at the White House on January 8, Stettinius met FDR with two department staffers in tow, James Dunn and Dr. Leo Pasvolsky.[74] No record exists as to what was discussed, but this was after FDR had read and responded to Stettinius's December 27 letter. The president, having told Stettinius to let Pell know, there existed no pressing need to bring it up. Also, given what happened the very next day, when Pell met FDR at the White House, it is difficult, if not impossible to believe that Stettinius raised the issue.

Around 10:30 on the morning of January 9, Pell stopped by Hackworth's office at the State Department. Before meeting with the president, Pell wanted to know if there had been any new developments in London since he had last met with Stettinius on December 21. Hackworth told Pell that there had been two new developments, both of which Pell already knew. First, the Commission had decided to appoint a "central investigating officer" to manage all cases. Second, and more important, the chairman of the UNWCC, Sir Cecil Hurst, had resigned allegedly due to declining health.[75] The *New York Times* reported on January 6 that Pell was the likely replacement, but Hackworth did not mention that to Pell.[76]

A telephone call then came in for Pell from the White House. They were moving his meeting with the president up fifteen minutes to 12:15 P.M. According to the State Department summary of the meeting, at that, Pell "took leave" and went to other appointments. Those included one at the War Department, but not before he scheduled a 2:45 P.M. meeting that afternoon with Stettinius, presumably to go over any details following his discussion with FDR.[77]

Pell recounted a slightly different version of this morning meeting. He wanted to know if there had been any change in his status, not just any changes that had taken place in London. Hackworth told Pell, "No, there had been no change."[78] Of course, there had been a major change regarding Pell's status. He would not be going back to London. Hackworth had decided to leave that detail to the president, despite orders to the contrary.

As with his previous meeting with FDR, the June 1943 appointment following his selection as U.S. representative to the UNWCC, we only have Pell's recollections of their January 9, 1945, discussion. Pell reported to the president his various activities on the Commission, including his efforts to move beyond existing international law to hold Axis war criminals responsible for all their crimes, including those against their own nationals, many of whom were Jews. Pell wrote that FDR "agreed" with his position that every member of the Gestapo should be brought to justice. As Pell understood it, the president had always agreed with him on that account. Toward the close of their discussion, Pell informed the president that the chairman of the Commission had resigned. At this, FDR told Pell to take over the position himself. According to Pell, FDR's final words to him were, "Go back as quickly as you can and get yourself appointed chairman."[79]

As unbelievable as it may be, just three days after telling Stettinius to go ahead and remove Pell, FDR told Pell not only to get back to work in London as soon as possible but also to take on an even more important post. Could FDR simply have forgotten that he had already consented to Pell's removal? FDR may have thought the budget issue was only a temporary obstruction. Perhaps he had changed his mind. Since the way was now open for Pell to become chair, maybe FDR wanted Pell to return. Or maybe the president was just trying to avoid an embarrassing situation with a close friend, knowing full well that what he was saying was simply not possible. One thing was sure; Herbert Pell was entirely unprepared for what was to happen next.

Assuming Pell's recollection of his meeting with FDR is accurate, and there is little reason to doubt it, things could not have gone better from his perspective.[80]

Later that day he wrote FDR that the conversation they had "was most satisfactory."[81] Not only had the president reassured Pell that he agreed with the positions he had taken on the Commission but FDR also said he wanted him to assume an even more prominent role, as the next chair.

A reenergized Pell returned that afternoon to the State Department to see Stettinius and make arrangements to get back to London as soon as possible, which, after all, was what the president had ordered him to do. Waiting for Pell in the secretary's office with Stettinius was Hackworth. In an offhanded manner, Hackworth callously informed Pell that notwithstanding what the president may have said, Pell would not be returning to London. When the last Congress adjourned back in December, he said, it had done so failing to vote for any appropriation for the War Crimes Commission. There was "nothing left to be done," Hackworth told him. Pell's office in London would have to be closed, and U.S. representation on the Commission would have to be assumed by "some other regular official," perhaps a War Department officer or even Ambassador Winant. It was all very simple and tidy; Congress was to blame. Pell's tenure on the UNWCC was over.[82]

Pell may have been politically naïve, but once he got over the shock, he quickly saw through Hackworth's pretext. Seething, an indignant Pell pointed out that Hackworth should have told him about it that morning.[83] At that, Stettinius interjected himself into the conversation, but in supporting his subordinate, he only made things worse. He explained to Pell that the president had already been informed of the situation prior to his meeting with Pell: "We had no reason to suppose that the president would not have the matter in mind when he talked with [you]." How could that be? Pell simply could not bring himself to believe it. It was unconscionable for Hackworth not to have told Pell in advance of the meeting, but Pell had come to expect such actions by Hackworth. Still incensed, Pell told both men that he had just discussed with the president both his work on the Commission and his getting back to London. Moreover, Pell said, "The President had approved of his becoming Chairman."[84]

Pell reiterated that Hackworth should have told him of the budget development prior to his meeting with the president. According to Pell, Hackworth replied with some pleasure, "You were the president's appointee and not mine, and it was none of my business to inform you."[85] Pell did not know just how far from the truth that statement was. The president, in fact, had told the State Department to let Pell know. It *was* Hackworth's "business" to tell him.

The State Department summary of the conversation recorded Hackworth replying even more duplicitously: "That he had only been asked [by Pell] regarding developments in London; that Mr. Pell was the president's appointee and that he, Mr. Hackworth, was not authorized to speak for the president nor could he properly anticipate the president in a matter peculiarly between him and Mr. Pell."[86] Again, dutifully supporting his subordinate, Stettinius agreed with Hackworth, stating that the legal adviser's "position was correct." He added, however, that had he been in on the morning meeting, he would have told Pell in advance about the budgetary problem.[87] That had to come as little consolation to Pell, who never thought much of Stettinius. Years later, Pell still had nothing positive to say about the secretary, calling him "one of the stupidest men that I have ever known."[88] Closing their conversation, Stettinius told Pell that he would discuss the matter with the president and contact him; barring that, Stettinius would have the president get in touch with Pell directly.[89]

As soon as Pell left the State Department, Stettinius wasted no time in calling the White House. Unable to speak with the president directly, he had Grace Tully write down a message. "The Secretary fears that Mr. Pell will insist on seeing you again," Tully recorded, "so he asks that you turn the whole thing over to him [Stettinius] to handle." Stettinius then asked Tully to tell FDR that he "will have to assign an Army Officer to carry on the work at least until June when the Congress may appropriate the necessary funds to take care of Mr. Pell's salary, etc."[90]

Had Stettinius completely forgotten about his December 27 memorandum and the president's reply? FDR had already agreed to all of this on January 6. Aware of the president's failing health, perhaps Stettinius was concerned that FDR had simply forgotten. Worse yet, at least from Stettinius's viewpoint, perhaps the president had changed his mind. That may explain why Stettinius floated the possibility that Congress might later appropriate funds for Pell. Why that could not happen until June, the secretary did not say. Nor was there any consideration as to how nonsensical it would be for Pell to wait six months before returning to his post. In any case, the content of Stettinius's dictation to Tully demonstrates convincingly that FDR did want—at least at that moment—Pell to return to London "quickly" and replace Hurst as UNWCC chair.

Upon leaving the State Department, Pell returned to his favorite haunt in Washington, the Metropolitan Club, to fire off a letter to the president. He was sure that FDR would not let such an outrage stand. Pell told the president how he had been handled at State, recounting both his morning and afternoon meetings with Hackworth. Pitting the department as working to embarrass them both, Pell wrote, "I suggested to Mr. Hackworth that it would have been better to have informed me of this [appropriations problem] before I went to the White House rather than let you and me make fools of ourselves discussing a subject which he knew to be impossible."[91]

Pell wanted to see FDR again as soon as possible to solve a problem that he believed was easily surmountable by presidential order. He told the president he felt he had "a right to ask for another interview," given what had happened. "It is needless for me to say that this will affect the prestige of the United States," Pell advised, and then added, "or at whom the blow is ultimately struck."[92] A pencil notation in a secretary's hand on the president's copy of Pell's letter spoke volumes: "not acknowledged."[93] A perfunctory telegram had been sent by Pa Watson instead: "No possible chance to arrange appointment for you with the President at present time."[94]

Despite what Stettinius had said, Pell could not bring himself to believe that his friend, the president had known about the problem when they met earlier that day. How could FDR not have told him? Certainly, he would have, had he known. Surely, FDR would not have betrayed a loyal and lifelong friend. How could the president have asked Pell to get back to London as quickly as possible and get appointed chair knowing that it was impossible? Pell could never bring himself to believe that FDR could have done such a thing, not then or ever.

FDR had appointed Pell as U.S. representative on the UNWCC back on June 10, 1943, with a scribble to Secretary of State Cordell Hull that read, "OK, FDR."[95] Nineteen months later, another presidential scribble to a different secretary of state approved Pell's removal from the UNWCC: "ERS Jr, OK—You do it—at last, FDR."[96]

Pell chose to believe that the State Department had orchestrated his removal against the desires of the president. And why had they done so? To Pell, "It was perfectly obvious that all this was designed to get me out because I had so vigorously upheld the cause of the victims in Germany."[97] Pell had taken up at the behest of the president the cause of seeking justice for the extermination of Europe's Jews and other minorities, and he was convinced the State Department removed him from his post for this very reason. Pell believed his personal reputation was at stake as well as the honor of the United States, to say nothing of the word of his friend the president.

Unwilling to go quietly (and inexplicably, no one had directly ordered him to remain silent), Pell was prepared to take his case to the American people, if it became necessary. Pell was too much of a gentleman, too loyal to the president to say anything about it, but Pell noticed his friend's condition. What Pell did next indicated that he believed the weary, overworked chief executive did not know all the facts or, worse, was being manipulated by the State Department.

Pell still had no idea of the extent to which the War Department had come up with a plan to seek justice for Nazi war crimes, including the Holocaust. Hackworth had kept all of that from Pell. The events of the next few weeks would show just how worried Pell was. It just might be that, from Pell's perspective, Hackworth and his allies at State had succeeded. There would be no justice for the persecuted and exterminated millions. Pell was not about to give up. Considering the stakes, he simply could not do so.

CHAPTER 11

STATE ACQUIESCES

"A Punishment That Is Speedy and Just—and Severe"

The great criticism of the United States in other countries is not based on a distrust of our intentions, but on a lack of confidence that we will carry them through.

Herbert C. Pell to President Franklin Roosevelt, March 5, 1945

Just two days after his appointment with the president, the dilemma of what to do about Axis atrocities against Axis nationals went public. On January 11, *New York Times* London correspondent John MacCormac reported that Sir Cecil Hurst had resigned as British member and chair of the UNWCC in protest against his country's failure to act on the American proposal to punish Axis nationals for atrocities against its own citizens. This contradicted earlier reports in the British press that indicated Hurst resigned for health reasons. MacCormac reported that this unexpected revelation was the likely reason for Pell's returning to the United States to meet with FDR. The timing of Hurst's resignation and Pell's meeting with the president seemed an obvious signal that Pell was to become the new chair. Pell and FDR did discuss Hurst's resignation and Pell taking over, but no one yet knew about Pell's removal by the State Department. That was to change very shortly.[1]

MacCormac specifically laid the blame for Hurst's resignation on the British Foreign Office and Foreign Secretary Anthony Eden. Pell had first proposed punishment for crimes against Jews in Germany and Hungary the previous March in what MacCormac described as "a dramatic speech." According to MacCormac, Pell was acting on "President Roosevelt's promise that these atrocities would be punished and he [Pell] said that the President had meant what he said." MacCormac had no idea, however, that Pell had been acting against the instructions of the State Department—or that State Department policy differed little from that of the British—consequently, his report suggested erroneously, "Another Anglo-American disagreement had been provoked." He also did not yet know—no one outside the administration did—that Pell had been removed.[2]

Pell did not make any immediate statement about his firing, nor did the State Department. Pell hoped he might still have an opportunity to meet with the president prior to FDR's leaving for Yalta and somehow get the decision reversed. Over the next week, press reports from London continued to suggest that Pell might become the next chair. Everyone seemed to be waiting for Pell's return and a public statement on the position of the United States regarding war crimes policy.[3]

On January 13 Hackworth granted an interview with a reporter from *Time* magazine on the condition that all information "was for background information only and was in no wise to be attributed." Among the questions posed to Hackworth was that "of atrocities by enemy nationals against its own nationals." According to his summary of the conversation, Hackworth "told him that that was a rather broad subject and that while we all deplored such atrocities . . . I was not prepared to say how that situation would be resolved." He did add, however, that he thought atrocities should be punished. As to Pell becoming the next chair of the UNWCC, Hackworth responded in perfect doublespeak: "The Commission would elect his [Hurst's] successor, but I had no way of telling who the successor might be." Hackworth was also asked if Pell was headed to Yalta with FDR. "I said," wrote Hackworth, "that I had no information on that question."[4]

With public interest in war criminals growing, Pell sent off another letter to the president on January 17. While still hoping for a personal meeting, Pell seemed resigned to his fate. He even apologized for his lack of information at their last meeting, as if it had been his own fault. With some humility, he told FDR, "I am awaiting your orders and those of the Secretary of State." This tone was quite different from that of his January 9 letter. Pell requested that FDR appoint him to the post of Librarian of Congress, "if for any reason" he could not return to London. The bulk of this letter related how he might succeed as librarian, despite having no previous experience for such a post.[5] Pell's motivation for this suggestion is not clear. Perhaps he was giving the president one last opportunity to purchase his silence about what had happened.

Pell received his answer from the president a week later in the form of a letter from Grace Tully, sent only after FDR had left for Yalta: "The President has asked me to acknowledge your letter of January 17 and to tell you he wishes much he could have had another opportunity to talk with you, but just at present this is impossible." FDR would keep Pell's request "in mind," Tully closed, and "arrange an appointment sometime later on."[6]

Pell expected the noncommittal response he received from FDR via Tully. He had already received the previous week a letter from Stettinius reiterating the reason he could not return to London, perhaps sent at the president's request. "As I explained to you in our conversation [on the ninth] . . . there is no available money with which to finance your work with the Commission."[7] Previously, when they had met, Stettinius had assured Pell he would discuss the matter with the president and let him know.[8] Although it had taken more than a week to get back to Pell, Stettinius had in fact spoken with FDR. "I promptly took the matter up with the President as I promised," he told Pell, "and I fear that he did not have a clear understanding of the matter at the time I discussed it with you." Hoping to put Pell off permanently and end any future discussion of the matter, Stettinius added, "He now fully realizes that because of the lack of funds it will be impossible for anyone to retain the position as American Representative on the War Crimes Commission until further funds are available. The President and I are deeply sorry that you cannot return to London."[9]

Stettinius's letter failed to silence Pell. If anything, it infuriated him further. Pell knew that it was not "impossible for anyone" to continue in London due to lack of funds.[10] Hodgson and several staff members, for example, were still in London representing the United States. Funds did exist, just not for Herbert Pell.

Stettinius did succeed in clearing up Pell's confusion about FDR's actions. How could the president have told Pell to get back to London and become chair if he knew it to be impossible? FDR had simply forgotten about the problem owing considerably to his failing health and the weight of other matters. As Stettinius gently put it, "He did not have a clear understanding of the matter."[11] This explanation made sense to Pell, to a degree, although he would have much preferred to have Stettinius tell him that FDR had changed his mind—that he knew about the problem but wanted Pell returned nonetheless.

The visible change in FDR's health was obvious to Pell, who saw the president for the first time in nearly a year and a half when they met on January 9.[12] An ill and distracted FDR might very easily have forgotten that he had acquiesced to Pell's removal. It is difficult to believe that a healthy FDR would have allowed State Department officials to ignore so blatantly his instructions that they inform Pell. He would not have allowed Hackworth or Stettinius to embarrass him in such a manner in front of his friend. From Pell's perspective, if FDR had remembered, someone in the State Department would have received at the very least a reprimand for not informing Pell prior to his meeting with the president.

Whatever the case, with FDR off to Yalta and the State Department aligned resolutely against him, Pell held out little hope for reversing his removal. Still, the president had not directly asked for his silence, nor had anyone else, although Hackworth had alluded to it in early December. But even if anyone had—except for FDR—it would not have meant much to a man like Pell. Biographer Leonard Baker wrote that Pell had no career ambitions or any "worry about future honors."[13] While this may have been true to a limited extent, Pell was quite concerned about protecting his reputation. He believed he had acted properly while on the Commission and that history would prove his actions appropriate, even noble, considering the scale of the Nazi crime. Moreover, he knew that he had been acting at the behest of the president.

Cast off nonetheless from the administration and resigned that his dismissal was probably irrevocable, Pell was free to go on the offensive. He felt he had to because no one had confided to him the extent of war crimes deliberations within the administration in Washington. Pell was careful, however, to castigate the State Department as acting in opposition to the president, which was what he believed had happened. Pell had three principal goals: protecting his own reputation, protecting the integrity of the United States, and seeing to it that the Allies sought justice for the Holocaust—and not necessarily in that order. He was convinced that it was his duty to ensure that the United States stood behind all its declarations. FDR had announced many times the United States' determination to bring all war criminals to justice. Although he was no longer American representative on the UNWCC, Pell still believed he was the man for the job.

Meanwhile, back in London on January 24, Commission members discussed the efficacy of the United States and the United Kingdom, issuing a joint statement regarding the UNWCC's "attitude towards recent press statements." Although the British representative said the Foreign Office would be "pleased to join in such a statement," an American military officer representing the United States in the absence of Pell and his assistant had instructions that "the United States Government was not prepared to take part in the proposed joint statement." At issue was "secrecy." The members elected to put off any decision on changing policy as it related to the press until later and after the election of a new chair in the wake of Hurst's resignation. Incredibly, according to the UNWCC minutes, "The [U.S.] State Department had requested that the election be postponed until Mr. Pell's return." Asked about when that might be, the acting American representative "stated that there was no objection to holding the election in a fortnight."[14] The Commission members were left to believe that Pell would return within two weeks, and it certainly seemed that upon his arrival he would become the next chair of the UNWCC. Of course, that was not to be.

Pell's next step was to return to the State Department and visit an old acquaintance, Joseph C. Grew. Grew was serving as acting secretary in the absence of Stettinius, who had accompanied the president to Yalta. Pell first met Grew in 1903 during a winter break from Harvard while skating on a frozen lake at Tuxedo Park. A young woman had fallen through the ice that day. Grew responded first, but he also fell in the icy water. Pell was next to attempt the rescue, and down he went. Luckily for all three, other rescuers using ropes and ladders pulled them out.[15] Pell now looked for similar unexpected heroics; perhaps Grew would see things Pell's way, although Pell held little hope of changing anything. It was at least worth an attempt to discuss the situation with him and see what might come of it.

Meeting with Grew on January 24, Pell explained in some detail his actions while on the Commission. Pell met with Hackworth in advance of his meeting with Grew, attempting to acquire as much information as he could. He should have known better. Hackworth was noncommittal to most of Pell's queries, suggesting Grew was the one with whom he should speak. Commenting on Pell's attitude, Hackworth noted, "Mr. Pell seemed to be in an agreeable frame of mind, but it was apparent from the general tenor of his conversation that he was hoping that he would be regarded as still in office awaiting a new appropriation."[16]

With Grew, Pell began by informing the acting secretary that several people had contacted him, he said, "to write and to undertake radio broadcasts explaining the work of the Commission." Grew took this as a threat. He believed Pell was insinuating that he would take his story fully to the press if he were not returned forthwith to London. Obviously prepared by Hackworth and informed of Pell's previous leaks to the press, Grew reminded Pell in the form of a rhetorical question that his work on the Commission was not for public consumption.[17]

According to Grew's summary of their conversation, he then asked Pell "point blank" if his statement was "intended to be in the nature of a threat." Pell stated that it was not, to which Grew replied, "But you have just told me that you were considering such publicity work and that it was in order to decide whether you should undertake it or not that you wanted to be sure of your future status."[18]

"I said to you only that I had been asked to undertake such publicity work," Pell quickly countered.[19]

Apparently pacified, Grew said, "The ethics of publicly discussing the work of the Commission would seem to me to be very questionable."[20]

Pell then suggested to Grew what he had previously put forward to both Hackworth and Stettinius. Why not just give him a position in the State Department or a commission in the army and send him back to London, thereby avoiding the budget problem? "Salary," Pell said, "was of no concern to him." Before Grew could respond, Pell made a counterproposal that the department should at least make some kind of a public statement explaining the reason for his removal and that his service had been "commendable."[21] If only Pell had given Grew time to respond.

Far from a threat, Pell seemed to be offering Grew a deal. If Grew were to announce to the press what had happened and why, making sure to praise Pell, Pell would be satisfied and remain silent—at least that was the implication. Apparently understanding Pell's proposition, Grew ended their conversation. He would think over the matter, Grew said, and telephone Pell at the Metropolitan Club with an answer in a day or two, adding, however, that Pell should not get his hopes up about anything changing anytime soon.[22]

Pell had laid his own trap for the State Department in attempting to get them to announce his removal from the UNWCC. From Pell's perspective, he would then be free to defend himself and respond to reporters' inquiries without any question of ethics. Pell was certain everyone would see the department's explanation for what it was—nothing more than a poorly disguised deceit.

In any case, with or without Pell's goading, the department could not wait much longer before making some announcement. Just as it had been during the interminable months-long delay in getting Pell to London after his appointment in the summer of 1943, the press and Commission members in London were beginning to wonder: where was Herbert Pell? Why had he not returned to London? Acting Secretary Grew offered the answer in a poorly written announcement to the press on January 26: "I am sorry this morning to have to announce that on account of the failure of the appropriation recommended by the Department of funds to cover the salary and expenses of Mr. Herbert C. Pell as American member of the United Nations War Crimes Commission, it will not be possible to return him to London."[23]

After expressing his and the department's appreciation for Pell's service, Grew then stated that Pell's deputy, Lieutenant Colonel Hodgson, would continue representing the United States in Pell's stead. Ill-considered to the point of recklessness, Grew gave no explanation as to how it was possible for Hodgson to be paid but not Pell. Trying to pass this announcement off as inconsequential to American policy aims, Grew noted, "There will be no diminution in the interest or activity of this Government in the work of the Commission or in the general subject of the punishment of war criminals."[24] Clearly, Grew was not thinking. This statement seemed to beg for questions from the press.

After Pell had been back in Washington for more than a month, it became public knowledge that Hurst had not resigned because he was ill; instead, it was because the British government failed to support the prosecution of Axis criminals for their crimes against Axis nationals, the very thing Pell himself had recommended the Commission do in March 1944. More than two weeks had passed since Pell met with the president, and he had still not returned to London. Many had expected him to replace Hurst and become chair, but the department announced Pell had been removed. It must have been obvious to everyone that Pell had been fired. The failure of Congress to appropriate funds was simply a convenient pretext. Given what had just transpired, did the State Department really expect anyone to believe that the United States was serious about pursuing war criminals?

Grew tried to deflect attention from his announcement concerning Pell by discussing Hungarian armistice terms. As soon as he paused, the gathered press began questioning Pell's removal: What did Grew mean "by the failure of the appropriations recommended for salaries"? Was Pell referred to specifically in the appropriation? Was Congress dissatisfied with Pell specifically or the Commission? How could Hodgson be retained if there were no funds? The most important question, "Will Mr. Pell be reappointed to this assignment?" was not answered.[25]

The Washington correspondent for the *New York Times,* Bertram D. Hulen, wasted no time in interviewing Pell about his dismissal. The title of Hulen's January 27 front-page article summed it up delicately: "Pell Leaves War Crimes Board; He Favored Wider Punishments."[26] The *Washington Post* was more straightforward in its conclusions about what had happened: "Pell Says Stand for Avenging German Jews Cost Him Post." The *Post* quoted Pell, asserting, "It is just damned nonsense that the reason for not returning me to London is lack of money." Moreover, the article noted, "Pell expressed the blunt view that technical questions of international law aside, crimes against racial minorities should be treated as 'crimes against humanity.'" Pell made clear that he was certain the opposition to his continued service on the Commission originated in the State Department, not the White House.[27]

The *Post* article then quoted Pell making a statement that must have made those members of the administration who were working on setting American war crimes policy, particularly the secretary of war, wince. In his own way, Herbert Pell had hit upon the most basic difficulty underlying any plan that was to hold Axis war criminals accountable for atrocities committed on the basis of racial persecution against its own nationals.

According to *Post* writer Ben W. Gilbert, "[Pell] sharply challenged the point of view that 'what a country does to its own people is its own business,' and [he] added that although 'technical students of international law' might feel that way, he was certain neither President Roosevelt or the mass of Americans felt that way." Henry L. Stimson, for one, would not have been as certain about that as was Pell. From Stimson's point of view—and in his own words—there existed "no reason in law or in justice why we should intervene in the matter to punish the Germans who had been guilty of killing the Jews than Germany would have the right to intervene in our country to punish the people who are lynching the Negroes."[28]

The last thing Stimson would have wanted was a public discussion about American racial persecution and the vicissitudes of international law. The revelations surrounding Pell's firing, however, afforded African Americans the opportunity to see the hypocrisy of it all—but what if they agreed with Pell? What if they, like Pell, were ready to challenge the idea that "what a country does to its own people is its own business"? Would this group of citizens demand the intervention of some other nation or nations in seeking punishment for racial persecution in America? Faced with such a threat, perhaps American leaders might take on the task themselves of rooting out racism at home.

The game was on. What quickly became known in the press as the "Pell Affair" was set to force the United States into being more up-front about its strategy for bringing Axis war criminals to justice. Any hopes that State Department officials may have had at putting off revealing plans for the prosecution of war criminals were seriously threatened by the growing controversy surrounding Pell's firing.

The United Press reported in the wake of Grew's announcement that the Hebrew Committee of National Liberation was "naturally apprehensive" about Pell's "withdrawal." That Committee pointed out the importance of Pell's enduring support for "a positive course of action on crimes committed against the Hebrew people," and it called on the United States to issue a statement "that crimes committed against Jews in Europe, irrespective of territory or citizenship of the victim, be considered as war crimes and punished as such." Of course, this was precisely what Pell for months had been advocating that the UNWCC do, and what he believed the president had directed him to do, contrary to the instructions of the State Department.[29]

From London, the Associated Press reported that "Allied diplomatic quarters" were quite surprised to learn of Pell's dismissal, since he was expected to become the Commission's new chair.[30] The American Jewish Conference sent letters of protest to Congress and to Acting Secretary Grew, urging that Pell be returned to London without delay.[31] Still others sent their protests directly to the White House.[32]

The next day Pell confided to another reporter his fears that both the United States and Great Britain "will lose leadership among European nations unless they adopt a strong policy toward Nazi war criminals." European nations, Pell observed, would begin to gravitate toward the Soviet Union, which was already meting out harsh punishment to Nazis for all their crimes. Pell had made a very similar point to Hackworth when they met on December 7, 1944.[33] He now felt free to say whatever was on his mind. From Pell's perspective, he was the injured party, and he had every right to speak out. In so doing, he believed he was not simply defending himself; he was defending his president and the honor of his country. As the controversy grew, however, it turned out that the State Department needed to defend itself, not Pell.

Following the botched announcement on January 26, 1945, and in the wake of Pell's public contention that he was fired for his stand on atrocities, Grew found that he was under increasing pressure to explain himself—and to clarify U.S. policy on war criminals. Just three days later, at a January 29 press conference, Grew did his best to do exactly that. The State Department's position on war criminals was "unchanged," Grew announced, and they intended to press for the appropriation dropped by Congress. In fact, he said, the Department had already prepared and sent to Congress a new request to fund U.S. representation on the UNWCC. What about Pell? Would he be returned once funding was made available? Grew declined to say, stating only, "I won't touch on that particular point today."[34] The implication was obvious; money would be sought, but not for Pell.

Columnist Drew Pearson then asked about Pell's contention that "dissatisfaction" existed within the State Department over his position that Nazi atrocities against German nationals, including German Jews, should be treated as war crimes. "Can you tell us, Sir, if the State Department differs with him in that point of view?" Rather than answer the question, Grew read from his prepared statement: "It is the policy of this Government that the Axis leaders and their henchmen who are guilty of war crimes shall be brought to the bar of justice. We in the Government have a definite program . . . which, I can assure you, is comprehensive and forthright." That proclamation satisfied no one, especially Pearson, who noted that Grew did not answer his question.[35]

Attempting to deflect attention from Pearson's question further, Grew announced he wanted to speak briefly "off the record." "This whole subject has a good many difficulties and thorny angles and one of the aspects of this whole subject is the security angle," he said. Thousands of Americans were prisoners of war in Nazi "hands today and the more this whole subject is publicly discussed at present, the greater will be the risk to our prisoners and you know what things the Nazis are capable of; that they will take very good steps to see that so far as possible all traces and evidence of these atrocities are blotted out."

Did Grew really expect the gathered press to believe that Nazis would exterminate American prisoners of war as part of a procedure to destroy evidence of other atrocities if the press continued to publicize war crimes policies? It was nonsensical to consider: committing one set of atrocities to obliterate evidence of another. Undeterred, Grew persisted, "That is the security angle of the whole problem today and it is an exceedingly important angle, and I merely wish, as I say, to pass that thought on to you as patriotic Americans because I think it is of the utmost importance." As if that was sufficient to silence critics like Pearson, Grew concluded, "That is all on the subject."[36]

Just one more question, Pearson said. To him, the main issue seemed "to be the definition of what a war crime is." Would Mr. Grew care to "clarify" what constitutes a war crime?

Grew replied, "Off the record, that is a very complicated subject, as you know. There has been plenty of discussion of it but I am not in a position to say that this is a crime, that is not a crime, or what is a crime."

Pressed again, Grew stated, "Off the record, there are many angles to the whole subject which we are exploring with the utmost determination," but he reiterated that he could not go any further on the matter or "specify exactly what is going to be considered a crime and what is not."

One final time Pearson attempted to confront Grew on the definition of the crimes. "Sir, you gave us a very helpful statement about the attitude of the State Department on the war crimes matter, but if I may say so, my particular question remains unanswered. Would you feel, Sir, that security angles would prevent you from answering that question? You recall what I asked?"

"I recall your question perfectly. Off the record, Mr. Pearson, I would prefer not to answer that question."[37]

Could it be that Grew fully appreciated what was at stake? Did he understand, as he put it, that one of the "good many difficulties and thorny angles" was safeguarding sovereignty, protecting America's social order at home? How could the United States participate in the prosecution of Nazis for crimes based on racial persecution while that same persecution persisted in America? To whatever extent he did grasp the problem, he was careful not to say.

Later that same day from New York, Pell responded to Grew's statements. The State Department's policy toward war criminals, he asserted, would ultimately be judged based upon whom they picked as representative on the UNWCC. That wasn't quite right, obviously, but based on what Pell knew at the time, it was accurate to him. He was, of course, pleased to hear that the department was pressing for funds. He was ready to return to his post, "but they know where I stand," he said. "I stand for hard, rough treatment of every war criminal. They know that I favor Nazis be brought to trial for atrocities against their own Jewish citizens, as well as for their atrocities against people in other countries."[38]

Pell was not about to let up. Grew had failed to clear up anything by not finalizing Pell's status at the press conference. "If I do go back," Pell announced, "it will be with the understanding that I shall not alter the principles I have expressed. I am for condign punishment, nothing less."[39]

Given the department's ongoing unwillingness to announce any specific policy, Pell was more confident than ever that he had been removed for his stance on atrocities against Axis nationals. And he believed the majority of Americans supported him. If department officials really wanted to end the controversy, they were going to have to be more specific about its "comprehensive and forthright" program. At the very least, they were going to have to announce that they supported Pell's ideas.

The following day in a *Washington Post* editorial titled "The Pell Affair," Grew came under the harshest attack yet. The *Post* editorial declared that the acting secretary had been "somewhat disingenuous" by blaming Congress in his first statement. While the appropriation problem was "technically" accurate, the article noted, Grew failed to mention that the department "did not try very hard" to get the appropriation. It was, actually, worse than that; the State Department had made sure the appropriation for Pell was quashed. "The real point at issue between Mr. Pell and the legal lights in the department," the *Post* continued, "is whether the persecution and wholesale murder by the Nazis of German Jews and other racial minorities in Germany are crimes which the United Nations have a right to punish." Pell believed they were, and so did the president, the editorial announced, even quoting FDR's March 24, 1944, statement in which he said, "All who share the guilt shall share the punishment." "But apparently," the *Post* editorial noted, "the President did not make the point clear enough to certain well-entrenched functionaries in the State Department." For Washington insiders, little doubt existed as to the identity of at least one of the "functionaries"—Green H. Hackworth.[40]

The *Post* editorial stated explicitly that the State Department maintained that no precedents existed for which the United Nations could punish Axis criminals for "crimes against humanity perpetrated on German soil." These fell within domestic jurisdiction. As the *Post* had it, this kind of "legalism . . . was responsible for the fiasco" of Versailles, and would certainly bring about another at the end of this war. Pointing out that Grew's second statement offered no definitive policy, the editorial demanded the State Department "take the American people into its confidence."[41]

On February 1, compelled by unceasing pressure, Grew made his third and most explicit pronouncement on American war crimes policy. Grew began, "The Department of State welcomes public discussion of the punishment of war criminals." Referring to several presidential "pledges" over the last three years as the basis for American policy, Grew announced the intention of the United States to bring all Axis criminals to justice for all their crimes. Working toward the "realization of the objectives stated by the President," he said, the State Department in consultation with officials in other departments had been working out proposals to bring Nazi criminals to justice "for the whole broad criminal enterprise devised and executed with ruthless disregard of the very foundation of law and morality, including offenses against the rules of war and against minority elements, Jewish and other groups, and individuals."[42]

Drew Pearson was not satisfied; did Grew's statement include Jewish minorities in Germany and satellite countries? "I think the statement is abundantly clear," Grew replied. To Pearson, the statement allowed for wiggle room. The British, he told Grew at the press conference, had stated publicly that the Allies had "no authority to punish Hitler and his crowd for crimes committed against their own people." The State Department had taken a similar view, he added, and as a result, Sir Cecil Hurst had resigned from the UNWCC and "the decision was reached not to send Mr. Pell back to the Commission." Such circumstances required greater specificity over jurisdiction. Pearson asked Grew if his recitation of the facts was correct.[43]

For background only, not for attribution, Grew reiterated his earlier stance that only the appropriation matter prevented Pell's return to the UNWCC. He made no other comment on Pearson's presentation. After pressing Grew on the details of the appropriation failure, Pearson asked if Pell might be returned to London once funds were made available. As before, Grew did not answer the question.

Pearson then said, "Sir, it seems to me that the crux of the whole misunderstanding . . . is one in which the United States Government should state clearly whether it does or does not favor the punishment of Nazis for crimes committed against Jewish nationals of Germany. This statement does not clarify that point to my satisfaction."

"I am afraid I differ with you on that point," Grew replied. Rereading his statement that Nazi war criminals would be brought to justice for crimes, including those "against minority elements" and "Jewish and other groups," Grew asked Pearson, "Cannot you get everything out of that?

"Yes, Sir," Pearson answered, but only if that also included German nationals.

An obviously frustrated Grew asked, "Is it absolutely necessary to mention the particular place?"

"Is it absolutely necessary to evade it?" Realizing he may have gone too far, Pearson added, "Even if you could say it off the record so that we could be sure of our interpretation."

Grew acquiesced: "I will say this, gentlemen, that I prefer to put this off the record for your guidance. That is very definitely our intention."

Still that was not good enough for Pearson. Grew then equivocated by noting that what the Allies did about war criminals was complicated by the involvement of many nations and that he could not discuss "the machinery or the types of courts or the way things are going to be done." Sensing that Grew was possibly preparing to move into the "security angle" in an attempt to cut him off again, Pearson attacked it—and Grew—directly.

"I am confused on one point," Pearson said. "The last time we met, you informed us that it might be unpatriotic to discuss this question of war crimes, but today this statement says it welcomes it."

Grew replied, "I don't want to argue this question. I am speaking off the record now. I do feel what I said the other day that there is a security angle involved here and I would have preferred not to go any further at the present time on this whole subject but in view of developments which have recently occurred and the desire of our people to know how we stand on this, I believed that it was necessary, in spite of what I said the other day, to give out this statement. I think that this may answer your question, your point which was well raised, I admit."

With Grew cornered, Pearson suggested that he do one of two things: amend the final paragraph with the phrase, "wherever these minorities may be found," or make an additional official statement that German nationals were specifically covered by the United States' war crimes policy. Turning to another State Department official present, Grew said, "I want to make it as clear as I can," suggesting they add "wherever they may be" to the final sentence so that it read, "including offenses against the rules of war and against minority elements, Jewish and other groups, wherever they may be."[44] In the end, the final statement was altered, but the meaning was the same: war criminals were to be brought to justice "for the whole broad criminal enterprise devised and executed with ruthless disregard of the very foundation of law and morality, including offenses, *wherever committed* [emphasis added], against the rules of war and against minority elements, Jewish and other groups, and individuals."[45]

Finally, after months of miscommunication, disagreement, and duplicity on the part of the State Department, Herbert Pell had succeeded —with the considerable help of the persistent Drew Pearson—in getting them to see things his way. He had forced the department to announce American intentions. For Pell, it turned out to be a pyrrhic victory. As Grew had announced it, under the leadership of the president, the United States had always been determined to bring war criminals to justice for all their crimes, including crimes committed against its own citizens. This was inaccurate, of course; it was true insofar as the president and Pell were committed to it, but it had only become American policy in the last few months, and it was not yet finalized. The president himself had yet to approve anything officially. But at least Pell had forced the State Department to announce it would bring Axis war criminals to justice for all their crimes, including those against its own nationals. The Allies would seek justice for the Holocaust.

Hackworth was then left to answer questions from journalists who wanted more information than Grew had offered and from his colleagues at State who could not understand how State had botched things so badly. On February 8 I. F. Stone of *The Nation* telephoned State and spoke directly with Hackworth, who dutifully recorded the conversation. Stone asked first about Pell. He understood that Pell had volunteered to serve without compensation, but that the department had said no. Hackworth told Stone that Title 31, Section 665, of the United States Code prohibited it as if that was the only reason Pell was prohibited from returning.[46] At any time, State or War—or some other department—could have made Pell a regular employee.

Stone asked for an accounting of State's effort to get the funding for Pell. Hackworth explained it to Stone in very much the same language that he had explained it in the letter he composed for Stettinius, which was sent to the president on December 27, 1944. Stone must have accepted it, but he then asked a question that must not have made Hackworth happy: "When [had] Mr. Pell been notified that he was out of office?" Hackworth answered that he "was not certain as to the exact date." He was certain, of course. He was the one who had told Pell on January 9. With this falsehood, Hackworth avoided being asked, and having to answer, why it had taken so long for State to inform Pell of the problem.[47]

Had State made a new request "for another appropriation?" Stone asked. Yes, they had, but Hackworth told Stone he "was not able to give him the exact date." Exact dates had apparently become difficult for Hackworth. Well, then, Stone wanted to know if "Mr. Pell would be returned to London" once Congress approved a new appropriation. For his memorandum, Hackworth recorded, "I said that I was unable to answer that question, since the matter would be one to be decided by the President."[48]

Nonplussed, Stone wondered why Pell simply couldn't operate as a dollar-a-year appointee. That was just not possible, Hackworth told Stone. Based on the law as it related to the President's Emergency Fund, the department "could not draw upon any appropriation for even the dollar a year." If there were any other questions or answers, Hackworth did not record them. He simply summed up their conversation in his memorandum by noting that "Mr. Stone had stated at the outset that he desired merely factual information and did not intend to quote me."[49]

Hackworth's colleague Dean Acheson had been paying attention to the row in the press. He wanted an update on "the war crimes situation." Hackworth tried to be as detailed as possible, and unlike his telephone conversation with Stone, this time he could remember exact dates. But he similarly obscured the truth, writing as if Pell had done great harm by his comments to the press. "This matter has recently become a tempest in a teapot for no good reason," Hackworth began, "owing in large measure to the fact that Mr. Pell is being pictured as a martyr to the cause of the Jews against alleged obstacles being advanced by the Department." Hackworth repeated yet again that only the appropriation issue ended Pell's service on the UNWCC, not his stand to seek justice for the Holocaust.[50]

"He was specifically told, following his return from London," Hackworth noted, "that all were agreed that punishment should be meted out in all these cases, and that it was merely a question of finding a proper and practical method of procedure." Hackworth explained to Acheson that State, War, Navy, and Justice had been working since August to study the development of a proper procedure for "pre-war atrocities against the Jews, and atrocities against German nationals in Germany." Of course, no one apparently felt it necessary to inform Pell that the ideas he had put forth on the UNWCC had been taken up by these departments until his December 7 meeting with Hackworth, and even then, it was in the vaguest of terms. "It was not possible to tell Mr. Pell just what line of procedure was being evolved," Hackworth explained to Acheson, "since the whole matter was regarded by the military authorities as involving elements of security." But the procedure, Hackworth told Acheson, was "sufficiently comprehensive to take care of the whole situation in which the Jews and others are interested." Hackworth wanted Acheson to understand that the entire dust-up in the press was all Pell's doing.[51]

Moreover, according to Hackworth, the State Department had gone to extensive lengths to convince Congress to appropriate funds, offering several examples. On November 27, three State staffers went to Congress and "appeared in support" of funding for Pell. One of the staffers, Katherine Fite, pointed "to the importance of the work of the Commission and the fact that Mr. Pell is our representative." The legal adviser even quoted what Fite had said. "She stated that the matter was 'of such importance and such great interest to our people, if not the world at large, that steps must be taken to deal with the matter.'" Another staffer, G. Howland Shaw, had even pointed to Pell's considerable experience as "a former member of Congress and a former Minister to Portugal and Hungary." Still, Hackworth told Acheson, the House committee failed to fund Pell's position on the UNWCC. A letter from Stettinius—authored by Hackworth, of course—to Senator McKellar, "calling his attention, in strong terms, to the importance attached by the Department to the continuance of the work," resulted in the Senate restoring Pell's funding. But somehow—Hackworth offered no explanation to Acheson—funding for Pell on the UNWCC was "eliminated in the conference between the Senate and the House on the bill as passed by the Senate." Consequently, when the bill was passed on December 22, funding for Pell on the UNWCC had been eliminated.[52]

Having narrated what happened—as he wished it to be known—and to reinforce the uprightness of all State's actions—especially his own—Hackworth related how State had informed Pell. "On January 9, the Secretary saw Mr. Pell, who had come down from New York, and explained the situation to him and stated that under the circumstances the Department was without authority to return him to London." And that was that, save for the "formal letter . . . to Mr. Pell explaining the exact nature of the difficulty." Pell's charge in the press that the funding issue was "damned nonsense," Hackworth made clear to Acheson, was itself just that: "damned nonsense."[53] If Acheson or anyone else in the department questioned Hackworth's recitation, no record of it exists. As for Pell, he held little hope of returning to the UNWCC. Short of presidential intervention, Pell was to remain consigned to the sidelines. There was not much left he could do or say until the president returned from Yalta.

On March 1, 1945, the president addressed a special joint session of Congress. Pell, like most Americans, paid close attention. Next to his performance following the Japanese attack on Pearl Harbor, this was perhaps his most stirring appearance before that body, but not just for what he had to say. Entering down the aisle in his homemade wheelchair, for the first time, he publicly acknowledged his incapacity. As only he could, he brushed his infirmity aside with considerable aplomb. "I hope you will pardon me for this unusual posture of sitting down during the presentation, but I know that you will realize that it makes it a lot easier for me not to have to carry about ten pounds of steel around on the bottom of my legs."[54]

Considering everything that had happened in the president's absence, Pell was as much as ever determined to see FDR now that he had returned. So Pell did what he had done so many times over the past year and a half; he wrote a personal letter to his friend. "I am glad to see your statement that war criminals would be punished," he began.[55] During the president's address to Congress, in explaining what "unconditional surrender" meant for Germany, he had included the promise of a "speedy and just—and severe" punishment for war criminals.[56] This, of course, was not the first time he had done so. Pell got right to his point. He had been the one, who, for more than a year, had been laboring to carry out the pledges of the president. "Had I not continuously pushed the Commission according to your instructions," he said, very little would have been accomplished.[57]

Although he left it unwritten, his question was clear enough: after all he had done for his friend, was FDR really going to abandon him?

Despite Grew's announcement, which was more than a month old by then, Pell alleged nothing positive had been done to move war crimes planning forward. While he should have known better, Pell still believed that the UNWCC was the prime locus for policy and that his return was necessary. Not only had State Department officials informed him that various departments were working on forming policy, it had also been announced publicly the previous month that a section had been created in the Office of the Army Judge Advocate General to gather war crimes evidence.[58] The UNWCC had become at best window dressing and, more likely, at least from the perspective of American officials, an unwanted appendage.

The president did not reply to Pell's March 5 letter for more than two weeks and then not before Pell had sent him a second request for an appointment.[59] He had "carefully examined" Pell's March 5 letter, FDR said, and talked the whole matter over with Stettinius, whom he had also asked to discuss the matter with Pell. FDR closed this brief letter suggesting that Pell "arrange with him [Stettinius] for an appointment." This was not what Pell wanted to hear. And like so many of his previous letters over the last year to Pell, this letter, at the request of the president, had been composed by Hackworth, and, as before, Pell had no awareness of that fact.[60] In an accompanying memorandum to the draft reply, over Grew's signature, Hackworth took one final parting shot at Pell. "He makes a number of extravagant statements [in his March 5 letter]," Hackworth wrote, "but I do not think that we need to go into them.[61] A proper accounting of State Department activities was the last thing Hackworth wanted.

FDR sent the suggested letter to Pell, having made no changes, just as he had done so many times before. But unlike previous letters to Pell that were signed fully, "Franklin D. Roosevelt," this letter contained only a hesitant and painfully scribbled "FDR."[62] The end was nearing for the president; in a little more than a month, he would be gone, and with him would go any hope Pell held onto that he might return to UNWCC—or some other position within the administration. But before that happened, Pell had a chance to answer the growing questions in Congress.

Pell had wanted desperately to meet with the president prior to testifying before the House Foreign Affairs Committee on March 22. It was only natural that Congress would get involved, having been blamed by the State Department for the appropriation problem. By then, a new appropriation was pending to fund

American expenses on the UNWCC.[63] The Foreign Affairs Committee wanted to know what had happened regarding Pell and his abrupt departure from the UNWCC. If American representation on the Commission was going to continue to receive funding, at the very least, the committee wanted an accounting of UNWCC accomplishments.

Meanwhile, the State Department made one last attempt to purchase Pell's cooperation prior to his testifying, sending him a letter over the signature of the secretary of state. "Upon my return [from Yalta] to Washington I had an opportunity to talk with the President," Stettinius wrote, "and hope that it will be possible for us to see each other soon as I have something to tell you which I know will be of interest to you."[64] Why not tell Pell what that "something" was? Did he really have something "of interest" for Pell, or was he trying to silence him before he testified? If that was Stettinius's purpose, it failed; Pell was determined to speak his mind before the Foreign Affairs Committee, which convened on March 22, 1945.

"The work of the Commission cannot remain a secret," demanded the House representative from New York, Emanuel Celler. A Democrat, Celler was, however, no friend of the State Department. In 1943 he had attacked department officials—and the president as well—for their "cold and cruel" policies on European refugees. He would go on to serve in the House almost fifty years. In the 1960s, he had a hand in drafting the Civil Rights Act of 1964 and the Voting Rights Act of 1965. But on this day, Celler was not particularly interested in righting wrongs done to minorities. He demanded congressional participation in war crimes planning. "Unless Congress steps in," he reiterated, "the whole program for the punishment of Axis criminals will remain a dark secret just as it was after the last war." Celler wanted to hear from Herbert Pell, as did everyone else.[65]

Before the committee, Pell testified that the Commission had examined some two thousand war crimes cases. In nearly half, it had recommended indictments be brought and trials undertaken in the countries of perpetration. However, it was not until December 1944 that charges were brought against Adolf Hitler. Only Allied governments could bring charges, and in this case, it was Czechoslovakia that finally proffered them. That none of the Big Three had done so, particularly the United States (the Soviet Union was not represented on the UNWCC), came as a shock and embarrassment to many. That little morsel led many on the committee to question the seriousness of American war crimes policy.[66]

Before ending his testimony, Pell emphasized that two major issues remained unresolved: one, punishing Nazis "for their treatment of minorities within

Germany and, two, setting up courts to try war criminals." Neither the British Foreign Office nor the American State Department, Pell asserted, had yet to move on these recommendations of the UNWCC, despite what Grew had previously announced. Another Democrat, Daniel J. Flood of Pennsylvania, expressed the outrage that many on the committee felt. "I think the whole question [of what to do about war criminals] has been very improperly handled. Definitions of war crimes have been entirely too vague," he said, adding, "There is an atmosphere of evasion about the whole issue."[67]

With his testimony, Pell had inaugurated a minor controversy—again—this time over the punishment of heads of state. The UNWCC formally answered the question of charges against Adolf Hitler on April 1, 1945, announcing that Hitler's name was at the top of one of five separate lists of war criminals.[68] Given what had taken place over the last two years or so between Pell and the State Department, it was fitting that such a thing was done on the first day of the month, April Fool's Day.

When the Commission began its work, its members had assumed that Heads of State would not be immune to prosecution, but as months passed, no nation had brought forth charges. The *New York Times* even reported that it was a dispute over "whether heads of States could be tried as common criminals . . . [that] led to the resignation of Herbert C. Pell." This was not true, but somehow, in the eyes of the public, Pell was perceived as the lone beacon demanding the punishment of all war criminals. Pell was not alone in his beliefs, and more to the point, he had not "resigned" over this dispute. Moreover, Pell cared as much, if not more, about the thousands of "lesser" criminals, who had participated personally in the killing of millions, than he did the major criminals.[69]

Americans, however, were more concerned with the notable and notorious. They wanted to know about Hitler and his henchmen. Thanks in large part to Pell, they then knew. That it had taken so much effort and so long to even get the announcement that Hitler had been charged gave Americans little confidence that the Allies would ever bring him to justice. When the Committee pointed out that the Moscow Declaration had reserved the punishment of major criminals for a later "joint decision," they were even less convinced.[70]

Following his congressional testimony and having received instructions from the White House to meet with the secretary of state, Pell was quite anxious to do so, especially given that Stettinius had written that he had "something of interest" to tell him. That meeting was not to happen anytime soon. Pell had come down with conjunctivitis. It would be "manifestly discourteous" for him to see the secretary just then, Pell told Stettinius by telegram on March 24.[71] He suggested they meet sometime during the week beginning April 9.[72]

Hoping against all hope that the president would agree to see him, Pell sent FDR another letter on April 5. His bitterness over his friend having abandoned him was quite apparent. For months, Pell had been seeking another interview with the president, to no avail. He had been the one who pursued FDR's agenda on the UNWCC, which had included forcing through a motion calling for crimes based on racial persecution to be treated as war crimes. He had done so only because he was certain he had the president's support. In the course of accomplishing that result "which I believed you desired," he told FDR bluntly, "I made a certain number of bitter enemies, or rather acquired the personal enmity of some of yours.[73]

Dispirited but not yet broken, Pell informed the president that he knew serious issues required extended consideration, but he had just about exhausted his patience. "The leading nation of the world," he wrote, "should take less than ten months to decide whether or not internal persecutions for race and religion are war crimes."[74] This was, in its simplest form, the basic problem. Predictably, Pell's letter was forwarded to the State Department for preparation of a reply.[75]

As suggested by the president, Pell finally did meet with Stettinius at 3:45 P.M. on April 12. The meeting lasted scarcely ten minutes and was interrupted numerous times by telephone calls. The two barely discussed war crimes policy. Stettinius did have that "something of interest" still to tell Pell. FDR had instructed Stettinius to inform Pell explicitly that he would not be going back to the UNWCC, but that he would not be repudiated either. More than that, if Pell wanted another post in the administration, he could have one—as long as it was not in the State Department. As Pell understood it, he could have just about any post he wanted. As he had done with the president in January, Pell asked Stettinius about being appointed librarian of Congress. With nothing specifically decided, Pell departed.[76]

Had FDR finally grasped what the State Department had done to Pell? Perhaps the president harbored some guilt over the abandonment of his friend. Whatever the motivation, for the moment, Pell seemed destined to rejoin the administration in some other capacity, but not in the State Department, and preferably as far removed from it as possible. Hopes for a speedy return—any return, in fact—were already dashed. Pell just did not yet know it.

Later that afternoon, Pell met his son, Claiborne, at the Metropolitan Club to discuss the events of the day. For the father, it had been an important one, and he was quite proud to talk about it. In the last few weeks he had forced the State Department to announce publicly it supported the one thing for which he had been fighting so resolutely for months—prosecution of all Axis war criminals for all their crimes, especially those against minorities wherever and whenever they occurred. And now he was able to tell his son about it. Moreover, he could proudly tell Claiborne that the president had not abandoned him after all. He was to return to the administration shortly, and, if he had his way, it would be in a position he coveted, as librarian of Congress.[77]

Just then, Massachusetts senator David Walsh arrived and informed Pell that FDR had died that very afternoon.[78] In fact, the president was pronounced dead just ten minutes before Pell met with Stettinius. We are left to wonder if Stettinius received word of what happened while Pell was in his office. The president's death was a double blow for Herbert Pell. He had lost his only chance to return to the administration, and personally he had just lost a lifelong friend.

FDR had failed to put in writing his directive that Pell be given a new post in his administration. For his part, Stettinius did not dictate the standard "Memorandum of Conversation" recording the details of his meeting with Pell. Perhaps the events of the day were too overwhelming for the secretary. Whatever the case, no official administration document recorded Pell having been offered any new position. Even if there had been a written record, it would not have mattered. FDR was gone, and Pell had no connections to Harry Truman, who, in any case, would have been under no obligation to honor FDR's promise to Pell.

In an odd turn of events, four days after the president's death and Pell's meeting with Stettinius, an investigator from the State Department traveled to New York to meet with the former American representative on the UNWCC. Of all things, the purpose was to discuss Pell's past confrontation with Lawrence Preuss.[79] A day or so after that, a letter for Pell arrived from Stettinius. Ironically, for the first and only time, the State Department acknowledged that FDR had asked them to reply to one of Pell's personal letters to the president. "The late President Roosevelt sent me your letter to him dated April 5 for the preparation of a reply for his signature." Stettinius was probably pleased to insult Pell this one last time. In what turned out to be his final opportunity, Pell's friend had not replied personally. Closing his brief but final brush-off, Stettinius wrote, "Under the circumstances, I assume our conversation of April 12th takes care of the matter."[80]

Pell spent the next several weeks pursuing an appointment in the Truman administration, but his efforts proved hopeless. As Dan Plesch notes in *Human*

Rights after Hitler, on May 23, 1945, Pell sent a long report to the White House detailing his efforts on the UNWCC and State obstructionism. Drew Pearson published Pell's report in its entirety on June 6 in his "Washington Merry-Go-Round." The story's headline was sensational: "U.S. Section of War Crimes Commission Has Not Yet Named for Trial a Single Nazi; Jackson Cannot Even Be Pinned Down to Chances of Convicting Any Group Before Christmas; Pell's Report Reveals Runaround by Some State Department Officials."[81] Of course, Pell's "secret report" was even more dramatic than Pearson's headline, detailing, as Plesch put it, "the whole sorry business."[82] How Pearson acquired Pell's report is not clear. Very likely, considering his anger over being let go and fear that the Allies would fail to seek justice for the Holocaust, Pell probably provided it himself. Unfortunately for Pell—and Pearson—the timing of the June 6 "Merry-Go-Round" could not have been worse.

The problem was that, most likely coincidentally, the White House released that same day the "Report to the President by Mr. Justice Jackson, June 6, 1945," detailing the specific crimes for which the Allies intended to bring Axis war criminals to justice. Jackson's report was accompanied by a statement of approval by the president.[83] Pearson and Pell's contention that the Allies had not yet taken proper action on war crimes consequently fell flat. For Pell, it must have been another painful embarrassment. It may also be possible, as Plesch notes, that the White House released the "Report to the President" in part to counteract Pell and Pearson.[84] Their partnership in early 1945 had then, after all, created quite a stir.

Jackson did not need Pell's report to produce his "Report to the President." After his appointment by Truman, Jackson worked swiftly to acquire as much information as possible about the work done to date on war crimes. By May 7 he had already consulted General William Donovan of the Office of Strategic Services, army and navy representatives, Colonel Murray C. Bernays in the War Department, two assistant attorneys general, Green Hackworth and Katherine Fite of the State Department, and Herbert C. Pell, former U.S. representative on the UNWCC. After that, on May 22, at the behest of Truman, Jackson traveled to Europe to gather additional information, returning in early June to compile his report with his growing staff.[85]

Although finding Hackworth "a competent and sympathetic man," Jackson's displeasure with the work of the State Department was obvious, if understated, when he noted, "We couldn't expect too much help from the State Department." As to the UNWCC and especially Pell, Jackson recalled that they "just didn't have authority or access to information." More to the point, "It had eminent men, and eminently able men. It was in a considerable row." One of those men, Herbert Pell, he observed, had left his position on the UNWCC "with a very strong bang at the State Department."[86]

Judging by Jackson's later work at the London Conference and the trial that followed, his meeting with Pell had been particularly helpful and illuminating. But it did not change Pell's status as it related to war crimes policy. His public life was over; it had gone the way of FDR. His contentious time as American representative on the UNWCC, however, was not without its accomplishments.

Throughout 1944 Pell had operated in relative anonymity. The American public knew of his position, but they had no idea what he was doing. Not until late January 1945 did the American people hear about his unceasing effort to move beyond existing international law. They did not know that the State Department had worked to delay Pell's departure in 1943. Nor did they know the department rejected his becoming chair of the Commission at the time of his appointment. The public did not know the department sent an assistant to London to undermine Pell. Worst of all, perhaps, they had no idea that the department had manipulated Pell with vague and contradictory instructions, composing one set of guidelines under the signature of the president and another under their own masthead. Pell himself did not know that either.

Pell believed that Nazi Germany had perpetrated an evil conspiracy against mankind from the moment Hitler became chancellor. As Pell understood it, the Allies needed bring all war criminals to justice for all their crimes, particularly their "crimes against humanity." He did not care to allocate justice selectively. He did not care about precedent. All Axis atrocities committed on the basis of racial, religious, and political persecution were crimes for which the Allies must seek punishment, regardless of the location of the crime or nationality of the victim, or even when it occurred. He did not care—or apparently consider—what that might mean at home. All these crimes were to come under the jurisdiction of the UNWCC. As he understood, that was what the president had wanted him to accomplish.

Despite repeated attempts by the State Department to silence him, Pell consistently refused to back down. Although he did not know it then, or probably thereafter, his decision to bring his problems to the attention of Morgenthau and the WRB eventually compelled the War Department to reevaluate its own position on war crimes. Indirectly, Herbert Pell had forced the secretary of war to grapple with the problem posed by the United States demanding Axis nationals be prosecuted for racial persecution against their own citizens.

With Bernays's conspiracy/criminal-organization plan and Chanler's aggressive warfare idea, a method had been found to hold Axis criminals responsible for atrocities committed against their own nationals and satellites. Administration officials came to realize that the American public, particularly the Jewish community, would not reconcile itself to a distortion in international law that accepted a distinction among victims of Axis atrocities. As this was considered in the fall of 1944 and early January 1945, no one bothered to tell Pell or the American people about it. Despite repeated presidential announcements that all war criminals would be brought to justice for all their crimes, officials in the State and War Departments remained concerned that any war crimes policy announcement might bring retribution against Allied prisoners of war or those held in concentration camps. Pell believed just the opposite: he was convinced, as were others, particularly WRB officials, that the assuredness of punishment might save lives.

Herbert Pell played a key role in arousing the press and public to what was taking place in Europe, thanks in large measure to the ill-advised manner with which the State Department removed him from the UNWCC. In the end, the new American position that all Axis war criminals would be prosecuted for crimes against humanity, including those against their own nationals, was incorporated into the London Agreement and Charter in August 1945, but in limited form, as will be seen. The most-remembered aspect of Nuremberg—the prosecution of Axis war criminals for crimes against humanity—is directly traceable to the actions of Herbert C. Pell. Pell, unknown today in almost every circle, made it all possible by his determined actions on the UNWCC and his refusing to go quietly after his removal.

Pell's decision to ignore the warnings that he not speak about Commission matters made it possible for Green Hackworth to have Pell removed from his post. At the same time, Pell's firing freed him to plead his case candidly before the press and public. By doing that, the battle over what to do about Axis crimes against Axis nationals, namely atrocities against the Jews, was revealed to the public. And as it turned out, what Pell told FDR on June 29, 1943, when he first met with the president to discuss his appointment to the UNWCC, became prophesy and, finally, his epitaph. "Many people were going to sacrifice their lives in this war," Pell had then said, adding, "I [stand] ready to sacrifice my reputation."[87]

Herbert C. Pell would have nothing further to offer the administration regarding American war crimes policy planning; Supreme Court Associate Justice Robert H. Jackson had assumed the task. It remained to be seen, however, what his considerable experience could bring to the problem of prosecuting Axis war criminals for crimes against humanity.

CHAPTER 12

JUSTICE JACKSON TAKES OVER

"I Have My Neck in the Noose"

We cannot successfully cooperate with the rest of the world in establishing a reign of law unless we are prepared to have that law sometimes operate against what would be our national advantage.

Robert H. Jackson, April 13, 1945

On April 22, 1945, Assistant Secretary of War John McCloy sent Judge Samuel Rosenman a memorandum containing eight possible candidates to take the lead in America's war crimes program. Of the eight, Associate Justice of the Supreme Court Robert H. Jackson seemed by far the most experienced choice, except for what hardship such a selection might cause to the Court schedule. Both McCloy and Rosenman wanted Jackson for the post.[1] Jackson always believed that FDR had spoken to Rosenman prior to his death about designating him for the post of chief American prosecutor. In his oral history, Jackson said, "I've always assumed, although I have no definite information to that effect, that Roosevelt had had some talk with Rosenman about designating me in that connection, which would have been in keeping with my former role in his administration."[2] Jackson had served FDR from March 1938 to January 1940 as solicitor general and after that as U.S. attorney general until 1941. FDR nominated Jackson as Associate Justice on June 12, 1941, and he was confirmed by the Senate on July 7.

Late in the afternoon of April 26, 1945, Rosenman telephoned Jackson from the White House. Rosenman had a proposal to convey from President Truman. The president wanted Jackson personally to lead and conduct the case against the major Axis war criminals. To avoid the press routinely camped out at the White House, Rosenman agreed with Jackson that it was better for them to meet at the Supreme Court Building.[3] Before agreeing to take on the task, Jackson needed to talk over a few issues.

That evening, Rosenman met Jackson in his chambers to discuss the details of the proposition. Not only did Truman want him to head the American delegation, he also wanted the United States to take the dominant role in prosecution of the Axis war criminals. While appreciative, Jackson was concerned. Two weeks earlier on April 13—just one day following the death of FDR—Jackson had delivered an address to the American Society of International Law during which he expressed a preference, he told Rosenman, for political disposition of war criminals.[4]

In his address, Jackson declared that he had no interest in entering "into any controversy as to what shall be done with war criminals, either high or humble." But that was not quite accurate. Jackson was entering into the controversy—a controversy made public thanks in large measure to Herbert C. Pell. Twice Jackson stated specifically that he was "not arguing against bringing those accused of war-crimes to trial." He was genuinely worried that the United States was preparing to participate in some sort of "phony" trial.[5] He was also keenly aware that bringing Axis war criminals before a legitimate court was fraught with any number of dangers, not the least of which was the possibility of seeing an accused war criminal go free if the evidence did not support a conviction. The American people, he feared, were not prepared for such an outcome. But if there was to be a judicial proceeding, Jackson believed that it must not come with a predetermined result. "If you are determined to execute a man in any case," he said, "there is no occasion for a trial; the world yields no respect to courts that are merely organized to convict."[6]

More significantly, Jackson was apprehensive about the potential reach of international law, and he opposed bringing Axis war criminals to justice through adjudication because of the impact it might have domestically. "We cannot successfully cooperate with the rest of the world in establishing a reign of law," he said, "unless we are prepared to have that law sometimes operate against what would be our national advantage."[7] As Jackson knew, the interests of justice did not always serve everyone equally in America. Jackson did not say so specifically, but in making this statement, he seemed to suggest that the advancement of international law might challenge the long-held presumption that national sovereignty is unassailable.

Where did Jackson stand on the issue? Would he really put the requirements of justice before the conflicting interests of the nation? He obviously did not yet know of the Bernays solution to what he had called "The Minorities Problem"; no one did outside of those involved in its conception. Jackson warned Rosenman at their meeting that if Truman were to appoint him, there might be some political fallout because of the speech he had given. Jackson believed his address was not necessarily "inconsistent" with the desires of the government to bring war criminals to trial, but he wanted Rosenman to understand the public stance he had taken. Jackson gave Rosenman two copies of the address. After a hurried reading right there in Jackson's chambers, Rosenman announced that "there was nothing embarrassing in it," and, more, that it was "entirely consistent" with American policy. It was not consistent, of course, but that did not seem to matter. Truman wanted Jackson.[8]

Jackson's address had suggested that he thought an international trial of war criminals might work against U.S. national interests. Jackson believed fervently in the rule of law; he might have to put justice before his nation, if he were to serve. At least, that was what he seemed to imply to Rosenman. As it turned out, going forward as chief prosecutor for the United States at Nuremberg, Jackson did everything in his power to protect the interests and sovereignty of the nation. If international law could be advanced through an international adjudication of war criminals, so be it, as long as it did not come at the expense of American autonomy to pursue its own national and international objectives. Jackson was not, it turned out, "prepared to have that law sometimes operate against what would be our national advantage." So much for cooperating with the rest of the world to establish a "reign of law."[9]

Jackson's work as Nuremberg prosecutor was not, of course, the first time he had thought seriously about the intersection of law, war, and justice. In August 1936, while head of the Tax Division of the Department of Justice, Jackson helped prepare FDR's famous "I Hate War" speech.[10] Photographs and newsreels of the speech show Jackson sitting proudly behind the president, who had said, recalling his experiences in World War I:

> I have seen war. I have seen blood running from the wounded. I have seen men coughing out their gassed lungs. I have seen the dead in the mud. I have seen cities destroyed. I have seen two hundred limping exhausted men

come out of line—the survivors of a regiment of one thousand that went
forward forty-eight hours before. I have seen children starving. I have seen
the agony of mothers and wives. I hate war. I have passed unnumbered
hours, I shall pass unnumbered hours, thinking and planning how war
may be kept from this Nation. I wish I could keep war from all Nations;
but that is beyond my power.[11]

Following his appointment as chief prosecutor on May 2, 1945, Jackson hoped
he just might begin to make the late president's wish—his own wish—if not
achievable, at least approachable, by creating international legal precedent that
promised punishment for those who carry out aggressive war.

Jackson was even more intimately involved in the intersection of international
law and war, and this time, not incidentally, the problems of race relations during
a several-month period in 1940 when FDR grappled with the issue of sending U.S.
destroyers to Great Britain in exchange for military bases. The president wanted
to help the British hold out against the Nazis, who were themselves struggling
with how to help the French survive the Nazi onslaught in the late spring and
early summer of 1940. An immediate issue for Churchill—at least until the French
surrendered—was whether to deploy the Royal Air Force fully in the skies over
France. FDR worried that if the British did so, in what he suspected was already
a lost cause—saving France—that it would render Britain defenseless against
Luftwaffe attacks that were sure to come. FDR ominously told Jackson, "We had
better be thinking about this. It is not much different than the questions we may
have to face if things continue as they are going now."[12]

After the fall of France on June 22, 1940, FDR was even more determined
to help the British, but the problem was how to do it in the face of complicated
diplomatic and political obstacles. In July FDR had accepted the Democratic
nomination for what would become an unprecedented third term. On top of that,
isolationists still held considerable sway in the nation, notwithstanding the loss
of France. Moreover, FDR initially believed any agreement that involved loaning,
gifting, or selling destroyers to the British needed congressional approval. He
wanted to avoid political difficulties at home, especially with Congress during an
election year, but he also needed to be mindful of existing international agreements circumscribing neutrals during wartime. His attorney general, Jackson,
played a crucial role in helping FDR navigate all these difficulties.

By August 1940 the president had decided on an exchange—destroyers
for bases—and to do so by issuing an executive order accompanied with an

explanation to Congress, which Jackson would draft. The president could fend off the isolationists by acquiring bases in the Caribbean to protect shipping headed to and from the Panama Canal, and bases in the North Atlantic to safeguard American merchant vessels headed to Britain. And, thanks to the legal opinion that Jackson provided, FDR could avoid seeking ratification of the deal in Congress because the destroyers being transferred to Britain were classified as obsolete. According to Jackson, "The President said to me with a chuckle, 'They [Congress] will get into a terrific row over your opinion instead of my deal, but after all, Bob, you are not running for office."[13]

But among all his considerations—fending off isolationists, satisfying the complaints of congresspersons at being disregarded, sustaining the needs of Britain and the political position of Churchill, to say nothing of protecting his reelection chances—according to Jackson, there was one issue "over and above all" that weighed on the president in contemplating a destroyers-for-bases exchange: taking on the burden of assuming control over the civilian population at the locations of the bases. According to Jackson, FDR had "warned that we must not in any way assume any responsibilities for government of the bases that could involve us in race relations there."[14] That a Democratic president who needed the southern vote to stay in office was concerned about race relations was certainly no surprise to Jackson. FDR was always a political animal—he reveled in it, in fact—but if race relations became part of any issue, as it sometimes did during his presidency, it was a rare occasion if he had not already given it considerable consideration, usually ahead of everyone else. The destroyers-for-bases deal could not be a quid-pro-quo exchange. The United States could not take free and clear possession of the bases. The deal had to be consummated in rent-free leases of the bases rather than their exchange for the destroyers.

Secretary of State Cordell Hull in his *Memoirs* had written that FDR was concerned about the "penurious condition of the native populations," because the deal would establish American bases in Antigua, British Guiana, Jamaica, St. Lucia, Bermuda, Newfoundland, and Trinidad.[15] But it was Jackson's recitation of FDR's reasoning for "preferring" to lease these bases that reveals unmistakably what was at issue, and is worth quoting here in full:

> On the islands, there was not legal discrimination and in fact very little of any kind. If the United States assumed sovereignty and continued the British policy, it would be in sharp conflict with southern practice and sentiment and would precipitate a row with southern representatives in

Congress. If the United States should attempt to change insular practice to conform to its own racial pattern, it would cause grave unrest in the islands. Therefore, he wanted the powers and responsibilities of the United States confined strictly to military installations and personnel, leaving civil government of the territory entirely to the British.[16]

Leaving no doubt about what Jackson noted as FDR's topmost consideration in the exchange, an early draft agreement stated that for the period of the leases (ninety-nine years) the United States would possess "all the rights, power, and authority within the bases" and areas close by as "if it were the sovereign of the territory." FDR made sure that this sovereignty clause was eliminated—on Jackson's advice—even though "preparation of the diplomatic documents," Jackson admitted, "was not [his] business."[17]

In terms of proscriptions related to international agreements, concern existed initially that the United States could not provide destroyers to Great Britain on the basis of the Hague Convention, which (among other aspects of defining war-making) made it illegal for any neutral country—in this case, the United States—to provide or fit out armed vessels to a belligerent—Britain.[18] FDR and his major subalterns—Cordell Hull, Sumner Welles, Henry Stimson, and Jackson—had come to view the German invasion of France, and Poland before that, as a violation of the Kellogg-Briand Pact, the 1928 agreement in which the signatories—which included Germany, Italy, and Japan—agreed to forgo war-making as a legal right. Consequently, any prohibitions of the Hague Conventions were superseded. As Jackson put it, "Hitler's war was one of naked aggression"; therefore, the United States had the right, "if not the duty," of "assisting the victims of such unlawful aggression."[19] On September 2, 1940, Britain and the United States concluded the agreement to exchange warships for bases.

The same legal reasoning—Axis violations of Kellogg-Briand—was used the following spring to justify lend-lease; this time put before Congress since the administration was no longer talking about exchanging "obsolete" materiel. In a March 1941 speech written for the Inter-American Bar Association, Jackson went on to explain the administration's thinking.[20] "Present aggressive wars are civil wars against the international community. . . . We are permitted to give to defending governments all the aid we choose."[21] He also pointed out, "It does not appear to be necessary to treat all wars as legal and just simply because we have no court to try the accused."[22] He could not have then guessed that, only four years later, he would play such a pivotal role in creating just such a court at Nuremberg.

Rosenman was scheduled to travel on May 2, 1945, to San Francisco, where the organizational meeting that set up the United Nations was taking place, but he would only make the trip if Jackson was willing to accept the appointment. Rosenman's task in San Francisco would be to present the American plan for prosecution of war criminals. President Truman wanted to move forward rapidly with a trial, continuing—as he would with other aspects of the Roosevelt administration—what he knew to be FDR's policy on war criminals. Truman believed—and told Jackson directly—that the justice's presence would have a beneficial effect on other countries, moving them toward agreement on an international military tribunal.[23]

On the afternoon of Sunday, April 29, Rosenman met with Jackson at his home. Jackson had prepared a memorandum for Rosenman to take to the president detailing the terms of his acceptance. At their meeting, the two men worked together to produce a draft of Executive Order 9547, which would announce Jackson's appointment.[24] On May 2, 1945, President Truman issued the executive order designating Jackson as U.S. chief prosecutor. This appointment was an important step on the road to Nuremberg. In the ensuing months, Jackson set the agenda and the tone for the London Conference, whose negotiations produced the Agreement and Charter of the International Military Tribunal, as well as the trial that followed.

With Jackson appointed, Rosenman traveled to San Francisco and presented the American trial plan. As Truman had hoped, general support in favor of a trial promptly developed. The British were committed, as the French seemed to be. Buoyed by Truman's confidence and the reports coming back from San Francisco, Jackson believed his appointment the key factor in producing the progress accomplished thus far.[25] The French and the Russians both informed Rosenman that they required clearance to continue. The representatives at San Francisco were having difficulty resolving the specifics; mired in the discussion of legal details, negotiations had stalled. But progress had been made, due in part to the reputation of Jackson. Representatives of the four Allied powers had agreed on basic issues. They resolved to move forward with an international military tribunal, a committee of four chiefs of counsel, a trial rather than summary execution of the major criminals, and a return of minor criminals with "fixed geographical location to the countries where their crimes were committed."[26]

San Francisco was a clear victory in favor of American ideas that were first put forth by Herbert C. Pell on the UNWCC. But everyone seemed to understand that a comprehensive agreement would require the work of legal minds because diplomatic representatives alone would not be able to fashion the complex international agreement necessary for the prosecution of war criminals.[27] Taking the initiative, likely in reaction to their surrendering to the initial American plan in San Francisco, the British proposed that further meetings take place in London. For the United States, the work was now under the direction of Jackson and the team he was speedily bringing together.

After spending the first half of May in Washington putting together his staff, Jackson traveled to Europe to gather information and organize his evidence-gathering apparatus. The work of preparing the American case against the principal war criminals could not wait for a signed agreement establishing an international military tribunal. Beyond this, Jackson believed his most important accomplishment was a successful press conference on May 28 in Paris.

Across Europe and in the United States, much confusion existed over the purpose and direction of war crimes policy, as well as anxiety over the sluggishness of the process. Jackson tried to convey the difficulties that lay ahead in constructing a trial protocol. Following the press conference, he believed that the journalists now understood it would take some time to bring war criminals to trial; consequently, they might exercise some patience in their reporting.[28]

Not much was accomplished in the two days of preliminary meetings in London that followed the press conference. Perhaps the most important thing to come out of these meetings was the appointment of British attorney general Sir David Maxwell Fyfe as Jackson's opposite number. To forge an agreement, Jackson needed a strong ally in the negotiations, and he now had one. But to make any real progress, all four Allied powers needed to meet. They scheduled further meetings in London for the next month, hoping representatives of all four powers would attend.

Jackson had begun to understand the extent of the difficulties of his task. Returning to the United States, he set to work, with the help of his growing staff, to produce the "Report to the President by Mr. Justice Jackson, June 6, 1945."[29] The White House released the report to the press, accompanied by a statement of approval from the president; widely published, it represented the official U.S. position statement on war criminals.[30] Prefacing the legal charges listed in his report, Jackson detailed the basic acts of the Nazi regime that first "outraged" the American people, among them "the cruelest forms of torture and the wholesale confiscation of property." The world, he wrote, had been witness to "persecution of the greatest enormity on religious, political and racial grounds." These crimes—and more—were all executed as part of a common plan of aggression. As the "Nazis swooped down upon nations they had deceived," Jackson wrote, they shamelessly violated international law, wiping out entire populations. The American people, Jackson asserted, had come to understand that these crimes had been "committed against us and against the whole of civilized nations."[31]

Using this recitation as his background, Jackson listed the specific crimes for which Axis war criminals would be brought to justice: atrocities and offenses against international law, including "atrocities and persecutions on racial or religious grounds, committed since 1933," and aggressive warfare. The first of these two was the very thing Herbert C. Pell had been working toward on the UNWCC. All persons to be prosecuted on these charges, Jackson added, had participated in "the formulation or the execution of a criminal plan." The Fourth Hague Convention provided the legal precedent.[32]

This preliminary list of crimes would undergo considerable alteration before the four principal Allied Powers agreed upon them, but as they appeared at this moment, it seemed Herbert Pell had won his battle. As Jackson had it, the United States was committed to the concept of prosecuting Axis war criminals for crimes of racial and religious persecution since 1933. If atrocities against German nationals were to be included—and there was nothing in Jackson's words that indicated they would not be—this then constituted a clear invasion of sovereignty. Jackson's reliance on the Fourth Hague Convention was a questionable precedent given his experience during the administration's debate over the destroyers for bases deal. A better justification was needed. Moreover, as written, the door might be opened to similar adjudications against all nations, including, obviously, the United States.

Jackson put his lead assistant, Sidney Alderman, on the task of finding a solution to the issue of sovereignty.[33] Alderman was an unexpected choice for the position, although he was fluent in both French and German, a sure advantage and important skill. By reputation alone, Jackson considered him "a very good advocate" and "fine courtroom lawyer."[34] When Jackson selected him, neither man had any recollection of ever having conversed with the other.

In his Washington apartment on the morning of May 3, Alderman read about Jackson's appointment over breakfast. Remarking casually to his wife, he noted what a prime assignment it would be to participate in such an undertaking. At his office later that morning, Alderman was beyond surprised when a secretary told him that the justice was on the phone and wanted a word with him.[35]

"Mr. Alderman, I suppose you have seen in the papers that I have my neck in the noose, and I want some other good necks in the noose with me and first of all, I want you."

Alderman replied, "Well, that is highly flattering, Mr. Justice, but just what do you mean?"

"I want you as my first assistant on this whole mission."

The two arranged to meet the following Monday, May 7, at which time Alderman was to give Jackson his answer. Alderman had some issues to overcome, mainly securing a leave of absence from his employer, the Southern Railway Company, but he already knew he wanted to participate. No lawyer could pass up this opportunity. At their meeting, he accepted Jackson's proposal.[36]

Alderman's appointment as Jackson's assistant came with its own irony. In the 1930s Alderman had helped prepare materials in opposition to FDR's court-packing plan, for which Jackson had been a principal advocate before a Senate committee. At the time of his appointment, Alderman was busy fighting the attorney general over antitrust charges as the Southern Railway Company's lead attorney. When Alderman told Jackson that detail at their meeting, Jackson replied, "Well, that is quite amusing because I have looked around as to where I can hang you on the government payroll and where I can get the best salary for you, and I find the best I can do is to have you appointed as special assistant to the Attorney General of the United States, Francis Biddle." Alderman was to be paid nine thousand dollars per annum, a considerable pay cut, but Alderman was unconcerned; the Southern Railway Company had already offered to make up any difference.[37] If only it had been that easy to find a place to "hang" Pell on the payroll, yet Pell's time had passed.

On June 14 Alderman dropped by the office of his new boss, the attorney general, to take care of some paperwork. "You needn't call me your new boss," Biddle told him. "I won't have a damn thing to do with you." Before Alderman could muster a response, Biddle added that Jackson was "a good picker." Although adversaries in the courtroom, Biddle nonetheless respected Alderman. His selection to work with Jackson, Alderman acknowledged, was, however, "strange." He was not a criminal lawyer, nor had he any significant experience in international law. The admission brought a wide smile to Biddle's face, who suggested to Alderman that that might be the very reason for his selection.[38]

Working through the next day at his temporary office at the Pentagon, Alderman readied for the coming departure of Jackson's staff to London, the date of which was still not firmly set. He probably also spent some time preparing for a meeting that was scheduled for the next day, June 16, to deal with the issue of sovereignty. Whatever his shortcomings—or recommendations—may have been, Alderman was just the next in line to attempt to deal with the jurisdiction problem. He had an opportunity to discuss the problem with Jackson the evening before the meeting.

As the two traveled back to the Supreme Court Building, Jackson told Alderman that the departure date for London had finally been set for June 19, the next Tuesday. This reminded Alderman of a story, and Jackson, he recalled, "always loved our southern stories." Alderman recounted it this way in his oral history:

> I told him about the Negro who had been convicted of first degree murder and was called up to stand before the judge. The judge announced to him the significance of the jury's verdict. . . . "The order of this court is that on Tuesday, the sixth day of August of this year, you will be taken by the sheriff of Guilford County to the state penitentiary in Raleigh, North Carolina. There you will be delivered to the warden of the state penitentiary and by him you will be taken into a specially prepared chamber, where a current of electricity will be passed through your body until you are dead, dead, dead. And may god have mercy on your soul!"
>
> Then the judge said to the Negro defendant, "Defendant, do you have anything to say?"
>
> The Negro said, "Boss Judge, Your Honor, you don't mean this here next coming Tuesday, do you?"

Thereupon, Alderman said to Jackson, "You don't mean this here next coming Tuesday, do you, for flying to Europe?" Jackson, Alderman observed, "got a great kick out of the story."[39]

These men were dealing with issues of tragic importance. Humor—to the extent this was humor at that time—was an absolute necessity. And in a very real sense, the task they were about to assume in London might well turn out to be—figuratively, at least—an execution of sorts. At least in Jackson's case, if he failed, his career would be seriously damaged, and the reputation of the United States would surely suffer. At this point, Jackson still had some ideas about possibly running for high office in the future, in addition to being the likely candidate as the next Chief Justice. Jackson had admitted the risks of their enterprise when he told Alderman on May 3 that he wanted "some other good necks in the noose" with him. Neither man would have acknowledged any inappropriateness in using such allusions and allegory; indeed, few would have found it inappropriate at that time in America. More to the point, however, neither man that day connected the racism inherent in Alderman's anecdote to the problem they were facing: how to seek justice for racial persecution abroad and sustain it at home. In fact, according to Alderman's recollection, the topic was not discussed, even though a meeting was set for the next day to deal with it.

On June 16 Alderman held a meeting on the matter of sovereignty. Among those in attendance was Colonel Bernays, the originator of the first half of the most probable solution, the conspiracy/criminal-organization plan. One of the other men present, Professor Hans Kelsen, a gifted and considerably experienced legal scholar, offered another option. In the 1930s, he had been removed from his position at the University of Cologne when the Nazis came to power, ultimately emigrating to the United States in 1940, a refugee of Nazi persecution. After delivering a series of well-received lectures at Harvard during the early war years, Kelsen took a position as visiting professor at the University of California, Berkeley. At the time of the meeting, Kelsen was serving as a legal adviser to the United Nations War Crimes Commission in Washington.[40]

Kelsen suggested that sovereignty could be worked around with a simple technical maneuver. German sovereignty, Kelsen insisted, temporarily did not exist. It had been seized by the Allied powers. If the Allied Control Council continued to assert sovereignty over the German nation and if the trial was held under its auspices, then under such a construction, the tribunal would be able to prosecute for atrocities committed, as Alderman later put it, "by Germans against Germans in Germany . . . matters which would ordinarily be completely outside the scope of international law."[41]

Bernays pointed out that the protocol in its present draft provided for the Allied Control Council to appoint the court. The Control Council could operate as a "ministerial agent" for the Allied powers. Another staff member at the meeting then reminded everyone that the unconditional surrender document signed by Admiral Karl Doenitz was the equivalent of a treaty that consigned sovereignty to the Allies. At this, Kelsen recommended that the Allies sign a new treaty delegating the Allied Control Council to exercise the sovereign powers of the former German state. An international tribunal appointed by the Allied Control Council could theoretically solve the sovereignty problem.[42]

No one made any comment on the considerable roadblocks to such a plan. In the first place, the Allied Control Council had no sovereignty at the time the crimes were committed. Also, Axis persecution of minorities was legal within Nazi Germany. Moreover, for the United States, treaties were considerably disadvantageous from a time standpoint, as they required Senate approval. The idea of utilizing a treaty had already been considered and dismissed for just such a reason. Nonetheless, those at the meeting seemed pleased with Kelsen's ideas.

With so much still unsettled within the American delegation, Jackson and his team of assistants traveled to London as scheduled the following week to begin negotiations to create a trial protocol under which Axis war criminals would be prosecuted. Representatives for the governments of the United Kingdom, France, the Soviet Union, and the United States officially met from June 26 to August 8, 1945. The result of this conference was, officially, the "London Agreement of August 8th 1945 and the Charter of the International Military Tribunal," which Jackson later labeled a "formal statement of the principles of substantive law and agreed-upon methods of procedure for the prosecution and trial of the major European war criminals."[43]

The negotiators labored under considerable pressure from the press and the public around the globe to reach an agreement and begin a trial as soon as possible. To accomplish this, the negotiators had to agree on several complicated issues. Alderman, Jackson's lead assistant, described them this way: "There were differences in concepts as to judicial process, as to procedure, as to what constitutes a fair trial, as to where the trial should be held, even as to substantive International law and definitions of war crimes."[44]

The task of creating a new legal procedure that each of the victorious Allied powers would find acceptable proved particularly difficult. The Soviet Union and France used a system of law commonly referred to as the continental system, an inquisitorial process. The United Kingdom and the United States, with some variations, used a system of common or Anglo-Saxon law, which is adversarial. In the inquisitorial system, the prosecutor is responsible for assembling and presenting all evidence to an examining judge, who then decides whether the accused should be brought to trial. A rule in the affirmative is tantamount to a finding of guilty; the burden of proof then falls upon the defendant. In the adversarial system, the burden of proof rests solely with the prosecution and features direct examination and cross-examination of witnesses before a judge who acts primarily as an arbiter.[45] The negotiation teams faced the problem of trying to forge a single prosecutorial method by merging portions of both systems—not an easy task.

On the question of defining which types of acts would be considered war crimes, Jackson later observed, "However great the superficial differences in institutions, it is surprising to find how much men of all nations, creeds, races and cultures agree on fundamental questions of right and wrong."[46] As accurate as Jackson's statement may have been in a general sense, the Allied powers experienced real difficulties on this issue. The French and Russians desired solely to prosecute Nazi war crimes, and who could blame them? These two nations had faced the full force of the land war in Europe.

The United States, with the British in tow, were both determined to bring Axis war criminals to justice for aggressive war and their crimes against humanity. They sought to prosecute the Nazis for their crimes but also wanted to give new meaning to the tens of millions of lost lives across the globe by making illegal forever wars of aggression for all nations, and not just for the Nazis; at least, this was Jackson's public stance. Privately, during the negotiations, this position was actually only a posture. Jackson was determined to apply crimes against humanity only to the Nazis. Consequently, this double-dealing contributed greatly to the contentiousness of the negotiations.

Despite complicated legal differences, the men of all four delegations who met in London possessed a common objective: the creation of some form of protocol establishing an international military tribunal. All four Allied powers united to bring to trial, convict, and punish the major European Axis war criminals.[47] Whether a joint four-power trial could accomplish this objective given the many difficulties, they did not yet know. Their goal might only be met through several separate trials held by each nation. Jackson more than once successfully wielded that possibility as a negotiation tactic. He grappled with another basic problem that needed to be surmounted: if Axis war criminals were to be brought to justice for all their crimes, including those against its own nationals—crimes against humanity—somehow the sovereignty of the United States must be protected.[48] This was problem not new, but it had become Jackson's. Seeking justice for the Holocaust, as obviously necessary as it seemed during the war, became even more a necessity with the liberation of the concentration camps in late spring 1945. The *seeking* of justice was well under way by then, owing especially to the efforts of Herbert C. Pell on the UNWCC, but what remained discomfortingly uncertain was whether there would be any meaningful justice.

CHAPTER 13

PROTECTING AMERICAN SOVEREIGNTY

"A Real Expression of Our Moral Judgment"

The way Germany treats its inhabitants, or any other country treats its inhabitants, is not our affair any more than it is the affair of some other government to interpose itself in our problems.

Robert H. Jackson, April 13, 1945

Before leaving for London, the American team had worked on a revised protocol that the four delegations would use as a starting point.[1] On June 14, 1945, Jackson sent a revised draft to the British, Soviet, and French Embassies in Washington.[2] The crimes for which war criminals would be charged had been slightly altered from those proposed in Jackson's report to Truman. Atrocities on grounds of racial persecution had been clarified, but any reference to preexisting international law and agreements had been removed. The draft read, "Atrocities and offenses, including atrocities and persecutions on racial or religious grounds, committed since 1 January 1933 in violation of any applicable provision of the domestic law of the country in which committed."[3] Among other difficulties, as it was then written, atrocities within Germany and satellite nations were beyond reach of the Allies.

The same day Jackson had drafts sent to the embassies, Nikolai V. Novikov, minister counselor of the Soviet Embassy in Washington, delivered to Jackson an aide-mémoire—a Russian-language original and an English translation—raising questions regarding the American plan. The Soviets were of the same mind as the American team regarding the need for swift negotiations and a subsequent speedy trial. Novikov was under instructions to negotiate with the American team, evidently unaware that a meeting had been set for London later in the month.[4] Consequently, Jackson was concerned that the Russians might not be represented there. Discussing the problem with President Truman before he left for London, the two agreed that if the Russians were not there by June 25, Jackson should wait another week. If they did not arrive, negotiations should commence without them. About the criminal charges, the Soviet aide-mémoire offered no criticisms, an omission that was not destined to last.[5]

The American delegation arrived in London late on Tuesday, June 19. The following afternoon, members of the American team held an informal meeting with British delegation representatives. The meeting began with a general discussion of American and British positions on the protocol. The British then shared their concerns about the possible length of a trial, suggesting that public interest would wane if it lasted more than two to three weeks. The discussion moved to the number of war criminals who might be prosecuted. The British preferred to keep the number small, perhaps as few as seven to ten; the Americans were considering a much larger number, as many as fifty.[6]

On Thursday, at a second preliminary meeting, British attorney general Fyfe brought up something that had bothered him about the protocol. Why, he wondered, did it provide for the appointment of the tribunal by the Allied Control Council? The British had no desire to delegate such a power to the council. Alderman chose that day not to go into Kelsen's plan for working around sovereignty in any detail, saving it for explanation at a later subcommittee meeting.[7]

By June 26 the French and the Soviet delegations had arrived in London, and Fyfe called to order the first official conference of the four Allied powers. After Fyfe's opening remarks reviewing the American plan, the lead Soviet representative, General I. T. Nikitchenko, recommended that they divide the plan into two parts, including a separate "agreement" between the four powers and a "statute" that would codify the rules and procedure of the trial.[8] This was a sensible suggestion to which the other delegations readily agreed. A disagreement developed, however, over what to call the statute.

By this point, the American delegation had realized an error in considering Kelsen's idea of a treaty. In different drafts, the statute had been titled as an "annex." Alderman did not like the use of "statute" in the least; he believed it would be interpreted in the United States as if it were an international treaty requiring Senate ratification. The Soviet delegation did not like the term "annex." To them, "annex" implied that the rules and procedure were secondary rather than an integral part of the agreement. At a subcommittee meeting on July 5 Alderman suggested the use of the word "charter." The word had been used for the Atlantic Charter to some success, he told the other delegates, and had not required treaty approval in the American Congress. Consequently, from that day forward the protocol became officially the "Agreement and Charter." Where this left Kelsen's plan, Alderman did not say, but a primary feature of it—utilization of a treaty—was no longer a consideration.[9]

Excluding the weekend, a drafting subcommittee met from July 5 to the afternoon of July 11 with the goal of resolving existing differences between the delegations. The resulting proposed protocol included an updated version of the crimes and a reworking of the concept of crimes against humanity. "Atrocities and persecutions and deportations on political, racial, or religious grounds" were now connected directly to Bernays's criminal conspiracy/criminal-organizations plan and Chanler's aggressive warfare approach. Such crimes thus fell within the jurisdiction of the Allies only if they occurred "in pursuance of the common plan or enterprise."[10] In other words, only Nazi atrocities in preparation of their conspiracy to commit aggressive warfare were adjudicable by the Allies.

The French and Soviet delegations were both opposed to the inclusion of the phrase "in pursuance of the common plan or enterprise." Although still unknown to the press and public, this concept had been a keystone of the American plan for war criminals since Bernays first introduced it the previous fall. To Jackson, the most important charge the Allies could bring was that the Nazis had executed a conspiracy to carry out an aggressive war. Every other charge from traditional war crimes to crimes against humanity was intrinsically connected with the notion of a greater conspiracy.[11]

Jackson was far from pleased with the work of the subcommittee. Alderman and the British representatives thought that considerable progress had been made toward agreement, and Alderman and Fyfe in particular were stunned by Jackson's displeasure. Not only was he prepared to scrap the work of the subcommittee, but at the plenary meeting on July 13, it became apparent Jackson was ready to call an end to the negotiations and proceed to trial separately. Whether Jackson's performance at the meeting was a calculated tactic to force an agreement from the other side or a real expression of his outlook at that moment is not clear; it was probably a little of both.[12]

The next morning, several American delegation members met with Jackson, attempting to get him to support the subcommittee draft as written.[13] In the afternoon, the American delegation held a short meeting to try to reach some resolution. Speaking against the subcommittee's revised protocol, Bernays thought his conspiracy/criminal-organization plan was in danger of not being carried out, and he had the Justice's ear. A tired and frustrated Jackson simply put on his hat and walked out in the middle of the discussion.[14]

With Jackson more determined than ever to make the conspiracy/criminal-organization plan for the purpose of carrying out aggressive war the centerpiece of the criminal charges, the American delegation submitted on July 19 a definition of "aggression" for inclusion in the protocol. At the plenary session held that day, the French immediately attacked the inclusion of any such definition. There was no precedent for such a thing in international law. Nikitchenko concurred: "In my opinion we should not try to draw up this definition for the future. . . . Our task should be to form the basis for the trial not of any criminals who may commit international crimes in the future but of those who have already done so."[15] Here was the essential difference. The French and the Soviets saw the coming trial and the protocol being created for it as case specific. Jackson wanted to make advancements in international law. But Jackson had a problem: how to make advancements in the law and at the same time protect American sovereignty?

Considerably less strident than he had been the previous week but still concerned that no agreement on the crimes might be reached, Jackson explained that he was "in agreement with a great deal" of the French and Soviet position, but he was determined to press his own ideas. "Our view is that this isn't merely a case showing that these Nazi Hitlerite people failed to be gentlemen in war; it is a matter of their having designed an illegal attack on the international peace, which to our mind is a criminal offense by common-law tests, at least, and the other atrocities were all preparatory to it or done in execution of it."[16]

The common plan/conspiracy to commit aggressive war plan, Jackson told the other delegates, was the only way to reach many of the guilty for whom specific evidence might be lacking. But more than that, Jackson was intimating that it was necessary to circumvent sovereignty issues. It was, he believed, the only way to hold Axis war criminals responsible for all their crimes, including atrocities against their own nationals. If Jackson could not get the other delegations to see it his way, he might have to pursue a course of separate trials.[17]

Jackson had kept the new secretary of state, James F. Byrnes, abreast of the development of the negotiations and on July 20 sent him an updated progress report.[18] Utterly frustrated by what he believed to be Soviet delaying tactics, Jackson now wanted to present a final offer to them. Byrnes wired a reply to Jackson on July 22, but Jackson did not receive it until the next day. Byrnes diplomatically suggested that he did not object to the tactic of a final offer, assuming it was "as close" to the Soviet position as Jackson was willing to go "without compromise of [a] fair judicial trial." Byrnes then recommended that Jackson might want simultaneously to present the Soviets an alternative plan that allowed for separate trials. Separate trials, Byrnes wrote, would "avoid some difficulties arising from differences in systems of jurisprudence, language and general approach to the problem." In any case, whether there would be one or several trials, Byrnes wanted Jackson to "avoid an embarrassing breakup of negotiations." These suggestions notwithstanding, Byrnes then gave Jackson a free hand in determining the final course of the negotiations, strengthening it by letting him know that both Stimson and McCloy concurred.[19]

On July 23, the Soviet delegation submitted revised versions of Article 6 of the Charter, the definition of the crimes, borrowing greatly from an earlier French submission.[20] This revision became the basis of discussion at the plenary meeting that day. It included no definition of aggression and no reference to a common plan or conspiracy. After Nikitchenko had introduced his version, Fyfe interjected for a few short minutes, fearing a coming explosion from Jackson and another threat to withdraw from the conference. Jackson surprised everyone, though, remaining calm and beginning his criticisms by saying in the most understated manner he could muster, "I think a great deal depends on what we are trying to accomplish by [this] definition, and I don't think this one accomplishes what the United States has had in mind to try to accomplish." It did not take him long, however, to verbalize his disgust. The protocol and subsequent trial must define the substantive international law under which the accused will be tried. Otherwise, he said, the trial would be a "travesty."[21]

Jackson then began a detailed examination of the Soviet version, indicating what it lacked and how and why the American version was better. Paragraph (b) of the Soviet version dealt with Axis atrocities: "Atrocities against the civilian population including murder and ill-treatment of civilians, the deportation of civilians to slave labour and other violations of the laws and customs of warfare." "From our point of view," Jackson said, "[it] does not reach all that we want to reach and reaches a good deal we would not want to reach. . . . The internal affairs of another government" had never been the "business" of the United States—"from time immemorial," as Jackson put it. "The way Germany treats its inhabitants, or any other country treats its inhabitants, is not our affair any more than it is the affair of some other government to interpose itself in our problems."[22]

In defending why it was necessary for these crimes to be "reached" using the charge of a criminal conspiracy to commit aggressive war, Jackson made it clear precisely what "our problems" were that the United States did not want "reached":

> We have some regrettable circumstances at times in our own country in which minorities are unfairly treated. We think it is justifiable that we interfere or attempt to bring retribution to individuals or states only because the concentration camps and the deportations were in pursuance of a common plan or enterprise of making an unjust or illegal war in which we became involved. We see no other basis on which we are justified in reaching the atrocities which were committed inside Germany, under German law, or even in violation of German law, by authorities of the German state. Without substantially this definition, we would not think we had any part in the prosecution of those things.[23]

There it was. The United States insisted that the trial of Axis war criminals set international precedent for the future in hopes of outlawing aggressive war, and at the same time demanded that no international precedent be set regarding crimes based on racial persecution unless connected to such a war. Why? The answer was just as Jackson stated it: to protect the sovereignty of the United States against accusations about its own "regrettable circumstances" at home.

It was obvious to almost every member of every delegation why the Soviet Union had objected so strenuously to basing the charges on a larger conspiracy to carry out aggressive warfare. It was no secret that the Soviet Union had participated in what many might consider aggressive warfare during the invasions of Poland and Finland in 1939. The Soviet delegation persisted until the last meeting of the conference that only Nazi crimes should come under the scope of the Agreement and Charter.

Jackson always maintained that Soviet insistence that justice be sought only for Nazi crimes was "the most serious disagreement" of the London Conference. On this point, Jackson claimed the United States would not compromise. In the Preface to his 1949 book on the negotiations, Jackson set the position of the United States this way: "The United States contended that the criminal character of such acts [Nazi war crimes and atrocities] could not depend on who committed them and that international crimes could only be defined in broad terms applicable to statesmen of any nation guilty of the proscribed conduct."[24] Jackson believed that at the time of the negotiations as well as later. But to be accurate, he should have added that these crimes had universal applicability as long as they did not include those based on racial persecution. Yes, the United States wanted to create international law applicable to all, but with one notable exception: crimes against humanity based upon racial, religious, or political persecution were only adjudicatable when connected to a conspiracy to commit a war of aggression. This specification was a necessity; certain "regrettable circumstances" at home in the United States demanded it. It was the only way, as Jackson had put it, to "reach all that we want to reach" and simultaneously protect what "we would not want to reach."[25]

At the plenary session the next day, July 24, the Soviets consented to Jackson's requirements on atrocities based on racial, religious, or political persecution. It was "quite acceptable," Nikitchenko said. In protecting the United States from charges of racial persecution at home, Jackson was also protecting the Soviet Union—and every other nation, for that matter, at least those that had not carried out aggressive warfare. Professor André Gros for the French was not so amenable. Jackson had "clearly explained" why racial and religious atrocities must be reached in such a way, he admitted, but he suggested Jackson was incorrect in his contention that other countries had not interfered in the internal affairs of other nations previously on such a basis. Giving no example in support, he then made a half-hearted suggestion that the wording be changed so that other justifications would be allowed for interventions against persecution. Fyfe took up the cause for Jackson and dismissed Gros's objection. Although the Soviet delegation had relented regarding atrocities—and the French, from this point forward, let the matter drop—the Soviets, for obvious reasons, were still determined that all the crimes be connected solely to Axis activities.

Before the next session the following day, the American and Soviet delegations both produced revised versions of Article 6. As the meeting commenced, in his own peculiarly British manner, Fyfe stated, "The drafts of the Soviet Union and the United States on article 6 have not got together so well." As far as atrocities went, the Soviet version was quite similar to that of the United States, but considerable disagreement still remained on almost everything else—and the United States still sought a specific definition of aggression that would apply to all nations at all times. The Soviets were entirely unwilling to compromise; only the Nazis were to be brought to justice for their aggression. As the discussions continued, Nikitchenko and Jackson agreed that since their first meeting they

were moving "backward" on the definition of crimes, notwithstanding having reached agreement on limiting atrocities to those committed pursuant to
aggressive warfare.[26]

With the prospects of a joint international trial looking doubtful, on the
morning of July 26, Jackson flew to Potsdam to confer with Secretary Byrnes. As
Jackson recorded in his diary, "The moment for leaving the conference seemed
strategic." In the previous week of negotiations, he had made several different
offers. One day he suggested that the effort for a joint trial should be abandoned,
and the four powers conduct separate trials. On another, Jackson said he would
recommend that the United States simply step out of the trial altogether and
leave it to the European nations. Finally, he offered that he would simply refer
the matter to the Potsdam Conference for a "political decision." In doing so,
Jackson hoped this final tactic of threatening to bring up the difficulties with
Stalin would pressure Nikitchenko to reach agreement.[27]

The Potsdam Conference between leaders of the United States, the Soviet
Union, and Great Britain began on July 17. Now that Nazi Germany had been
defeated, the Allied powers resolved at Potsdam to implement agreements reached
earlier at Yalta; the three victorious Allied powers divided Germany and Austria
into four occupation zones, as well as dividing the cities of Berlin and Vienna
into four sectors. A provisional border between Germany and Poland was also
established. President Truman, Prime Minister Churchill, and Prime Minister
Clement Atlee, who replaced Churchill during the middle of the conference,
were all deeply mistrustful of Premier Stalin and concerned over the communist
governments being installed in Soviet-occupied territories. Truman obliquely
informed Stalin about the atomic bomb, and near the end of the conference, he
gave Japan an ultimatum to surrender or face destruction. The conference was
not a particularly cooperative get-together. Given the uncertain relationship
between the United States and the Soviet Union, Jackson was concerned that
the leaders at Potsdam might conclude a political agreement regarding a trial
contrary to his desires.

Jackson arrived in Potsdam July 26 and met with Secretary Byrnes that same
night. He began by telling Byrnes of the difficulties and "run-around" the Soviets
had been giving him during the negotiations. Byrnes interjected and told Jackson
that he completely understood; after all, he was negotiating with the Soviets
himself. As Jackson noted in his diary, "He [Byrnes] felt that the only way to get
along with the Russians was to have as few joint enterprises as possible because
we were simply unable to see things alike and there were always the same kind

of misunderstandings and charges of bad faith."[28] But did this mean that Byrnes wanted to pull out of a joint trial?

Jackson went on to list the differences between the American and Soviet positions, the most important being the definition of the crimes. Byrnes told Jackson that he was in complete agreement with his stance that the crimes not be limited to the Axis powers only. He was much less supportive of Jackson's effort on atrocities. "He did not think much of our efforts to go back [before] the commencement of the war and try to reach atrocities committed by Germany against her own people," Jackson recorded. If he explained to Jackson why he thought it was a bad idea, Jackson did not record it.[29] Byrnes obviously wanted to protect the racial order at home. As a South Carolina senator in 1938, for example, Byrnes had publicly joined with southern conservatives in killing the Wagner antilynching bill.[30]

Executive secretary of the NAACP Walter White had attended the Senate sessions daily, hoping to witness the passing of a bill he had fought for over much of his career. During his filibustering remarks, Byrnes turned at his desk, pointed a finger directly at White, and attacked him personally: "What legislation will he next demand of the Congress of the United States? Will he demand that Congress enact legislation to punish the officials who fail to protect Negroes in the right to stop at hotels where white persons are entertained? . . . I do not know, but I know that he will make other demands and that those who are willing to vote for this bill will acquiesce in his subsequent demands."[31]

It is easy to imagine Byrnes admonishing Jackson with similar predictions if the Allies attempted to create international precedent in bringing Nazis to justice for all their atrocities. In time, the NAACP would have something to say about the meaning of Nuremberg and American racism, but that was a few months away. At that moment, neither White nor anyone else in America had any idea of the lengths to which representatives of the United States had gone to protect American sovereignty.

Before leaving Byrnes that night, Jackson reiterated his desire to conclude an agreement that created a joint four-power trial, and he voiced his concern that it might not come to fruition. Mindful of Byrnes's earlier admonition, Jackson said that he did not want to embarrass him or President Truman since they were at that very moment negotiating with Stalin. According to Jackson, Byrnes told him not to worry if he could not come to an agreement. He also went a step further than he did in his earlier communication, telling Jackson directly that he "thought it would be the best solution if we could agree on a definition of crimes and then we each try his own criminals by his own procedure."[32] Jackson did not note in his diary his immediate reaction to this proposition.

Back in London, Jackson did not want to continue negotiations immediately. Instead, he prepared three documents; the third, he noted, was "a memorandum of other changes in the agreement and charter necessary to our acceptance."[33] This document, dated July 31, 1945, and annotated with Jackson's handwritten changes, reflected the position of Jackson and the United States following Potsdam.[34] The last paragraph stated that Jackson was authorized by his government to conclude an agreement for separate trials if they could not agree on the procedure for a joint trial. As Byrnes had instructed, Jackson on behalf of the United States suggested he would seek agreement on the charges and then proceed separately.[35]

When the negotiations recommenced on August 2, 1945, they had reached a critical stage. Each delegation had copies of the latest American documents, including a revision of Article 6, the definition of the crimes that gave titles to the three main definitions: "The Crime of War," "War Crimes," and "Crimes Against Humanity." During the discussion that morning about evidentiary rights for the defense, Jackson called for an absolute resolution to the question of joint or separate trials. Nikitchenko, however, continued to press other details.[36]

Lord Chancellor William Jowitt, who was presiding after the announcement on August 1, 1945, of his election as part of the new Labour government in the United Kingdom, adroitly pushed ahead with the negotiations. But Jackson also continued to stress his point, saying again that separate trials would be much simpler and infinitely less time consuming. Nikitchenko then let Jackson and all the delegates know that the Soviets would only agree to a joint trial. This was why they had come to London, despite any difficulties Jackson cared to point out.[37] Nikitchenko seemed ready to reach agreement on all remaining points of difference, because he had likely received instructions from Moscow to move the process forward.

Jowitt then brought up perhaps the most important article of the charter. "Now, gentlemen, we have got Article 6." He suggested they go through the latest American draft of Article 6, point by point. Without waiting for anyone to concur, he began reading the first sentence. Nikitchenko made it clear that would not be necessary. He asked for three minor alterations in the wording of the articles. Jackson was pleased. "It sounds all right to me," he said.

Nikitchenko asked if they might dispense with the title designations for each crime that had just been added, but he was ready to concede that point as soon as Jowitt said that it was "rather convenient to have it in." Nikitchenko agreed quickly, saying, "We don't think that of great importance." The delegates agreed to keep them but decided to change "The Crime of War" to "Crimes Against Peace." There was only one remaining point of contention, and it was also dispensed with quickly. The delegates agreed that the seat of the International Military Tribunal would be Berlin and that the first trial would take place in the city of Nuremberg.[38]

Barring any unforeseen problems, the Agreement and Charter then only needed editing with the latest changes and translation into the separate languages. Nikitchenko had, he said, taken it upon his own "personal responsibility" in agreeing to the language of Article 6, the crimes, but he did not expect that it would be overruled from above. Jackson wanted to know when he might have official approval, and Nikitchenko said it should come in a day or two at most. On August 7, 1945, what everyone believed to be the final draft of the Agreement and Charter was distributed to the delegations—with one small but important correction to come later.[39]

That evening, the British delegation hosted an informal dinner for all the representatives at Claridge's Hotel. Before sitting for dinner, Lord Chancellor Jowitt made a speech belittling his own participation in the conference. Jackson spoke next. According to Alderman's recollection, he made "as customary a most excellent short speech." The "excellent" part, Alderman said, "was customary, not the short."[40]

After these and two brief addresses from Nikitchenko and then one by a member of the French delegation, it was pointed out that no one had spoken on behalf of the war criminals. The new British foreign minister, Ernest Bevin, took up that cause. He had "considerable sympathy" for them, he said. The waiting to be hanged was as bad as the actual hanging, he noted. He hoped the "chief prosecutors would not leave the poor criminals in suspense too long."[41]

The formal signing of the Agreement and Charter was scheduled for Church House in downtown London at 11:00 A.M., August 8, 1945. The ceremonial signing took place on schedule before a packed room of movie and still photographers. "The Agreement was signed this morning," Bernays related to colleague Colonel Ammi Cutter, "in front of more cameras than I knew were in the European Theatre."[42]

There were, actually, several signings. Each representative required an original in his own language and a copy of the originals in each of the others' respective languages, including separate copies for the United States and Great Britain to account for spelling and punctuation differences.[43] After the photographers had finished recording the signings for posterity, Soviet professor A. N. Trainin took the opportunity to make a brief speech thanking the other delegations and announced that his boss at the negotiations, General I. T. Nikitchenko, had been chosen as Soviet chief of counsel for the forthcoming trial.[44]

Later that day, following a 3:00 P.M. meeting of the heads of the delegations, Jackson delivered an address on the meaning of the signing from the NBC Radio facilities located at London's BBC headquarters. The address aired at 5:30 P.M. New York time, just two hours after it was announced in the United States that the Soviet Union had declared war on Japan and invaded Manchuria. Jackson's address would have to compete first with the aftereffects of Hiroshima and then with the Soviet announcement.

Those listening at home on the radio that evening heard Jackson read out that "for the first time, four of the most powerful nations have agreed not only upon the principle of liability for war crimes and crimes of persecution, but also upon the principle of individual responsibility for the crime of attacking the international peace." Leaders of nations that make aggressive war, he said, would now be held accountable. Moreover, the legal definitions under which the Allies will try the Nazis were "general definitions." He said, "They impose liability upon war-making statesmen of all countries alike." To Jackson, this was a considerable accomplishment and one, he hoped, that would reverberate in the years to come. "If we can cultivate in the world the idea that aggressive war-making is the way to the prisoner's dock rather than the way to honors, we will have accomplished something toward making the peace more secure."[45]

"Mutual concessions," he told his fellow Americans, had to be made to create a workable and acceptable legal procedure to try the defendants. Such was the price of international cooperation. He spoke of the difficulties still ahead: the "tedious prospect" of a trial conducted in four languages and the possibility of it becoming extremely long-lasting, and the overarching danger to the peace and prosperity of mankind if the world came to regard the procedure as political rather than judicial. That the victors would be sitting in judgment over the vanquished, he said, "however unfortunate it may be," was necessary. The Germans could hardly be expected to try themselves. "We must make clear to the Germans," he continued, "that the wrong for which their fallen leaders are on trial is not that they lost the war, but that they started it."[46]

"Four of the most powerful nations," as Jackson identified them, had announced that aggressive war was an international crime. He hoped that the trial would legitimate this concept as a precedent in international law for all time to come. At the end of his address, just before he noted again the difficulty of his task still ahead, he reiterated why the London Agreement and Charter and the trial to be carried out under its auspices was so significant: "I therefore want to make clear to the American people that we have taken an important step forward in this instrument in fixing individual responsibility of war mongering, among whatever peoples, as an international crime." To this he added, "We have taken another [important step] in recognizing an international accountability for persecutions, exterminations and crimes against humanity when associated with attacks on the peace of the international order."[47]

Not incidentally, a typographical error in the transcription of the different versions of the Agreement and Charter had accidentally abrogated the requirement that "murder, extermination, enslavement, deportation, and other inhumane acts committed against any civilian population, before or during the war" had to be connected to aggressive warfare to be considered criminal. Alderman had noticed the problem on August 23, 1945, and discussed it with Katherine Fite, whose services were on loan to Jackson from the State Department.

The next day Alderman brought up the problem with Jackson directly. A "discrepancy," he said, existed between the Russian-language version and the English- and French-language versions of the Charter. At an exceedingly important location in the text—Article 6, paragraph (c), the definition of "crimes against humanity"—the Russian version contained a comma; the other versions contained a semicolon. The English language version of the August 8 Charter read:

> (c) CRIMES AGAINST HUMANITY: namely, murder, extermination, enslavement, deportation, and other inhumane acts committed against any civilian population, before or during the war; or persecutions on political, racial or religious grounds in execution of or in connection with any crime within the jurisdiction of the Tribunal, whether or not in violation of the domestic law of the country where perpetrated.[48]

The punctuation mark in question appeared between the words "the war" and "or persecutions." Such a construction, if allowed to stand, would mean that only racial, religious, and political persecutions needed to be connected to aggressive warfare to be considered a criminal act.[49]

Jackson agreed with Alderman that the comma in the Russian-language version was indeed the correct punctuation; the semicolons in the English- and French-language versions were not. The intention had always been that all stated crimes against humanity "before or during the war" were only criminal if connected to aggressive warfare, not just racial, religious, and political persecutions. Jackson told Alderman not to worry about the discrepancy; the correction could easily be made, and a simple emendation to the protocol could be prepared and signed by the four powers.

Perhaps if the transcription error had made racial, religious, and political persecutions criminal whether or not they were committed "in execution of or in connection with any crime within the jurisdiction of the Tribunal," Jackson might have been more worried. In any case, as Jackson noted, "The correction made a limitation in the definition of crimes against humanity, which would run in the interest of the defendants rather than against their interest."[50] With that, the semicolon in the English and French versions was changed to match the comma in the Russian version, and all named crimes against humanity, in every version of the protocol, could be adjudicated only when committed "in execution of or in connection with any crime within the jurisdiction of the Tribunal, whether or not in violation of the domestic law of the country where perpetrated."[51]

Just three months after the end of World War II in Europe, and as the war was ending in the Pacific, the Allies had announced it was time to end a category of warfare. So important was this to Jackson, in later years, he even came to regard the outcome of the trial as secondary to the establishment of the concept that wars of aggression were unlawful and immoral acts.[52] As difficult as the negotiations had been for the Allied powers attempting to reach agreement on a trial protocol, still other problems stood in the way of bringing the defendants to trial. Jackson told biographer Eugene C. Gerhart some years later, "This is the first case I have ever tried when I had first to persuade others that a court should be established, help negotiate its establishment, and when that was done, not only prepare my case but find myself a courtroom in which to try it."[53]

The chosen location for the trial—Nuremberg, in the American Occupation Zone—was nearly destroyed, like so many other cities in Europe. Eighty-five percent of the city was in ruin, and no single block was intact. In almost every section of the city, there was no power, no running clean water, no working sewer system, no public transportation, no infrastructure at all, and there was little hope of fixing any of those problems anytime soon. American prosecution team member Major Frank B. Wallis recorded in his diary on his first night in what was left of the city, September 7, 1945: "Nuremberg is completely wrecked—the worst I have seen. The people are living in caves and cellars. . . . I talked with one of the military government officers, who told me that the policy they are following is this—everyone who was a Nazi is fired from his job—if he is a lawyer he is disbarred, etc., if he owned a business it is shut up. Then in order to get a food ration card he must register for work with the military government, and he is put to work at manual labor."[54] Not everyone, of course, was so fortunate. The smell of death still hung in the air.

The Palace of Justice, the complex of buildings that would hold the trial, like the rest of the city was in shambles. A large part of the roof was missing, apparently from Allied bomb damage. Windows were blown out, and walls were pockmarked by numerous bullets. While it would take a considerable amount of reconstruction to make ready, its imposing structure offered many advantages, not the least of which was its capacity to hold numerous prisoners and transport them to the courtroom via secure passageways. But more than that, as Sidney Alderman put it, "I could imagine nothing more fitting than that we should hold the trial of these major Nazi criminals in this ancient courthouse in the Mecca of Naziism."[55] In gold lettering on the walls of the courtroom, Alderman noted, were the "old Latin maxims, *Fiat justitia ruat coelum* and *Justitia est fundamentum regem regiis*" (Let justice be done though the heavens should fall. Justice is the foundation of any solid state).

Nuremberg, the location for Hitler's most impressive rallies, had also been the locus for the proclamation of the Nuremberg Laws in September 1935 that had taken from German Jews not just their property but their rights as well. While Jackson always maintained Nuremberg was chosen for practical reasons, the site was philosophically and historically appropriate. Jackson and his staff would spend the next three and a half months—August 8 to November 20, 1945—preparing the case against the accused. Still others would do the massive work to set up the building and its infrastructure.

The trial began November 20, 1945, in the Main Courtroom of the Palace of Justice. The dark-paneled courtroom was tightly packed to accommodate spectators, visiting dignitaries, members of the press, four teams of prosecutors, defense attorneys, the twenty-two defendants, court reporters and clerks, camera operators, a sound monitor, a dozen interpreters sequestered behind glass partitions, and the military police. Bright klieg lights illuminated the proceedings to facilitate the filming of every tribunal session. In a corner next to the interpreters' booths was a small sound control room where technicians monitored the operation of the simultaneous interpretation system that made the four-language trial possible.

At 10:00 A.M. a marshal announced, "All rise, the Tribunal will now enter." The four judges and their alternates walked into the courtroom and took their seats at the bench. Justice Lawrence, president of the tribunal, struck his gavel and began the trial. After a few preliminary remarks, he said, "The Trial which is now about to begin is unique in the history of the jurisprudence of the world and it is of supreme importance to millions of people all over the globe."[56] As the *New York Times* reported it, the "History-Making Case" had started. The former leaders of Nazi Germany were now "defendants in the greatest trial of modern times."[57]

On November 21, 1945, the president of the Nuremberg War Crimes Tribunal, Lord Justice Geoffrey Lawrence, announced, "I will now call upon the defendants to plead guilty or not guilty to the charges against them. They will proceed in turn to a point in the dock opposite to the microphone." Standing before the tribunal, defendant Hermann Göring replied, "Before I answer the question of the Tribunal whether or not I am guilty . . . ," but Justice Lawrence stopped him instantly. "I informed the Court that defendants were not entitled to make a statement. You must plead guilty or not guilty." Incensed at the rebuke, an indignant Göring responded, "I declare myself in the sense of the Indictment not guilty." Promptly, and with obvious petulance, Göring returned to his seat.

One by one, the other defendants in the courtroom that day stood before the tribunal, the prosecution teams of the four victorious Allied powers, and the worldwide press to assert their innocence. Five followed Göring's lead, declaring themselves not guilty *in the sense of the indictment*. The pleas completed, Göring, no doubt wanting to address the tribunal on the legality of the proceedings, yet again attempted to interrupt, only to be censured by Justice Lawrence: "You are not entitled to address the Tribunal except through your counsel, at the present time."[58]

Perhaps the most anticipated moment of the trial was then at hand. Chief Prosecutor for the United States Robert H. Jackson gave the now-famous opening address:

> May it please Your Honors: The privilege of opening the first trial in history for crimes against the peace of the world imposes a grave responsibility. The wrongs which we seek to condemn and punish have been so calculated, so malignant, and so devastating, that civilization cannot tolerate their being ignored, because it cannot survive their being repeated.

Forced to speak slowly so a bank of interpreters could translate his words into three additional languages—French, Russian, and German—Jackson's remarks seemed overenunciated as they resonated throughout the courtroom. "That four great nations, flushed with victory and stung with injury," he continued, "stay the hand of vengeance and voluntarily submit their captive enemies to the judgment of the law is one of the most significant tributes that Power has ever paid to reason."[59]

Jackson's opening comments filled the remainder of the day. His first task was to dismiss the notion that Nuremberg was simply "victors' justice." He went on to catalog Nazi excesses and abuses against its own citizens as well as those of conquered nations: wholesale arrests of Nazi opponents; beatings and killings; the segregation of certain individuals and groups into concentration camps; and, as we now tally, the mass extermination of approximately 6,000,000 European Jews and approximately 6,000,000 others, including Gypsies, Serbs, Poles, German opponents of Nazism, homosexuals, Jehovah's Witnesses, the disabled, and other "undesirables."[60]

Jackson committed the final segment of his address to the legal issues: justifying why the conduct of aggressive war was a crime, why government officials were personally liable, and explaining the validity of indicting the principal Nazi agencies and the German Armed Forces High Command as criminal organizations. He did not explain—nor justify—why crimes of humanity were only crimes for which the Allies could seek punishment because they were carried out as part of a conspiracy to commit aggressive warfare.

Jackson gave but one brief acknowledgment of the president under whom he had long served, the man he always thought most responsible for his standing before the tribunal that day. The Agreement and Charter under which the trial was at that moment being carried out came about, he said, "Following the instructions of the late President Roosevelt" and a decision taken at Yalta.[61] He made no mention of the formation and work of the UNWCC or, obviously, of what Herbert Pell had worked for at the behest of the president. There was no reason Jackson should have, of course. His address was about the law, the accused and their crimes, and, he anticipated, the significance of the trial to the future of international law and justice.

Concluding his opening address, Jackson intoned, "The real complaining party at your bar is Civilization. . . . [The world] does expect that your [the tribunal's] juridical action will put the forms of International Law, its precepts, its prohibitions and, most of all, its sanctions, on the side of peace, so that men and women of good will, in all countries, may have 'leave to live by no man's leave underneath the law.'"[62]

Jackson's colleagues in the courtroom, the tribunal members, the press, and the public all considered the address a great achievement. A report by Ivan H. Peterman in the *Philadelphia Inquirer* expressed widely received praise: "Eloquent but unrestrained, bitter but convincing, Justice Jackson delivered scathing charges for four hours, punctuating his lengthy 61-page indictment with horror figures and facts which fell like triphammer blows upon the ears of the accused." The defendants, "blinking before the bar of justice," as Peterman put it, "shrank and seemed overwhelmed."[63] Jackson, the country lawyer who never attended college, who rose to the highest bench in the United States, at that moment had become the most famous jurist on the planet.

The Nuremberg War Crimes Trial lasted 218 days. The prosecution called only thirty-three witnesses, relying primarily on documentary evidence. The defense nearly doubled that number, calling sixty-one witnesses. Nineteen defendants testified on their own behalf. Trial transcripts were kept in all four languages; the English-language version numbers more than seventeen thousand pages. The prosecution examined more than one hundred thousand captured Nazi documents and scrutinized ten thousand of those for possible use at the trial. Ultimately, of those, four thousand were translated into each of the four languages and introduced by the prosecution.[64]

More than 100,000 feet of film and 25,000 still photographs were brought to Nuremberg. Eighteen hundred photographs were introduced as evidence. At its peak, the American prosecution team numbered 654, including lawyers, secretaries, interpreters, and translators. The other three delegations combined numbered nearly the same. The American delegation also provided all security for the trial as well as administrative services to the many members of the international press gathered to witness the trial. Approximately 50 million pages of typed and mimeographed material were produced. Each day of the 218 days of the trial, a team of twelve interpreters translated the proceedings simultaneously, and transcripts were later produced in all four languages.[65]

On October 7, 1946, Jackson reported the results of the trial to U.S. president Truman. His report was widely reprinted in the press. The tribunal found nineteen of twenty-two defendants guilty on at least one of the charges. Twelve were sentenced to death, three to life terms in prison, and four to prison terms of ten to twenty years. To accomplish such a result, Jackson asserted that "the four dominant powers of the earth" had "for the first time made explicit and unambiguous" what had been formerly only "implicit in International Law." The United States, the Soviet Union, Great Britain, France, and nineteen other adherents had declared that "to prepare, incite, or wage a war of aggression, or to conspire with others to do so, is a crime against international society, and that to persecute, oppress, or do violence to individuals or minorities on political, racial, or religious grounds in connection with such a war, or to exterminate, enslave, or deport civilian populations, is an international crime, and that for the commission of such crimes individuals are responsible."[66]

At face value, making such crimes implicit in international law was quite an accomplishment. But the crime of aggression remained undefined. The Soviets had objected to defining it during the London negotiations, and the United States had acquiesced in order to reach agreement. Moreover, racial, religious, and political persecutions were only international crimes when committed in connection with such a war.

Still, Jackson concluded, the Allies had "put International Law squarely on the side of peace as against aggressive warfare, and on the side of humanity as against persecution." Of course, here he neglected the qualifier. That matter notwithstanding, to underscore this penultimate point on the trial and the law under which it was conducted, Jackson chose to quote Woodrow Wilson. The Nuremberg Trial and the law code created for it had done "more than anything in our time to give to International Law what Woodrow Wilson described as 'the kind of vitality it can only have if it is a real expression of our moral judgment.'" A nice quote, indeed, but certainly one that did not direct credit appropriately.

After all, the World War I Allies had failed to conduct any substantive war crimes trials, nothing on an international scale, and perhaps worst of all, nothing for the Armenian genocide. Flaws and limitations aside, the Allies of World War II did conduct an international trial, and they did seek justice for the Holocaust, thanks in large measure to the consistency of FDR, the loyalty—and fortitude—of his lifelong friend Herbert C. Pell, and the legal expertise of Robert H. Jackson to see the trial through to the sentencing of the accused.

CONCLUSION

"Freedom Means the Supremacy of
Human Rights Everywhere"

*I realize that American leadership will involve costs that we have
never met; responsibilities that we have never faced; problems that
we have never considered, but I see no reason to think that we are
unable to meet these costs, or that the responsibilities and problems
will be better faced by anyone else.*

Herbert C. Pell, Summer 1945

In one respect, this book recounts a familiar story: the role of domestic politics in
shaping international policy. In this circumstance, however, the subject matter is
especially remarkable. Policymakers were trying to find a way to seek justice for
the Holocaust, a crime so vast and unprecedented in scale, so evil in its execution
that even today it almost defies comprehension. But when it came to making
a decision about how to prosecute Nazi crimes against humanity, domestic
policy needs constrained the application and extension of justice. Nevertheless,
one of the most staggering crimes of human history offered an unprecedented
opportunity for the advancement of human rights.

Many certainly thought as much at the time. General Eisenhower thought
so when he sent communiqués to both Washington and London suggesting
that members of the press and legislatures be sent to see what the would-be
thousand-year Reich had carried out. He viewed the horror firsthand on April
12, 1945. Writing of his experience three years later in his memoir *Crusade in*

Europe, he noted, "I have never felt able to describe my emotional reactions. . . . I have never at any other time experienced an equal sense of shock."[1]

Many American congressmen also thought so when, on taking up the invitation of Eisenhower, they visited Dachau, Buchenwald, and Dora—just three of twenty-three main camps (some estimates put the total number of camps where the Nazis carried out their crimes in the years 1933–45 at as many as twenty thousand).[2] In their May 8, 1945, statement to the press, the congressmen reported finding "the extent, devices, methods, and conditions of torture almost beyond the power of words to describe." What took place at the camps, they announced, had been "no less than organized crime against civilization and humanity."[3]

Vincent Tubbs, a war correspondent for the *Baltimore Afro-American,* gave his readers a devastatingly stark portrayal of the atrocities in his "Inside View of Nazi Horror Camp." "The closer we got to the place," he wrote, "the more peculiar the air smelled. It was like burning brown sugar with a low, sour stench of unwashed bodies." He went on to describe the same images that other newspapers had been reporting: "the charred bodies of uncountable men lay in tangled heaps, still smoldering and giving off this bluish smoke and sickening odor." Human limbs "looked like water pipes or chair legs. . . . Torsos were little more than skeletons with skin on them."[4]

"On the road and in the nearby towns that afternoon and following day," Tubbs reported, "survivors dressed in convict-striped muslin kissed the hands and feet of American soldiers." Tubbs became part of his own story. "A man of 60 with tears in his eyes and a boy of 15 who didn't have enough water in his body to cry if he'd tried, came and kissed my hand." Tubbs noted that this camp was located just a short walking distance from Landsberg prison, "where Hitler wrote 'Mein Kampf.'" What he observed was just so unbelievable, even to him, that he wrote poignantly, "On my honor it was one of the most inhumane attempts at race extermination any people ever suffered."[5]

Chief of the Morale Branch of the army, Frederick Osborn, spent just one day at Dachau. During the First World War, he had been a volunteer for the Red Cross. Of that experience, he wrote, "Nothing I saw in France seemed unexpected. The dead, the wounded on the battlefield and in the hospitals, the hasty burials behind the lines, the intoning of the priest over the rough coffins, dim over the noise of the guns, and the smell of gunpowder mixed with the sickly sweet smell of bodies too long unburied." With the detachment expected of men of his class, he observed, "It was all part of the story of the human race over the millennia of years, as real and natural as the scenes at home. It was hard, like an injury or an illness, but it was real and never unexpected." Recalling his visit to Germany in 1945, Osborn said, "In contrast, the day I spent at Dachau in World War II affected me deeply. I was never quite the same after that. . . . Ahead lay the unfolding of a new world, not measurable in any terms of the past history of man."[6]

No one who bore witness to what happened in the camps could help being forever changed. Ever since, even those who only experience the Holocaust through books and films, in classrooms, and at museums have been similarly transformed. The lesson of this war, it seems, is that the capacity of humankind for malevolence is unbounded. If ever there had been an opportunity to find meaning from unprecedented death and destruction this must have been it. An evil so unparalleled in human history required a response.

The aims of the Fascist powers and the racist ideology underpinning them had led the Allies to respond with an opposing statement of principles. A racist war seeking global domination obligated the defense of liberty, equality, and human rights—and demanded their universal application. At the urging of FDR, and from the beginning of American entry into the war, the Allies had presented World War II as an ideological struggle between good and evil. In actuality, the president had been pushing this idea through rhetoric and policy even before America's entry into the war.

At the Brooklyn Academy of Music on November 1, 1940, while seeking a then unprecedented third term, FDR reminded American voters, "We are a nation of many nationalities, many races, many religions—bound together by a single unity, the unity of freedom and equality. Whoever seeks to set one nationality against another, seeks to degrade all nationalities. Whoever seeks to set one race against another, seeks to enslave all races. Whoever seeks to set one religion against another, seeks to destroy all religion."[7] This was the same president who said on January 6, 1941, in his annual message to Congress, that "we look forward to a world founded upon four essential freedoms": "freedom of speech and expression," "freedom of religion," "freedom from want," and "freedom from fear." For obvious reasons, we know the address today as "The Four Freedoms." He had something else of note to say that day lost in the simplicity of his larger message:

> Since the beginning of our American history, we have been engaged in change—in a perpetual peaceful revolution—a revolution which goes on steadily, quietly adjusting itself to changing conditions—without the concentration camp or the quick-lime in the ditch. The world order which

we seek is the cooperation of free countries, working together in a friendly, civilized society . . . [where] freedom means the supremacy of human rights everywhere.[8]

Americans have always liked powerful rhetoric, particularly when it recalls our most deeply held assumptions about the country and its mission, and even more so when it is spoken so eloquently.

FDR's choice of counterpositioning American ideals as against those of the Nazis by declaring the steady and "peaceful" development of American history toward realizing these freedoms "without the concentration camp or the quick-lime in the ditch" was stunning for a speech delivered in January 1941. It is reasonable to conclude that FDR's approach for the development of a plan to seek justice for the Holocaust can be found in these words—"a revolution which goes on steadily, quietly adjusting itself to changing conditions."[9]

FDR's broad vision expressed in the Four Freedoms underlay the less elegant but no less important eight-point Atlantic Charter issued on August 14, 1941.[10] Among other things, it promised the protection of peoples to determine their own destinies and the restoration of "sovereign rights and self-government . . . to those who have been forcibly deprived of them." Promising "that all men in all the lands may live out their lives in freedom from fear and want," the charter assured that a renewed effort will be undertaken toward "the abandonment of the use of force" and toward limiting "the crushing burden of armaments" following the Nazi defeat.[11] Back in 1936, with the help of Robert Jackson, FDR had said it more simply: "I hate war."[12]

Embedded in all these ideas, however, was the paramount importance of sovereignty—the independence of free people everywhere to determine the course of their own lives and their own nations. One wonders the degree to which FDR recognized that this promise of the Atlantic Charter posed so many dilemmas—politically, legally, and morally—in war. Moreover, he must have known that the idea put forth in the charter to establish "a wider and permanent system of general security" required a diminution of sovereignty and would not come easy for Americans.

The "Declaration by United Nations" on January 1, 1942, gave full expression of these tenets with every signatory subscribing to the "purposes and principles embodied" in the Atlantic Charter. At the same time, this declaration seemed to make implicit that the exigencies of war could put sovereignty on hold. "Being convinced that complete victory over their enemies is essential to defend life, liberty, independence and religious freedom, and to preserve human rights and justice in their own lands as well as in other lands," the signatories affirmed themselves "engaged in a common struggle against savage and brutal forces seeking to subjugate the world."[13] To preserve these values in one's own nation—to the extent they existed—was one thing, but to pursue them in other nations was something else altogether. High ideals are difficult for one nation to foist upon another, especially when those ideas are incompletely realized at home. The effort to seek justice for the Holocaust demonstrated that difficulty all too well.

The Allied powers had declared World War II a struggle not just to defend but also to extend Western democratic ideals. These values—life, liberty, and freedom—had been augmented to include the moral principle of human rights and the legal principle of justice for all peoples. However, those ideals, both old and new, were themselves applied unequally in Allied nations, including in the United States. But here, in this declaration, the signatories were calling for the application of these principles "in their own lands as well as others." As Churchill later noted, "The Declaration could not by itself win battles, but it set forth who we were and what we were fighting for."[14]

The dissemination of this rhetoric—and the problems created by doing so—continued throughout the war years. It was present to some degree in every pronouncement on war crimes, most obviously perhaps in FDR's March 24, 1944, statement on atrocities, which had been so important to Herbert Pell on the UNWCC. "The United Nations," the president had then pledged, "are fighting to make a world in which tyranny and aggression can not exist; a world based upon freedom, equality and justice; a world in which all persons regardless of race, color or creed may live in peace, honor and dignity."[15] And it was certainly present in Robert Jackson's opening statement at Nuremberg when he said, "The wrongs which we seek to condemn and punish have been so calculated, so malignant, and so devastating, that civilization cannot tolerate their being ignored, because it cannot survive their being repeated."[16]

Following the trial at Nuremberg, the victorious Allied powers had initially planned to hold subsequent international trials to bring so-called lesser criminals to justice. Political and practical difficulties between the United States, the Soviet Union, the United Kingdom, and France ended that strategy even before the first trial concluded.

On December 20, 1945, the Allied Control Council issued Control Council Law No. 10. The Control Council operated as a military governing body in the occupation zones in Germany. Control Council Law No. 10 authorized the occupying powers to bring additional war criminals to justice in separate trials within each zone under an updated list of acts recognized as crimes. "Crimes against Humanity" were no longer linked to a conspiracy to commit aggressive war.[17] Just like that, with no discussion or apparently any worries about "regrettable circumstances" in the United States in which "minorities are unfairly treated," the requirement that crimes based on racial, religious, or political persecution be connected to aggressive war was abrogated. There need not have been any concern, of course. The jurisdiction of Control Council Law No. 10 was limited to the occupation zones in Germany. Moreover, any subsequent trials were not international trials.

Between December 1946 and April 1949 the United States held twelve additional trials in the American-occupied zone of Germany.[18] The judges and prosecutors were all Americans; Brigadier General Telford Taylor served as chief counsel for the prosecution. As Arieh Kochavi noted in *Prelude to Nuremberg*, although it had not been required, many judges convicted war criminals in these trials for crimes against humanity only when those crimes were connected with other charges.[19]

Before the subsequent trials played themselves out, the United Nations General Assembly recognized "genocide" as an international crime in December 1946. Two years later, on December 9, 1948, the General Assembly approved the Convention on the Prevention and Punishment of the Crime of Genocide and announced unequivocally that genocide was a crime whether or not committed in time of war. Article II defined genocide as "acts committed with intent to destroy, in whole or in part, a national, ethnical, racial or religious group." Article I stated "that genocide, whether committed in time of peace or in time of war, is a crime under international law." Paradoxically, Nuremberg's circumscription of crimes against humanity provided the impetus for Raphael Lemkin's effort to push for its recognition as an international crime at the United Nations. Lemkin was the originator of the term "genocide."[20]

Legal scholar William Schabas argues that it "seems likely that . . . there would have been no need to define genocide as a distinct international crime" without the limitations placed on crimes against humanity at Nuremberg.[21] The London Charter had circumscribed "crimes against humanity" with its connection to aggressive war. The Nuremberg tribunal had ruled that the Nazi "policy of terror was certainly carried out on a vast scale," but that the prosecution had not "satisfactorily proved" that those acts carried out before the war were done in execution of a conspiracy to commit aggressive war.[22] Lemkin and others, therefore, were motivated to pursue codification of genocide with the United Nations.[23]

Of course, genocide is not the same as crimes against humanity in a strictly legal sense. But, as Schabas put it, they "certainly belong to the same *genus* of international crime."[24] Although Nuremberg's "crimes against humanity" was limited to a connection with aggressive war, in addition to "murder, extermination, enslavement, deportation, and other inhumane acts committed against any civilian population, before or during the war," it did include the codification that "persecutions on political, racial or religious grounds" were a crime "whether or not in violation of the domestic law of the country where perpetrated."[25] The Convention on the Prevention and Punishment of the Crime of Genocide required that persecutions must result in large-scale exterminations (national, ethnical, racial, or religious) before such actions can be considered to rise to the level of an international crime.[26] Take note, however, that in the wake of Nuremberg, "genocide" (and war crimes for that matter) has become a recognized international crime; "crimes against humanity" has not. In other words, the London Charter's proscription against "persecutions on political, racial or religious grounds," restricted though they were, are still not a codified international crime as of the time of this writing.

The American effort to restrict crimes against humanity in the London Charter was not just a legal distraction. It mattered as well to the Soviet Union, Great Britain, and France, all of whom had their own reasons to circumscribe the scope of jurisdiction. For American policymakers, sovereignty—protecting the existing social order in the United States, was a major consideration. Jackson and Byrnes had found it so important a restriction that they were willing to blow up the entire international agreement and hold separate trials.

From a twenty-first-century perspective, it is easy to assert that the Allied rhetoric for fighting the war and the scope of the Nazi crimes themselves as well as the fraudulent ideal underlying their commission (the Nazi conception of an Aryan master race) should have made more impact on those responsible for American war crimes policy planning. Perhaps it should have caused them to move beyond the need to protect the social order in America. That would not have been an easy thing to do, however, considering the state of American morality on racial matters at the time. Doing such a thing, moreover, would have revoked the principle of state sovereignty, something no nation was willing to abandon then or now.

As Jackson put it, "The most significant results of applying these definitions [conspiracy, crimes against peace, war crimes, crimes against humanity] as the laws of nations are to outlaw wars of aggression and to lift to the level of an international offense the persecution of minorities for the purpose of clearing the road to war."[27] Circumscribed though it was by the need to protect sovereignty, nonetheless, it was an important initial step in the advancement of human rights and international law. Jackson, though, always retained his lawyer's perspective: "it would be extravagant to claim" that Nuremberg could "make aggressive war or persecution of minorities impossible just as it would be extravagant to claim that our federal laws make federal crime impossible. . . . But we cannot doubt that they strengthen the bulwarks of peace and tolerance."[28]

Roy Wilkins of the NAACP wrote in *The Crisis* shortly after the conclusion of the trial that the verdict had been generally hailed, but he pointed out that had the virtual annihilation of Jews in Europe not been connected with Germany's implementation of aggressive warfare, the Nazis would not have been prosecuted. Wilkins concluded, "It is thus possible for any nation to grievously mistreat any minority within its borders without fear of punishment before a world tribunal, so long as the mistreatment is not part of warfare against another nation." Where was the trial against the grievous mistreatment of minorities in America? "America," Wilkins wrote, "may continue to mistreat its Negro minority without being hauled before any world court." Wilkins closed his editorial by stating that Nuremberg went "only part way; the next hope of all minorities lies in the United Nations where through long and painful argument, devious and delaying committee action, and political power trading, it may be possible to establish and correct some of the crimes against minority and so-called backward peoples."[29]

While Jackson has received considerable scholarly and popular attention for Nuremberg, when it came to seeking justice for crimes against humanity, he was implementing what Pell had worked toward on the UNWCC at the behest of FDR and against so many obstacles. But Jackson fully agreed with the president's secretary of war, Henry L. Stimson, who wanted Nuremberg to be an effort seek justice, not vengeance, as long as seeking justice for the Holocaust did not create a boomerang effect back in the United States. Pell, for his part, had not been concerned about any impact that seeking justice for racial persecution in Europe might have on the United States. Pell, Stimson, and Jackson were each trying to implement FDR's wartime promise of "All who share the guilt shall share the punishment."[30]

Appreciating the meaning of this discussion of sovereignty is not meant to obscure what I have attempted to reveal in the breadth of this book: the monumental—and contested—effort undertaken by American and Allied representatives to seek justice for the Holocaust. Considering the politics, personalities, and the momentum of events, the results were likely the most that could have been achieved. Among the many protagonists in this book, acting on behalf of their country as they saw it—Cordell Hull, Green Hackworth, Henry Morgen-thau, Josiah DuBois, Henry Stimson, Murray C. Bernays, William Chanler, and so many others—two deserve a final accounting. One, President Franklin D. Roosevelt, known by so many—and for so much—deserves greater credit for his steadfast determination that the Allies seek justice for the Holocaust, however accomplished. The other, Herbert Pell, although known to so few, deserves recognition—even gratitude—for his unheralded efforts on the UNWCC.[31]

We can never know with any certainty what might have happened had FDR not passed away in April 1945. We can be confident, however, that he would have accepted the London Agreement and Charter as worked out by Jackson. He understood the "regrettable circumstances" as well as any politician could. He knew that sovereignty mattered to Americans through his experience getting the nation ready for—and its citizens comfortable with—the responsibilities that come with entering another world war. As a Democrat who needed the southern vote, he understood the potential domestic political consequences had crimes against humanity not been connected to aggressive war. More than that, no matter how he may have felt about America's unequal social order, he believed any change had to come from within and that it could not come immediately. When it came to Nazi war crimes and the Holocaust, FDR led a successful effort to seek justice.[32] His purpose was to make sure, to the extent that it was possible, that "All who share the guilt shall share the punishment."

Through his decades-long relationship with FDR, Pell observed the leadership qualities of his friend. In May 1945 he shared it with his son: "The real leader is always he who can know men and use them. For such people, the greatest necessity is willingness at all times to accept responsibility and to make decisions. Of course, consult people . . . but when a decision has to be made, make it." Pell added, almost as an afterthought, "I have said nothing about character, because that has to be assumed. Without character, nothing can be done."[33]

Of course, FDR's "use" of people was not always something to emulate. If there is fault to be found, we can certainly find it in FDR's reliance on the State Department to support Pell on the UNWCC. But it was not as if FDR had any other choice, given the demands of his job and, later, his declining health. But he knew his friend Pell. He knew how Pell thought and what he thought, particularly as it related to America's place in the world. And FDR had observed Pell's character through years of politics and campaigns, and through his correspondence as his ambassador.

Pell in his parlor later in life. *Courtesy of Distinctive Collections, University of Rhode Island Library.*

Still, by 1942–43 FDR fully understood the attitudes and tendencies—even the animosity—some of the leaders at State held toward him. Given Pell's relationship with the department, FDR had to know that Pell did not fit with that crowd—that his selection of Pell for the UNWCC would not be well taken. But that was how the president liked to operate. In this case, his selection of Pell guaranteed conflicting views on war crimes and atrocities procedures, thus ensuring that all would have to rely on presidential guidance along the way and ultimately for final decisions. FDR probably did not expect Hackworth's maneuverings, however. In the end, although he did not live to see it, the president did achieve his promise, broadly defined, of justice for war crimes and atrocities.

To his credit, Pell never expressed any outright animosity for how the president had treated him at the end. He could never bring himself to believe that FDR abandoned him. Pell accepted that, as his representative on the UNWCC, he worked for the president, not the man he once called "Frank." Pell's own experience in public life and his observations of FDR likely helped him understand that people and reputations and friendships were secondary to policy needs. And Herbert Pell was not one to dwell too much on public disappointments, real or perceived. Already by May 1945, he had moved on to a degree, writing proudly to his son, "Your career, which is now my great interest, seems to be starting very well."[34] Pell's interest in Claiborne's career, of course, had been under way by then for quite some time.

After his departure from the Roosevelt administration, Pell became quite circumspect about his own career. Upon turning seventy in 1954, Pell wrote Claiborne that he would "never in his life come across a man who has been freer ... [and] on the whole ... happier" than his own father.[35] Pell's apparent contentment with the trajectory of his life, however, must have masked a frustration over the lack of any public acknowledgment of his work on the UNWCC. At one time he had expected that it would become the most recognized accomplishment of his career.

Pell came to look upon his brief tenure on the Commission as just one part of his varied and fortunate life. Given what happened, to have done anything else probably would have been too much to bear. Besides, it would have been a vanity inappropriate for a gentleman-aristocrat who believed, like his friend FDR, in the requirements of noblesse oblige. Pell passed his post–World War II years quietly as a man of leisure, enjoying travel, books, and grandchildren, and never sure that his actions on the UNWCC had meant something. What he likely considered his greatest accomplishment took place in 1960.

On Tuesday, November 8—election night in the United States—Pell surged through the crowd at the Providence, Rhode Island, Sheraton-Biltmore Hotel, single-mindedly keen to congratulate his son, Claiborne, on his election to the U.S. Senate. Even at age seventy-six, the six-feet-five, barrel-chested gentleman still possessed an enormous presence. Intercepted by reporters, the senior Pell, noted by them as a former one-term congressman, ambassador to Portugal and Hungary, and seasoned political manager of Al Smith and Franklin Roosevelt—from 1943 to 1945 he had also served as U.S. representative on the UNWCC, but these reporters, like most other Americans, were completely unaware of that—announced with pride, "I have run for public office and have handled campaigns, but no campaign in which I was interested has given me anything like the pleasure and happiness I have now." Asked if he had any role in his son's success, Pell enthusiastically responded, "I certainly did!" Before his son's wincing managers could interject, Pell explained, self-effacingly and no doubt with a wry smile, "I stayed away."[36] Although Pell had been away from public service since January 1945, he would have liked nothing more than to have helped his son campaign. Pell's role in his son's success, however, was assured long before that election season.

Pell died not long thereafter in the summer of 1961 while taking one of his grandsons on a tour of Europe, a favorite activity since he was a young man. He was surely trying to pass on his own love for travel to his grandson. Pell spent his final day, of all places, in Germany. He died of a heart attack while crossing a street in Munich.[37]

Two years later, on Sunday, August 25, 1963, a plaque was dedicated in his honor at Trinity Church, Newport, Rhode Island. Such plaques are traditionally supposed to highlight the most notable accomplishments of the person honored. In Pell's case, there was one conspicuous omission. Herbert Claiborne Pell, the "kind and beloved public servant & scholar," had served as a congressman and ambassador, but nowhere was it noted that he had served as U.S. representative on the UNWCC.[38] Perhaps this was fitting in one way. Pell himself never quite understood what he had accomplished. He was not the only one, then or now.

The Reverend Canon Lockett Ford Ballard delivered the sermon in Pell's honor. Regrettably, the reverend knew very little about the man of whom he was speaking. At least Pell's service on the UNWCC was given a brief mention: "After the victory of World War II, Mr. Pell served as the American Member of the United Nations Commission for the Investigation of War Crimes." This, of course, was not quite accurate. Pell was long gone from the Commission before the end of the war, and the Commission had become mostly irrelevant by that time. But that was not the worst of it.

Reverend Ballard told those in attendance, "I do not know if Herbert Claiborne Pell ever fully understood the horrible strength on which Hitler flashed to his few years of conquest."[39] Pell understood it all too well and more than most. Even before the outbreak of war, he was one who had fully grasped the dangers of Hitler and his fascist ideology. And for a time, as American representative on the UNWCC, against every obstruction put up by the U.S. State Department, he fought continuously to do something about it.

Forty-eight years later, in January 2009, Pell's son, Claiborne, was eulogized by longtime friends, including former president Bill Clinton. From the podium—directly in front of his father's plaque—Clinton said of Claiborne, "He was the right kind of aristocrat: a champion by choice, not by circumstance, of the common good and our common future and our common dreams, in a long life of grace, generous spirit, kind heart, and determination right up to the very end." These words for the son would have fit well for the father, perhaps even better, particularly because of his service on the UNWCC.

Claiborne spent much of his life trying to live up to his father's expectations and accomplishments —especially what he considered his father's greatest, seeking justice for the Holocaust. Claiborne's work produced a long list of his own achievements that served so many: Pell Grants, the National Endowment for the Arts, and the National Endowment for the Humanities, to name three. In his final year in the Senate in 1996, Claiborne voted against the Defense of Marriage Act, which called for a ban on the recognition of same-sex marriage (it passed, but was eventually ruled unconstitutional in 2013).[40]

His father, Herbert Pell, believed the United States was the greatest nation on earth and, therefore, had to do great things. To his son Claiborne, he wrote, a year before his service on the UNWCC that America should "run and control the world after the war, suppressing disorder wherever it may arise and protecting justice all over the surface of the globe."[41] This was why he acted as he had on the UNWCC at the behest of his friend the president and on behalf of Europe's minorities. Following his removal from the UNWCC, he stated it more fully:

> I realize that American leadership will involve costs that we have never met; responsibilities that we have never faced; problems that we have never considered, but I see no reason to think that we are unable to meet these costs, or that the responsibilities and problems will be better faced by anyone else. On balance, I am in favor of the United States taking the lead, but if we take it, we must take it firmly. We cannot refuse responsibility. We cannot wait months while pettifoggers consider precedents. When a present problem demands a present answer, that answer must be given at once, and as well as possible, without waiting for months of fruitless consultation.[42]

On November 13, 1945, ten months after his removal from the UNWCC and two months after the birth of his first grandson—Herbert Claiborne "Bertie" Pell III—Pell wrote Claiborne's wife, Nuala, offering some advice on his new grandson's life and some recollections—and assessments—on his own. "I am working and thinking now to give him, after my time," he wrote, "a happy and contented life." Of his own time, he allowed, "I have had my share. I know of no one who has been so well served by fortune. . . . It is for me to repay to the future as much as I can of the debt which I owe the past."[43]

The previous evening, Pell gave an address at Vassar Temple in Poughkeepsie, New York, titled "The Prosecution of War Criminals." The *Poughkeepsie Journal* labeled it, modestly, "a subject he has been actively concerned with as a former United States Representative to the War Crimes commission."[44] Prior to his talk, in the afternoon, he sat in on a meeting with a group hoping to locate the newly formed United Nations at Hyde Park in honor of the late president. They asked Pell to consider speaking in favor of the idea. He did not really want to do it, he told Nuala, but he would if he felt there was a chance of its success. "I have carried worse things through in my time," he wrote.[45] Indeed he had. Through it all, his loyalty to FDR had endured. Although the United Nations headquarters ultimately was not destined for Hyde Park, at least it was close by and in the same state.

ABBREVIATIONS

Alderman, "Reminiscences" | Sidney S. Alderman, The Reminiscences of Sidney S. Alderman; Oral History Research Office, Columbia University, N.Y.

Bernays, "Personal Report to Mrs. Bernays" | Murray C. Bernays, "Personal Report to Mrs. Murray C. Bernays," June 10, 1945, Box 1, Correspondence June–July 1945, MCBP

Conspiracy | Conspiracy, Box 5, Records Relating to German War Crimes 1942–1946, Records of the Legal Adviser

CPP | Claiborne Pell Papers, Distinctive Collections, University of Rhode Island Library, Kingston, R.I.

State Dept.'s Policy Committee Papers (1942–44) | State Department's Policy Committee Papers (1942–44), Folder 2 of 2, Box 5, Records Relating to German War Crimes 1942–1946, Records of the Legal Adviser

EAC | European Advisory Committee

Establishment of Commission | Establishment of Commission, Box 6, Records of US Participation in UN War Crimes Commission 1943–1949, Records of the Legal Adviser

FDR | Franklin D. Roosevelt

FDRL | Franklin Delano Roosevelt Library, Hyde Park, N.Y.

FDRP | Franklin D. Roosevelt Papers, FDRL, Hyde Park, N.Y.

General Correspondence | General Correspondence, HCPP

HCP | Herbert C. Pell

HCP, "Reminiscences" | The Reminiscences of Herbert C. Pell, Oral History Research Office, Columbia University, N.Y.

HCPP | Herbert C. Pell Papers, FDRL, Hyde Park, N.Y.

Hull, Cordell | Hull, Cordell, Box 10, 9–General Correspondence, HCPP

IMT | International Military Tribunal

Jackson, "Justice Jackson's Story" | Robert Houghwout Jackson, "Justice Jackson's Story," Container 191, Folder 9, Biographical File, 1936–1970, n.d., Robert H. Jackson Papers, Manuscript Division, Library of Congress, Washington, D.C.

Jackson Diary | Robert H. Jackson, Container 95, Diary kept by Jackson, 27 Apr.–19 Nov. 1945, Pre-Trial Material, Nuremberg War Crimes Trial, Legal File, 1919–1962, n.d., Robert H. Jackson Papers; Manuscript Division, Library of Congress, Washington, D.C.

MCBP | Murray C. Bernays Papers, American Heritage Center, Laramie, Wyo.

McCloy Correspondence | ASW 370.8 Germany to 15 September 1944, Box 26, Formerly Security-Classified Correspondence of John J. McCloy, 1941–45, War Department, Office of the Assistant Secretary of War, Records of the Office of the Secretary of War (1890–09/18/1997), RG 107, NACP

NACP | National Archives at College Park, College Park, Md.

OF5152 | OF 5152–War Crimes Investigating Commission 1942–45, Official File, FDRP

Oral History Research Office | Oral History Research Office, Columbia University, N.Y.

Pell, Claiborne | Pell, Claiborne 1943–60, Box 19, General Correspondence

Pell Correspondence | Pell Correspondence, Box 5, Records Relating to German War Crimes 1942–1946, Records of the Legal Adviser

Records of the Legal Adviser | Records of the Legal Adviser Relating to War Crimes, RG 59, NACP

RG | Record Group

Roosevelt, FD 1929–35 | Roosevelt, FD 1929–35, Box 24, General Correspondence

Roosevelt, FD 1936–45 | Roosevelt, FD 1936–45, Box 25, General Correspondence

Stimson Diary | Henry Lewis Stimson Papers (MS 465), Manuscripts and Archives, Yale University Library, New Haven, Conn.

Trial and Punishment of War Criminals | Trial and Punishment of War Criminals: A Summary Statement on Treasury Department Participation in Molding the United States Recommendations for Treating War Criminals, Reparations and War Crimes, Box 396—Final Draft of 1067, Sub-Series 12: Germany Is Our Problem, Series 1: General Correspondence, 1933–1945, Henry Morgenthau Jr. Papers, FDRL

Untitled Recollections, May 1945 | Untitled Recollections of Tenure on the UNWCC, May 1945, War Crimes Commission: Pell Notes and Statements, Box 28, General Correspondence

UNWCC | United Nations War Crimes Commission

USFET | United States Forces European Theater

War Crimes Commission | War Crimes Commission, Box 170, President's Secretary File, FDRL

War Crimes Commission: Correspondence | War Crimes Commission: State Department, Box 28, General Correspondence

War Crimes Commission: State Department | War Crimes Commission: State Department, Box 28, General Correspondence

War Crimes—Correspondence with Mr. Pell | War Crimes—Correspondence with Mr. Pell, Box 6, Records Relating to US Participation in the UN War Crimes Commission 1943–1949, Records of the Legal Adviser, RG 59, NACP

War Crimes—Miscellaneous Correspondence 1943 | War Crimes—Miscellaneous Correspondence January–December 1943, Box 5, Records Relating to German War Crimes 1942–1946, Records of the Legal Adviser

War Crimes—Miscellaneous Correspondence 1944 | War Crimes—Miscellaneous Correspondence January–December 1944, Box 5, Records Relating to German War Crimes 1942–1946, Records of the Legal Adviser

Winant | Winant, John G. (folder), Box 29, General Correspondence
WJC | World Jewish Congress
WRB | War Refugee Board

NOTES

Preface

1. Jackson, *Report of Robert H. Jackson*, 423.

Introduction

Epigraph: HCP to Claiborne Pell, September 9, 1942, CPP.

1. United States Congress, Senate Committee on Foreign Relations, and United States Department of State, *Decade of American Foreign Policy*, 13.

2. During World War II, the term "Holocaust" was not used to define the Nazi attempt to exterminate European Jews. In February 1944, for example, Herbert C. Pell wrote of atrocities against and exterminations of German Jews as fitting within President Franklin D. Roosevelt's phrase "crimes against humanity" (HCP to FDR, February 16, 1944, Roosevelt, FD 1936–45). Pell believed that these crimes as well as similar Nazi crimes against enemy nationals "because of race, religion or political opinion" must be treated as war crimes (HCP to FDR, March 5, 1945, Roosevelt, FD 1936–45). Dan Plesch points out that "beginning with the United Nations Declaration on the Persecution of Jews of 1942, the term 'extermination' of the Jews was in general use among the Allies and was an accepted concept within the commission" (*Human Rights after Hitler*). Today, we commonly use the term "The Holocaust" to define that extermination; however, debate still exists among scholars over the precise definition of the term. Some—perhaps most—use the term exclusively for the attempted extermination of European Jewry, while others use the term to encompass all Nazi attempts at extermination. Because this book centers on Pell's effort to include atrocities against German Jews as well as all those targeted for persecution and extermination based on race, religion, or politics, as war crimes, the term "Holocaust" is used in the title and throughout the book. For more on the origin of the term, see Ofer, "Linguistic Conceptualization of the Holocaust in Palestine and Israel," and Petrie, "Secular Word Holocaust."

3. The Soviet Union and France both used a system of law commonly referred to as the continental system, an inquisitorial process. The United Kingdom and the United States, with some variations, used a system of common or Anglo-Saxon law, which is adversarial.

4. The Allies indicted twenty-four defendants, two of whom for reasons noted below were not prosecuted, and one was tried in absentia: Martin Bormann (in absentia), Karl Dönitz, Hans Frank, Wilhelm Frick, Hans Fritzsche, Walther Funk, Hermann Göring, Rudolf Hess, Alfred Jodl, Ernst Kaltenbrunner, Wilhelm Keitel, Gustav Krupp von Bohlen und Halbach (deemed too elderly to stand trial), Robert Ley (committed suicide prior to the trial), Baron Konstantin von Neurath, Franz von Papen, Erich Raeder, Joachim von Ribbentrop, Alfred Rosenberg, Fritz Sauckel, Dr. Hjalmar Schacht, Baldur von Schirach, Arthur Seyss-Inquart, Albert Speer, and Julius Streicher.

5. The bibliography for Nuremberg is considerable. For trial participants, see, for example, Andrus, *I Was the Nuremberg Jailer*, 203–6; Calvocoressi, *Nuremberg*, 117–27; Glueck, *The Nuremberg Trial and Aggressive War*, 91–103; Harris, *Tyranny on Trial*, 491–571; Martin, *Inside Nürnberg*, 122–23; Speer, *Inside the Third Reich*, 519–24; Sprecher, *Inside the Nuremberg Trial*, 144–58; Storey, *The Final Judgment?* 180–91; Taylor, *Nuremberg and Vietnam*, 625–41. For others, see, for example, Bass, *Stay the Hand of Vengeance*, 203–5; Borgwardt, *New Deal for the World*, 196–247; Davidson, *Trial of the Germans*, 586–94; Gerhart, *America's Advocate*, 407–54; Irving, *Nuremberg*, 312; Persico, *Nuremberg*, 435–43; Plesch, *America, Hitler, and the UN*, 101–18; Plesch, *Human Rights after Hitler*, 8, 59, 171, 196, 204; Robertson, *Crimes against Humanity*, 203–42; Smith, *Reaching Judgment at Nuremberg*, 299–306; Tusa and Tusa, *Nuremberg Trial*, 491; Woetzel, *Nuremberg Trials in International Law*, 218–32.

6. Sarah Klebnikov, interview with author, New York, November 1, 2001.

7. IMT, *Trial of the Major War Criminals*, 2:431.

8. IMT, *Trial of the Major War Criminals*, 2:431–32.

9. IMT, *Trial of the Major War Criminals*, 2:104.

10. See Schabas, *Unimaginable Atrocities*, 12.

11. Robert Houghwout Jackson, "'Worst Crime of All,'" *New York Times*, September 8, 1945.

12. IMT, *Trial of the Major War Criminals*, 2:118.

13. IMT, *Trial of the Major War Criminals*, 2:119.

14. IMT, *Trial of the Major War Criminals*, 2:431.

15. Jackson, "'Worst Crime of All.'" A close reading of this article shows that Jackson relied heavily on his March 27, 1941, speech to the Inter-American Bar Association.

16. Storey, *The Final Judgment?* 114–15; Tusa and Tusa, *Nuremberg Trial*, 160.

17. IMT, *Trial of the Major War Criminals*, 2:434.

18. Raymond Daniell, "War-Crimes Court Sees Horror Films," *New York Times*, November 30, 1945.

19. Daniell, "War-Crimes Court Sees Horror Films."

20. IMT, *Trial of the Major War Criminals*, 2:434.

21. Daniell, "War-Crimes Court Sees Horror Films."

22. Quoted in Conot, *Justice at Nuremberg*, 149; Tusa and Tusa, *Nuremberg Trial*, 160. For more on Gilbert and his discussions with the defendants, see Gilbert, *Nuremberg Diary*.

23. Kimball, *The Juggler*, 4.

24. Kimball, *The Juggler*, 4.

25. For more on the debate over rescuing the Jews, see Breitman and Lichtman, *FDR and the Jews;* Breitman and Kraut, *American Refugee Policy and European Jewry;* Lipstadt, *Beyond Belief;* Rosen, *Saving the Jews;* Wyman, *Abandonment of the Jews.*

26. IMT, *Trial of the Major War Criminals*, 2:98–99.

27. For more on the UNWCC's significance, see Plesch, *Human Rights after Hitler.*

Chapter 1

Epigraph: HCP quoted in Baker, *Brahmin in Revolt*, 121–22.

1. HCP, "Reminiscences," 295.

2. "Battle of Washington," *Time*, August 8, 1932.

3. Black, *Franklin Delano Roosevelt*, 240–42; Brands, *Traitor to His Class*, 258–59; Dallek, *Franklin D. Roosevelt and American Foreign Policy, 1932–1945*, 124–25; Smith, *FDR*, 282–85. For a detailed examination, see Dickson and Allen, *Bonus Army.*

4. The only other Democratic presidents in that period were Grover Cleveland, 48.9 percent in 1884, and Woodrow Wilson who received 41.8 percent in 1912 and 49.2 percent in 1916.

5. HCP to FDR, November 8, 1932, Roosevelt, FD 1929–35.

6. HCP to FDR, November 8, 1932, Roosevelt, FD 1929–35. Pell's "equal footing" reference also related to the two men's shared view of how in part to address the inequities that helped bring about the Great Depression. Pell often wrote to FDR in a way that offered multiple meanings.

7. "Surprising Their Friends, The Quiet Marriage of Miss Kernochan and Mr. Herbert C. Pell," *New York Times*, February 24, 1883.

8. Quoted in Baker, *Brahmin in Revolt*, 46.

9. HCP, "Reminiscences," 157. See also Baker, *Brahmin in Revolt*, 55–56.

10. Quoted in Baker, *Brahmin in Revolt*, 57.

11. HCP, "Reminiscences," 14.

12. HCP, "Reminiscences," 64.

13. HCP, "Reminiscences," 59. See also Baker, *Brahmin in Revolt*, 31–32.

14. HCP, "Reminiscences," 62–63. See also Baker, *Brahmin in Revolt*, 34.

15. HCP, "Reminiscences," 58.

16. Franklin D. Roosevelt, untitled English class paper/speech, April 15, 1903, Harvard College, Notes and Papers, Course Papers, Papers Pertaining to Family, Business and Personal affairs, 1882–1945, FDRP. See also Black, *Franklin Delano Roosevelt*, 27.

17. HCP to Claiborne Pell, February 21, 1938, CPP.

18. Quoted in Baker, *Brahmin in Revolt*, 88. See also Blayney, *Democracy's Aristocrat*, 59–61.

19. HCP, "Reminiscences," 284.

20. "Tammany to Name New Party Chief," *New York Times*, June 10, 1921.

21. HCP, "Reminiscences," 296. See also Baker, *Brahmin in Revolt*, 97.

22. Blayney, *Democracy's Aristocrat*, 61–62.

23. "Democrats Seek a State Chairman," *New York Times*, June 30, 1921.

24. See Baker, *Brahmin in Revolt*, 101–2.

25. Jeremiah Mahoney, The Reminiscences of Jeremiah Mahoney, Oral History Research Office, Columbia University, N.Y., 5. Also quoted in Baker, *Brahmin in Revolt*, 99, and Blayney, *Democracy's Aristocrat*, 62.

26. Baker, *Brahmin in Revolt*, 97–99. Some thirty years after the event, Pell attempted to remain the sober, unaligned aristocrat politician, noting in his oral history only that "very shortly thereafter I was installed in the office of State Chairman" (HCP, "Reminiscences," 296).

27. Blayney, *Democracy's Aristocrat*, 47.

28. HCP to Claiborne Pell, October 11, 1943, Pell, Claiborne.

29. Baker, *Brahmin in Revolt*, 120.

30. Quoted in Blayney, *Democracy's Aristocrat*, 63.

31. HCP, "Reminiscences," 329.

32. Quoted in Baker, *Brahmin in Revolt*, 121–22.

33. Lawrence Deutzman of the *Smithtown Messenger*.

34. "Klan Is Denounced by Chairman Pell," *New York Times*, August 15, 1924. See also Baker, *Brahmin in Revolt*, 125.

35. HCP, "Reminiscences," 352–53. See also Blayney, *Democracy's Aristocrat*, 65.

36. "Klan Is Denounced by Chairman Pell."

37. HCP to Henry Drayton, November 11, 1935, Drayton, Henry 1934–41, Box 6, General Correspondence. See also Blayney, *Democracy's Aristocrat*, 65.

38. Baker, *Brahmin in Revolt*, 123.

39. "F. D. Roosevelt May Make Smith Speech," *New York Times*, May 27, 1924.

40. "To Pick Man Today to Nominate Smith," *New York Times*, June 21, 1924.

41. Joseph M. Proskauer, The Reminiscences of Joseph M. Proskauer, Oral History Research Office, Columbia University, N.Y., 5. See also Finan, *Alfred E. Smith*, 178.

42. Roosevelt and Shalett, *Affectionately*, 184. See also Smith, *FDR*, 210.

43. Osborne, "Frederick Osborn," v; Shapiro, "In Memory of Frederick H. Osborn," iii. Osborn was one of the founding members of the American Eugenics Society in 1926, and two years later he joined the Galton Society. British mathematician and naturalist Francis Galton first coined the word "eugenics" in 1881. Over time, the American Eugenics Society became the best-funded and most-supported eugenics organization in the world, receiving considerable money from the Rockefeller Foundation and Kellogg's Race Betterment Foundation ("Background Note," in Frederick Osborn Papers; Mehler, "History of the American Eugenics Society," 40, 113.). By the 1930s Osborn was then the leading figure in the American eugenics movement; he authored what had become the standard text in the field, *Preface to Eugenics*, in 1940. At one time, he was a reluctant admirer of the Nazi sterilization program, calling it the "most important experiment which has ever been tried" and its sterilization program "excellent," while he simultaneously condemned Nazi antisemitism (Frederick Osborn, "Summary of the Proceedings of the Conference on Eugenics in Relation to Nursing," February 24, 1937, American Eugenics Society Papers: Conference on Eugenics in Relation to Nursing; see also Kühl, *Nazi Connection*, 75). At his passing, colleague Richard H. Osborne noted that Frederick Osborn is recognized as

the "catalyst for the creation of a new multidisciplinary area . . . term[ed] social biology" (Osborne, "Frederick Osborn," v; Shapiro, "In Memory of Frederick H. Osborn," iii).

44. Osborn and Osborn, *Voyage to a New World,* 70–71.

45. Roosevelt and Shalett, *Affectionately,* 184.

46. Farley, *Jim Farley's Story,* 4.

47. Roosevelt and Shalett, *Affectionately,* 185.

48. Farley, *Jim Farley's Story,* 4.

49. Roosevelt and Shalett, *Affectionately,* 185.

50. Roosevelt and Shalett, *Affectionately,* 186.

51. "Scenes and Foibles of the Convention," *New York Times,* July 10, 1924.

52. HCP, "Reminiscences," 333.

Chapter 2

Epigraph: HCP to FDR, November 8, 1932, Roosevelt, FD 1929–35.

1. HCP, "Reminiscences," 369. Also quoted in Baker, *Brahmin in Revolt,* 172.

2. HCP, "Reminiscences," 380. Also quoted in Baker, *Brahmin in Revolt,* 176.

3. Blayney, *Democracy's Aristocrat,* 1.

4. Baker, *Brahmin in Revolt,* 140.

5. Baker, *Brahmin in Revolt,* 152.

6. Quoted in Blayney, *Democracy's Aristocrat,* 76.

7. HCP to FDR, November 8, 1932, Roosevelt, FD 1929–35.

8. Blayney, *Democracy's Aristocrat,* 77.

9. "Haiti to Control Its Own Finances," *New York Times,* April 18, 1934; "Sings to Two Presidents," *New York Times,* April 18, 1934.

10. Luncheon in Honor of the President of Haiti, 1:00 P.M., April 17, 1934, White House Usher's Log, FDRP.

11. HCP, "Reminiscences," 457–58.

12. FDR, meeting with HCP, 11:45 A.M., April 18, 1934, White House Stenographer's Diary, FDRP.

13. HCP, "Reminiscences," 457.

14. FDR, meeting with HCP, 12:15 P.M., January 22, 1935, White House Stenographer's Diary, FDRP; FDR, meeting with HCP, 12:15 P.M., January 22, 1935, Grace Tully Appointment Diary, FDRP.

15. Brands, *Traitor to His Class,* 441–43; Dallek, *Franklin D. Roosevelt and American Foreign Policy,* 95–97. For more on the United States and the World Court, see Dunne, *United States and the World Court;* Fleming, *United States and the World Court.*

16. FDR, *Public Papers and Addresses of Franklin D. Roosevelt,* 4:40–41.

17. FDR, *Public Papers and Addresses of Franklin D. Roosevelt,* 4:41.

18. FDR, *Public Papers and Addresses of Franklin D. Roosevelt,* 5:289.

19. "Coughlin Opposes World Court Entry," *New York Times,* January 21, 1935.

20. "Coughlin Asserts America 'Retains Her Sovereignty,'" *New York Times,* January 30, 1935.

21. Quoted in Dallek, *Franklin D. Roosevelt and American Foreign Policy,* 96.

22. FDR Lunch—Herbert Pells and Neson Brown—Drive through Woods, 1:00 P.M., June 9, 1935, Grace Tully Appointment Diary, FDRP.

23. FDR (Tea), Mr. and Mrs. Herbert Pell, Mr. and Mrs. Frederick Osborn at Hyde Park, 5:00 P.M., September 21, 1935, Grace Tully Appointment Diary, FDRP; FDR (Tea), Mr. and Mrs. Herbert Pell, Mr. and Mrs. Frederick Osborn at Hyde Park, 5:00 P.M., September 21, 1935, White House Stenographer's Diary, FDRP.

24. HCP to FDR, February 17, 1936, Roosevelt, FD 1936–45.

25. HCP to FDR, February 17, 1936, Roosevelt, FD 1936–45. See also Blayney, *Democracy's Aristocrat*, 77.

26. HCP, "Reminiscences," 396.

27. HCP, "Reminiscences," 392. See also Baker, *Brahmin in Revolt,* 157–61; Blayney, *Democracy's Aristocrat,* 77–80.

28. Quoted in Baker, *Brahmin in Revolt,* 159–60.

29. HCP, "Reminiscences," 396–97.

30. HCP, "Reminiscences," 396–97. Also quoted in Baker, *Brahmin in Revolt,* 177.

31. FDR Meeting with HCP, 11:00 A.M., April 21, 1937, White House Stenographer's Diary, FDRP.

32. HCP, "Reminiscences," 398.

33. Baker, *Brahmin in Revolt,* 179.

34. HCP to FDR, April 19, 1937, Roosevelt, FD 1936–45.

35. Baker, *Brahmin in Revolt,* 169.

36. HCP, "Reminiscences," 423.

37. HCP, "Reminiscences," 424–25. According to Dominic Tierney, Germany sent 200 tanks, 840 aircraft, and between 14,000 and 16,000 troops into Spain (Tierney, *FDR and the Spanish Civil War,* 20). For Italian troop numbers in Spain between November 1936 and March 1939, see Appendix C in Coverdale, *Italian Intervention in the Spanish Civil War,* 417.

38. HCP, "Reminiscences," 425.

39. Farago, *Game of the Foxes,* 488.

40. Quoted in Baker, *Brahmin in Revolt,* 185.

41. HCP to FDR, September 18, 1937, CPP. A copy of this letter in the HCPP at the FDRL is apparently misdated as September 11, 1937. Curiously, both copies are signed, "Bertie Pell" (HCP to FDR, September 11, 1937, Roosevelt, FD 1936–45).

42. HCP to FDR, September 18, 1937, CPP.

43. HCP to FDR, March 2, 1938, CPP.

44. FDR to HCP, March 18, 1938, CPP.

45. HCP to FDR, April 22, 1938, CPP.

46. FDR to HCP, May 12, 1938, CPP.

47. FDR to HCP, May 12, 1938, CPP.

48. HCP to FDR, May 31, 1938, CPP.

49. HCP to FDR, May 31, 1938, CPP.

50. HCP, "Reminiscences," 441.

51. HCP to FDR, September 26, 1938, CPP. See also Baker, *Brahmin in Revolt,* 186–87.

52. FDR to HCP, October 17, 1938, CPP.

53. HCP to FDR, October 21, 1938, CPP. See also Baker, *Brahmin in Revolt,* 191–94; Blayney, *Democracy's Aristocrat,* 92–93.

54. FDR to HCP, March 18, 1938, CPP.

55. FDR to HCP, November 12, 1938, CPP.

56. FDR, *Public Papers and Addresses of Franklin D. Roosevelt,* 7:597–98. See also Black, *Franklin Delano Roosevelt,* 490–92; Smith, *FDR,* 426–27.

57. HCP to FDR, December 15, 1938, CPP.

58. FDR, *Public Papers and Addresses of Franklin D. Roosevelt,* 8:1–2.

59. FDR to HCP, January 10, 1939, CPP.

60. HCP to FDR, February 11, 1939, CPP.

61. HCP to FDR, April 15, 1939, CPP.

62. Blayney, *Democracy's Aristocrat,* 93.

63. HCP, "Reminiscences," 443–44. Also quoted in Baker, *Brahmin in Revolt,* 196.

64. HCP, "Reminiscences," 447. Also quoted in Baker, *Brahmin in Revolt,* 197.

65. See Blayney, *Democracy's Aristocrat,* 107–8n32. See also Farago, *Game of the Foxes,* 417.

66. Blayney, *Democracy's Aristocrat,* 92.

67. Blayney, *Democracy's Aristocrat,* 93.

68. Baker, *Brahmin in Revolt,* 213.

69. Quoted in Blayney, *Democracy's Aristocrat,* 95–96.

70. "Pell to Motor from Lisbon to Budapest Post" (unidentified clipping), CPP.

71. HCP to FDR, April 2, 1941, Roosevelt, FD 1936–45.

72. HCP to FDR, April 2, 1941, Roosevelt, FD 1936–45. Quoted in Blayney, *Democracy's Aristocrat,* 96.

Chapter 3

Epigraph: HCP to FDR, June 24, 1943, Roosevelt, FD 1936–45.

1. Stimson Diary, December 7, 1941. See also Hull and Berding, *Memoirs of Cordell Hull,* 1095.

2. Stimson Diary, December 7, 1941.

3. Stimson Diary, December 7, 1941.

4. FDR, *Public Papers and Addresses of Franklin D. Roosevelt,* 10:514–15.

5. FDR, *Public Papers and Addresses of Franklin D. Roosevelt,* 10:523–24.

6. "Churchill Wears Life Saver's Garb," *New York Times,* December 23, 1941.

7. Winston Churchill, "Address to Joint Session of US Congress [December 26,] 1941," National Churchill Museum, accessed December 30, 2018, https://www.nationalchurchill museum.org/churchill-address-to-congress.html.

8. China, Australia, Belgium, Canada, Costa Rica, Cuba, Czechoslovakia, Dominican Republic, El Salvador, Greece, Guatemala, Haiti, Honduras, India, Luxembourg, Netherlands, New Zealand, Nicaragua, Norway, Panama, Poland, South Africa, Yugoslavia.

9. Mexico (June 5, 1942), Philippines (June 10, 1942), Ethiopia (July 28, 1942), Iraq (January 16, 1943), Brazil (February 8, 1943), Bolivia (April 27, 1943), Iran (September 10, 1943), Colombia (December 22, 1943), Liberia (February 26, 1944), France (December

26, 1944), Ecuador (February 7, 1945), Peru (February 11, 1945), Chile (February 12, 1945), Paraguay (February 12, 1945), Venezuela (February 16, 1945), Uruguay (February 23, 1945), Turkey (February 24, 1945), Egypt (February 27, 1945), Saudi Arabia (March 1, 1945).

10. Churchill, *Grand Alliance,* 683.

11. FDR, *Public Papers and Addresses of Franklin D. Roosevelt,* 11:3.

12. Churchill, *Grand Alliance,* 683.

13. HCP to FDR, April 2, 1941, Roosevelt, FD 1936–45.

14. Quoted in Baker, *Brahmin in Revolt,* 213.

15. HCP, "Reminiscences," 501–2. Also quoted in Baker, *Brahmin in Revolt,* 234.

16. Farago, *Game of the Foxes,* 416–23. See also Baker, *Brahmin in Revolt,* 220–23; Blayney, *Democracy's Aristocrat,* 102–4.

17. HCP, "Reminiscences," 510. See also Baker, *Brahmin in Revolt,* 235.

18. Bárdossy to HCP, August 2, 1941, Hull, Cordell.

19. Bárdossy to HCP, August 2, 1941, Hull, Cordell.

20. HCP, Untitled Report on the Treatment of Jews in Hungary, n.d. [August 1941], Hull, Cordell.

21. Quoted in Baker, *Brahmin in Revolt,* 229.

22. Quoted in Baker, *Brahmin in Revolt,* 230.

23. HCP, "Reminiscences," 520.

24. Houseguests, Hyde Park—Mrs. Franklin D. Roosevelt Jr., Mr. and Mrs. Clarence Pell, Mr. and Mrs. Meyer (Left 9:40), Judge Samuel I. Rosenman (Left 3:00), February 1, 1942, White House Usher's Log, FDRP.

25. "Samuel I. Rosenman, 77, Dies; Coined New Deal for Roosevelt," *New York Times,* June 25, 1973.

26. Baker, *Brahmin in Revolt,* 238.

27. HCP, "Reminiscences," 527.

28. Quoted in Baker, *Brahmin in Revolt,* 243.

29. Quoted in Baker, *Brahmin in Revolt,* 245.

30. The communiqué was signed by the Netherlands, Yugoslavia, and Luxembourg on behalf of Belgium, Greece, Luxembourg, Norway, Netherlands, Poland, Czechoslovakia, Yugoslavia, and the French National Committee in London.

31. "1,000,000 Jews Slain by Nazis, Report Says 'Slaughterhouse' of Europe under Hitler Described in London," *New York Times,* June 30, 1942.

32. "Allies Are Urged to Execute Nazis," *New York Times,* July 2, 1942.

33. Franklin D. Roosevelt, "Statement by the President," August 21, 1942, OF5152. Also quoted in Kochavi, *Prelude to Nuremberg,* 33; Rosen, *Saving the Jews,* 237.

34. W. H. Lawrence, "President Warns Atrocities of Axis Will Be Avenged," *New York Times,* August 22, 1942; Rosen, *Saving the Jews,* 237.

35. FDR, "Statement by the President," October 7, 1942, OF5152.

36. Chronological Summary of Telegrams regarding the Establishment of the United Nations War Crimes Commission, n.d. [1945?], Miscellaneous—War Crimes (Folder 1 of 2), Box 4, Records Relating to German War Crimes 1942–1946, Records of the Legal Adviser; Berge and Cox, "Memorandum for the Attorney General," May 12, 1943, War

Criminals, Box 68, Oscar Cox Papers, FDRL. For a detailed account on the establishment of the UNWCC, see Kochavi, *Prelude to Nuremberg*; Plesch, *Human Rights after Hitler.* For the official UNWCC history, see United Nations War Crimes Commission, *History of the United Nations War Crimes Commission and the Development of the Laws of War.* For information on the connections between World Wars I and II and international law, see Lewis, *Birth of the New Justice.*

37. Bathurst, "United Nations War Crimes Commission," 567–68.

38. For example, see the "German Policy of Extermination of the Jewish Race," which was released to the press by the U.S. State Department, December 17, 1942.

39. "11 Allies Condemn Nazi War on Jews," *New York Times,* December 18, 1942.

40. Telford Taylor called the lack of American attention to the plight of Jews in Europe "astonishingly . . . shameful." According to Taylor, the trial at Nuremberg did the most to inform Americans about the mass exterminations that took place during the war. He didn't himself become aware of the extent of the tragedy until he became involved in the trial (*Anatomy of the Nuremberg Trials*, 29).

41. Only after March 11 did things begin to move forward, when the British informed Secretary Hull that all the Allied nations had responded (Berge and Cox, "Memorandum for the Attorney General," May 12, 1943, War Criminals, Box 68, Oscar Cox Papers, FDRL).

42. Freeman Matthews, telegram to the Secretary of State, March 5, 1943, Establishment of Commission.

43. Hull, memorandum for FDR, March 30, 1943, OF5152.

44. Hull, memorandum for FDR, March 30, 1943, OF5152. See also Kochavi, *Prelude to Nuremberg,* 51.

45. Berge and Cox, "Memorandum for the Attorney General," May 12, 1943, War Criminals, Box 68, Oscar Cox Papers, FDRL.

46. Hull to HCP, December 28, 1943, Hull, Cordell.

47. The three Justice Department officials were Louis B. Schwartz, Louis Hector, and Douglas Maggs (Francis Biddle to Hull, March 6, 1943, Establishment of Commission).

48. Francis Biddle to Hull, March 6, 1943, Establishment of Commission.

49. Hull to the Attorney General, March 31, 1943, War Crimes—Miscellaneous Correspondence 1943.

50. Hull, memorandum for FDR, March 30, 1943, OF5152.

51. The four other suggestions were Roland S. Morris, U.S. ambassador to Tokyo during World War I and professor of international law at the University of Pennsylvania; Wendell Berge, assistant attorney general in charge of the Criminal Division; Charles Warren, a "practicing lawyer with special interest in constitutional history"; and George Rublee, "an able practicing lawyer with some experience in the international field" (Hackworth to Sumner Welles, March 16, 1943, War Crimes—Miscellaneous Correspondence 1943).

52. Hackworth to Sumner Welles, March 16, 1943, War Crimes—Miscellaneous Correspondence 1943. Also quoted in Kochavi, *Prelude to Nuremberg,* 51.

53. HCP to Claiborne Pell, March 17, 1943, Pell, Claiborne.

54. Hackworth, "Confidential" letter to Sumner Welles, March 17, 1943, War Crimes—Miscellaneous Correspondence 1943.

55. Hackworth, "Confidential" letter to Sumner Welles, March 17, 1943, War Crimes—Miscellaneous Correspondence 1943.

56. Later conflicts between Hackworth and Pell tend to reinforce the conclusion that Hackworth saw himself as the perfect candidate to represent the United States on the UNWCC. Hackworth, "Confidential" letter to Sumner Welles, March 17, 1943, War Crimes—Miscellaneous Correspondence 1943.

57. FDR, memorandum for the Attorney General, April 1, 1943, OF5152.

58. Francis Biddle to Hull, April 1, 1943, War Crimes—Miscellaneous Correspondence 1943.

59. Hull, memorandum for FDR, May 21, 1943, War Crimes—Miscellaneous Correspondence 1943.

60. Francis Biddle, memorandum for FDR, June 22, 1943, OF5152. Although Biddle did not note it, Glueck was an active member of the London International Assembly. See Plesch, *Human Rights after Hitler*, 161.

61. Homer Cummings to FDR, December 17, 1942, OF5152.

62. Sheldon Glueck to M. H. McIntyre, October 15, 1942, OF5152.

63. Grace Tully, memorandum for FDR, June 10, 1943, OF5152. Michael Blayney incorrectly implies that it was at Hull's suggestion that FDR appoint Pell (Blayney, *Democracy's Aristocrat*, 120). According to Arieh Kochavi, Hull only "acquiesced" in Pell's appointment (Kochavi, *Prelude to Nuremberg*, 52). Pell reported in his 1953 oral history that FDR had ordered his appointment over the objections of the State Department (HCP, "Reminiscences," 530). See also Baker, *Brahmin in Revolt*, 257.

64. FDR to HCP, June 14, 1943, Roosevelt, FD 1936–45.

65. Quoted in Baker, *Brahmin in Revolt*, 245.

66. FDR (Lunch) with HCP, 1:00 P.M., April 8, 1943, Grace Tully Appointment Diary, FDRP; FDR (Lunch) with HCP, 1:00 P.M., April 8, 1943, White House Stenographer's Diary. FDRP; FDR (Lunch) with HCP, 1:00 P.M., April 8, 1943, President's Appointment Index, FDRP.

67. McIntyre to Glueck, September 10, 1942; McIntyre to Felix Frankfurter, November 12, 1942; FDR, "Memorandum for Mac," November 11, 1942: all from OF5152.

68. Homer Cummings to FDR, December 17, 1942; McIntyre to Glueck, September 10, 1942; McIntyre to Felix Frankfurter, November 12, 1942; FDR to Cummings, December 21, 1942: all from OF5152.

69. When Hull resigned from the State Department, Pell thanked him for their twenty-five-year acquaintance, writing, "I have always valued your friendship, not only for itself but as a tribute for I know it is not given to unworthy people" (HCP to Hull, November 27, 1944, Hull, Cordell).

70. Blayney, *Democracy's Aristocrat*, 119–20.

71. HCP, "Reminiscences," 530.

72. HCP, "Reminiscences," 530. The other possibility was G. Howland Shaw (Hackworth, memorandum to Shaw and Welles, June 29, 1943, War Crimes—Miscellaneous Correspondence 1943).

73. Grace Tully, memorandum for FDR, June 10, 1943, OF5152.

74. Blayney, *Democracy's Aristocrat*, 120.

75. Quoted in Kimball, *The Juggler*, 7.

76. Watson and Petre, *Father, Son & Co.*, 33.

77. Watson and Petre, *Father, Son & Co.*, 43–45.

78. Edwin Black, *IBM and the Holocaust*, 71–72; Watson and Petre, *Father, Son & Co.*, 43–45.

79. HCP to Thomas J. Watson, n.d., Watson, Thomas, Box 28, General Correspondence.

80. Thomas J. Watson, telegram to HCP, July 2, 1943, Watson, Thomas, Box 28, General Correspondence.

81. Black, *IBM and the Holocaust*, 52–74, 292–374.

82. For a positive account of IBM's wartime activities, see Pugh, *Building IBM*; Watson and Petre, *Father, Son & Co.*

83. In *The Nuremberg Trial* by Ann and John Tusa, the equipment provision by IBM is noted as a "loss leader." The Tusas imply that the free provision of the system at Nuremberg led to its purchase and installation at the United Nations in New York (Tusa and Tusa, *Nuremberg Trial*, 97). While no evidence seems to exist to refute this observation, another possible motivating factor for IBM's free provision of the system was as an effort to temper or absolve the company from its indirect participation in the Holocaust. A search of the online archives for the IBM Corporation has revealed a significant list of documents concerning the IBM interpretation system. IBM, however, in reply to an email from the author stated they would not release any document classified as "IBM Internal Use Only." See Cox, "Interpretation Factor."

84. Black, *IBM and the Holocaust*, 72–73.

85. FDR to HCP, June 14, 1943, Roosevelt, FD 1936–45.

86. Christopher Gray, "Inside the Union Club, Jaws Drop," *New York Times*, February 11, 2007.

87. When he was in London for his service on the UNWCC, as was to be expected, Pell joined the Athenaeum Club (HCP to Adolf Berle, May 4, 1944, War Crimes—Miscellaneous Correspondence 1944).

88. Roberta Barrows, "Memorandum For: The Record," June 24, 1943, OF5152.

89. Roberta Barrows, "Memorandum For: The Record," June 24, 1943, OF5152.

90. HCP to FDR, June 24, 1943, Roosevelt, FD 1936–45. Also quoted in part in Blayney, *Democracy's Aristocrat*, 120.

91. HCP to FDR, June 24, 1943, Roosevelt, FD 1936–45; HCP, "Reminiscences," 530.

92. HCP to Leroy King, November 8, 1944, King, LeRoy, Box 11, General Correspondence.

93. FDR, *Public Papers and Addresses of Franklin D. Roosevelt*, 13:198.

94. Quoted in Kimball, *The Juggler*, 98.

95. *Foreign Relations of the United States*, 594.

96. HCP to FDR, March 8, 1944, War Crimes Commission.

97. Pell had remained since his term in Congress ever fearful of the isolationist elements in the United States, and, apparently, feared FDR might not run for another term, or if he ran, might not win. He wrote his son in February 1943, "The situation at home looks

very bad to me. It seems almost certain that the Isolationists will either win the next election, or at least be able to prevent the United States taking any serious part in the preservation of world order" (HCP to Claiborne Pell, February 11, 1943, Pell, Claiborne).

98. Baker, *Brahmin in Revolt*, 255; Blayney, *Democracy's Aristocrat*, 118–19.

99. HCP to Leroy King, September 29, 1944, King, LeRoy, Box 11, General Correspondence.

100. Letter to Clarence Pell, April 18, 1944, Pell, Clarence, Box 20, General Correspondence.

101. FDR, "Statement on the Murder of French Hostages," October 25, 1941, OF5152. See also Gilbert, *Second World War*, 247; Kochavi, *Prelude to Nuremberg*, 15.

102. Quoted in Baker, *Brahmin in Revolt*, 121–22.

103. Quoted in Baker, *Brahmin in Revolt*, 230.

104. See, for example, Conot, *Justice at Nuremberg*, 10; Harris, *Tyranny on Trial*, 5; Kochavi, *Prelude to Nuremberg*, 51–52; Smith, *Road to Nuremberg*, 10, 19. According to Telford Taylor, Pell was a "friend" of FDR who had become "sensitive to ethnic factors in New York politics" (Taylor, *Anatomy of the Nuremberg Trials*, 26).

105. Pell was so pleased with his telegram and especially the reply he received from the president, he copied both the lines from the Bible and FDR's reply in a letter to his son (HCP to Claiborne Pell, February 15, 1943, Pell, Claiborne).

106. HCP to Claiborne Pell, February 15, 1943, Pell, Claiborne. Also quoted in Baker, *Brahmin in Revolt*, 245–46.

Chapter 4

Epigraph: Pell, "Reminiscences," 569. See also Baker, *Brahmin in Revolt*, 254–55.

1. HCP to FDR, June 24, 1943, Roosevelt, FD 1936–45.

2. HCP, Untitled Recollections, May 1945.

3. Bishop, "Lawrence Preuss."

4. HCP, "Reminiscences," 531; Notes of Service with UNWCC, n.d. [April? 1945], War Crimes Commission: Pell Notes and Statements, Box 28, General Correspondence. See also Baker, *Brahmin in Revolt*, 256–57; Kochavi, *Prelude to Nuremberg*, 52.

5. HCP, "Reminiscences," 531.

6. Hackworth, memorandum to Shaw and Welles, June 29, 1943, War Crimes—Miscellaneous Correspondence 1943.

7. HCP, Notes of Service with UNWCC, n.d. [April? 1945], War Crimes Commission: Pell Notes and Statements, Box 28, General Correspondence. See also Kochavi, *Prelude to Nuremberg*, 143–44; Wyman, *Abandonment of the Jews*, 258.

8. Hackworth, memorandum to Shaw and Welles, June 29, 1943, War Crimes—Miscellaneous Correspondence 1943; FDR to HCP, June 14, 1943, Roosevelt, FD 1936–45.

9. Jeremiah Mahoney, "The Reminiscences of Jeremiah Mahoney," Oral History Research Office, 5. Also quoted in Baker, *Brahmin in Revolt*, 99, and Blayney, *Democracy's Aristocrat*, 62.

10. Matthews, telegram to the Secretary of State, March 5, 1943, Establishment of Commission.

11. Both Assistant Attorney General Wendell Berge and Assistant Solicitor General Oscar Cox had wanted the attorney general to consider taking the post, writing, "We believe it would greatly enhance the prestige of the project for punishment of Axis war criminals if you could accept Chairmanship of the preliminary conference on organization of the Commission" (Berge and Cox, "Memorandum for the Attorney General," May 12, 1943, War Criminals, Box 68, Oscar Cox Papers, FDRL, 7).

12. Hull, telegram to Matthews, June 28, 1943, Establishment of Commission. See also Kochavi, *Prelude to Nuremberg*, 52.

13. HCP to FDR, July 15, 1943, OF5152.

14. See also Baker, *Brahmin in Revolt*, 257–58; Blayney, *Democracy's Aristocrat*, 119–20; Kochavi, *Prelude to Nuremberg*, 53–54; Wyman, *Abandonment of the Jews*, 258.

15. HCP to FDR, July 15, 1943, OF5152.

16. Shaw to HCP, July 16, 1943, War Crimes Commission: State Department.

17. The British Foreign Office routinely communicated to the State Department by sending messages through the American Embassy in London. John Gilbert Winant, telegram to the Secretary of State, July 13, 1943, War Crimes—Miscellaneous Correspondence 1943.

18. Shaw to HCP, July 16, 1943, War Crimes Commission: State Department.

19. Olive Pell to FDR, n.d. [August 1943], Roosevelt, FD 1936–45.

20. Hull, telegram to HCP, August 11, 1943, War Crimes Commission: State Department. The State Department had telegraphed London on August 5 requesting an update on when the UNWCC might meet. The Foreign Office replied via the American Embassy in London on August 7 that they had sent a communication to the "United Nations," but that it might take "a month or six weeks" before they could begin to proceed (Hull to FDR, September 7, 1943, OF5152).

21. HCP, telegram to FDR, August 9, 1943, OF5152.

22. HCP to FDR, August 10, 1943, Roosevelt, FD 1936–45. Pell used multiple methods in his effort to reach the president. In this letter he was reiterating what he wrote to FDR the previous day: "Can I see you this week or next Hyde Park or Washington about War Guilt Commission to which you appointed me[?] Feel it to be important that we should leave as soon as possible so as to support your recent statements[.] Please answer Garden City Hotel" (HCP, telegram to FDR, August 9, 1943, OF5152). The phrase "War Guilt Commission" was often used as shorthand for the more formal name, the United Nations Commission for the Investigation of War Crimes.

23. FDR, *Public Papers and Addresses of Franklin D. Roosevelt*, 12:306.

24. FDR, *Public Papers and Addresses of Franklin D. Roosevelt*, 12:327-28

25. FDR, *Public Papers and Addresses of Franklin D. Roosevelt*, 12:338–39.

26. HCP to FDR, August 28, 1943, Roosevelt, FD 1936–45.

27. HCP to FDR, August 28, 1943, Roosevelt, FD 1936–45.

28. FDR, memorandum for the Secretary of State, September 2, 1943, War Crimes Commission, President's Secretary File, FDRP. Also quoted in Baker, *Brahmin in Revolt*, 257.

29. Hull to FDR, September 7, 1943, OF5152.

30. "Press Release from the White House," June 28, 1943, War Crimes—Miscellaneous Correspondence 1943. The Foreign Office made its displeasure clear in a July 13 message:

"As this appointment [of Pell] had been made public we have decided to make a similar announcement of the appointment of Sir Cecil Hurst as the British representative. His Majesty's Embassy at Washington were instructed to inform the United States Government in advance of our intention to do this" (Winant, telegram to the Secretary of State, July 13, 1943, War Crimes—Miscellaneous Correspondence 1943). See also Kochavi, *Prelude to Nuremberg*, 52–53.

31. FDR, memorandum to HCP, September 8, 1943, OF5152. On September 8, having not yet received Hull's forwarded memorandum from the president, Pell telegrammed the president asking for a meeting since he planned on being in Washington the following week. "I should be very grateful if you would let me see you next week. I believe it to be important to success of War Guilt Commission." The president had Grace Tully reply and ask Pell to refer to Hull's letter, adding he might be available to meet with Pell the following week (Grace Tully to HCP, September 9, 1943, OF5152; HCP, telegram to FDR, September 8, 1943, OF5152).

32. Hackworth, memorandum for Matthews and Dunn, September 14, 1943, War Crimes—Miscellaneous Correspondence 1943.

33. Winant, telegram to the Secretary of State, September 1, 1943 (received September 6), Establishment of Commission.

34. Welles, *Sumner Welles*, 199.

35. According to the FDRL's in-house database, Grace Tully's appointment diary recorded FDR and Hull meeting for lunch privately at 1:00 P.M. on Monday, August 9, and again on Monday, August 16, 1943. On Tuesday, August 10, Hull was at the White House for a 12:15 P.M. meeting with the president that also included Sumner Welles, Norman Davis, Dr. Isaiah Bowman, and Dr. Leo Pasvolsky. Benjamin Welles's account in *Sumner Welles* suggests that Hull presented FDR his ultimatum at the August 10 meeting. This is highly suspect, given Sumner Welles's presence at the meeting. Hull would not have been so foolish to do such a thing in front of Sumner Welles and others. Irwin Gellman reports that Hull presented FDR his ultimatum on Monday, August 15. This, of course, could not have been the case and was perhaps an error in typesetting (Gellman, *Secret Affairs*, 317; Welles, *Sumner Welles*, 346).

36. See, in particular, Welles, *Sumner Welles*, 1–3.

37. Welles, *Sumner Welles*, 340.

38. Roosevelt, *This I Remember*, 63. FDR also recounted the confrontation to Assistant Secretary of State Adolf Berle. See Welles, *Sumner Welles*, 345.

39. Welles, *Sumner Welles*, 379–80.

40. Gellman, *Secret Affairs*, 317.

41. Hull and Berding, *Memoirs of Cordell Hull*, 1230.

42. Winant, telegram to the Secretary of State, September 22, 1943, Establishment of Commission.

43. Winant, telegram to the Secretary of State, September 1, 1943 (received September 6), Establishment of Comission.

44. Hull, "Airgram" to Winant, September 25, 1943, Establishment of Commission.

45. Hull, "Airgram" to Winant, September 25, 1943, Establishment of Commission.

46. HCP, "War Guilt Commission," September 17, 1943, Hull, Cordell.

47. HCP, "War Guilt Commission," September 17, 1943, Hull, Cordell.

48. HCP, "War Guilt Commission," September 17, 1943, Hull, Cordell.

49. HCP to Hull, September 23, 1943, Hull, Cordell.

50. Pell wrote, "May I take the liberty of suggesting that copies of these reports and clippings be sent to me. I realize that the organization has not been made and that the field of the Commission has not been settled, but I think it would be a good thing if I were in on the discussions of the subject and that I should have as much information as possible sent to me in small doses as it comes along" (HCP to Shaw, October 12, 1943, State Department: Shaw 1943, Box 26, General Correspondence).

51. For Hull's perspective on the conference, see Hull and Berding, *Memoirs of Cordell Hull*, 1274–91.

52. The nations represented at the meeting were Australia, Belgium, Canada, China, Czechoslovakia, Greece, India, Luxembourg, the Netherlands, New Zealand, Norway, Poland, the Union of South Africa, the United Kingdom of Great Britain and Northern Ireland, the United States of America, Yugoslavia, and the French Committee of National Liberation (Winant, telegram to the Secretary of State, October 21, 1943, Establishment of Commission). As Dan Plesch noted, many members of the London International Assembly represented their nations on the UNWCC. The assembly consisted of exiled European governments and began meeting in 1941. The Soviets sent an observer; the United States and Britain did not (Plesch, *Human Rights after Hitler*, 54–55).

53. "War Crimes' Listing to Be Started Soon," *New York Times*, October 21, 1943.

54. Winant, telegram to the Secretary of State, October 26, 1943, War Crimes—Miscellaneous Correspondence 1943; "War Crimes' Listing to Be Started Soon."

55. W. H. Lawrence, "Accord in Moscow," *New York Times*, November 2, 1943.

56. U.S. Department of State, "Declaration of German Atrocities in State Department Bulletin No. 228," November 6, 1943 (released to the press November 1), War Crimes Commission: State Department. See Taylor, *Anatomy of the Nuremberg Trials*, 26–27.

57. Stettinius, memorandum for FDR, November 4, 1943, White House, Box 4, Records Relating to German War Crimes 1942–1946, Records of the Legal Adviser. Pell was concerned equally that the secretary appointed to serve him in London would not be traveling with him. Pell hated to fly and traveled to Europe by ship whenever he could. He wrote the president on November 11, "I would, of course, like to have her [Olive Pell] help in the domestic installation of my establishment, and I certainly should have the secretary of the [U.S.] Commission, Miss Grigsby, with me. It will not be easy, in fact, it will be extremely difficult, to begin the work without adequate staff, and at the same time be obliged to hunt lodgings and manage my proper social intercourse with my colleagues." Pell was used to discussing details with the president and was probably trying to intimate just how disorganized the State Department was regarding his travel arrangements. Of course, these were hardly details with which Pell should bother the president, but that's what friends did (HCP to FDR, November 11, 1943, Roosevelt, FD 1936–45).

58. Ralph W. S. Hill, "United States Commission for the Investigation of War Crimes," November 9, 1943, War Crimes—Miscellaneous Correspondence 1943.

59. HCP, memorandum, December 23, 1943, War Crimes Commission: Pell Notes and Statements, Box 28, General Correspondence.

60. Hill, "United States Commission for the Investigation of War Crimes," November 9, 1943, War Crimes—Miscellaneous Correspondence 1943.

61. HCP to the Secretary of State, November 11, 1943, War Crimes—Miscellaneous Correspondence 1943.

62. HCP to FDR, November 11, 1943, Roosevelt, FD 1936–45. See also Wyman, *Abandonment of the Jews,* 258.

63. HCP, "Reminiscences," 543.

64. HCP, "Reminiscences," 533. Also quoted in Baker, *Brahmin in Revolt,* 260.

65. Stettinius, telegram to London, November 5, 1943, War Crimes—Miscellaneous Correspondence 1943. See also Wyman, *Abandonment of the Jews,* 258.

66. The purpose of such a committee would serve to limit the authority of the Commission and, therefore, the governments in exile and lesser Allies. See Kochavi, *Prelude to Nuremberg,* 55–56, 93; Winant, telegram to the Secretary of State, October 21, 1943, Establishment of Commission.

67. Kochavi, *Prelude to Nuremberg,* 53–54.

68. HCP to "Mama," July 3, 1943, Pell, Mrs. Herbert, Sr., Box 20, General Correspondence.

69. Following his unceremonious removal, Pell worked hard to promote the work he did on the Commission, but while serving he tended to minimize the importance of his own contributions. See Blayney, *Democracy's Aristocrat,* 135–38.

70. HCP to the Secretary of State, May 2, 1944, War Crimes Commission: Reports and Printed Material, Box 28, General Correspondence.

71. In a 1931 article, for example, Pell envisioned the future necessity of an alliance between Soviet Russia and the United States in opposition to a "united Europe" ("Preparing for the Next War," Speeches, Articles and Reprints, 1918–59, Box 31, Speech and Writings File, HCPP).

72. HCP, "Reminiscences," 569. See also Baker, *Brahmin in Revolt,* 254–55.

73. Pell wrote to Secretary Hull on November 11, "I believe that the business of my Committee will be to take its part in the great effort to prevent a third war rather than merely to act as an instrument of vengeance for past wrongs" (HCP to the Secretary of State, November 11, 1943, War Crimes—Miscellaneous Correspondence 1943). See also Baker, *Brahmin in Revolt,* 255; Blayney, *Democracy's Aristocrat,* 118–19.

74. HCP, "Reminiscences," 570.

Chapter 5

Epigraph: FDR to HCP, March 1, 1944, Roosevelt, FD 1936–45.

1. HCP, "Reminiscences," 534–37.

2. Although Pell did not identify the specific book, it could only have been Alphonse Dunoyer, *The Public Prosecutor of the Terror, Antoine Quentin Fouquier-Tinville; Tr. from the French of Alphonse Dunoyer by A. W. Evans. With a Photogravure Frontispiece and Fourteen Other Illustrations*; HCP, "Reminiscences," 569.

3. Dunoyer, *Public Prosecutor of the Terror,* 299.

4. Dunoyer, *Public Prosecutor of the Terror,* 304.

5. According to UNWCC minutes, the Commission dealt with the issue of "superior orders" on August 22, September 19, September 26, and October 6, 1944. In its October 6 "Explanatory Memorandum to Accompany the Draft Convention for the Establishment of a United Nations War Crimes Court," the Commission decided "that it is better to leave it to the Court itself in each case to decide what weight should be attached to a plea of superior orders" (United Nations War Crimes Commission, "Folder UNWCC—Indexes [with Supplements] to Minutes and Documents—Meetings 0-38—S-1804-0001-0001," United Nations Archives and Records Management Section, https://search.archives.un.org/unwcc-indexes-with-supplements-to-minutes-and-documents-meetings-01-38).

6. Pell noted in his 1953 oral history, "When the French Revolution was well under way a great many of the government officials were holdovers from the old administration. There was a considerable feeling for royalism. Royalist and anti-government plots were going on all over the country. The Committee of Public Safety was organized. Fouquier-Tinville was put in charge of it, and the Terror began. A considerable number of people were executed. Many of them would have been perhaps put only in jail, a good many of them should have been let go completely; many of them were innocent, a great many of them were harmless. However, the net result of Fouquier-Tinville's activities was that royalism was suppressed. I felt we were facing the same situation in Germany" (HCP, "Reminiscences," 569–70). These ideas were not those of Dunoyer's *Public Prosecutor of the Terror,* but must have come from Pell's own study of the French Revolution.

7. In early July FDR had asked Grace Tully to acknowledge his receipt of both Glueck's "Editor's Note," a future introductory chapter for a text on war crimes policy, and his article "Trial and Punishment of the Axis War Criminals," noting that both would be forwarded to Herbert Pell. Grace Tully to Glueck, July 22, 1943, Roosevelt, FD 1936–45.

8. HCP to Breckinridge Long, November 11, 1943, State Department Correspondence 1941–1946 and Undated, Box 26, General Correspondence.

9. Pell wrote in his 1953 oral history, "I had received no instructions from the department or from the government—or practically none" (HCP, "Reminiscences," 568).

10. Glueck, "Trial and Punishment of the Axis War Criminals," September 1942, OF5152, 22.

11. Glueck, "Trial and Punishment of the Axis War Criminals," September 1942, OF5152, 22–23.

12. Glueck, "Trial and Punishment of the Axis War Criminals," September 1942, OF5152, 21–22.

13. Glueck, "Trial and Punishment of the Axis War Criminals," September 1942, OF5152, 27.

14. In February 1943 Pell's assistant Lawrence Preuss notified officials back at the State Department that Pell had formalized his plans "before his departure from the United States" (Preuss to Sandifer, February 3, 1944, War Crimes Commission: State Department).

15. Hull to HCP, December 28, 1943, Hull, Cordell. See also Baker, *Brahmin in Revolt,* 273.

16. Winant, telegram to the Secretary of State, September 1, 1943 (received September 6), Establishment of Commission; Hull, "Airgram" to Winant, September 25, 1943, Establishment of Commission.

17. Hull to HCP, December 28, 1943, Hull, Cordell.

18. United Nations War Crimes Commission, "Folder UNWCC—Indexes (with Supplements) to Minutes and Documents—Meetings 01-38—S-1804-0001-0001."

19. Preuss to Sandifer, February 3, 1944, War Crimes Commission: State Department; State Department Policy Committee, "The Definition of War Crimes in Relation to Crimes against Jews in Axis Countries (Le-2)," May 19, 1944, State Dept.'s Policy Committee Papers (1942–44). See also Kochavi, *Prelude to Nuremberg*, 143–44; Wyman, *Abandonment of the Jews*, 257–58; Blayney, *Democracy's Aristocrat*, 123–25.

20. In his 1953 oral history, Pell noted, for example, "I had the advantage of not being a lawyer at all, associating with first-class experts in international law. I could make suggestions as a layman and they never felt that they were attacking my professional pride when they criticized or explained errors that I was making, which they wouldn't have liked to have done among themselves" (HCP, "Reminiscences," 577).

21. HCP to Claiborne Pell, February 25, 1944, Pell, Claiborne.

22. HCP to G. Howland Shaw, December 16, 1943, War Crimes Commission: State Department.

23. Preuss to Sandifer, January 22, 1944, War Crimes Commission: State Department.

24. By the time of Preuss's letter to Sandifer, Pell and Preuss had attended four meetings of the UNWCC (December 2, 1943, and January 4, January 11, and January 18, 1944). Based on UNWCC minutes, the two worked without discord. See UNWCC minutes and documents, "Folder UNWCC—Indexes (with Supplements) to Minutes and Documents—Meetings 01-38—S-1804-0001-0001."

25. Pell began his January 27 letter to FDR mentioning that he read "with great interest" the statement establishing the War Refugee Board. Pell went so far as to quote it back to the president (HCP to FDR, January 27, 1944, Roosevelt, FD 1936–45). See Kochavi, *Prelude to Nuremberg*, 145.

26. FDR, memorandum for the Secretary of War, August 26, 1944, White House Correspondence 1-1-44–9-21-45, Box 15, Top Secret Correspondence, 07/1940–09/18/1947, Records of the Office of the Secretary of War, RG 107, NACP. See also Kochavi, *Prelude to Nuremberg*, 145.

27. Preuss to Sandifer, February 3, 1944, War Crimes Commission: State Department.

28. Glueck, "Trial and Punishment of the Axis War Criminals," September 1942, OF5152, 22–23.

29. Blayney argued that Pell's love for animals helps explain his desire to prosecute the Nazis for crimes against the Jews. Pell had often expressed his hatred of animal cruelty in any form and routinely sought to mitigate it (Blayney, *Democracy's Aristocrat*, 121–23).

30. Preuss to Sandifer, February 3, 1944, War Crimes Commission: State Department.

31. HCP to FDR, January 27, 1944, Roosevelt, FD 1936–45.

32. HCP to Breckinridge Long, January 28, 1944, War Crimes—Correspondence with Mr. Pell.

33. Breckinridge Long to HCP, February 10, 1944, War Crimes—Miscellaneous Correspondence 1944.

34. Hackworth, memorandum to Breckinridge Long, February 9, 1944, War Crimes—Miscellaneous Correspondence 1944.

35. Breckinridge Long, memorandum to Mr. Hackworth, February 7, 1944, War Crimes—Miscellaneous Correspondence 1944.

36. Simpson, *Splendid Blond Beast*, 165–66.

37. The Commission dropped the technical committee on January 25, 1944 (UNWCC, "Folder UNWCC—Indexes (with Supplements) to Minutes and Documents—Meetings 01-38—S-1804-0001-0001."

38. Hackworth, memorandum to Breckinridge Long (unsent), February 9, 1944, War Crimes—Miscellaneous Correspondence 1944.

39. Hackworth, memorandum to Breckinridge Long (unsent), February 9, 1944, War Crimes—Miscellaneous Correspondence 1944.

40. FDR to HCP, February 12, 1944, War Crimes—Correspondence with Mr. Pell. Unaware that the letter was not written by FDR, Leonard Baker in his biography of Pell concluded that letter implied the Commission "should become involved in the mechanics of seeking justice rather than only gather evidence as Cordell Hull had suggested." Despite his being mistaken about the authorship of the "My dear Bertie" letter, nonetheless, Baker was quite correct in its implication (Baker, *Brahmin in Revolt*, 273–74).

41. Stettinius to HCP, February 15, 1944, Written Instructions to Commissioner, Folder 1 of 2, Box 6, Records Relating to US Participation in UN War Crimes Commission 1943–1949, Records of the Legal Adviser.

42. Hull, memorandum for FDR, February 9, 1944, War Crimes—Correspondence with Mr. Pell; Stettinius to HCP, February 15, 1944, Written Instructions to Commissioner, Folder 1 of 2, Box 6, Records Relating to US Participation in UN War Crimes Commission, Records of the Legal Adviser.

43. FDR, *Public Papers and Addresses of Franklin D. Roosevelt*, 12:327.

44. HCP to FDR, February 16, 1944, Roosevelt, FD 1936–45.

45. FDR asked the State Department on February 22 to compose this reply. The president made no changes to it (Stettinius, memorandum to FDR, February 29, 1944, War Crimes—Correspondence with Mr. Pell).

46. FDR to HCP, March 1, 1944, Roosevelt, FD 1936–45.

47. Lawrence Preuss reported to State the details about what Pell received when (State Department Policy Committee, "The Definition of War Crimes in Relation to Crimes against Jews in Axis Countries [Le-2]," May 19, 1944, State Dept.'s Policy Committee Papers [1942–44]).

48. HCP, "Reminiscences," 578–79.

49. HCP to Winant, April 3, 1944, Winant.

50. United Nations War Crimes Commission, "Folder UNWCC—Legal Committee (Committee III Documents III 1–III 118 [Incomplete]—15854)," United Nations Archives and Records Management Section, https://search.archives.un.org/unwcc-legal-committee-committee-iii-documents-iii-1-iii-118-incomplete.

51. State Department Policy Committee, "The Definition of War Crimes in Relation to Crimes against Jews in Axis Countries (Le-2)," May 19, 1944, State Dept.'s Policy Committee Papers (1942–44).

52. FDR to HCP, March 1, 1944, Roosevelt, FD 1936–45.

53. State Department Policy Committee, "The Definition of War Crimes in Relation to Crimes against Jews in Axis Countries (Le-2)," May 19, 1944, State Dept.'s Policy Committee Papers (1942–44); HCP to FDR, April 3, 1944, Roosevelt, FD 1936–45. See also Kochavi, *Prelude to Nuremberg*, 147.

54. HCP to FDR, March 16, 1944, Roosevelt, FD 1936–45. The March 1 letter signed by the president had included an addendum that the contents were for Pell's "confidential guidance" only (FDR to HCP, March 1, 1944, Roosevelt, FD 1936–45). See also Kochavi, *Prelude to Nuremberg*, 146.

55. HCP to FDR, March 16, 1944, Roosevelt, FD 1936–45.

56. FDR, "Radio Bulletin No. 72," March 24, 1944, Roosevelt, FD 1936–45.

57. Although this was the strongest statement FDR had made to date on Jews and the Holocaust, the final version of the address was not as strong as Morgenthau had hoped. Presidential special counsel Sam Rosenman altered the text for the president, moving mention of atrocities against Jews from the first to the fourth paragraph, based primarily on political considerations in an election year. See Wyman, *Abandonment of the Jews*, 256. Robert Rosen in *Saving the Jews* (609n29) downplays the importance of Rosenman's editing, given the strength of the final statement. If there was indeed a real concern about the political consequences of speaking out in favor of saving the Jews in an election year, Rosenman's alterations were not nearly enough to alleviate that problem. The statement stands as a strong denunciation of atrocities against many groups, especially the Jews, and promises punishment.

58. FDR, "Radio Bulletin No. 72," March 24, 1944, Roosevelt, FD 1936–45.

59. FDR, "Radio Bulletin No. 72," March 24, 1944, Roosevelt, FD 1936–45.

60. Pell wrote Gil Winant in early April, "I do not care whether it is done by the War Crimes Commission or by some other body, but it seems to me that so far there is no other organization equipped to set up the means of reaching this problem as effectively as we can" (HCP to Winant, April 3, 1943, Winant).

61. FDR, "Radio Bulletin No. 72," March 24, 1944, Roosevelt, FD 1936–45.

62. State Department Policy Committee, "The Definition of War Crimes in Relation to Crimes against Jews in Axis Countries (Le-2)," May 19, 1944, State Dept.'s Policy Committee Papers (1942–44).

63. FDR, "Radio Bulletin No. 72," March 24, 1944, Roosevelt, FD 1936–45.

64. FDR to HCP, March 1, 1944, Roosevelt, FD 1936–45.

65. FDR, "Radio Bulletin No. 72," March 24, 1944, Roosevelt, FD 1936–45.

66. HCP to Hull, March 24, 1944, Hull, Cordell.

67. State Department Policy Committee, "The Definition of War Crimes in Relation to Crimes against Jews in Axis Countries (Le-2)," May 19, 1944, State Dept.'s Policy Committee Papers (1942–44). See also Kochavi, *Prelude to Nuremberg*, 147.

68. Hull to HCP, March 13, 1944, Written Instructions to Commissioner, Folder 1 of 2, Box 6, Records Relating to US Participation on UN War Crimes Commission, Records of the Legal Adviser.

69. See Simpson, *Splendid Blond Beast,* 165–66.

70. Hull's summary of the proposed State Department instructions for Pell contained considerably less detail than did the instructions to Pell. The president probably read only the slimmed-down version in the memorandum. It is certainly possible, if not likely, that Hull purposely kept his memorandum limited in detail for the president, assuming that the president would not want to examine the more detailed instructions, given the pressures on his time. A more conspiratorial view, however, is also possible. Give to the president, who was a lawyer, a simplified version. Give to Pell, who was not a lawyer, a more complex, legalistic set of instructions. In any case, neither document—the instructions to Pell or Hull's memorandum—discusses crimes against German nationals, while the "president's" letter does (Hull, memorandum for FDR, February 9, 1944, War Crimes—Correspondence with Mr. Pell).

71. FDR to HCP, February 12, 1944, War Crimes—Correspondence with Mr. Pell.

72. Stettinius to HCP, February 15, 1944, Written Instructions to Commissioner, Folder 1 of 2, Box 6, Records Relating to US Participation in UN War Crimes Commission, Records of the Legal Adviser.

73. FDR to HCP, March 1, 1944, Roosevelt, FD 1936–45.

74. Hull to HCP, March 13, 1944, Written Instructions to Commissioner, Folder 1 of 2, Box 6, Records Relating to US Participation on UN War Crimes Commission, Records of the Legal Adviser.

75. HCP, "Personal to the Secretary of State," April 24, 1944, War Crimes Commission: State Department; HCP, "Reminiscences," 584–87. See also Blayney, *Democracy's Aristocrat,* 124–25; Kochavi, *Prelude to Nuremberg,* 147; Wyman, *Abandonment of the Jews,* 258.

76. HCP, "Personal to the Secretary of State," April 24, 1944, War Crimes Commission: State Department; HCP, "Reminiscences," 584–87. See also Blayney, *Democracy's Aristocrat,* 124–25; Kochavi, *Prelude to Nuremberg,* 147; Wyman, *Abandonment of the Jews,* 258.

77. HCP, "Reminiscences," 587.

78. Roosevelt, *This I Remember,* 329.

79. For a specific examination of FDR's health, see Ferrell, *Dying President.* See also Evans, *Hidden Campaign.*

80. Tully, *F.D.R.,* 273–74.

81. Ferrell, *Dying President,* 147.

82. Roosevelt, *This I Remember,* 343.

83. FDR, "Radio Bulletin No. 72," March 24, 1944, Roosevelt, FD 1936–45.

84. HCP, "Reminiscences," 584–603. Pell was very outspoken about State Department antisemitism in a letter to David Drucker of the International Lawyers Committee. Pell noted, "One [of the reasons for the 'soft-peace' for Germany] is anti-Semitism [*sic*],

which is, to a large extent, prevalent in the State Department" (HCP to David Drucker, September 28, 1945, War Crimes Commission: Correspondence).

85. HCP, Untitled Recollections, May 1945. Pell used the document as a rough draft for a shorter version sent to David Niles at the White House on May 23, 1945 (HCP to David Niles, May 23, 1945, War Crimes Commission: Correspondence). Pell likely gave a copy of this letter to Drew Person, who published portions of it in "The Washington Merry-Go-Round" on June 6, 1945. Pearson called it "Pell's Secret Report" (Drew Pearson, "The Washington Merry-Go-Round," June 6, 1945, Drew Pearson's Washington Merry-Go-Round, American University Library—Special Collections, Washington, D.C.).

86. Wyman, *Abandonment of the Jews*, 190.

87. HCP to Hull, March 24, 1944, Hull, Cordell.

88. HCP to Hull, June 20, 1944, Hull, Cordell.

89. HCP to Hull, March 24, 1944, Hull, Cordell.

Chapter 6

Epigraph: HCP, "War Guilt Commission," September 17, 1943, Hull, Cordell.

1. HCP to FDR, March 8, 1944, War Crimes Commission.

2. HCP to FDR, March 8, 1944, War Crimes Commission.

3. HCP to FDR, April 3, 1944, Roosevelt, FD 1936–45. Also quoted in Kochavi, *Prelude to Nuremberg*, 147.

4. HCP to FDR, April 3, 1944, Roosevelt, FD 1936–45; HCP to Hull, April 3, 1944, Hull, Cordell; HCP to Winant, April 3, 1944, Winant.

5. HCP to Hull, April 3, 1944, Hull, Cordell.

6. HCP to Winant, April 3, 1944, Winant.

7. HCP to FDR, April 3, 1944, Roosevelt, FD 1936–45.

8. Kochavi, *Prelude to Nuremberg*, 148.

9. Preuss to Sandifer, February 3, 1944, War Crimes Commission: State Department.

10. State Department Policy Committee, "The Definition of War Crimes in Relation to Crimes against Jews in Axis Countries (Le-2)," May 19, 1944, State Dept.'s Policy Committee Papers (1942–44); Preuss to Sandifer, February 3, 1944, War Crimes Commission: State Department. See also Kochavi, *Prelude to Nuremberg*, 144.

11. FDR requested State compose his reply on April 1. The reply was written by Green Hackworth (Hull, memorandum for the president, April 4, 1944, War Crimes—Miscellaneous Correspondence 1944).

12. Hackworth to HCP for signature of the president, April 4, 1944, War Crimes—Miscellaneous Correspondence 1944; FDR to HCP, April 5, 1944, Roosevelt, FD 1936–45.

13. FDR to HCP, March 1, 1944, Roosevelt, FD 1936–45.

14. Hackworth to HCP for signature of the president, April 4, 1944, War Crimes—Miscellaneous Correspondence 1944; FDR to HCP, March 1, 1944, Roosevelt, FD 1936–45.

15. FDR to HCP, March 1, 1944, Roosevelt, FD 1936–45.

16. HCP to the Secretary of State, May 2, 1944, War Crimes Commission: Reports and Printed Material, Box 28, General Correspondence. The creation of a lasting international

criminal court had been debated in the interwar years in the League of Nations and more recently in the London International Assembly. See Plesch, *Human Rights after Hitler,* 58.

17. Following the dissolution of the technical committee, the Commission created three separate committees: Committee I—The Committee on Facts and Evidence, Committee II—The Committee on Means and Methods of Enforcement, and Committee III—The Committee on Legal Questions. See Kochavi, *Prelude to Nuremberg,* 93–94, 148–49; Frank Roberts to Winant, February 24, 1944, War Crimes Commission: Reports and Printed Material, Box 28, General Correspondence.

18. HCP to Berle, May 4, 1944, War Crimes—Miscellaneous Correspondence 1944; HCP to Stettinius, April 18, 1944, War Crimes Commission: State Department.

19. HCP to Hull, March 24, 1944; Hull, Cordell.

20. Hull, telegram to HCP, March 31, 1944, War Crimes—Miscellaneous Correspondence 1944.

21. Hull, telegram to Stettinius, March 31, 1944, War Crimes—Miscellaneous Correspondence 1944.

22. FDR to HCP, March 1, 1944, Roosevelt, FD 1936–45.

23. State Department Policy Committee, "The Definition of War Crimes in Relation to Crimes against Jews in Axis Countries (Le-2)," May 19, 1944, State Dept.'s Policy Committee Papers (1942–44); HCP to FDR, April 3, 1944, Roosevelt, FD 1936–45. See also Kochavi, *Prelude to Nuremberg,* 147.

24. According to the instruction, "The Department is of the opinion that to assume to punish officials of enemy governments for action taken against their own nationals pursuant to their own laws would constitute an assumption of jurisdiction probably unwarranted under international law" (Hull to HCP, March 13, 1944, Written Instructions to Commissioner, Folder 1 of 2, Box 6, Records Relating to US Participation on UN War Crimes Commission, Records of the Legal Adviser).

25. Hull to HCP, March 13, 1944, Written Instructions to Commissioner, Folder 1 of 2, Box 6, Records Relating to US Participation on UN War Crimes Commission, Records of the Legal Adviser.

26. HCP to Stettinius, April 18, 1944, War Crimes Commission: State Department.

27. HCP to Berle, May 4, 1944, War Crimes—Miscellaneous Correspondence 1944.

28. Berle, memorandum to Hackworth, May 13, 1944, War Crimes—Miscellaneous Correspondence 1944.

29. Just who was on this "policy committee" or how long it had been in operation is not stated in the documents. This is the first mention of any such committee existing within the State Department. Who the "two officers" were is not provided either. The most likely candidates were Green Hackworth and Lawrence Preuss (Hackworth to Berle, May 15, 1944, War Crimes—Miscellaneous Correspondence 1944).

30. Berle to HCP, May 16, 1944, War Crimes—Miscellaneous Correspondence 1944.

31. HCP to Berle, May 23, 1944, War Crimes Commission: Correspondence.

32. HCP to Berle, May 23, 1944, War Crimes Commission: Correspondence.

33. Berle to HCP, May 16, 1944, War Crimes—Miscellaneous Correspondence 1944.

34. State Department Policy Committee, "The Definition of War Crimes in Relation to Crimes against Jews in Axis Countries (Le-2)," May 19, 1944, State Dept.'s Policy Committee Papers (1942–44).

35. "The Scope and Definition of War Crimes—Summary (Le-4)," May 20, 1944, State Dept.'s Policy Committee Papers (1942–44). The "policy committee" also produced a longer document accompanying the "Summary": "The Definition and Scope of War Crimes (Le-3)," May 20, 1944, State Dept.'s Policy Committee Papers (1942–44).

36. Although not stated, presumably that meant September 1, 1939, in Europe. "The Scope and Definition of War Crimes—Summary (Le-4)," May 20, 1944, State Dept.'s Policy Committee Papers (1942–44).

37. "The Scope and Definition of War Crimes—Summary (Le-4)," May 20, 1944, State Dept.'s Policy Committee Papers (1942–44).

38. HCP to Berle, June 5, 1944, War Crimes Commission: Correspondence.

39. See also Kochavi, *Prelude to Nuremberg,* 149.

40. Hackworth, memorandum to Berle, June 12, 1944, War Crimes—Correspondence with Mr. Pell.

41. Berle replied to Pell following communication from Hackworth, writing him on June 13: "The Department has been working on an instruction, which is now being cleared with the appropriate departments. I hope it will come relatively soon. When it comes out it should settle a good many questions which have been bothering us all." Pell probably received this letter simultaneously with the president's June 13 letter, offering specifically that the War and Navy Departments had become involved in war crimes policy planning (Berle to HCP, June 13, 1944, War Crimes–Correspondence with Mr. Pell).

42. Hurst to Eden, May 31, 1944, War Crimes Commission: Correspondence. The British government decided on June 28, 1944, to reject the proposals contained in Hurst's letter, adopting a policy similar to the State Department that concluded that crimes against German Jews did not fall within existing war crimes laws. For more on British war crimes policy planning, see, in particular, Kochavi, *Prelude to Nuremberg,* 151–55.

43. HCP to FDR, June 5, 1944; Roosevelt, FD 1936–45.

44. FDR to HCP, March 1, 1944, Roosevelt, FD 1936–45.

45. Hull, memorandum to FDR, June 13, 1944, War Crimes—Correspondence with Mr. Pell.

46. FDR to HCP, June 13, 1944, Roosevelt, FD 1936–45.

47. HCP to Hull, June 20, 1944, Hull, Cordell. Also quoted in Kochavi, *Prelude to Nuremberg,* 149.

48. HCP to Hull, June 20, 1944, Hull, Cordell.

49. The Navy Department sent an approval letter on June 22, and the War Department did similarly on June 23 (Hull, memorandum for FDR, June 28, 1944, White House, Records of the Legal Adviser); Stimson Diary, November 21, 1944. See also Kochavi, *Prelude to Nuremberg,* 149.

50. Hull, memorandum for FDR, June 28, 1944, White House, Records of the Legal Adviser.

51. Kochavi, *Prelude to Nuremberg,* 150.

52. FDR, "Radio Bulletin No. 72," March 24, 1944, Roosevelt, FD 1936–45.

53. FDR, *Public Papers and Addresses*, 11:3–5.

54. Stimson believed FDR was "the poorest administrator" he ever worked with (Stimson Diary, March 28, 1943). See also Morgenthau, *Mostly Morgenthaus*, 373.

55. Quoted in Smith, *Road to Nuremberg*, 13–14.

56. Arieh Kochavi concludes otherwise, writing, "If Roosevelt had not been indifferent to the war crimes issue or had he any established conception about them, he might have more carefully examined the principles laid down in the [June 28] memorandum." Kochavi did not take into account the declining health of the president, and he did not note that the State Department had written FDR's "My dear Bertie" letters. Believing the president composed those letters helps create the impression that FDR was "indifferent" to war crimes policy. Whatever the level of FDR's conception of war crimes policy and the degree to which he examined the memorandum does not automatically mean FDR was indifferent. The memorandum, moreover, contained so many conditionals, it would have been difficult for FDR, even reading them closely, to conclude that they rose to the level of principles. However, Kochavi is quite right that had FDR read the memorandum closely he "would have realized that [it] diverged, at the very least, from the sprit of his own previous statements" (Kochavi, *Prelude to Nuremberg*, 150).

57. Hull, memorandum for FDR, June 28, 1944, White House, Records of the Legal Adviser; Hull to HCP, July 15, 1944, War Crimes Commission: State Department.

58. Hull to HCP, July 15, 1944, War Crimes Commission: State Department.

59. On February 3, 1944, Lawrence Preuss reported to the State Department that Pell had actually formed this idea prior to arriving in London (Preuss to Sandifer, February 3, 1944, War Crimes Commission: State Department).

60. Hull to HCP, July 15, 1944, War Crimes Commission: State Department.

61. Hull to HCP, July 15, 1944, War Crimes Commission: State Department.

62. Hull to HCP, March 13, 1944, Written Instructions to Commissioner, Folder 1 of 2, Box 6, Records Relating to US Participation on UN War Crimes Commission, Records of the Legal Adviser.

63. FDR to HCP, March 1, 1944, Roosevelt, FD 1936–45.

64. Kochavi, *Prelude to Nuremberg*, 149.

65. HCP to FDR, February 16, 1944, Roosevelt, FD 1936–45.

66. See, for example, Hitler, Johnson, and Chamberlain, *Mein Kampf*.

67. HCP to FDR, February 16, 1944, Roosevelt, FD 1936–45.

68. FDR to HCP, March 1, 1944, Roosevelt, FD 1936–45.

69. Hull to HCP, July 15, 1944, War Crimes Commission: State Department.

70. FDR to HCP, March 1, 1944, Roosevelt, FD 1936–45.

71. Hull to HCP, July 15, 1944, War Crimes Commission: State Department.

72. Up until March 19, 1944, Hungary was a satellite of Germany, and therefore, according to the State Department, Hungarian Jews were beyond the protection of the Allies or jurisdiction of the UNWCC. After Germany occupied Hungary, the status of Hungary's Jews becomes less clear (Kochavi, *Prelude to Nuremberg*, 149).

73. Kochavi, *Prelude to Nuremberg*, 155–56.

Chapter 7

Epigraph: HCP to Hull, June 20, 1944, Hull, Cordell. Also quoted in Kochavi, *Prelude to Nuremberg,* 149.

1. Morgenthau, *Mostly Morgenthaus,* 305, 350–53; Glueck, "Trial and Punishment of the Axis War Criminals."

2. DuBois told Morgenthau, "On the way over in the plane, White and your dad sat together, and though I wasn't deliberately eavesdropping, it was obvious from the conversation that what they were talking about was the whole notion of how we should get reparations from Germany. And by the time we arrived in England, there was no question in my mind that your dad was at this point completely convinced that the approach that the State Department had suggested was the wrong approach. . . . So at that point he began pushing what later became known as the so-called Morgenthau Plan for Germany, and wherever he went, whoever he talked to, he would hammer his point home" (quoted in Morgenthau, *Mostly Morgenthaus,* 353). Fred Smith believed the Morgenthau Plan grew out of a meeting between Eisenhower, Morgenthau, and his aides. "On August 7 1944 at approximately 12:35 P.M. in a tent in southern England, the Morgenthau Plan was born. Actually, it was General Dwight D. Eisenhower who launched the project. . . . The subject first came up at lunch in General Eisenhower's mess tent" (quoted in Bacque, *Other Losses,* 197). Smith was overemphasizing the importance of Eisenhower regarding the origins of the Morgenthau Plan, although Eisenhower's support for a harsh postwar policy was particularly important to Morgenthau. At a meeting back in Washington with his staff on August 18, 1944, Morgenthau made it clear that an immediate purpose of his meeting with Eisenhower was to discover his position. "We got down to the Southern part of England where his headquarters were . . . and we started right in with General Eisenhower to find out where he stood on this business of how he is going to treat Germany when he first gets in" (Henry Morgenthau and Judiciary Subcommittee, *Morgenthau Diary,* 414).

3. According to Henry Morgenthau III, his father was predisposed to want a harsh peace imposed on Germany. He wrote that Morgenthau "had inherited his own father's [Henry Morgenthau Sr.] hatred of the Germans and a fear that after each successive war they would reemerge even stronger unless their military-industrial base was dismantled" (Morgenthau, *Mostly Morgenthaus,* 361).

4. The degree to which Churchill was for or against the Morgenthau Plan was ever shifting. Churchill gave Morgenthau the "impression" of support at a two-hour lunch meeting in London on August 10 when the two met in London, then came out against it initially at the Quebec Conference, and one day later did a complete 180 and supported it. Churchill's support or lack thereof was always politically motivated and likely connected to his effort to secure postwar loans for Great Britain (Morgenthau, *Mostly Morgenthaus,* 361).

5. Henry Morgenthau III argues that while White should be credited with the origins of the Morgenthau Plan, Morgenthau himself was the primary author (Morgenthau, *Mostly Morgenthaus,* 353, 364).

6. Trial and Punishment of War Criminals.

7. Morgenthau and Judiciary Subcommittee, *Morgenthau Diary,* 892. On September 4 at an earlier group meeting, Morgenthau informed staff members that Herbert Pell had urged him to get involved in war crimes policy. Harry Dexter White said at the meeting, "DuBois who had talked to Pehle [*sic*—Pell] in London about the war criminals concluded that they have done next to nothing [on a list of war criminals to be summarily shot upon capture]." Morgenthau added, "I got that from Pehle [*sic*—Pell], and then asked DuBois to see Pehle [*sic*—Pell]" (Morgenthau and Judiciary Subcommittee, *Morgenthau Diary,* 486).

8. Trial and Punishment of War Criminals.

9. Trial and Punishment of War Criminals. For Kochavi's account of Pell's approaching the WRB, see Kochavi, *Prelude to Nuremberg,* 155–57.

10. Trial and Punishment of War Criminals.

11. Trial and Punishment of War Criminals.

12. Trial and Punishment of War Criminals.

13. Hackworth quoted Pell's July 27 telegram, which was received on July 28. Green H. Hackworth, "Urgent" memorandum to the acting secretary (Stettinius), July 29, 1944, War Crimes—Miscellaneous Correspondence 1944.

14. Hackworth, "Publicity," n.d. [November 15–16, 1944?], Pell Correspondence. Back on February 20, 1944, Pell had moved that all UNWCC minutes be marked "Secret" rather than "Confidential." An article in the *Manchester Guardian* had apparently been written based on UNWCC minutes. According to the July 11 UNWCC minutes, Pell's attitude had changed regarding publicity, and he moved that a committee be formed. "Mr. PELL raised the question whether the time had not come to appoint a committee to issue communiques from time to time regarding the Commission's work. The policy of avoiding publicity had been adopted at a moment when the Commission's proceedings could be best conducted by strict secrecy, but it was now, in his opinion, putting the Commission in a false position. The general public did not understand that the Commission had at present a strictly limited task." The UNWCC approved the setting up of just such a committee (UNWCC, "Folder UNWCC—Indexes [with Supplements] to Minutes and Documents—Meetings 01-38—S-1804-0001-0001").

15. Pell wrote that he was reporting what he had "already" sent two days earlier on July 27 (HCP, "Personal and Confidential to the Secretary" [Hull], July 29, 1944, Jews 1944–1945, Box 11, General Correspondence).

16. Quoted in Kochavi, *Prelude to Nuremberg,* 149–50.

17. HCP, "Personal and Confidential to the Secretary" [Hull], July 29, 1944, Jews 1944–1945, Box 11, General Correspondence.

18. UNWCC, "Folder UNWCC—Indexes (with Supplements) to Minutes and Documents—Meetings 01-38—S-1804-0001-0001."

19. According to Hackworth's memorandum, "Commander Gary who has to do with war crimes in the Navy Department" also approved of the telegram (Hackworth, "Urgent" memorandum to the acting secretary [Stettinius], July 29, 1944, War Crimes—Miscellaneous Correspondence 1944).

20. HCP, memorandum to the Secretary of State Re: Statement on the Origin and Composition of the Commission, August 5, 1944, War Crimes—Miscellaneous Correspondence 1944.

21. HCP, memorandum to the Secretary of State Re: Statement on the Origin and Composition of the Commission, August 5, 1944, War Crimes—Miscellaneous Correspondence 1944.

22. HCP, memorandum to the Secretary of State Re: Statement on the Origin and Composition of the Commission, August 5, 1944, War Crimes—Miscellaneous Correspondence 1944.

23. Back on March 13, the War Department suggested to State that a representative from the War Department be placed on the Commission to assist Pell. Pell wanted Major Robert Grant of the U.S. Air Corps, who was already in London, appointed as his assistant. However, the War Department had already decided on Lieutenant Colonel Hodgson and was preparing to send him over. The State Department acquired FDR's approval only after the fact. In an unsent memorandum by Green Hackworth (he wrote two) explaining to Hull what had transpired, Hackworth wrote, "Personally, I think the suggestion of representatives of both the War and Navy Departments working with Mr. Pell is a good idea, but I do not know how Mr. Pell would feel in the matter." The Navy Department had suggested they have someone in London with Pell as well, but it was only the War Department's selection that was sent to London. On May 23, Lieutenant Colonel Joseph V. Hodgson from the Judge Advocate General's Office was officially appointed Pell's assistant to replace the recently removed Lawrence Preuss (Hackworth, memorandum to the Secretary of State [1 of 2—Unsent], May 22, 1944, War Crimes—Miscellaneous Correspondence 1944; Hackworth memorandum to the Secretary of State [2 of 2—Unsent], May 22, 1944, War Crimes—Miscellaneous Correspondence 1944; Hull, memorandum to FDR, May 23, 1944, War Crimes—Miscellaneous Correspondence 1944).

24. The "Statement on the Origin and Composition of the Commission" had already been sent to the United States and Argentina for release (HCP, memorandum to the Secretary of State Re: Statement on the Origin and Composition of the Commission, August 5, 1944, War Crimes—Miscellaneous Correspondence 1944, Records of the Legal Adviser).

25. Winant, telegram to State Department, August 3, 1944, War Crimes—Miscellaneous Correspondence 1944.

26. HCP, memorandum to the Secretary of State Re: Statement on the Origin and Composition of the Commission, August 5, 1944, War Crimes—Miscellaneous Correspondence 1944.

27. Trial and Punishment of War Criminals.

28. Trial and Punishment of War Criminals.

29. Trial and Punishment of War Criminals.

30. Trial and Punishment of War Criminals.

31. HCP to Grace Tully, August 14, 1944, Pell, Herbert, President's Personal File, FDRP.

32. FDR, memorandum to Grace Tully, August 24, 1944, Pell, Herbert, President's Personal File, FDRP.

33. Grace Tully to HCP, August 25, 1944, Roosevelt, FD 1936–45.

Chapter 8

Epigraph: Stimson and McCloy, "Memorandum of Conversation," September 8, 1944, McCloy Correspondence.

1. Morgenthau and Judiciary Subcommittee, *Morgenthau Diary*, 414–15.

2. Morgenthau and Judiciary Subcommittee, *Morgenthau Diary*, 415.

3. According to Henry Morgenthau III, Hull had no "consistent policy" regarding postwar Germany, but that "his attitude shifted perhaps more in reaction to how he was treated personally than because he held to any basic tenets" (Morgenthau, *Mostly Morgenthaus*, 364).

4. Morgenthau and Judiciary Subcommittee, *Morgenthau Diary*, 416. Also quoted in Morgenthau, *Mostly Morgenthaus*, 364; Blum, *From the Morgenthau Diaries*, 3:341.

5. Morgenthau and Judiciary Subcommittee, *Morgenthau Diary*, 416–17. Also quoted in Morgenthau, *Mostly Morgenthaus*, 364; Blum, *From the Morgenthau Diaries*, 3:341.

6. Morgenthau and Judiciary Subcommittee, *Morgenthau Diary*, 416. See also Morgenthau, *Mostly Morgenthaus*, 364; Blum, *From the Morgenthau Diaries*, 3:341. Morgenthau III reorders the conversation and has Morgenthau saying this to Hull after Hull had mentioned what he said at the Moscow Conference. According to the Morgenthau Diary, the conversation occurred the other way around.

7. Blum, *From the Morgenthau Diaries*, 3:342.

8. Blum, *From the Morgenthau Diaries*, 3:342–43; Morgenthau, *Mostly Morgenthaus*, 365.

9. Stimson Diary, August 21, 1944.

10. Morgenthau reached this conclusion after meeting with Stimson and McCloy for lunch on August 23. Stimson indicated as much in his diary, writing at the end of a long day and after a dinner meeting with State Department officials on the night of the twenty-second, "I am rather disappointed with the day and am coming to the conclusion that there isn't much that I can do short of what I can talk over with the President when I see him personally. This is always a problem which cannot be very accurately prophesied." Stimson had not met with the president since June and he was concerned about FDR's state of health and mind (Morgenthau and Judiciary Subcommittee, *Morgenthau Diary*, 426–27; Stimson Diary, August 22, 1944).

11. Stimson wrote in his diary, "The problem of the three great powers (U.S., U.K., and Russia) [is] to keep Germany from attacking the world again during the necessarily long period which will pass before the present poisoned generation of German youth reaches and passes their maturity and goes off the world stage" (August 22, 1944).

12. Stimson Diary, August 23, 1944.

13. Stimson Diary, August 23, 1944.

14. Morgenthau and Judiciary Subcommittee, *Morgenthau Diary*, 425–27; Stimson Diary, August 23, 1944. See also Morgenthau, *Mostly Morgenthaus*, 366.

15. Stimson wrote that choosing southern Germany as the American occupation zone "keeps us away from Russia. . . . Let her do the dirty work but don't father it" (Stimson, "Brief for Conference with the President, August 25, 1944," in Stimson Diary).

16. Stimson, "Brief for Conference with the President, August 25, 1944," in Stimson Diary.

17. Indicative of just how distanced Stimson had been to that point about activities relating to concentration camps in Germany, he was under the mistaken impression that the Gestapo was in charge of it all. See Smith, *Road to Nuremberg,* 53.

18. Stimson, "Brief for Conference with the President, August 25, 1944" in Stimson Diary.

19. Stimson Diary, August 25, 1944; Blum, *From the Morgenthau Diaries,* 3:347–48; Morgenthau and Judiciary Subcommittee, *Morgenthau Diary,* 440–42, 447; Morgenthau, *Mostly Morgenthaus,* 367.

20. Blum, *From the Morgenthau Diaries,* 3:347; Smith, *Road to Nuremberg,* 25.

21. Stimson Diary, August 25, 1944; Blum, *From the Morgenthau Diaries,* 3:347–48; Morgenthau and Judiciary Subcommittee, *Morgenthau Diary,* 440–42; Morgenthau, *Mostly Morgenthaus,* 367.

22. FDR, memorandum for the Secretary of War, August 26, 1944, White House Correspondence 1-1-44-9-21-45, Box 15, Top Secret Correspondence, 07/1940–09/18/1947, Records of the Office of the Secretary of War, RG 107, NACP. See also Blum, *V Was for Victory,* 348–49; Hull and Berding, *Memoirs of Cordell Hull,* 1602–1603; Morgenthau, *Mostly Morgenthaus,* 367–68.

23. Blum, *From the Morgenthau Diaries,* 3:350.

24. Trial and Punishment of War Criminals; Smith, *American Road to Nuremberg,* 8, 21–22.

25. Trial and Punishment of War Criminals; Smith, *American Road to Nuremberg,* 21–23.

26. Trial and Punishment of War Criminals; Smith, *American Road to Nuremberg,* 21–23.

27. Trial and Punishment of War Criminals; Smith, *American Road to Nuremberg,* 21–23.

28. Trial and Punishment of War Criminals.

29. Kochavi, *Prelude to Nuremberg,* 156.

30. Morgenthau and Judiciary Subcommittee, *Morgenthau Diary,* 447.

31. McCloy, Telephone Conversation with Secretary Stimson, 12:30 P.M., August 28, 1944, McCloy Correspondence; Smith, *American Road to Nuremberg,* 8, 23.

32. McCloy to Freeman Matthews (Office of European Affairs, State Department), August 28, 1944, McCloy Correspondence.

33. Quoted in Blum, *From the Morgenthau Diaries,* 3:352. See also Morgenthau, *Mostly Morgenthaus,* 369.

34. Morgenthau and Judiciary Subcommittee, *Morgenthau Diary,* 464.

35. Morgenthau and Judiciary Subcommittee, *Morgenthau Diary,* 465. This suggested policy directive actually appeared back in April 1944 in a document titled "Combined Civil Affairs Committee" produced for the Combined Chiefs of Staff "Directive for Military Government in Germany Prior to Defeat or Surrender" (April 17, 1944, Treatment of Germany, Box 5, Top Secret Correspondence, 07/1940–09/18/1947, RG 107, NACP).

36. The military occupation administration was instructed to carry out a series of measures, which included the following instruction: "You will take immediate steps to abrogate or declare null and void all laws, decrees, regulations or aspects of laws which discriminate on the basis of race, color, creed or political opinions. All persons who are detained or placed in custody by the Nazis on these grounds will be released" (Morgenthau and Judiciary Subcommittee, *Morgenthau Diary*, 468).

37. Henry Morgenthau III was convinced that FDR was following a usual policy of obfuscation (Morgenthau, *Mostly Morgenthaus*, 369).

38. Blum, *From the Morgenthau Diaries*, 3:352; Morgenthau, *Mostly Morgenthaus*, 369; Morgenthau and Judiciary Subcommittee, *Morgenthau Diary*, 506–7.

39. Morgenthau and Judiciary Subcommittee, *Morgenthau Diary*, 486. See also Smith, *Road to Nuremberg*, 34.

40. Morgenthau and Judiciary Subcommittee, *Morgenthau Diary*, 486–87.

41. Morgenthau and Judiciary Subcommittee, *Morgenthau Diary*, 487.

42. Morgenthau and Judiciary Subcommittee, *Morgenthau Diary*, 508.

43. Blum, *From the Morgenthau Diaries*, 3:359; Morgenthau and Judiciary Subcommittee, *Morgenthau Diary*, 503, 522, 524; Morgenthau, *Mostly Morgenthaus*, 370–72; Smith, *Road to Nuremberg*, 34.

44. Blum, *From the Morgenthau Diaries*, 3:359–60; Morgenthau and Judiciary Subcommittee, *Morgenthau Diary*, 526; Smith, *Road to Nuremberg*, 35.

45. Stimson, "Secretary of War's Comments on Suggested Recommendations of Treatment of Germany from the Cabinet Committee September 5, 1944," Germany, Box 5, Top Secret Correspondence, 07/1940–09/18/1947, RG 107, NACP. See also Morgenthau and Judiciary Subcommittee, *Morgenthau Diary*, 530–32; Smith, *Road to Nuremberg*, 37; *American Road to Nuremberg*, 30; Stimson and Bundy, *On Active Service in Peace and War*, 569–73.

46. Hull, "Suggested Recommendations on the Treatment of Germany from the Cabinet Committee for the President," September 4, 1944, Germany, Box 5, Top Secret Correspondence, 07/1940–09/18/1947, RG 107, NACP.

47. Hull and Berding, *Memoirs of Cordell Hull*, 1609.

48. Stimson Diary, September 6, 1944; Stimson and Bundy, *On Active Service in Peace and War*, 473.

49. Stimson Diary, September 6, 1944; Stimson and Bundy, *On Active Service in Peace and War*, 374.

50. Morgenthau and Judiciary Subcommittee, *Morgenthau Diary*, 536.

51. Stimson wrote in a later memorandum, "[Punishment] was not argued at all at the last hearing for I had not had an opportunity to see Mr. Morgenthau's proposition but I have since read it and it seems to me violative of our entire constitutional history" (Stimson and McCloy, "Memorandum of Conversation," September 8, 1944, McCloy Correspondence).

52. Stimson Diary, September 7, 1944.

53. Stimson Diary, September 7, 1944.

54. Trial and Punishment of War Criminals; Smith, *American Road to Nuremberg*, 21–23.

55. Hull, "Suggested Recommendations on the Treatment of Germany from the Cabinet Committee for the President," September 4, 1944, Germany, Box 5, Top Secret Correspondence, 07/1940–09/18/1947, RG 107, NACP.

56. Combined Civil Affairs Committee, "Directive for Military Government in Germany Prior to Defeat or Surrender," April 17, 1944, Germany, Box 5, Top Secret Correspondence, 07/1940–09/18/1947, RG 107, NACP.

57. Stimson Diary, September 8, 1944.

58. Stimson and McCloy, "Memorandum of Conversation," September 8, 1944, McCloy Correspondence.

59. Stimson and McCloy, "Memorandum of Conversation," September 8, 1944, McCloy Correspondence.

60. Preuss to Sandifer, February 3, 1944, War Crimes Commission: State Department.

61. Hull to HCP, July 15, 1944, War Crimes Commission: State Department.

62. Stimson and McCloy, "Memorandum of Conversation," September 8, 1944, McCloy Correspondence.

63. Stimson and McCloy, "Memorandum of Conversation," September 8, 1944, McCloy Correspondence.

64. Stimson Diary, September 8, 1944.

65. Stimson Diary, September 9, 1944. See also Smith, *Road to Nuremberg,* 42.

66. Stimson, memorandum to FDR, September 9, 1944, in Stimson Diary. Also quoted in Morgenthau and Judiciary Subcommittee, *Morgenthau Diary,* 613; Smith, *American Road to Nuremberg,* 30–31.

67. Stimson, memorandum to FDR, September 9, 1944, in Stimson Diary. See also Kochavi, *Prelude to Nuremberg,* 157; Morgenthau and Judiciary Subcommittee, *Morgenthau Diary,* 613–14; Smith, *Road to Nuremberg,* 42–43; Smith, *American Road to Nuremberg,* 30–31.

68. Stimson, memorandum to FDR, September 9, 1944, in Stimson Diary.

69. Combined Civil Affairs Committee, "Directive for Military Government in Germany Prior to Defeat or Surrender," April 17, 1944, Germany, Box 5, Top Secret Correspondence, 07/1940–09/18/1947, RG 107, NACP.

70. Stimson Diary, September 11, 1944. See also Smith, *Road to Nuremberg,* 43.

Chapter 9

Epigraph: Bernays, "Trial of European War Criminals," September 15, 1944, Box 4, Trial & Punishment, MCBP.

1. Stimson Diary, September 11, 1944.

2. Stimson Diary, September 12, 1944.

3. Stimson wrote, "Do not think an extended or detailed reply would be helpful to FDR" ("In Re Treatment of Germany, Reply to Latest Morgenthau Memorandum" [unsent draft], September 12, 1944, McCloy Correspondence).

4. Bundy wrote, "My thoughts run along the following lines: Our fundamental belief is that all men throughout the world have, in the long run, the right to be free human beings. That means that each man is entitled not only to freedom of worship and freedom

of speech but in order to have freedom from want and from fear men must be free to work at what they are best fitted for and to receive a fair reward for the toil" (Bundy, memorandum for McCloy, September 13, 1944, McCloy Correspondence).

5. Bundy, memorandum for McCloy, September 13, 1944, McCloy Correspondence.

6. Colonel William D. Hohenthal, memorandum to John J. McCloy, September 12, 1944, McCloy Correspondence.

7. For other accounts of Bernays's early role in creating the foundation for the London Charter, see Conot, *Justice at Nuremberg*, 10–13; Kochavi, *Prelude to Nuremberg*, 157–60, 205–12; Smith, *Road to Nuremberg*; Smith, *American Road to Nuremberg*, 10–11, 33, 52–56, 93, 98, 140; Taylor, *Anatomy of the Nuremberg Trials*, 4, 35–37; Tusa and Tusa, *Nuremberg Trial*, 54–58.

8. Hackworth, "Urgent" memorandum to the acting secretary (Stettinius), July 29, 1944, War Crimes—Miscellaneous Correspondence 1944.

9. Bernays, "Personal Report to Mrs. Bernays."

10. Pehle, memorandum for Stettinius, August 28, 1944, Box 1, Miscellaneous & Undrafted, MCBP.

11. Bernays, "Personnel Security Questionnaire," September 7, 1942, Box 1, Military Records and Miscellaneous, MCBP; Untitled Biographical Material, n.d., Box 1, Miscellaneous & Undrafted, MCBP.

12. "Hella" was the name reported in the *New York Times* article on the wedding ("Bridegroom Takes Name of His Bride," *New York Times*, October 16, 1917). According to Bernays's Security Questionnaire, his wife's name was "Hertha (also known as Isott) Bernays" (Bernays, "Personnel Security Questionnaire," September 7, 1942, Box 1, Military Records and Miscellaneous, MCBP).

13. "Bridegroom Takes Name of His Bride."

14. This was the title of Larry Tye's 1998 biography of Edward L. Bernays. According to Tye, Edward L. Bernays "almost single-handedly fashioned" the profession of public relations (Tye, *Father of Spin,* vii).

15. Tye, *Father of Spin*, 1–2.

16. Tye, *Father of Spin*, 148.

17. Bernays, Untitled Biographical Material, n.d., Box 1, Miscellaneous & Undrafted, MCBP.

18. Bernays, "Personal Report to Mrs. Bernays."

19. Bernays, "Personal Report to Mrs. Bernays."

20. Bernays, "Personal Report to Mrs. Bernays."

21. Bernays, "Personal Report to Mrs. Bernays." I have been unable to locate the intital document.

22. Bernays, "Personal Report to Mrs. Bernays."

23. Marcus's story did not stop there. In late 1947 Marcus, then a reservist, received permission from the War Department to serve as a military adviser to the Jewish paramilitary force in the British Mandate of Palestine, provided that he disguise himself. Thus, Colonel "Mickey" Marcus became "Michael Stone," arriving in Tel Aviv in January 1948. Just a few months later, as Michael Stone, he became Israel's first army general in

more than twenty-one hundred years. His story was the basis of *Cast a Giant Shadow* in 1966, starring Kirk Douglas as Marcus. See Berkman, *Cast a Giant Shadow;* Halperin and Kreinik, *Mickey Marcus;* Zabecki, "Israel's Greatest Military Commander since Judas."

24. Bernays, "Personal Report to Mrs. Bernays."

25. Bernays, "Personal Report to Mrs. Bernays."

26. The document was probably the aide-mémoire from Halifax to Hull on August 19, 1944 (United States Department of State, *Foreign Relations of the United States,* 1:1351–53). See also Smith, *American Road to Nuremberg,* 16–17.

27. Hackworth apparently never sent his reply.

28. Bernays, "Personal Report to Mrs. Bernays."

29. Bernays, "Personal Report to Mrs. Bernays."

30. Bernays, "Personal Report to Mrs. Bernays."

31. Bernays, "Personal Report to Mrs. Bernays"; Smith, *Road to Nuremberg,* 56.

32. Bernays, "Trial of European War Criminals," September 15, 1944, Box 4, Trial & Punishment, MCBP.

33. Bernays, "Trial of European War Criminals," September 15, 1944, Box 4, Trial & Punishment, MCBP.

34. Bernays, "Trial of European War Criminals," September 15, 1944, Box 4, Trial & Punishment, MCBP.

35. Bernays, "Trial of European War Criminals," September 15, 1944, Box 4, Trial & Punishment, MCBP.

36. See United States Department of State, *Conference at Quebec.*

37. Stimson Diary, September 16–17, 1944.

38. Stimson Diary, September 20, 1944.

39. Morgenthau and Judiciary Subcommittee, *Morgenthau Diary,* 624–28.

40. Stimson Diary, September 20, 1944.

41. Bernays, "Personal Report to Mrs. Bernays"; Smith, *American Road to Nuremberg,* 37–38.

42. Stimson Diary, September 27–October 1, 1944.

43. Drew Pearson, "The Washington Merry-Go-Round," September 21, 1944, Box 6, Folder 2, Drew Pearson's Washington Merry-Go-Round, American University Library—Special Collections, Washington, D.C.

44. Stimson Diary, September 23–24, 1944.

45. Stimson and Bundy, *On Active Service in Peace and War,* 578.

46. Stimson, memorandum for FDR, September 15, 1944, Germany, Box 5, Top Secret Correspondence, 07/1940–09/18/1947, RG 107, NACP.

47. Stimson Diary, October 3, 1944.

48. Bernays, "Personal Report to Mrs. Bernays"; Stimson Diary, October 24, 1944.

49. Bernays, "Personal Report to Mrs. Bernays."

50. Bernays, "Personal Report to Mrs. Bernays."

51. Stimson and McCloy, "Memorandum of Conversation," September 8, 1944, McCloy Correspondence.

52. Stimson Diary, October 24, 1944.

53. Stimson Diary, October 25, 1944.

54. Following the disallowed attempt at UNWCC publicity in August 1944, the Commission and Pell continued their work. According to UNWCC minutes, Pell was particularly involved in discussions over a proposed United Nations Military Tribunal (UNWCC, "Folder UNWCC—Indexes [with Supplements] to Minutes and Documents—Meetings 01-38—S-1804-0001-0001").

55. Stimson Diary, October 27, 1944.

56. Stimson Diary, October 3, 1944.

57. For Harriman's account of his time as Roosevelt's envoy, see Harriman and Abel, *Special Envoy to Churchill and Stalin.*

58. Stimson Diary, October 23, 1944.

59. McKinzie and Osborn, "Oral History Interview with Frederick Osborn" (Garrison, N.Y.), Harry S. Truman Library, 3. See also Osborn and Osborn, *Voyage to a New World,* 88–89.

60. Frederick Henry Osborn was born March 21, 1889, in the family home on the corner of Lexington Avenue and Thirty-Sixth Street in New York City. Herbert C. Pell was born in similar environs on February 16, 1884, in his family home on East Twenty-Third Street.

61. H. I. Brock, "Army's Morale Builder," *New York Times,* September 7, 1941; Collier, "Decaying Depot Is Resurrected in Garrison," *New York Times,* July 27, 1966.

62. Osborn and Osborn, *Voyage to a New World,* 15.

63. See Baker, *Brahmin in Revolt,* 5–10; Osborn and Osborn, *Voyage to a New World,* 15–25; HCP, "Reminiscences," 1–37.

64. Osborn considered these men honest, able, and apolitical government servants, but he never thought of them as friends. They were not men of Osborn's social standing; they were administrators, men with talent but lacking in pedigree and the benefits of good breeding (McKinzie and Osborn, "Oral History Interview with Frederick Osborn" [Garrison, N.Y.], Harry S. Truman Library, 14–15).

65. Stimson Diary, October 23, 1944.

66. Stimson Diary, October 23, 1944.

67. Root, Bacon, and Scott, *Addresses on Government and Citizenship.*

68. Stimson Diary, October 23, 1944.

69. Stimson Diary, October 23, 1944.

Chapter 10

Epigraph: HCP, Untitled Recollections, May 1945.

1. Stimson Diary, August 25, 1944; Kochavi, *Prelude to Nuremberg,* 207–9; Smith, *Road to Nuremberg,* 68–74; Smith, *American Road to Nuremberg,* 11–12, 41–44.

2. Smith, *American Road to Nuremberg,* 49, 57.

3. Katherine Fite, memorandum to Hackworth, November 10, 1944, Conspiracy.

4. Fite, memorandum to Hackworth, November 10, 1944, Conspiracy; Fite, memorandum to Hackworth, November 14, 1944, Atrocities Against Jews, Box 5, Records Relating to German War Crimes 1942–1946, Records of the Legal Adviser; Fite, memorandum to Mr. Hackworth, November 15, 1944, Conspiracy; Fite, memorandum to Mr. Hackworth,

November 13, 1944, Conspiracy; Fite, memorandum to Hackworth, November 14, 1944, Conspiracy; Hackworth, memorandum for McCloy, November 16, 1944, War Crimes—Miscellaneous Correspondence 1944.

5. Fite, memorandum to Hackworth, November 14, 1944, Atrocities Against Jews, Box 5, Records Relating to German War Crimes 1942–1946, Records of the Legal Adviser; Hackworth, memorandum for McCloy, November 16, 1944, War Crimes—Miscellaneous Correspondence 1944.

6. FDR, "Radio Bulletin No. 72," March 24, 1944, Roosevelt, FD 1936–45.

7. Hackworth, Draft for McCloy—War Department [Not Used], n.d. [November 10–15, 1944], Russia and Italy, Box 5, Records Relating to German War Crimes 1942–1946, Records of the Legal Adviser.

8. Hackworth, Draft for McCloy—War Department [Not Used], n.d. [November 10–15, 1944], Russia and Italy, Box 5, Records Relating to German War Crimes 1942–1946, Records of the Legal Adviser.

9. Bernays, "Personal Report to Mrs. Bernays."

10. Finding Aid, Green H. Hackworth Papers, Library of Congress, Washington, D.C.

11. Hackworth, "Publicity," n.d. [November 15–16, 1944?], Pell Correspondence.

12. Hackworth, "Urgent" memorandum to the acting secretary (Stettinius), July 29, 1944, War Crimes—Miscellaneous Correspondence 1944.

13. Hackworth, "Publicity," n.d. [November 15–16, 1944?], Pell Correspondence.

14. Frederick Kuh, "Loopholes for German Killers," *PM*, September 17, 1944; Kuh, "Cordell Hull: Hitler Isn't on War Guilt List," *PM*, September 25, 1944.

15. Kuh, "Loopholes for German Killers."

16. According to the UNWCC minutes, "The CHAIRMAN agreed that these leakages were most regrettable, himself having been accused in the Press of saying that the policy of the Governments was not to put Hitler on the list! In regard to the 'arch-criminals' he hoped that the Quebec Conference had now taken a decision which would put an end to the Press agitation" (UNWCC, "Folder UNWCC—Indexes [with Supplements] to Minutes and Documents—Meetings 01-38—S-1804-0001-0001").

17. Hackworth, "Publicity," n.d. [November 15–16, 1944?], Pell Correspondence.

18. Kuh, "Cordell Hull: Hitler Isn't on War Guilt List." Hugh Ballie, head of the United Press (1933–55), described Kuh as "a studious, quiet type with great ability at developing sources" (Baillie, *High Tension*, 77).

19. Hackworth, "Publicity," n.d. [November 15–16, 1944?], Pell Correspondence.

20. Although Hackworth didn't specify, it was Preuss's February 3 letter to Sandifer (Preuss to Sandifer, February 3, 1944, War Crimes Commission: State Department).

21. Hackworth, "Publicity," n.d. [November 15–16, 1944?], Pell Correspondence.

22. Fite, "Memorandum of Conversation," October 5, 1944, War Crimes—Miscellaneous Correspondence 1944.

23. Hackworth, "Publicity," n.d. [November 15–16, 1944?], Pell Correspondence.

24. Hackworth, "Publicity," n.d. [November 15–16, 1944?], Pell Correspondence.

25. FDR, "Radio Bulletin No. 72," March 24, 1944, Roosevelt, FD 1936–45.

26. Hackworth, "Publicity," n.d. [November 15–16, 1944?], Pell Correspondence.

27. Fite, memorandum to Hackworth, November 13, 1944, Conspiracy.

28. HCP to Hull on "Draft Convention for Establishment of a United Nations War Crimes Court," October 19, 1944, War Crimes Commission: Reports and Printed Matter, Box 28, General Correspondence.

29. HCP, "Personal to the Secretary of State," April 24, 1944, War Crimes Commission: State Department.

30. Hull and Berding, *Memoirs of Cordell Hull,* 1715; "Mr. Hull Resigns," *Time,* December 4, 1944.

31. HCP, "Personal" to Stettinius, October 30, 1944, War Crimes Commission: State Department.

32. Stettinius, memorandum for Grace Tully, November 9, 1944, War Crimes Commission; Stettinius, memorandum for FDR, November 9, 1944, War Crimes Commission.

33. HCP to Stettinius, November 13, 1944, War Crimes Commission: State Department.

34. Stettinius to HCP, November 24, 1944, War Crimes Commission: State Department.

35. Hackworth, "Memorandum of Conversation," December 7, 1944, Pell Correspondence; HCP, Untitled Recollections, May 1945.

36. Hackworth, "Memorandum of Conversation," December 7, 1944, Pell Correspondence.

37. Hackworth, "Memorandum of Conversation," December 7, 1944, Pell Correspondence.

38. Hackworth, "Memorandum of Conversation," December 7, 1944, Pell Correspondence.

39. Hackworth, "Memorandum of Conversation," December 7, 1944, Pell Correspondence.

40. HCP, "Reminiscences," 587.

41. According to Pell biographer Leonard Baker, "On December 11 [1944], Pell had wired Roosevelt that a crisis was developing within the War Crimes Commission, referring to the genocide question. Pell said he had reported this to the State Department but also wished to bring it directly to the President's attention" (Baker, *Brahmin in Revolt,* 300–301).

42. Similar to how the State Department stalled Pell's getting to London, they delayed Davies's trip. As Dan Plesch has noted, Davies was still waiting on State for his travel arrangements at the time of FDR's death (Plesch, *Human Rights after Hitler,* 166); Smith, *Road to Nuremberg,* 90.

43. Smith, *Road to Nuremberg,* 86–87; Kochavi, *Prelude to Nuremberg,* 160, 209.

44. Baker, *Brahmin in Revolt,* 301.

45. Hackworth to Stettinius, December 26, 1944, Pell Correspondence; Stettinius to FDR (draft unsent), December 26, 1944, Pell Correspondence; Stettinius, memorandum for FDR, December 27, 1944, War Crimes Commission.

46. Stettinius, memorandum for FDR, December 27, 1944, War Crimes Commission.

47. Stettinius, memorandum for FDR, December 27, 1944, War Crimes Commission.

48. According to Pell's appointment letter from the president, his salary was to be nine thousand dollars per annum (FDR to HCP, June 14, 1943, Roosevelt, FD 1936–45).

49. Stettinius to Senator McKellar, December 8, 1944, Pell Correspondence.

50. The internal State Department account of the budgetary issue noted, "The [deficiency] bill was finally passed with the item eliminated" (Kurth, Status of War Crimes Commission, December 23, 1944, Pell Correspondence); Stettinius, memorandum for FDR, December 27, 1944, War Crimes Commission; Stettinius to Senator McKellar, December 8, 1944, Pell Correspondence. See also Baker, *Brahmin in Revolt,* 303–4.

51. Kurth, Status of War Crimes Commission, December 23, 1944, Pell Correspondence.

52. Stettinius, memorandum for FDR, December 27, 1944, War Crimes Commission.

53. Section 213 of the Independent Offices Act made it possible for the State Department (or any other) to cover the expenses of American participation on the Commission provided regular employees were used (Kurth, Status of War Crimes Commission, December 23, 1944, Pell Correspondence).

54. Stettinius, memorandum for FDR, December 27, 1944, War Crimes Commission.

55. Morgenthau and Judiciary Subcommittee, *Morgenthau Diary,* 875.

56. Stimson to the Secretary of State, November 27, 1944, War & Navy 1st Person, Box 4, Records Relating to German War Crimes 1942–1946, Records of the Legal Adviser. Also quoted in Smith, *Road to Nuremberg,* 90.

57. Hackworth, memorandum to Stettinius, December 22, 1944, War Crimes—Miscellaneous Correspondence 1944.

58. Stettinius, memorandum for FDR, December 27, 1944, War Crimes Commission.

59. Anna Roosevelt, memorandum to Grace Tully, January 3, 1945, War Crimes Commission.

60. Devised by Aristide Briand, French foreign minister, and Frank Kellogg, U.S. secretary of state, the Kellogg-Briand Pact made illegal all future wars of aggression. The Reichstag in Berlin ratified the pact on February 6, 1929, by a vote of 288 to 127. By the end of that year, a total of sixty-three nations had become signatories.

61. FDR, memorandum for the Secretary of State, January 3, 1945, War Crimes Commission.

62. FDR, memorandum for the Secretary of War, August 26, 1944, White House Correspondence, 1-1-44–9-21-45, Box 15, Top Secret Correspondence, 07/1940–09/18/1947, Records of the Office of the Secretary of War, RG 107, NACP. See also Blum, *From the Morgenthau Diaries,* 3:348–49; Hull and Berding, *Memoirs of Cordell Hull,* 1602–1603; Morgenthau, *Mostly Morgenthaus,* 367–68. FDR also spoke of a Nazi "conspiracy" during his January 6, 1942, State of the Union message.

63. Civil Affairs was the army group assigned to overseeing the planning of Allied occupation. Bradley F. Smith incorrectly deduces that the content of the memorandum was conceived by Rosenman (see Smith, *Road to Nuremberg,* 119–20, 275n114).

64. Stimson wrote to McCloy on November 28 that Chanler's idea was "a little in advance of the progress of international thought" (Stimson to McCloy, November 28, 1944, Box 3, January 1943–December 1944, War Department, Office of the Assistant Secretary of War (1890–09/18/1947), Records of the Office of the Secretary of War, RG 107, NACP). Also quoted in Bush, "'The Supreme . . . Crime' and Its Origins," 2358; Taylor, *Anatomy of the Nuremberg Trials,* 38.

65. Bush, "'The Supreme . . . Crime' and Its Origins," 2363; Taylor, *Anatomy of the Nuremberg Trials*, 38.

66. Quoted in Bush, "'The Supreme . . . Crime' and Its Origins," 2358n2101. William C. Chanler, memorandum to McCloy, December 1, 1944, Box 3, January 1943–December 1944, War Department, Office of the Assistant Secretary of War (1890–09/18/1947), Records of the Office of the Secretary of War, RG 107, NACP.

67. Stimson, memorandum to FDR, September 9, 1944, in Stimson Diary.

68. Francis Biddle, memorandum for FDR, June 22, 1943, OF5152; see also Marrus, *Nuremberg War Crimes Trial*, 30–34. For a more detailed discussion of staff deliberations, see Smith, *Reaching Judgment at Nuremberg*, 144–51; Smith, *Road to Nuremberg*, 49–56, 117–22.

69. Stettinius, memorandum for FDR, December 27, 1944, War Crimes Commission.

70. Stimson Diary, November 21, 1944.

71. FDR meeting with Secretary of State Edward R. Stettinius Jr., Assistant Secretary Charles E. Bohlen, December 30, 1944, White House Stenographer's Diary, FDRP; FDR meeting with Secretary of State Edward R. Stettinius Jr., Assistant Secretary Charles E. Bohlen, December 30, 1944, Grace Tully Appointment Diary, FDRP.

72. FDR meeting with Secretary of State Edward R. Stettinius Jr., Undersecretary Joseph Grew, Assistant Secretary Clayton, Assistant Secretary Dean Acheson, Assistant Secretary Green H. Hackworth, Assistant Secretary Charles E. Bohlen, January 2, 1945, White House Stenographer's Diary, FDRP; FDR meeting with Secretary of State Edward R. Stettinius Jr., Undersecretary Joseph Grew, Assistant Secretary Clayton, Assistant Secretary Dean Acheson, Assistant Secretary Green H. Hackworth, Assistant Secretary Charles E. Bohlen, January 2, 1945, Grace Tully Appointment Diary, FDRP.

73. Hackworth, memorandum to Acheson, February 13, 1945, Pell Correspondence.

74. FDR meeting with Secretary of State Edward R. Stettinius Jr., James C. Dunn, Dr. Leo Pasvolsky, January 8, 1945, Grace Tully Appointment Diary, FDRP; FDR meeting with Secretary of State Edward R. Stettinius Jr., James C. Dunn, Dr. Leo Pasvolsky, January 8, 1945, White House Stenographer's Diary, FDRP.

75. Hackworth, "Memorandum of Conversation," January 9, 1945, Pell Correspondence.

76. "Pell May Head Crimes Board," *New York Times*, January 6, 1945.

77. Hackworth, "Memorandum of Conversation," January 9, 1945, Pell Correspondence. There is no record of Pell having met with anyone that day at the War Department.

78. HCP, Untitled Recollections, May 1945. In his 1953 oral history, Pell wrote, "[I] asked him if there had been any changes during the month that I had been in America or anything to interfere with my return to England. He said, 'No, nothing.' The only change was what I already knew, that Sir Cecil Hurst had resigned as chairman" (HCP, "Reminiscences," 589). Pell gives a similar recitation in a letter to FDR January 9, 1945, and in a June 1945 letter to Gil Winant (June 29, 1945, Winant); HCP to FDR, January 9, 1945, Roosevelt, FD 1936–45.

79. HCP, Untitled Recollections. In his 1953 oral history, Pell recorded the final words of their conversation this way: "The last words that President Roosevelt said to me, as I

left his office, were, 'Goodbye, Bertie. Good luck to you. Get back to London as quick as you can and get yourself elected chairman.' The words were important and I remember them" (HCP, "Reminiscences," 590). See also Baker, *Brahmin in Revolt*, 301–2. In a June 29, 1945, letter to Gil Winant, Pell wrote the president told him, "Go back to London as soon as you can and be elected chairman" (HCP to Winant, June 29, 1945, Winant).

80. Although no other record exists of what transpired, Pell never wavered on the material substance of his meeting with FDR in several retellings (see previous footnote).

81. HCP to FDR, January 9, 1945, Roosevelt, FD 1936–45.

82. HCP, Untitled Recollections, May 1945; Hackworth, "Memorandum of Conversation," January 9, 1945, Pell Correspondence; Pell, Letter to Gil Winant, June 29, 1945, Winant; Letter to FDR, January 9, 1945; HCP, "Reminiscences," 590. See also Baker, *Brahmin in Revolt*, 302.

83. The State Department summary of the meeting noted Pell was "somewhat indignant" over his treatment (Hackworth, "Memorandum of Conversation," January 9, 1945, Pell Correspondence).

84. Hackworth, "Memorandum of Conversation," January 9, 1945, Pell Correspondence.

85. Pell, Untitled Recollections, May 1945. In his oral history, Pell wrote, "I said, 'Why didn't you tell it to me before I went over to see the President.' He said, "It was none of my business to tell you that. In any case you're the President's appointee and not mine." HCP, "Reminiscences," 590.

86. Hackworth, "Memorandum of Conversation," January 9, 1945, Pell Correspondence.

87. Hackworth, "Memorandum of Conversation," January 9, 1945, Pell Correspondence.

88. HCP, "Reminiscences," 590. See also Baker, *Brahmin in Revolt*, 302.

89. Hackworth, "Memorandum of Conversation," January 9, 1945, Pell Correspondence.

90. Grace Tully, memorandum for FDR, January 9, 1945, OF5152. Also quoted in Baker, *Brahmin in Revolt*, 303.

91. HCP to FDR, January 9, 1945, Roosevelt, FD 1936–45.

92. HCP to FDR, January 9, 1945, Roosevelt, FD 1936–45.

93. HCP to FDR, January 9, 1945, Roosevelt, FD 1936–45.

94. Edwin M. Watson, telegram to HCP, January 16, 1945, OF5152.

95. Grace Tully, memorandum for FDR, June 10, 1943, OF5152.

96. Stettinius, memorandum for FDR, December 27, 1944, War Crimes Commission.

97. HCP, Untitled Recollections, May 1945.

Chapter 11

Epigraph: HCP to FDR, March 5, 1945, Roosevelt, FD 1936–45.

1. John MacCormac, "Britain Ignores War-Crime Plans, American Proposals Approved by United Nations Group—Chairman Resigns," *New York Times,* January 11, 1945. See also Baker, *Brahmin in Revolt,* 304–5.

2. MacCormac, "Britain Ignores War-Crime Plans, American Proposals Approved by United Nations Group—Chairman Resigns."

3. "Viscount Finlay in War Crimes Post," *New York Times,* January 16, 1945; "Plan for Hitler Trial Reported Abandoned," *Washington Post,* January 16, 1945; John MacCormac, "Big Three Divided on War Criminals," *New York Times*, January 19, 1945.

4. Hackworth, "Memorandum of Conversation," January 13, 1945, Pell Correspondence.

5. Pell wrote, "It is true that I am not a Librarian but I have already given about $12,000 worth of books to the Library. In any case I had no experience of legislative work when I went to Congress and did not do badly there. I had no experience of politics when I was made State Chairman of New York. Although not the most important member of the dominant group, I had something to do with the earliest development of conditions which you so brilliantly carried forward which kept Democratic Governors and Senators in New York from Miller to Dewey. I had no experience of diplomacy when you sent me to Portugal or of international negotiations when I went to London. I think I could succeed as Librarian. I shall be grateful if you would keep this thought in mind. I should immensely prefer the Library to any other available office" (HCP to FDR, January 17, 1945, Roosevelt, FD 1936–45).

6. Grace Tully to HCP, January 24, 1945, Roosevelt, FD 1936–45.

7. Stettinius to HCP, January 17, 1945, War Crimes Commission: Correspondence.

8. Hackworth, "Memorandum of Conversation," January 9, 1945.

9. Stettinius to HCP, January 17, 1945, War Crimes Commission: Correspondence.

10. Stettinius to HCP, January 17, 1945, War Crimes Commission: Correspondence.

11. Stettinius to HCP, January 17, 1945, War Crimes Commission: Correspondence.

12. Pell wrote in his 1953 oral history that one of the main reasons he never was able to see FDR after their final meeting on January 9 was the president's failing health (HCP, "Reminiscences," 601).

13. Baker, *Brahmin in Revolt*, 308–9.

14. UNWCC, "Folder UNWCC—Indexes (with Supplements) to Minutes and Documents—Meetings 01-38—S-1804-0001-0001."

15. Baker, *Brahmin in Revolt*, 306–7.

16. Hackworth, "Memorandum of Conversation," January 24, 1945, EW 1–2245 to 1–3145, 740.00116, Box 3592, Central Decimal File 1945–49, RG 59, NACP.

17. Grew, "Memorandum of Conversation," January 24, 1945, Pell Correspondence.

18. Grew, "Memorandum of Conversation," January 24, 1945, Pell Correspondence.

19. Grew, "Memorandum of Conversation," January 24, 1945, Pell Correspondence.

20. Grew, "Memorandum of Conversation," January 24, 1945, Pell Correspondence.

21. Grew, "Memorandum of Conversation," January 24, 1945, Pell Correspondence.

22. Pell also asked to be allowed to examine any recent Commission documents "so that he might use them in preparing his final report, if such a report were to be submitted" (Grew, "Memorandum of Conversation," January 24, 1945, Pell Correspondence).

23. "Press Notice No. 66," January 26, 1945, Press Releases, Newspaper Clippings, Purport Sheets, Publications, etc., Box 5, Records Relating to German War Crimes 1942–1946, Records of the Legal Adviser; "Memorandum of the Press and Radio News Conference, Friday, January 26, 1945." Prior to releasing the statement, Grew telephoned Pell and read it to him. Pell agreed to its release as worded. In addition, Grew told Pell he was free to call at Hackworth's office to review Commission documents so that he might prepare a final report (Grew, "Memorandum of Conversation," January 26, 1945, 740.00116, EW 1–2245 to 1–3145, Box 3592, Central Decimal File 1945–49, RG 59, NACP).

24. "Press Notice No. 66," January 26, 1945, Press Releases, Newspaper Clippings, Purport Sheets, Publications, etc., Box 5, Records Relating to German War Crimes 1942–1946, Records of the Legal Adviser; "Memorandum of the Press and Radio News Conference, Friday, January 26, 1945."

25. "Memorandum of the Press and Radio News Conference, Friday, January 26, 1945."

26. Bertram D. Hulen, "Pell Leaves War Crimes Board; He Favored Wider Punishments," *New York Times*, January 27, 1945.

27. Ben W. Gilbert, "Pell Says Stand for Avenging German Jews Cost Him Post," *Washington Post*, January 27, 1945.

28. Stimson and McCloy, "Memorandum of Conversation," September 8, 1944, McCloy Correspondence.

29. United Press, "Jewish Group Supports Pell," *New York Times*, January 27, 1945.

30. Associated Press, "Surprise Expressed in London," *New York Times*, January 27, 1945.

31. "Protest Sent to Washington," *New York Times*, January 28, 1945.

32. Baker, *Brahmin in Revolt*, 309–10.

33. United Press, "Pell Fears Split over War Crimes," *New York Times*, January 28, 1945. Pell said to Hackworth on December 7, 1944, "[If] the United States did not take the lead promptly in these [war crimes] matters, such countries as Greece, Yugoslavia and Czechoslovakia would gravitate toward the Soviet Union" (Hackworth, "Memorandum of Conversation," December 7, 1944, Pell Correspondence).

34. Grew, telegram to American Embassy, January 30, 1945, EW 1–2245 to 1–3145, 740.00116, Box 3592, Central Decimal File 1945–49, RG 59, NACP; "Memorandum of the Press and Radio News Conference, Friday, January 26, 1945"; "Grew Tells Stand on War Crimes," *New York Times*, January 30, 1945. See also Kochavi, *Prelude to Nuremberg*, 160.

35. Grew, telegram to American Embassy, January 30, 1945. See also "Grew Tells Stand on War Crimes."

36. "Memorandum of the Press and Radio News Conference, Friday, January 26, 1945."

37. "Memorandum of the Press and Radio News Conference, Friday, January 26, 1945."

38. "'Must Be Tough,' Says Pell," *New York Times*, January 30, 1945.

39. "'Must Be Tough,' Says Pell."

40 "Pell Affair," *Washington Post*, January 31, 1945. See also Baker, *Brahmin in Revolt*, 314–15; Blayney, *Democracy's Aristocrat*, 128; Kochavi, *Prelude to Nuremberg*, 160–61.

41. "Pell Affair."

42. "Memorandum of the Press and Radio News Conference, Thursday, February 1, 1945."

43. "Memorandum of the Press and Radio News Conference, Thursday, February 1, 1945."

44. "Memorandum of the Press and Radio News Conference, Thursday, February 1, 1945."

45. Grew, "Statement by Acting Secretary of State Joseph C. Grew," February 1, 1945, EW 2–145 to 3–2645, 740.00116, Box 3596, Central Decimal File 1945–49, RG 59, NACP; "Memorandum of the Press and Radio News Conference, Thursday, February 1, 1945"; Roberta Barrows, "Memorandum For: The Record," June 24, 1943, OF5152. Also quoted in Baker, *Brahmin in Revolt*, 316; Blayney, *Democracy's Aristocrat*, 128; Kochavi, *Prelude to Nuremberg*, 161.

46. Hackworth, "Memorandum of Conversation," February 8, 1945, Pell Correspondence.

47. Hackworth, "Memorandum of Conversation," February 8, 1945, Pell Correspondence.

48. Hackworth, "Memorandum of Conversation," February 8, 1945, Pell Correspondence.

49. Hackworth, "Memorandum of Conversation," February 8, 1945, Pell Correspondence.

50. Hackworth, "Memorandum of Conversation," February 8, 1945, Pell Correspondence.

51. Hackworth, "Memorandum of Conversation," February 8, 1945, Pell Correspondence.

52. Hackworth, "Memorandum of Conversation," February 8, 1945, Pell Correspondence.

53. Hackworth, "Memorandum of Conversation," February 8, 1945, Pell Correspondence.

54. FDR, *Public Papers and Addresses of Franklin D. Roosevelt*, 13:570.

55. HCP to FDR, March 5, 1945, Roosevelt, FD 1936–45.

56. FDR, *Public Papers and Addresses of Franklin D. Roosevelt*, 13:575.

57. HCP to FDR, March 5, 1945, Roosevelt, FD 1936–45.

58. Hackworth, "Memorandum of Conversation," December 7, 1944, Pell Correspondence; United Press, "U.S. Sets Up Own Commission," *New York Times*, February 1, 1945.

59. HCP to FDR, March 5, 1945, Roosevelt, FD 1936–45. Pell also took the time to send a telegraph to Grace Tully on March 4 requesting a meeting with the president. The telegram is mentioned in Grace Tully to HCP, March 17, 1945, Roosevelt, FD 1936–45. Having received no reply from Tully, Pell sent a letter to Tully requesting the same on March 13 (HCP to Grace Tully, March 13, 1945, Roosevelt, FD 1936–45). Hearing from Tully that the president could not see him just then, Pell sent another letter directly to FDR with similar appeals to his March 5 letter. "If nothing is done about this [war crimes policy]," he wrote, "there will be a hideous wave of cynicism which will go a long way toward making the establishment of world order difficult—if not impossible" (HCP to FDR, March 19, 1945, Roosevelt, FD 1936–45). On March 21 presidential secretary William D. Hassett replied to Pell's March 19 letter, stating that the president "deeply appreciates his continuing interest," but that "there was no immediate prospect of making an appointment" (Hassett to HCP, March 21, 1945, War Crimes Commission: Correspondence). The following day, FDR replied to Pell's original March 5 letter (FDR to HCP, March 22, 1945, Roosevelt, FD 1936–45).

60. Hackworth to Watson, March 19, 1945, EW 2–145 to 3–2645, 740.001146, Box 3596, Central Decimal File 1945–49, RG 59, NACP; Watson to Hackworth, March 17, 1945, EW 2–145 to 3–2645, 740.001146, Box 3596, Central Decimal File 1945–49, RG 59, NACP.

61. Grew to FDR, March 21, 1945, EW 2–145 to 3–2645, 740.001146, Box 3596, Central Decimal File 1945–49, RG 59, NACP.

62. FDR to HCP, March 22, 1945;, Roosevelt, FD 1936–45.

63. On March 1, 1945, the *Washington Post* reported that the House Appropriations Committee had approved at the end of February a twenty-five-thousand-dollar fund to cover American expenses on the UNWCC ("Pell to Appeal for Restoration to War Crime Unit," *Washington Post*, March 1, 1945).

64. Stettinius to HCP, March 14, 1945, EW 2–145 to 3–2645, 740.001146, Box 3596, Central Decimal File 1945–49, RG 59, NACP.

65. Associated Press, "Congress Asked to Raise Lid off Secrecy of War Crimes Unit," *Washington Post*, March 23, 1945; Samuel A. Tower, "Celler Asks Light on War Criminals," *New York Times*, March 23, 1945. For more on Congress and refugees, see Young, *Why We Fight*, 135–64.

66. Associated Press, "Congress Asked to Raise Lid off Secrecy of War Crimes Unit"; Tower, "Celler Asks Light on War Criminals."

67. Associated Press, "Congress Asked to Raise Lid off Secrecy of War Crimes Unit"; Tower, "Celler Asks Light on War Criminals."

68. Clifton Daniel, "Heads of States Will Not Escape War Crime Penalties, Allies Decide," *New York Times,* April 2, 1945.

69. Daniel, "Heads of States Will Not Escape War Crime Penalties, Allies Decide."

70. United States Congress, Senate Committee on Foreign Relations, and U.S. Department of State, *A Decade of American Foreign Policy,* 13.

71. HCP, telegram to Stettinius, March 24, 1945, EW 3–2745 to 4–1945, 740.001146, Box 3597, Central Decimal File 1945–49, RG 59, NACP.

72. HCP to Stettinius, March 29, 1945, EW 3-2745 to 4-1945; 740.001146, Box 3597, Central Decimal File 1945–49, RG 59; NACP.

73. HCP to FDR, April 5, 1945, EW 3-2745 to 4-1945, 740.001146, Box 3597, Central Decimal File 1945–49, RG 59, NACP.

74. HCP to FDR, April 5, 1945, EW 3-2745 to 4-1945, 740.001146, Box 3597, Central Decimal File 1945–49, RG 59, NACP.

75. FDR, memorandum to Stettinius, April 9, 1945, EW 3–2745 to 4–1945, 740.001146, Box 3597, Central Decimal File 1945–49, RG 59, NACP.

76. Baker, *Brahmin in Revolt,* 317–18; HCP to the Secretary of State, April 19, 1945, War Crimes Commission: State Department; HCP, "Reminiscences," 601–3.

77. HCP, "Reminiscences," 601.

78. HCP, "Reminiscences," 601.

79. HCP to the Secretary of State, April 17, 1945; War Crimes Commission: State Department.

80. Stettinius to HCP, April 14, 1945, War Crimes Commission: State Department.

81. Pearson's article is available in full in Plesch, *Human Rights after Hitler,* 167–70. See also Drew Pearson, "The Washington Merry-Go-Round, June 6, 1945," Washington Research Library Consortium, https://auislandora.wrlc.org/islandora/object /pearson%3A15930#page/1/mode/1up.

82. Plesch, *Human Rights after Hitler,* 167.

83. Truman, *Memoirs,* 346–47.

84. As Plesch put it, "Another [interpretation] is that Pell and Pearson were sufficiently well connected to press the administration as effectively as they had, and that Truman's action of June 6, 1945 came about, at least partly, to defuse the public pressure from Pell and Pearson" (Plesch, *Human Rights after Hitler,* 167).

85. Gerhart, *America's Advocate,* 311; Jackson, "Justice Jackson's Story," 1118.

86. "Justice Jackson's Story," 1084–85.

87. HCP, "Reminiscences," 569. See also Baker, *Brahmin in Revolt,* 254–55. For other authors' conclusions about the significance of Pell, see Baker, *Brahmin in Revolt,* 319–31; Blayney, *Democracy's Aristocrat,* 135–38; Kochavi, *Prelude to Nuremberg,* 136, 170–71, 241. Marrus wrote of Pell that he was in large measure responsible for what was ultimately

incorporated in Article 6(c) of the London Charter (Marrus, *Nuremberg War Crimes Trial,* 186). See also Plesch, *Human Rights after Hitler,* 8, 164, 171, 194.

Chapter 12

Epigraph: Jackson, "Rule of Law among Nations," 294.

1. Taylor, *Anatomy of the Nuremberg Trials,* 40.

2. Jackson, "Justice Jackson's Story," 1028.

3. Jackson Diary, April 27, 1945; "Justice Jackson's Story," 1032.

4. Jackson Diary, April 27, 1945. Ann and John Tusa report that Jackson's address "seems to have been shown" to Truman, convincing him that Jackson "was the man for the job" (Tusa and Tusa, *Nuremberg Trial,* 69).

5. Jackson, "Justice Jackson's Story," 1026–27.

6. Jackson, "Rule of Law among Nations," 293.

7. Jackson, "Rule of Law among Nations," 294.

8. Jackson Diary, April 27, 1945.

9. Jackson, "Rule of Law among Nations," 294

10. Jackson and Barrett, *That Man,* xv.

11. FDR, *Public Papers and Addresses of Franklin D. Roosevelt,* 5:289.

12. Jackson and Barrett, *That Man,* 86.

13. Jackson and Barrett, *That Man,* 99.

14. Jackson and Barrett, *That Man,* 100.

15. Quoted in Jackson and Barrett, *That Man,* 100. For the secretary of state's account of the destroyers for bases deal, see Hull and Berding, *Memoirs of Cordell Hull,* 830–43.

16. Jackson and Barrett, *That Man,* 100–101.

17. Jackson and Barrett, *That Man,* 100–101.

18. Jackson and Barrett, *That Man,* 96, 102–3.

19. Jackson and Barrett, *That Man,* 103.

20. Jackson, "Address of Robert H. Jackson," 348–59.

21. Jackson, "Address of Robert H. Jackson," 353.

22. Jackson, "Address of Robert H. Jackson," 350.

23. Jackson Diary, April 30, 1945.

24. "Justice Jackson's Story," 1038–41.

25. From Jackson's Diary, "May 4, 1945: 4 o'clock. Attorney General Biddle called to relate that he had just heard from [Columbia University law professor Herbert] Wechsler at San Francisco, who reports that since my appointment was announced, the British position has shifted considerably and they are much more friendly to the proposal.... 7 P.M. Judge Rosenman called from San Francisco. ... He says there is considerable modification in the British position since the appointment was announced, they now [are] taking the position if two of their major allies want the procedure indicated they, of course, would cooperate.... The general attitude, of course, favors the trials" (Jackson Diary, May 4, 1945). Kochavi credits the British move toward supporting a trial to mere expediency and does not mention the significance of Jackson's presence (Kochavi, *Prelude to Nuremberg,* 219).

Bradley Smith's books *Road to Nuremberg,* and *The American Road to Nuremberg* were published prior to the availability of Jackson's papers. Consequently, he makes no mention of the possibility of Jackson's appointment helping move the British toward agreement. For his discussion of the British change of position, see Smith, *Road to Nuremberg,* 220–23.

26. Jackson Diary, May 4, 1945.

27. "Justice Jackson's Story," 1051–52.

28. Jackson Diary, May 28, 1945.

29. Jackson was assisted in creating the report by Colonel Murray C. Bernays, Gordon Dean, Francis Shea, Sidney Alderman, and Ensign William E. Jackson (Jackson's son) ("Justice Jackson's Story," 1118).

30. President Truman called this report the "keynote for our policy" (Truman, *Memoirs,* 346–47).

31. Jackson, *Report of Robert H. Jackson,* 49–50.

32. *Report of Robert H. Jackson,* 50. The full charges as of June 6, 1945, were:

"Atrocities and offenses against person or property constituting violations of International Law, including the laws, rules, and customs of land and naval warfare. The rules of warfare are well established and generally accepted by the nations. They make offenses of such conduct as the killing of the wounded, refusal of quarter, ill treatment of prisoners of war, firing on undefended localities, poisoning of wells and streams, pillage and wonton destruction, and ill treatment of inhabitants in occupied territories.

"Atrocities and offenses, including atrocities and persecutions on racial or religious grounds, committed since 1933. This is only to recognize the principles of criminal law as they are generally observed in civilized states. These principles have been assimilated as a part of International Law at least since 1907. The Fourth Hague Convention provided that inhabitants and all belligerents shall remain under the protection and rule of 'the principles of the law of nations, as they result from the usage established among civilized peoples, from the laws of humanity and the dictates of the public conscience.'

"Invasions of other countries and initiation of wars of aggression in violation of International Law or treaties."

33. Alderman, "Reminiscences," 902.

34. Jackson, "Justice Jackson's Story," 1073.

35. Alderman, "Reminiscences," 796–98.

36. Alderman, "Reminiscences," 798–99.

37. Alderman, "Reminiscences," 800–802.

38. Alderman, "Reminiscences," 808.

39. Alderman, "Reminiscences," 900–901.

40. Ladavac, "Biographical Note and Biography (Hans Kelsen)." For more on the life and legal career of Hans Kelsen see Rigaux, "The European Tradition in International Law."

41. Alderman, "Reminiscences," 902–4.

42. Alderman, "Reminiscences," 904–5, 931.

43. Jackson, *Report of Robert H. Jackson,* iii.

44. Alderman, "London Negotiations for War Crimes Prosecutions," May 1, 1952, Container 112, Correspondence A (Alderman on London), Post-Trial Material, Robert H. Jackson Papers, Manuscript Division, Library of Congress, Washington, D.C. This text was later published as a chapter in Dennett, Johnson, and World Peace Foundation, *Negotiating with the Russians.*

45. For more on variations between legal systems, see Fyfe, *1st Earl of Kilmuir,* 88.

46. Robert Houghwout Jackson, Untitled Text for C. L. Sulzberger, March 9, 1946, Releases, Records of the Office of Chief of Counsel for War Crimes, National Archives at College Park Collection of World War II War Crimes Records, RG 238, NACP.

47. Alderman, "London Negotiations for War Crimes Prosecutions," May 1, 1952, Container 112, Correspondence A (Alderman on London), Post-Trial Material, Robert H. Jackson Papers, Manuscript Division, Library of Congress, Washington, D.C.

48. See also Marrus, *Nuremberg War Crimes Trial,* 45; Schabas, *Unimaginable Atrocities,* 108–9.

Chapter 13

Epigraph: Jackson, *Report of Robert H. Jackson,* 331.

1. American delegates included: Representative Robert H. Jackson, Associate Justice, Supreme Court, and Assistants Major General William J. Donovan, director, Office of Strategic Services; Colonel Murray C. Bernays, U.S. Army; Sidney S. Alderman, associate counsel; Francis Shea, assistant attorney general; William Dwight Whitney, associate counsel; Lieutenant Gordon Dean, U.S. Navy; Lieutenant James Donovan, U.S. Navy; Ensign William E. Jackson, U.S. Navy; Major Lawrence Coleman, U.S. Army; and Mrs. Elsie L. Douglas, secretary to Mr. Justice Jackson.

2. Jackson, *Report of Robert H. Jackson,* 55–60.

3. Jackson, *Report of Robert H. Jackson,* 57.

4. Jackson, *Report of Robert H. Jackson,* 61; Alderman, "London Negotiations for War Crimes Prosecutions," May 1, 1952, Container 112, Correspondence A (Alderman on London), Post-Trial Material, Robert H. Jackson Papers, Manuscript Division, Library of Congress, Washington, D.C., 15–16.

5. Jackson Diary, June 16, 1945.

6. Alderman, "London Negotiations for War Crimes Prosecutions," May 1, 1952, Container 112, Correspondence A (Alderman on London), Post-Trial Material, Robert H. Jackson Papers, Manuscript Division, Library of Congress, Washington, D.C., 18.

7. Alderman, "Reminiscences," 930–931.

8. Alderman, "London Negotiations for War Crimes Prosecutions," May 1, 1952, Container 112, Correspondence A (Alderman on London), Post-Trial Material, Robert H. Jackson Papers, Manuscript Division, Library of Congress, Washington, D.C., 23; Jackson, *Report of Robert H. Jackson,* 71.

9. Alderman, "Reminiscences," 1025–27.

10. Jackson, *Report of Robert H. Jackson,* 197.

11. Alderman, "Reminiscences," 1071–72; Jackson, *Report of Robert H. Jackson,* vii–viii.

12. Alderman, "Reminiscences," 1063–66; Jackson, *Report of Robert H. Jackson,* 211–42.

13. The members were Francis Shea, William Dwight Whitney, and Lieutenant Gordon Dean.

14. Alderman, "Reminiscences," 1068–69.

15. Jackson, *Report of Robert H. Jackson,* 295–98.

16. Jackson, *Report of Robert H. Jackson,* 299.

17. Jackson, *Report of Robert H. Jackson,* 300.

18. The text of this report has not been found, but can be reconstructed from the text of Byrnes's reply. James Francis Byrnes, telegram to Jackson, July 22, 1945, Container 110, State Department, Official File, Legal File, Robert H. Jackson Papers, Manuscript Division, Library of Congress, Washington, D.C.

19. James Francis Byrnes, telegram to Jackson, July 22, 1945.

20. Jackson, *Report of Robert H. Jackson,* 327.

21. Jackson, *Report of Robert H. Jackson,* 329–30.

22. Jackson, *Report of Robert H. Jackson,* 331

23. Jackson, *Report of Robert H. Jackson,* 333. Also quoted in Marrus, *Nuremberg War Crimes Trial,* 45; Schabas, *Unimaginable Atrocities,* 108.

24. Alderman, "Reminiscences," 1071; Jackson, *Report of Robert H. Jackson,* viii.

25. Jackson, *Report of Robert H. Jackson,* 331.

26. Jackson, *Report of Robert H. Jackson,* 360–79.

27. Jackson Diary, July 26, 1945.

28. Jackson Diary, July 26, 1945.

29. Jackson Diary, July 26, 1945.

30. See Robertson, *Sly and Able,* 282–86.

31. Quoted in Robertson, *Sly and Able,* 285.

32. Jackson Diary, July 26, 1945.

33. Jackson Diary, July 30, 1945.

34. Alderman, "Memorandum of Suggestions by the United States in the Draft Agreement and Charter Submitted by the Subcommittee," July 31, 1945, Container 97, Pre-Trial Material, Nuremberg War Crimes Trial, Legal File, 1919–1962, n.d., Robert H. Jackson Papers, Manuscript Division, Library of Congress, Washington, D.C. Alderman signed the version of the document in the published report, but Jackson was doubtlessly its author. One can only guess why Jackson chose to have this document circulated under the signature of Alderman rather than his own. Perhaps he wished to maintain a stronger negotiating position. In any case, the threat contained in this document helped coerce the Soviets to agree to a joint trial.

35. Alderman, "Memorandum of Suggestions by the United States in the Draft Agreement and Charter Submitted by the Subcommittee," July 31, 1945, Container 97, Pre-Trial Material, Nuremberg War Crimes Trial, Legal File, 1919–1962, n.d., Robert H. Jackson Papers, Manuscript Division, Library of Congress, Washington, D.C.; Jackson, *Report of Robert H. Jackson,* 397.

36. Jackson, *Report of Robert H. Jackson,* 412–13.

37. Jackson spent considerable time at this session discussing the problems of

conducting a multilanguage trial. At a critical moment, Jackson suggested translation and interpretation difficulties might make a joint trial impossible. "We, in the United States, try issues in courts that are somewhat appalling to other peoples in the length of our trials and the scope of our questions, and I have had some experience trying them. But this trial has a scope that is utterly beyond anything that has ever been attempted that I know of, in judicial history, and we must attempt to do it in four languages. I have been having a great deal to do with the preparation for the case for trial. This book, in my hand, of over a hundred pages, for example, is a mere outline, mere index, setting forth the documents in the case against Hermann Göring. It involves decades of time. It involves operations, almost daily operations, which we would classify as criminal under any definition. Now if that has to be translated into four languages and then be the subject of examination in court, we are undertaking a tremendous task and our professional reputations are at stake. . . . I would much rather see us agree the trial is impossible than to demonstrate that the trial is impossible" (Jackson, *Report of Robert H. Jackson*, 412–15).

38. Jackson, *Report of Robert H. Jackson*, 416–19.

39. Jackson, *Report of Robert H. Jackson*, 419.

40. Alderman, "Reminiscences," 1193–94.

41. Alderman, "Reminiscences," 1194–95.

42. Bernays to Ammi Cutter, August 8, 1945, Box 1, Correspondence Aug–Oct 1945, MCBP.

43. Alderman, "Reminiscences," 1202.

44. Professor Trainin along with General Nikitchenko signed for the Soviet Union.

45. "The Texts of the War Crimes Committee Report and the Jackson Statement," *New York Times*, August 9, 1945.

46. "The Texts of the War Crimes Committee Report and the Jackson Statement."

47. "The Texts of the War Crimes Committee Report and the Jackson Statement."

48. Jackson, *Report of Robert H. Jackson,* 423.

49. See Kochavi, *Prelude to Nuremberg,* 166.

50. Alderman, "Reminiscences," 1266.

51. Jackson, *Report of Robert H. Jackson,* 423.

52. Jackson, "Justice Jackson's Story," 1453.

53. Gerhart, *America's Advocate,* 353.

54. Frank B. Wallis, Frank B. Wallis Diary, Rauner Special Collections Library, Dartmouth College, Hanover, N.H., 73.

55. Alderman, "Reminiscences," 1093.

56. IMT, *Trial of the Major War Criminals,* 1:28–29.

57. "Abroad," *New York Times*, November 25, 1945.

58. IMT, *Trial of the Major War Criminals,* 2:97.

59. IMT, *Trial of the Major War Criminals,* 2:98–99.

60. See Spector and Rozett, *Encyclopedia of the Holocaust.*

61. IMT, *Trial of the Major War Criminals,* 2:142.

62. IMT, *Trial of the Major War Criminals,* 2:154.

63. Ivan H. Peterman, "Nazi Crimals Cringe under Jackson Lashing," *Philadelphia Inquirer*, November 22, 1945. See also Gerhart, *America's Advocate,* 364.

64. Jackson, *Report of Robert H. Jackson*, 432–40.
65. Jackson, *Report of Robert H. Jackson*, 432–40.
66. Jackson, *Report of Robert H. Jackson*, 437.

Conclusion

Epigraph: HCP, Untitled Recollections, May 1945.

1. Eisenhower, *Crusade in Europe*, 408–9.
2. Young, *Why We Fight*, 159–61.
3. Quoted in Young, *Why We Fight*, 161.
4. Vincent Tubbs, "Inside View of Nazi Horror Camp," *Baltimore Afro-American*, May 19, 1945.
5. Tubbs, "Inside View of Nazi Horror Camp."
6. Osborn and Osborn, *Voyage to a New World*, 60–61.
7. FDR, *Public Papers and Addresses of Franklin D. Roosevelt*, 9:537.
8. FDR, *Public Papers and Addresses of Franklin D. Roosevelt*, 9:672.
9. FDR, *Public Papers and Addresses of Franklin D. Roosevelt*, 9:672.
10. H. W. Brands labeled the Atlantic Charter "inelegant but artful—as artful in places as diplomatic prose ever gets" (Brands, *Traitor to His Class*, 608).
11. FDR, *Public Papers and Addresses of Franklin D. Roosevelt*, 10:314–15.
12. FDR, *Public Papers and Addresses of Franklin D. Roosevelt*, 5:289.
13. FDR, *Public Papers and Addresses of Franklin D. Roosevelt*, 11:3.
14. Churchill, *Grand Alliance*, 683.
15. FDR, "Radio Bulletin No. 72," March 24, 1944, Roosevelt, FD 1936–45.
16. IMT, *Trial of the Major War Criminals*, 2:98–99.
17. Article II listed the crimes as follows:

   (a) Crimes against Peace. Initiation of invasions of other countries and wars of aggression in violation of international laws and treaties, including but not limited to planning, preparation, initiation or waging a war of aggression, or a war of violation of international treaties, agreements or assurances, or participation in a common plan or conspiracy for the accomplishment of any of the foregoing.

   (b) War Crimes. Atrocities or offenses against persons or property constituting violations of the laws or customs of war, including but not limited to, murder, ill treatment or deportation to slave labour or for any other purpose, of civilian population from occupied territory, murder or ill treatment of prisoners of war or persons on the seas, killing of hostages, plunder of public or private property, wanton destruction of cities, towns or villages, or devastation not justified by military necessity.

   (c) Crimes against Humanity. Atrocities and offenses, including but not limited to murder, extermination, enslavement, deportation, imprisonment, torture, rape, or other inhumane acts committed against any civilian population, or persecutions on political, racial or religious grounds whether or not in violation of the domestic laws of the country where perpetrated.

    (d) Membership in categories of a criminal group or organization declared criminal by the International Military Tribunal.

IMT, *Trials of War Criminals before the Nuernberg Military Tribunals under Control Council Law No. 10*, 15:23–34. See also Kochavi, *Prelude to Nuremberg*, 168.

    18. Doctors' Trial (December 9, 1946–August 20, 1947), Milch Trial (January 2–April 14, 1947), Judges' Trial (March 5–December 4, 1947), Pohl Trial (April 8–November 3, 1947), Flick Trial (April 19–December 22, 1947), IG Farben Trial (August 27, 1947–July 30, 1948), Hostages Trial (July 8, 1947–February 19, 1948), RuSHA Trial (October 20, 1947–March 10, 1948), Einsatzgruppen Trial (September 29, 1947–April 10, 1948), Krupp Trial (December 8, 1947–July 31, 1948), Ministries Trial (January 6, 1948–April 13, 1949), and the High Command Trial (December 30, 1947–October 28, 1948). For more on the subsequent trials, see Buscher, *U.S. War Crimes Trial Program in Germany;* Taylor, *Final Report to the Secretary of the Army on the Nuernberg War Crimes Trials under Control Council Law No. 10.*

    19. See Kochavi, *Prelude to Nuremberg*, 167–69. A directive issued by the Joint Chiefs of Staff ("Directive on the Identification and Apprehension of Persons Suspected of War Crimes or Other Offenses and Trial of Certain Offenders" JCS 1023/10) made United States Forces European Theatre (USFET) responsible for cases involving "lesser offenders" of all four categories of crimes listed in the London Charter and Agreement since January 30, 1933, which included racial and religious persecution. After meetings between Jackson's staff and USFET representatives in December 1945, the conclusion was reached that it would simply not be feasible for USFET to handle so many cases. USFET would, therefore, only take on cases related to war crimes and concentration camps. German courts would have to take on all other atrocity cases, specifically racial and religious persecutions, as a "test of German regeneration" (Ziemke, *U.S. Army in the Occupation of Germany*, 394–95).

    20. Lemkin, *Axis Rule in Occupied Europe*, 79–95. During his remarks at a conference celebrating the sixtieth anniversary of the Genocide Convention in 2007 at Case Western University, Henry T. King, member of the American prosecutorial team at Nuremberg, recounted a chance encounter he had with Lemkin at the Grand Hotel in Nuremberg in 1946. Lemkin relayed to King that he was thoroughly disappointed in what happened at Nuremberg; at the time, King thought Lemkin just another "crank." In his remarks at the conference, King praised Lemkin's "vital role in pushing genocide as an international crime and in the development of the United Nations Convention on Genocide" (King, Ferencz, and Harris, "Origins of the Genocide Convention," 13–14). See also Schabas, "Origins of the Genocide Convention," 35; Schabas, *Unimaginable Atrocities*, 109.

    21. Schabas, "Origins of the Genocide Convention," 53.

    22. IMT, *Trial of the Major War Criminals*, 22:497.

    23. Schabas, "Origins of the Genocide Convention," 35.

    24. Schabas, "Origins of the Genocide Convention," 51.

    25. Jackson, *Report of Robert H. Jackson*, 423.

    26. For a more thorough analysis of the origins of the Genocide Convention, see Schabas, "Origins of the Genocide Convention"; Schabas, *Genocide in International Law;* Schabas, *Unimaginable Atrocities.*

27. Jackson, *Report of Robert H. Jackson,* ix.

28. Jackson, *Report of Robert H. Jackson,* 439.

29. Wilkins, "Not Far Enough," *The Crisis,* November 1946, 328.

30. FDR, "Radio Bulletin No. 72," March 24, 1944, Roosevelt, FD 1936–45.

31. Dan Plesch concluded that "the establishment of crimes against humanity was the greatest achievement of the Nuremberg IMT." While noting the work of Jackson, Truman, the other delegations at the London conference, and the commissioners on the UNWCC, Plesch wrote that "it was Pell, almost alone though with the strategic but flickering support of FDR and latterly of Morgenthau, that succeeded in taking action" (Plesch, *Human Rights after Hitler,* 171).

32. Plesch, *Human Rights after Hitler,* 51.

33. HCP to Claiborne Pell, May 17, 1945; Pell, Claiborne.

34. HCP to Claiborne Pell, May 17, 1945; Pell, Claiborne.

35. HCP to Claiborne Pell, January 16, 1954, CPP.

36. Robert E. Smith, "Ambassador-at-Large," *The Harvard Crimson,* November 18, 1960. See also Blayney, *Democracy's Aristocrat,* 137.

37. Baker, *Brahmin in Revolt,* 330.

38. Reverend Canon Lockett Ford Ballard, "A Sermon Eulogy Delivered in Trinity Church Newport, Rhode Island, in Memory of Herbert Claiborne Pell, Sunday August 25, 1963," Speeches, Articles and Reprints 1918–1969, Box 31, Speech and Writings File, HCPP.

39. Reverend Canon Lockett Ford Ballard, "A Sermon Eulogy Delivered in Trinity Church Newport, Rhode Island, in Memory of Herbert Claiborne Pell, Sunday August 25, 1963," Speeches, Articles and Reprints 1918–1969, Box 31, Speech and Writings File, HCPP.

40. For more on the life of Claiborne Pell, see Miller, *An Uncommon Man.*

41. HCP to Claiborne Pell, September 9, 1942, CPP.

42. HCP, Untitled Recollections, May 1945.

43. HCP to Nuala Pell, November 13, 1945, Pell, Claiborne.

44. "Pell to Address Vassar Temple Men," *Poughkeepsie Journal,* November 9, 1945.

45. HCP to Nuala Pell, November 13, 1945.

BIBLIOGRAPHY

Archives and Manuscript Collections

American Heritage Center, Laramie, Wyo.
    Murray C. Bernays Papers
American University Library—Special Collections, Washington, D.C.
    Drew Pearson's "Washington Merry-Go-Round"
Oral History Research Office, Columbia University, New York, N.Y.
    The Reminiscences of Sidney S. Alderman
    The Reminiscences of Jeremiah Mahoney
    The Reminiscences of Herbert C. Pell
    The Reminiscences of Joseph M. Proskauer
American Philosophical Society, Philadelphia, Pa.
    Frederick H. Osborn Papers
Franklin D. Roosevelt Library, Hyde Park, N.Y.
    Oscar Cox Papers
    Henry Morgenthau Jr. Papers
    Herbert C. Pell Papers
    Franklin D. Roosevelt Papers
Manuscript Division, Library of Congress, Washington, D.C.
    Joseph E. Davies Papers
    Green H. Hackworth Papers
    Cordell Hull Papers
    Robert H. Jackson Papers
    Breckenridge Long Papers
    Papers of the NAACP
National Archives, College Park, Md.
    Record Group 59, General Records of the Department of State
    Record Group 107, Records of the Office of the Secretary of War
    Record Group 238, National Archives at College Park Collection of World War
        II War Crimes Records

Harry S. Truman Library, Independence, Mo.
    "Oral History Interview with Frederick Osborn" (Garrison, N.Y.)
Rauner Special Collections Library, Dartmouth College, Hanover, N.H.
    Frank B. Wallis Diary
Distinctive Collections, University of Rhode Island Library, Kingston, R.I.
    Claiborne Pell Papers

Periodicals and News Services Cited

Associated Press
Baltimore Afro-American
CNN
Crisis, The
Harvard Crimson, The
New York Times
Philadelphia Inquirer
PM
Poughkeepsie Journal
Time
Washington Post

Books

Andrus, Burton C. *I Was the Nuremberg Jailer*. 1st American ed. New York: Coward-McCann, 1969.

Bacque, James. *Other Losses: An Investigation into the Mass Deaths of German Prisoners at the Hands of the French and Americans after World War II*. 2nd rev. ed. Boston: Little Brown, 1999.

Baker, Leonard. *Brahmin in Revolt: A Biography of Herbert C. Pell*. New York: Doubleday, 1972.

Baillie, Hugh. *High Tension: The Recollections of Hugh Baillie*. New York: Harper, 1959.

Bass, Gary Jonathan. *Stay the Hand of Vengeance: The Politics of War Crimes Tribunals*. Princeton Studies in International History and Politics. Princeton, N.J.: Princeton University Press, 2000.

Berkman, Ted. *Cast a Giant Shadow: The Story of Mickey Marcus Who Died to Save Jerusalem*. Carpinteria, CA: Manifest Publications, 1999.

Black, Conrad. *Franklin Delano Roosevelt: Champion of Freedom*. New York: Public Affairs, 2003.

Black, Edwin. *IBM and the Holocaust: The Strategic Alliance between Nazi Germany and America's Most Powerful Corporation*. New York: Crown Publishers, 2001.

Blayney, Michael Steward. *Democracy's Aristocrat: The Life of Herbert C. Pell*. Lanham, Md.: University Press of America, 1986.

Blum, John Morton. *From the Morgenthau Diaries: Years of War, 1941–1945*. Vol. 3. Boston: Houghton Mifflin, 1967.

————. *V Was for Victory: Politics and American Culture during World War II*. New York: Harcourt Brace Jovanovich, 1976.

Borgwardt, Elizabeth. *A New Deal for the World: America's Vision for Human Rights*. Cambridge, Mass..: Belknap Press of Harvard University Press, 2005.

Brands, H. W. *Traitor to His Class: The Privileged Life and Radical Presidency of Franklin Delano Roosevelt*. New York: Doubleday, 2008.

Breitman, Richard, and Alan M. Kraut. *American Refugee Policy and European Jewry, 1933–1945*. Bloomington: Indiana University Press, 1987.

Breitman, Richard, and Allan J. Lichtman. *FDR and the Jews*. Cambridge, Mass.: Belknap Press of Harvard University Press, 2013.

Buscher, Frank M. *The U.S. War Crimes Trial Program in Germany, 1946–1955*. Contributions in Military Studies. New York: Greenwood Press, 1989.

Calvocoressi, Peter. *Nuremberg: The Facts, the Law, and the Consequences*. New York: Macmillan, 1948.

Churchill, Winston. *The Grand Alliance*. Boston: Houghton Mifflin, 1950.

Conot, Robert E. *Justice at Nuremberg*. New York: Harper & Row, 1983.

Coverdale, John F. *Italian Intervention in the Spanish Civil War*. Princeton, N.J.: Princeton University Press, 1975.

Dallek, Robert. *Franklin D. Roosevelt and American Foreign Policy, 1932–1945*. New York: Oxford University Press, 1979.

Davidson, Eugene. *The Trial of the Germans: An Account of the Twenty-Two Defendants before the International Military Tribunal at Nuremberg*. Columbia: University of Missouri Press, 1997.

Dennett, Raymond, Joseph Esrey Johnson, and World Peace Foundation. *Negotiating with the Russians*. [Boston]: World Peace Foundation, 1951.

Dickson, Paul, and Thomas B. Allen. *The Bonus Army: An American Epic*. New York: Walker & Co., 2004.

Dunne, Michael. *The United States and the World Court, 1920–1935*. New York: St. Martin's Press, 1988.

Dunoyer, Alphonse. *The Public Prosecutor of the Terror, Antoine Quentin Fouquier-Tinville; Tr. from the French of Alphonse Dunoyer by A. W. Evans. With a Photogravure Frontispiece and Fourteen Other Illustrations*. New York: G. P. Putnam's Sons, 1913.

Eisenhower, Dwight D. *Crusade in Europe*. Baltimore: Johns Hopkins University Press, 1997.

Evans, Hugh E. *The Hidden Campaign: FDR's Health and the 1944 Election*. Armonk, N.Y.: M. E. Sharpe, 2002.

Farago, Ladislas. *The Game of the Foxes: The Untold Story of German Espionage in the United States and Great Britain during World War II*. New York: D. McKay Co., 1972.

Farley, James A. *Jim Farley's Story: The Roosevelt Years*. New York: Whittlesey House, 1948.

Ferrell, Robert H. *The Dying President: Franklin D. Roosevelt, 1944–1945*. Columbia: University of Missouri Press, 1998.

Finan, Christopher M. *Alfred E. Smith: The Happy Warrior*. New York: Hill and Wang, 2002.

Fleming, Denna Frank. *The United States and the World Court, 1920–1966.* Rev. ed. New York: Russell & Russell, 1968.

Foreign Relations of the United States, Conferences at Cairo and Tehran, 1943. Washington, D.C.: U.S. Government Printing Office, 1961.

Fyfe, David Patrick Maxwell. *1st Earl of Kilmuir, Political Adventure, the Memoirs of the Earl of Kilmuir.* London: Weidenfeld and Nicolson, 1964.

Gellman, Irwin F. *Secret Affairs: Franklin Roosevelt, Cordell Hull, and Sumner Welles.* Baltimore: Johns Hopkins University Press, 1995.

Gerhart, Eugene C. *America's Advocate: Robert H. Jackson.* Indianapolis: Bobbs-Merrill, 1958.

Gilbert, G. M. *Nuremberg Diary.* [New York:] New American Library, 1961.

Gilbert, Martin. *The Second World War: A Complete History.* New York: H. Holt, 1989.

Glueck, Sheldon. *The Nuremberg Trial and Aggressive War.* New York: A. A. Knopf, 1946.

Halperin, Judith, and Phyllis Kreinik. *Mickey Marcus: The Story of Colonel David Marcus.* New York: Bloch, 1949.

Harriman, W. Averell, and Elie Abel. *Special Envoy to Churchill and Stalin, 1941–1946.* New York: Random House, 1975.

Harris, Whitney R. *Tyranny on Trial: The Trial of the Major German War Criminals at the End of World War II at Nuremberg, Germany, 1945–1946.* Rev. ed. Dallas: Southern Methodist University Press, 1999.

Hitler, Adolf, Alvin Saunders Johnson, and John Chamberlain. *Mein Kampf, Complete and Unabridged, Fully Annotated.* New York: Reynal & Hitchcock, 1939.

Hull, Cordell, and Andrew Henry Thomas Berding. *The Memoirs of Cordell Hull.* New York: Macmillan Co., 1948.

International Military Tribunal. *Trial of the Major War Criminals before the International Military Tribunal, Nuremberg, 14 November 1945–1 October 1946.* 42 vols. Vol. 2. Nuremberg, Germany: n.p., 1947.

International Military Tribunal. *Trials of War Criminals before the Nuernberg Military Tribunals under Control Council Law No. 10; Nuernberg, October 1946–April 1949.* 15 vols. Vol. 15. Buffalo, NY: W. S. Hein, 1997.

Irving, David John Cawdell. *Nuremberg, the Last Battle.* London: Focal Point, 1996.

Jackson, Robert Houghwout. *Report of Robert H. Jackson, United States Representative to the International Conference on Military Trials, London, 1945.* Washington, D.C.: U.S. Government Printing Office, 1949.

Jackson, Robert Houghwout, and John Q. Barrett. *That Man: An Insider's Portrait of Franklin D. Roosevelt.* Oxford: Oxford University Press, 2003.

Kimball, Warren F. *The Juggler: Franklin Roosevelt as Wartime Statesman.* Princeton, N.J.: Princeton University Press, 1991.

Kochavi, Arieh J. *Prelude to Nuremberg: Allied War Crimes Policy and the Question of Punishment.* Chapel Hill: University of North Carolina Press, 1998.

Kühl, Stefan. *The Nazi Connection: Eugenics, American Racism, and German National Socialism.* New York: Oxford University Press, 1994.

Lemkin, Raphael. *Axis Rule in Occupied Europe.* Washington, D.C.: Carnegie Endowment for International Peace, Division of International Law, 1944.

Lewis, Mark. *The Birth of the New Justice: The Internationalization of Crime and Punishment, 1919–1950.* Oxford Studies in Modern European History. Oxford: Oxford University Press, 2014.

Lipstadt, Deborah E. *Beyond Belief: The American Press and the Coming of the Holocaust, 1933–1945.* New York: Free Press, 1986.

Marrus, Michael Robert. *The Nuremberg War Crimes Trial, 1945–46: A Documentary History.* Bedford Series in History and Culture. Boston: Bedford Books, 1997.

Martin, Roy A. *Inside Nürnberg: Military Justice for Nazi War Criminals.* Shippensburg, Pa.: White Mane Books, 2000.

"Memorandum of the Press and Radio News Conference, Friday, January 26, 1945." In *Press Conferences of the Secretaries of State, 1922–1973.* 15 microfilm reels. Wilmington, Del.: Scholarly Resources, 1970.

"Memorandum of the Press and Radio News Conference, Thursday, February 1, 1945." In *Press Conferences of the Secretaries of State, 1922–1973.* 15 microfilm reels. Wilmington, Del.: Scholarly Resources, 1970.

Miller, G. Wayne. *An Uncommon Man: The Life and Times of Senator Claiborne Pell.* Hanover, N.H.: University Press of New England, 2011.

Morgenthau, Henry, and Judiciary Subcommittee to Investigate the Administration of the Internal Security Act and Other Internal Security Laws. *Morgenthau Diary (Germany).* Washington, D.C.: U.S. Government Printing Office, 1967.

Morgenthau, Henry, III. *Mostly Morgenthaus: A Family History.* New York: Ticknor & Fields, 1991.

Osborn, Frederick Henry, and Joan Annet Osborn. *Voyage to a New World, 1889–1979: A Personal Narrative.* Garrison, N.Y.: Osborn, 1979.

Persico, Joseph E. *Nuremberg: Infamy on Trial.* New York: Viking, 1994.

Plesch, Daniel. *America, Hitler and the UN: How the Allies Won World War II and Forged a Peace.* London: I. B. Tauris, 2011.

———. *Human Rights after Hitler: The Lost History of Prosecuting Axis War Crimes.* Washington, D.C.: Georgetown University Press, 2017.

Pugh, Emerson W. *Building IBM: Shaping an Industry and Its Technology.* History of Computing. Cambridge, Mass.: MIT Press, 1995.

Robertson, David. *Sly and Able: A Political Biography of James F. Byrnes.* New York: Norton, 1994.

Robertson, Geoffrey. *Crimes against Humanity: The Struggle for Global Justice.* New York: New Press, 2000.

Roosevelt, Eleanor. *This I Remember.* New York: Harper, 1949.

Roosevelt, Franklin D. *The Public Papers and Addresses of Franklin D. Roosevelt.* 13 vols. New York: Russell & Russell, 1969.

Roosevelt, James, and Sidney Shalett. *Affectionately, F.D.R.* New York: Harcourt, 1959.

Root, Elihu, Robert Bacon, and James Brown Scott. *Addresses on Government and Citizenship.* Cambridge, Mass.: Harvard University Press, 1916.

Rosen, Robert N. *Saving the Jews: Franklin D. Roosevelt and the Holocaust.* New York: Thunder's Mouth Press, 2006.

Schabas, William. *Genocide in International Law: The Crime of Crimes.* 2nd ed. Cambridge: Cambridge University Press, 2009.

———. *Unimaginable Atrocities: Justice, Politics, and Rights at the War Crimes Tribunals.* Oxford: Oxford University Press, 2012.

Simpson, Christopher. *The Splendid Blond Beast: Money, Law, and Genocide in the Twentieth Century.* New York: Grove Press, 1993.

Smith, Bradley F. *The American Road to Nuremberg: The Documentary Record, 1944–1945.* Stanford, Calif.: Hoover Institution Press, 1982.

———. *Reaching Judgment at Nuremberg.* New York: Basic Books, 1977.

———. *The Road to Nuremberg.* New York: Basic Books, 1981.

Smith, Jean Edward. *FDR.* New York: Random House, 2007.

Spector, Shmuel, and Robert Rozett. *Encyclopedia of the Holocaust.* Facts on File Library of World History. New York: Facts on File, 2000.

Speer, Albert. *Inside the Third Reich: Memoirs.* [New York:] Macmillan, 1970.

Sprecher, Drexel A. *Inside the Nuremberg Trial: A Prosecutor's Comprehensive Account.* Lanham, Md.: University Press of America, 1999.

Stimson, Henry Lewis, and McGeorge Bundy. *On Active Service in Peace and War.* New York: Harper, 1948.

Storey, Robert Gerald. *The Final Judgment? Pearl Harbor to Nuremberg.* San Antonio, Tex.: Naylor, 1968.

Taylor, Telford. *The Anatomy of the Nuremberg Trials: A Personal Memoir.* New York: Knopf, 1992.

———. *Final Report to the Secretary of the Army on the Nuernberg War Crimes Trials under Control Council Law No. 10.* Buffalo, N.Y.: W. S. Hein & Co., 1997.

———. *Nuremberg and Vietnam: An American Tragedy.* Chicago: Quadrangle Books, 1970.

Tierney, Dominic. *FDR and the Spanish Civil War: Neutrality and Commitment in the Struggle That Divided America.* American Encounters / Global Interactions. Durham, N.C.: Duke University Press, 2007.

Truman, Harry S. *Memoirs.* Garden City, N.Y.: Doubleday, 1955.

Tully, Grace G. *F.D.R., My Boss.* New York: C. Scribner's Sons, 1949.

Tusa, Ann, and John Tusa. *The Nuremberg Trial.* 1st American ed. New York: Atheneum, 1984.

Tye, Larry. *The Father of Spin: Edward L. Bernays and the Birth of Public Relations.* New York: Crown Publishers, 1998.

United Nations War Crimes Commission. *History of the United Nations War Crimes Commission and the Development of the Laws of War.* London: Her Majesty's Stationery Office, 1948.

United States Department of State. *The Conference at Quebec, 1944.* Washington, D.C.: U.S. Government Printing Office, 1972.

———. *Foreign Relations of the United States: Diplomatic Papers, 1944.* Vol. 1. Washington, D.C.: U.S. Government Printing Office, 1944.

United States Congress, Senate Committee on Foreign Relations, and United States Department of State. *A Decade of American Foreign Policy; Basic Documents, 1941–49.* Washington, D.C.: U.S. Government Printing Office, 1950.

Ware, Gilbert. *William Hastie: Grace under Pressure.* New York: Oxford University Press, 1984.

Watson, Thomas J., and Peter Petre. *Father, Son & Co.: My Life at IBM and Beyond.* New York: Bantam Books, 1990.

Welles, Benjamin. *Sumner Welles: FDR's Global Strategist: A Biography.* Franklin and Eleanor Roosevelt Institute Series on Diplomatic and Economic History. New York: St. Martin's Press, 1997.

Woetzel, Robert K. *The Nuremberg Trials in International Law.* London: Stevens; Praeger, 1960.

Wyman, David S. *The Abandonment of the Jews: America and the Holocaust, 1941–1945.* New York: New Press, 2007.

Young, Nancy Beck. *Why We Fight: Congress and the Politics of World War II.* Lawrence: University Press of Kansas, 2013.

Ziemke, Earl Frederick. *The U.S. Army in the Occupation of Germany, 1944–1946.* Washington, D.C.: Center of Military History, U.S. Army, 1975.

Disssertations and Theses

Cox, Graham. "The Interpretation Factor: Overcoming the Language Barrier at the Trial of the Major War Criminals before the International Military Tribunal at Nuremberg." MA thesis, University of Houston, 2003.

Mehler, Barry Alan. "A History of the American Eugenics Society, 1921–1949." PhD dissertation, University of Illinois at Urbana-Champaign, 1988.

Journal Articles

Bathurst, M. E. "The United Nations War Crimes Commission." *American Journal of International Law* 39, no. 3 (July 1945): 565–70.

Bishop, William W., Jr. "Lawrence Preuss, 1905–1956." *American Journal of International Law* 50, no. 4 (October 1956): 907–9.

Bush, Jonathan A. "'The Supreme . . . Crime' and Its Origins: The Lost Legislative History of the Crime of Aggressive War." *Columbia Law Review* 102, no. 8 (2002): 2324–424.

Jackson, Robert Houghwout. "Address of Robert H. Jackson, Attorney General of the United States, Inter-American Bar Association, Havana, Cuba, March 27, 1941." *American Journal of International Law* 35, no. 2 (March 27, 1941): 348–59.

———. "Rule of Law among Nations: Address Delivered before the American Society of International Law, Washington D.C., April 13, 1945." *American Bar Association Journal* 31, no. 6 (June 1945): 290–94.

King, Henry T., Jr., B. B. Ferencz, and W. R. Harris. "Origins of the Genocide Convention." *Case Western Reserve Journal of International Law* 40, no. 1 (2008): 13–34.

Ladavac, Nicoletta Bersier. "Biographical Note and Biography (Hans Kelsen)." *European Journal of International Law* 9, no. 2 (1998): 391–400.

Ofer, Dalia. "Linguistic Conceptualization of the Holocaust in Palestine and Israel, 1942–53." *Journal of Contemporary History* 31, no. 3 (1996): 567–95.

Osborne, Richard H. "Frederick Osborn: Humanist." *Social Biology* 29, nos. 1–2 (spring–summer 1982): v–vii.

Petrie, Jon. "The Secular Word Holocaust: Scholarly Myths, History, and 20th-Century Meanings." *Journal of Genocide Research* 2, no. 1 (March 2000): 31–63.

Rigaux, François. "The European Tradition in International Law: Hans Kelsen." *European Journal of International Law* 9, no. 2 (1998): 325–43.

Schabas, William. "Origins of the Genocide Convention: From Nuremberg to Paris." *Case Western Reserve Journal of International Law* 10, no. 1 (2008): 35–55.

Shapiro, Harry L. "In Memory of Frederick H. Osborn." *Social Biology* 29, nos. 1–2 (spring–summer 1982): i–iv.

Zabecki, David T. "Israel's Greatest Military Commander since Judas." *Military History* 15, no. 1 (April 1998): 3.

Online Sources

Pearson, Drew. "The Washington Merry-Go-Round, June 6, 1945." Washington Research Library Consortium, https://auislandora.wrlc.org/islandora/object /pearson%3A15930#page/1/mode/1up.

United Nations War Crimes Commission. "Folder UNWCC—Indexes (with Supplements) to Minutes and Documents—Meetings 01-38—S-1804-0001-0001." United Nations Archives and Records Management Section, https://search.archives.un.org /unwcc-indexes-with-supplements-to-minutes-and-documents-meetings-01-38.

———. "Folder UNWCC—Legal Committee (Committee III) Documents III 1—III 118 (Incomplete)—15854." United Nations Archives and Records Management Section, https://search.archives.un.org/unwcc-legal-committee-committee-iii -documents-iii-1-iii-118-incomplete.

INDEX